AMERICAN MANNERS & MORALS

W9-CDA-894

Domestic tranquillity in old New England

"JOHN AND ABIGAIL MONTGOMERY," BY JOSEPH DAVIS, 1836

By

MARY CABLE

and

THE EDITORS OF AMERICAN HERITAGE

The Magazine of History

EDITOR IN CHARGE

WENDY BUEHR

PUBLISHED BY

AMERICAN HERITAGE PUBLISHING CO., INC., New York

AMERICAN MANNERS & MORALS

A PICTURE HISTORY
OF HOW WE BEHAVED
AND MISBEHAVED

© 1969 by American Heritage Publishing Co., Inc. All rights reserved under Berne and Pan-American Copyright Conventions. Reproduction in whole or in part without permission is prohibited. Printed in the United States of America. Standard Book Number: (regular edition) 8281-0023-3, (deluxe edition) 8281-0031-4. Library of Congress Catalog Card Number: 72-80958.

Frontiersmen frolicking at work

FOLIO
917.3
C115a

"FLAX SCUTCHING BEE," BY LINTON PARK, 1860

23067

AMERICAN HERITAGE
BOOK DIVISION

EDITORIAL DIRECTOR
Richard M. Ketchum

GENERAL EDITOR
Alvin M. Josephy, Jr.

Staff for this Book

EDITOR
Wendy Buehr

ART DIRECTOR
Mary Ann Joulwan

PICTURE EDITOR
Meryle R. Evans

ASSOCIATE EDITOR
Margot Brill

COPY EDITOR
Brenda Bennerup

ASSISTANT EDITOR
Susan D. Eikov

ASSISTANT PICTURE EDITOR
Sara H. Hudson

CONTRIBUTING EDITOR
Kristi Witker

EDITORIAL ASSISTANTS
Constance Turnbull
Shelley Benoit
Nancy Richardson

EUROPEAN BUREAU
Gertrudis Feliu, *Chief*

AMERICAN HERITAGE
PUBLISHING CO., INC.

PRESIDENT
James Parton

CHAIRMAN, EDITORIAL COMMITTEE
Joseph J. Thorndike

EDITOR, AMERICAN HERITAGE MAGAZINE
Oliver Jensen

SENIOR ART DIRECTOR
Irwin Glusker

PUBLISHER, AMERICAN HERITAGE MAGAZINE
Darby Perry

Endsheets: detail from a British calico depicting high life, country style, as it was lived among the English and their American cousins, c. 1820. Collection of Elinor Merrell, New York.

Contents

Dance hall denizens in the early 1900's

"HAYMARKET" (DETAIL), BY JOHN SLOAN, 1907

Preface

In these pages, we have endeavored to give something more than a catalog of quaint facts about the customs of our ancestors. Outmoded rituals can make entertaining reading for their own sake, but they can also tell us much about the hopes and aspirations of the people who have chosen to live by them. Manners and morals derive, after all, from the system of values men set upon life itself.

The first Americans, confronted with a vast and intimidating wilderness and an infinity of possibilities both wonderful and terrifying, had barely set sail before their leader, John Winthrop, proposed a new code of conduct to guide them in their enterprise. "The ligamentes of this body . . . are loue. . . . Wee must be knitt together in this worke as one man, wee must entertaine each other in brotherly Affeccion, wee must be willing to abridge our selues of our superfluities, for the supply of others necessities, wee must vphold a familiar Commerce together in a meekenes, gentlenes, patience and liberallity, wee must delight in eache other, make others Condicions our owne reioyce together, mourne together, labour, and suffer together, allwayes haueing before our eyes our . . . Community. . . ."

Winthrop's "Modell of Christian Charity" worked for a time, but as a code of behavior it was bound to lose its relevance in a land where newness was ever alluring and conditions always changing. Countless other Americans—preachers, jurists, charlatans, social arbiters, philosophers, "scribbling women," and just plain folks—have since left their marks upon our customs, and we have grown from a land of isolated settlements, each living by laws unto itself, into a nation where the manners and morals of different sorts of people are at least widely tolerated if not wholly endorsed. This book describes some of the personalities and events that have helped to bring about this evolution of the American character.

In a sense, almost any facet of life can be turned to account in such a study: legislation, entertainments, literature, fashions, attitudes toward sex, social institutions, our pleasures and our pains, all reflect deep-seated ideas of right and wrong. All these ingredients are to be found in the chapters, contemporary writings, and picture portfolios that follow, and certain immutable strains begin to emerge.

It is astonishing, for example, to observe how the Puritan ethic has endured. The few hundred New England Puritans were on their way to being outnumbered and overruled even in the second generation. Yet, their strong sense of guilt, their industry, and their curious combination of materialism and idealism have persisted and are regarded today by the rest of the world as typically American qualities.

What is usually called the Victorian Age in America was also largely home grown; there was as much of Cotton Mather as of Victoria in its spirit. Even in 1790, Europeans were complaining that Americans were prudes, and the criticism of our Puritan-Victorian standards could still be heard in 1914. Thus, this book gives a good deal of space to the nineteenth century, for it was a pivotal time in our social history and can be credited with much of the behavior ever since.

If the female seems to dominate our story, it is because, to a surprising extent, she has been the guardian of our manners and morals. Lord Chesterfield's sweeping pronouncement, "Women, then, are only children of a larger growth," would have met with a chilly reception in pioneer America, where both men and women agreed that the bumbling male should acquiesce to this creature "of finer clay" in matters of behavior. Men of all classes were too busy to give much time to such problems, for there was no genuine leisure class like that which existed in Europe, and the few men who concerned themselves much with social niceties were laughed at. Martin Van Buren, for one, may have lost a presidential election because he loved a ceremonious dinner party and spent too much money on chandeliers and silk tassels for the White House.

Indeed, ceremony of any sort has had an uncertain career in America, a fact that many Europeans have noted with mixed denunciations and envy. Virginia Woolf, once questioned by *Cosmopolitan* for her opinion of her American cousins, wrapped it up nicely: "The Americans never sit down to a square meal. They perch on steel stools and take what they want from a perambulating rail. The Americans have swallowed their dinner by the time it takes [an Englishman] to decide whether the widow of a general takes precedence of the wife of a knight commander of the Star of India. . . . But the best way of illustrating the difference . . . is to bid you observe that while we have shadows that stalk behind us, they have a light that dances in front of them. That is what makes them the most interesting people in the world—they face the future, not the past." — *The Editors*

Like it was in 1968

PHOTOGRAPH BY DON SNYDER, 1968

A Fresh Start

In which Numerous Vexed & Troubled Englishmen, together with Germans, Dutchmen, Swedes, & Africans, arrive on our Shores, and Many Mix't Customs begin to be Forged into an American Morality

The first New England colonists were proud of the thoroughness with which they discarded European corruption. "It may be said that, in a Sort, they began the World a New," wrote one of their descendants, a century later. In their own eyes they were not beginning a new world, but resurrecting the ancient one of the Children of Israel. They were happy to be alone in the wilderness, where, as Governor William Bradford of Plymouth put it, their children would not be "drawn away by evil examples into extravagant and dangerous courses, getting the reins off their necks and departing from their parents." What, then, was the Pilgrims' distress when, in the fifth year, they found that the Devil had crossed the Atlantic, too, and in all that great wilderness had settled not twenty-five miles from Plymouth?

The offending settlement consisted of a number of indentured servants, brought over by one Captain Wollaston and three or four "gentlemen of quality" with a view to starting a plantation and trading post. But Wollaston quickly grew discouraged with bleak New England and sailed to Virginia, taking with him some of the servants, whom he sold to tobacco planters at a fine profit. While he was gone, one of the gentlemen, Thomas Morton, entered into league with the remaining servants and gave them their freedom in return for their support. Morton named the settlement Ma-re Mount— Mount by the Sea—but the Pilgrim Fathers soon had reason to call it Merry Mount; the sound of its revelry apparently could be heard twenty-five miles away. Bradford wrote in *Of Plimoth Plantation* that Morton had become "lord of misrule, and maintained (as it were) a schoole of Athisme." Making friends with the Indians, Morton and his cohorts spent a great deal of time "quaffing and drinking both wine and strong waters in great exsess, and, as some reported, 10 *li.* worth in a morning. They allso set up a May-pole, drinking

Embroidering on tales of the American Eden, an Englishman created this imaginary wilderness scene to frame a shuttered travel mirror, perhaps as a going-away present.

and dancing aboute it many days togeather, inviting the Indean women, for their consorts, dancing and frisking togither, (like so many fairies, or furies rather,) and worse practises."

May-day celebrations were not sanctioned by the Bible. Even more pagan and abhorrent in the eyes of the Puritan were the dancing and the songs the renegades sang, one being of Morton's own composition. It began:

Children dancing around a Maypole

> *Drinke and be merry, merry, merry boyes,*
> *Let all your delight be in Hymen's joyes,*
> *Io to Hymen, now the day is come,*
> *About the merry Maypole take a Roome.*
> *Make greene garlons, bring bottles out;*
> *And fill sweet Nectar, freely about.*
> *Lasses in beaver coats, come away,*
> *Yee shall be welcome to us night and day.*

According to Bradford, it went on like that, "tending to lasciviousness."

Several unsuccessful attempts were made to rid the countryside of Morton's disturbing influence and his economic competition (he threatened to corner the fur trade by offering muskets to the Indians, rather than the beads and Bible lessons they were likely to get at Plymouth). Bradford decided that Morton must be stopped, and he sent Captain Miles Standish with a small force to arrest him. According to Standish, he found Morton and his fellows too drunk to offer resistance. According to Morton, "Captain Shrimp," as he called Standish, and his band of "Moles" surprised him when most of his comrades were off on a trading expedition. At any rate, Morton was brought back to Plymouth and left to shift for himself on a lonely island for a month "without gun, powder, or shot or dog or so much as a knife to get any thing to feed upon." But some of his Indian cronies brought him what he needed, including "bottles of strong liquor . . . so full of humanity are these infidels before those Christians." After that, the Pilgrim Fathers sent him back to England. Thus evil was routed (temporarily) from Massachusetts.

Unlike orthodox Calvinists, who believed that man was totally depraved and might be saved only by God's Grace, it was the Puritans' conviction that they had made a covenant, a bargain with God: by promising to live by the Bible in every aspect of their lives, and by doing good works, they would be granted success in this world and salvation in the next. Governor John Winthrop told them that in this unique moral venture they would be "as a Citty upon a Hill." And "if wee shall deale falsely with our god in this worke wee have undertaken and soe cause him to withdrawe his present help from us, wee shall be made a story and a by-word."

Their God was inscrutable and subject to sudden tempers, the causes of which were usually beyond the understanding of "This sinfull creature, frail and vain This lump of wretchedness, of sin and sorrow"—as man was described by the Puritan poet Anne Bradstreet. Man was powerless to save himself if God had predestined him to damnation; but up until the moment of death, there was always the chance that God would grant him a "converting experience" and a place among the Elect. God sometimes gave notice of his wrath by means of earthquakes and hurricanes, sometimes through visitations of illness and death. When Cotton Mather had a toothache, he prayed God to let him know what sin he had committed with his teeth. Even the most

trivial mishaps were taken as evidence of heavenly displeasure. Judge
Samuel Sewall, an old-school Puritan, upset a can of water and "made that
Reflection that our Lives would shortly be spilt." When John Winthrop's son
found that a mouse had been eating part of his prayer book, he thanked God
for having curbed the mouse's appetite before it ate the Psalms.

An ailing Puritan, while waiting for the doctor, prayed for forgiveness
of his sins, and his neighbors helped him—for it was a Puritan precept that
every man was his brother's keeper. A person whom we would call a busybody
was simply doing his Christian duty in seventeenth-century New England.
Sewall, whose life spanned the last half of the century and the first quarter
of the next, recorded in his diary that he often went about Boston giving unsolicited advice. For example, when his friend Reverend Josiah Willard
acquired a wig, Sewall went at once to call on him and "enquired of him what
Extremity had forced him to put off his own hair, and put on a Wigg? He
answered, none at all. But said that his Hair was streight, and that it parted
behinde. Seem'd to argue that men might as well shave their hair off their
head, as off their faces. I answered men were men before they had hair on
their faces, (half of mankind have never any). God seems to have ordain'd our
Hair as a Test, to see whether we can bring our minds to be content to be at
his finding; or whether we would be our own Carvers, Lords, and come no
more at Him. Allow me to be so far a *Censor Morum* for this end of the Town.
[Willard] seem'd to say would leave off his Wigg when his hair was grown."

Massachusetts Bay seal, 1680

Puritan manners and morals were in many ways unique. Nevertheless, the
Massachusetts settlers could not leave their background completely behind;
and with them aboard their little ships, besides such things as English pewter,
wheelbarrows, doublets, apple seeds, plowshares, hemp cord, and conserve
of wormwood (a seasick remedy), they brought English standards of gentility,
English forms of address and behavior, English law, the English language,
and those embryonic notions of man's freedom that, since the Magna Carta,
had set England apart from Europe. Not that the Puritans were democrats.
Said John Winthrop, "If we should change from a mixt aristocratie to a mere
Democratie, first we should have no warrant in scripture for it: there was no
such government in Israel. . . . A Democratie is, amongst most civil nations,
accounted the meanest and worst of all forms of government." But, un-
wittingly, the Bay colonists left the door open for democracy by turning away
from feudalism and hereditary aristocracy. The colonists were freeholders.
And when a group of English lords of the Puritan persuasion proposed to
emigrate to Massachusetts on condition that they and their heirs would be
the aristocrats of the colony and the founders of a colonial House of Lords,
John Cotton, acting as spokesman for the Bay magistrates, replied that while
the colony welcomed persons of a "noble or generous family with a spirit
and gifts fit for government," yet it might happen that "God should not delight to furnish some of their posterity with gifts fit for magistracy." The noble
lords stayed home.

Christian soldiers marching onward

The Bay colonists were only in favor of freedom of thought if it was their
own. For them, liberty was the privilege of attending to the word of God,
interpreting it in the Puritan way, and keeping their covenant with Him. The
Salem pastor, Francis Higginson, spoke for all when he said "we have here
the true Religion . . . we doubt not but God will be with us, and if God be
with us, who can be against us?" Dissenters either kept their views to them-

selves or were asked to leave the colony. As another Puritan minister put it, dissidents "shall have free Liberty to keep away from us, and such as will come to be gone as fast as they can, the sooner the better." The people of Massachusetts were somewhat more humane with dissenters than the English, preferring to send them into the wilderness rather than to burn them (but then, in England, there was no wilderness to send them into).

At the Bay colony, only church members could vote, and joining the church was like joining an exclusive club, except that the qualifications were spiritual, not temporal. Applicants had to convince the elders and the congregation "that they are true beleevers, that they have beene wounded in their hearts for the originall sinne, and actuall transgressions, and can pitch upon some promise of free grace in the Scripture, for the ground of their faith, and that they finde their hearts drawne to beleeve in Christ Jesus, for their justification and salvation . . . and that they know competently the summe of Christian faith."

It was a tall order, and only one-fifth of the adults of John Winthrop's Boston were able to fill it. God in His wisdom usually chose His Saints from "the better sort," the leading families of the community. But it sometimes happened, disconcertingly, that a son would become a Saint and not his father, or a humble cowherd and not the well-off farmer who employed him. The colony's leaders were anxious to prevent too much power from falling into the hands of any one group. As they had rejected a hereditary nobility, so they feared "leveling"; nor did they want an imbalance of power in favor of either clergy or magistracy. According to John Cotton, it was "most wholsome for Magistrates and Officers in Church and Commonwealth, never to affect more liberty and authority than will do them good. . . . There is a straine in a mans heart that will sometime or other runne out to excesse, unlesse the Lord restraine it, but it is not good to venture it: It is necessary therefore, that all power that is on earth be limited, church-power or other."

In a theocratic state, as in a communist one, no man, woman, or child is excused from continual dedication to duty. A Sabbath day in Puritan Massachusetts, while affording rest from physical work, called for spiritual efforts that in our time are expected only in religious orders. Let us say that it is the year 1650, a January Sabbath, and we are attending meeting in one of the outlying villages of the Bay colony—Ipswich, perhaps, or Hingham. The meetinghouse is unpainted, inside or out, and has a weathercock on top instead of a "popish" cross (Saint Peter's having heard the cock crow gives that bird a holy association). The interior of the meetinghouse is unheated. Some of the congregation have brought foot stoves (brass boxes filled with hot coals, the cause of more than one disastrous fire); others sit in wolfskin bags, or have brought along a well-behaved dog to lie on their feet. The winter light that falls through the small windows is barely enough to illumine our psalmbooks. The sermon goes on for at least two hours. Many of the congregation take notes—a good way of staying attentive, for there is a fine for falling asleep. Near the pulpit, a two-foot-high hourglass marks the time. Each time its course is run, it is discreetly turned over by the tithingman. The tithingman also prevents anyone from leaving early and keeps a disciplinary eye on the children; but his chief duty is to collect the offerings.

The women and girls sit together on one side of the middle aisle, the men on the other, and the boys on the steps of the chancel, where no nonsense is

King David, fabled Psalmist, was cited in a 1684 almanac (above). A system for improving colonial harmony is below.

possible. Pews and seats are assigned by the church committee in order of social rank. The magistrates sit in front; then the people who have brought with them from England the right to be called Mister or Madam, taking precedence over the artisans, who call themselves Goodman and Goodwife. They are followed by the laborers, who are addressed by their first names only and sit at the back. High up in the gallery are the white bond servants, with Negro and Indian bond servants and slaves behind them.

A portable foot warmer for church

The meetinghouse is not called a church, for that word smacks of popery. There is no kneeling; the people stand during prayers and psalm singing. When they rise, the pew seats are pushed back, like seats in a modern theater. When it is time to sit again, which may be as much as two hours later, the banging down of seats is deafening. There is no organ and probably there is no other musical instrument, although a trumpet, drum, or flute would be acceptable because they are mentioned in the Bible. Someone gives the key for the next psalm and the congregation is off and away: *off* being the right word when it comes to key, for these are people who have had little to do with music.

Psalm singing had earlier been one of the consolations and glories of the Protestant movement, with many of the tunes adapted from spirited ballads, hornpipes, and even courtly love songs. Despite the encouragement that appeared on the *Bay Psalm Book*—"If any be merry, let him sing psalms"— much of the joy and inspiration had gone out of singing. The Puritan repertoire had been winnowed to a few austere songs, retranslated direct from the Hebrew, lest Anglican theology corrupt the true message. The congregation was forced to labor over such unsingable lines as this recasting of Psalm 137:

> *The rivers on of Babilon there when we did sit downe:*
> *Yea even then we mourned, when wee remembered Sion.*
> *Our harpe wee did hang it amid upon the willow tree,*
> *Because there they that us away led in captivitie,*
> *Requir'd of us a song, thus asks mirth; us waste who laid*
> *Sing us among a Sions song unto us then they said.*

A reader "lined out" a phrase at a time, with the congregation repeating after him, thus doubling both length and tedium.

At the end of the morning, those among the congregation who lived nearby went home for a meal prepared the day before. (There were fines for preparing meals on Sunday; also for performing any other housework, traveling, shaving, running, kissing, or having sexual intercourse. Parents of children born on the Sabbath were likely to be fined for the latter offense, for it was generally believed that a child born on the Sabbath must have been conceived on the Sabbath.) Those who lived farther away retired to the noonhouse, a small, fire-warmed building near the meetinghouse, where they ate something they had brought with them, conversed (but only on religious topics), and then returned to the meetinghouse for an afternoon much like the morning.

Perhaps someone brought a newborn baby to be baptized: better the risk of exposing a young infant to cold and wind than the horror of its dying at home unbaptized and going at once to hell. Considerable imagination could be exercised by the parents in choosing a name: besides common English ones—John, Thomas, Richard, Henry—any name in the Old Testament from Ahab to Zerubbabel was considered beautiful. There was also a fashion for names like Gift-of-God, Kill-sin, Fly-fornication, Joy-from-Above, Zealous, and the like. One of Governor Winthrop's grandchildren was called Waitstill. A girl child of a couple named Cheeseman, baptized in the womb for fear of a stillbirth, went through a long life under the name of Creature.

Sometimes the meeting was enlivened by someone making a public confession—perhaps of legally punishable sins, such as cheating or fornication, or perhaps of inwardly tormenting sins, like pride or envy. For a Puritan, relief of a bad conscience was as painful and necessary as having a tooth pulled. (The most famous and impressive example of a public confession was that of Judge Samuel Sewall, who a few years after the Salem witchcraft trials, stood up in meeting and expressed remorse for his part in the condemnations.) Or the solemnity of the meetinghouse might be suddenly disrupted by a Quaker, dressed in sack cloth—or even stark naked—to demonstrate that the trappings of rank were meaningless.

The Sabbath day meeting was one of two important events of the week; the other occurred on Thursday evenings, when another sermon, thinly disguised as a "lecture," and generally known as "the Great and Thursday," was delivered from the same pulpit to the same congregation. Under penalty of fine, everyone attended, unless he were absent from town or very ill. The sermons and lectures were stern stuff indeed. Delivered in what was called "the plain style," with no Latin quotations or other forms of literary ostentation, they were designed to scarify a sinner into repentance and to counteract any smugness that the Devil might have implanted in sinners already repented. "Every natural man and woman is born full of sin, as full as a toad of poison," said Thomas Hooker on one occasion. The plain style, though very plain indeed for the most part, had its moments of hard-hitting and vivid phraseology, and few could doubt that hell was a real and frightful place.

Clergymen in New England did not speculate about theological problems. The Saints already knew the Truth; it was all there in the Bible. The only question was how to apply God's manual of instruction to the practical issues of daily living. One way was to promote literacy, so that as many people as possible could read the Scriptures and take notes at meeting. When, in 1647, the Great and General Court of Massachusetts ordered each town of the Bay colony with a population of fifty householders or more to provide a teacher for children and bond servants, the purpose was not to "educate" in our understanding of the word, but to promote the True Religion. "Xerxes did die And so must I" read a verse in an early primer, deftly combining a use of the letter x, a bit of history, and some practical Puritan wisdom.

America's universities had their start in the seventeenth century. With more than fifteen thousand English-speaking colonists settled in New England—over a hundred of them graduates of Cambridge and Oxford—there was strong motivation to transplant England's system of higher learning. On October 28, 1636, the Massachusetts General Court agreed to give £400 "towards a schoale or colledge." Within two years a board of overseers had secured a small house and a tract of land adjoining Cambridge's cow yards, had fenced off the area, and had chosen a master. Fortunately for the institution's future, an enthusiastic supporter named John Harvard died about that time, leaving a significant legacy and a library of four hundred volumes. The court promptly named the community's pride Harvard.

Colonists in the South, on the other hand, commenced life in the New

(Continued on Page 24)

The Devil, as incarnated in Boston

Jamestown: 1612

America's first permanent settlement, as ruled by Lawes Devine, Morall, and Martiall. *Excerpts from the code, drafted by Sir Thomas Dale, appear below.*

Euerie man and woman duly twice a day vpon the first towling of the Bell shall vpon the working daies repaire vnto the Church, to hear diuine Service. . . . He that vpon pretended malice, shall murther or take away the life of any man, shall bee punished with death. No man shal commit the horrible, and detestable sins of Sodomie vpon pain of death; & he or she that can be lawfully conuict of Adultery shall be punished with death. No man shall rauish or force any woman, maid or Indian, or other, vpon pain of death, and . . . he or shee, that shall commit fornication, and euident proofe made thereof, for their first fault shall be whipt. . . . He that shall rob the store of any commodities . . . whether prouisions of victuals, or of Arms, Trucking stuffe, Apparrell, Linnen, or Wollen, hose or Shoes, Hats or Caps, Instruments or Tooles of Steele, Iron, &c. . . . shall bee punished with death. What man or woman soeuer, shall rob . . . any vineyard . . . or steale any eares of the corne growing . . . shall be punished with death. No manner of person whatsoeuer, shall dare to detract, slaunder, calumniate, or vtter unseemely, and unfitting speeches, either against his Maiesties Honourable Councell for this Colony . . . or against the zealous endeauors, & intentions of the whole body of Aduenturers for this pious and Christian Plantation. . . . No man of what condition soeuer shall barter, trucke, or trade with the Indians, except he be thereunto appointed by lawful authority. . . . No man shall rifle or dispoile, by force or violence, [or] take away any thing from any Indian comming to trade, or otherwise, upon paine of death. No man shall dare to kill, or destroy any Bull, Cow, Calfe, Mare, Horse, Colt, Goate, Swine, Cocke, Henne, Chicken, Dogge, Turkie, or any tame Cattel or Poultry . . . whether his owne, or appertaining to another man, without leave from the Generall, upon paine of death in the Principall, and in the accessary, burning in the Hand, and losse of his eares, and unto the concealer of the same foure and twenty houres whipping, with addition of further punishment. . . . There shall no man or woman, Launderer or Laundresse, dare wash any vnclean Linen . . . or throw out the water or suds of fowle cloathes, in the open streete, within the Palizadoes. . . . Nor shall anyone aforesaid, within lesse than a quarter of one mile from the Palizadoes, dare to doe the necessities of nature, since by these vnmanly, slothfull, and loathsome immodesties, the whole Fort may bee choaked, and poisoned with ill aires. . . . Euery man shall haue an especiall and due care, to keepe his house sweete and cleane, as also so much of the streete as lieth before his door, and . . . set his bedstead whereon he lieth, that it may stand three foote at least from the ground. . . . Euery tradsman in their seuerall occupation . . . shall duly and daily attend his worke . . . vpon perill for his first fault, and negligence therein, to haue his entertainment checkt for one moneth . . . for his third, one yeare, and if he continue . . . to the Gally for three yeare. . . . No man or woman . . . shall runne away to any sauage Weroance else whatsoeuer.

*Free spirits who found England confining
were urged to go to Virginia. Eager breeders,
like those shown, made the best colonists.*

World with different ideas in their heads. Though they came from the same stock as New Englanders—the middle and lower classes of England, with a handful of settlers claiming descent from titled families—there was never the deep-rooted moral Idea to bind them together. The problem of founding a college never had the same urgency—William and Mary was not chartered until 1693. The Virginia immigrants did not come in shiploads of families with the object of founding a religious-minded community. Mostly Anglicans, they were not fleeing religious persecution, and they were more interested in this world than the next one. Usually they came independently and without wives, just as gold prospectors went west in a later era. Most women arrived in groups, some of them by their own choosing, others apparently sold by their parents or guardians or simply kidnapped under the auspices of the Virginia Company. Still other women came as indentured servants, or were erstwhile denizens of London gaols. On at least one occasion, the city of London sent more than a hundred orphans—both boys and girls—to be bound out to planters. Until after mid-century the men in Virginia greatly outnumbered the women and social life was far from normal. Unlike the patriarchal, close-knit Puritan family, the southern family continued to follow the ancient European pattern—a loosely structured gathering of master, servants, and slaves, of husband, wife, mistresses, and children.

Through luck or opportunism, it was possible for immigrants with modest capital—and even for indentured servants—to rise in the world like kites in a windy sky. In 1629 seven of the forty-four burgesses who formed the Virginia governing body had been servants only a few years before; in 1662 there were nineteen. These newly rich landowners, however, made it difficult for later immigrants to emulate them. They snapped up the land by the thousands of acres, so that before the end of the century, persons without capital had to become tenants of the earlier arrivals or else travel beyond the settled regions to the Indian-haunted frontier. By 1750 the land and government of Virginia was chiefly in the hands of about a hundred "First Families of Virginia," and they did not let it go until the Civil War.

During most of the seventeenth century, African slaves were no more numerous in the South than in the North. Until 1664, Dutch ships representing Dutch interests monopolized the slave trade. The supply, therefore, was limited, and so was the demand. But gradually, the Virginia plantations grew larger. Tobacco quickly exhausted the soil, and new fields had constantly to be cleared. The blacks survived the climate and hard work better than white bond servants and were therefore a better investment. In those days, very few people had any moral scruples about slavery. It was a fact of life the world over, even among West Africans whose tribes kept the slavers supplied. (There was an often overlooked distinction, however: slaves in Africa were not necessarily bound for life. Like white bond servants in America, they could become free and even rise to important positions.)

In the middle colonies, only the Quakers and the Mennonites opposed slavery (although many Quakers were slaveowners). In Boston, Samuel Sewall published America's first pamphlet against it, *The Selling of Joseph*, and noted in his diary, "I essay'd . . . to prevent Indians and Negroes being Rated with Horses and Hogs; but could not prevail." Cotton Mather, on the other hand, in a sermon to Negroes, informed them that God had appointed them to the role of slave. But New England's economy was unsuited to slavery.

Farms were small and at best not very productive. Winters were hard. Early prosperity came from fishing and fur trading, which did not require a multiplicity of hands. Later, New England's wealth depended on overseas trade, and merchants found it more profitable to deal in slaves than to own them. Indeed, after 1700, there were complaints in the South that the Yankees were bringing them too many.

Relieved of manual labor, landed Virginians were free to imitate English lords of the manor. Instead of going to London to see the queen, they went to Williamsburg to flock around His Majesty's royal governor, who kept miniature court there. Sir William Berkeley, who served twice, did much to shape seventeenth-century Virginian social attitudes. He encouraged Royalist sympathizers to immigrate, reinforcing the local partiality for the English caste system, and he thanked God that there were no free schools or presses in Virginia, "for learning has brought disobedience and heresy and sects into the world; and printing has divulged them and libels against the government. God keep us from both." With much flogging and many executions, Berkeley put down a rebellion of dissatisfied landowners. Charles II, certainly no democrat, recalled him for his excesses, remarking, "the old fool has hanged more people in that naked Country, than I have done for the murder of my Father." Of those rebels who survived, some moved to the frontier, "the back country," and others stayed on their small farms and made the best of things.

Geography also had a strong effect on Virginian manners and morals. The coastline from Maryland to Georgia abounds in rivers and inlets—the Chesapeake Bay alone has 3,500 miles of coastline—obviating any urgent need for good roads. Planters built their houses by riversides and shipped their barrels of tobacco from their own wharves. Thus they could live like English landed gentlemen and engage in trade without having to associate with tradesmen—for the sale of the tobacco was handled by London factors.

Indirectly, it was geography that also fostered the tradition of "southern hospitality." There were almost no towns and thus very few inns. Planters, leading isolated lives on their domains, were always glad to see a new face; sometimes they would station a servant by the track or waterway where travelers might pass by, in order to extend an invitation for a meal or the night. This custom of private hospitality revived a medieval tradition that had been somewhat forgotten by English country gentlemen as they grew more sophisticated and acquired London houses.

Hospitality was also high among the virtues extolled in Henry Peacham's *The Compleat Gentleman*, 1662, an English etiquette book familiar to every literate colonist, North and South, but taken more seriously in the South. The book stressed fortitude, prudence, justice, liberality, courtesy, and leadership. A southern gentleman was expected to have pleasing manners, converse well, dance, ride, and be familiar with music and literature. Above all, he was to be moderate in all things, including intellectual endeavors; it was not thought meet for a gentleman to become too proficient, for that smacked of work—and a gentleman, by definition, was a man who did no physical labor.

Seventeenth-century etiquette books did not concern themselves with the petty details of behavior. Young men of "the better sort" were expected to know by a kind of osmosis how to bow to a lady or how to make a toast; if they had to seek such information from books, they were clearly not gentlemen. As James I once said to his old nurse, when she asked him to make her

Virginia slaves crating a tobacco shipment

son a gentleman, "I can make him a Lord—but a gentleman, never." Richard Alestree's *The Gentleman's Calling*, first printed in London about 1660, was to be found in many colonial libraries. It preached much the same message as *The Compleat Gentleman*, but in typical seventeenth-century style leaned heavily on religious precepts and biblical texts. Pointing out that "the lower rank of men fetch their meer Necessaries out of the Earth; which being, as it were, hardned and petrified by Adam's Sin, must be mollified and suppled with their Sweat, before it will become penetrable . . . whilst Gentlemen sweat only at the Engagements of their Sports, or by the Direction of the Physician, to digest their Fulness of Bread," the author cited Deuteronomy 6:11 as an explanation: the rich are "Heirs of the Israelites Blessing . . . who were to possess Houses full of all good Things which they filled not, and Wells digged which they digged not, Vineyards and Olive-trees, which they planted not." Wealth brings with it education, time, and authority: but the gentleman must have care how he handles these precious items or he will become "a troubler of his own House, to whom Solomon (Proverbs 11:29) assigns no other Inheritance but the Wind." The author admonishes that the gentleman gets no credit for having been born rich. "God in his Wisdome, discerning that Equality of Conditions would breed Confusion in the World, had ordered several States, designed some to Poverty, others to Riches, only annexing to the Rich the Care of the Poor, yet that rather as an Advantage, than a Burden, a Seed of more Wealth both Temporal and Eternal. Now in this Division of Men, those on whom he hath caused the better Lot to fall, can owe it to nothing but his gracious Disposal. . . . Every Rich Man is God's Steward."

Despite wide circulation of *The Gentleman's Calling* and *The Compleat Gentleman*, which emphasized the rich man's duty toward the poor, social consciousness was not a seventeenth-century characteristic in the South. Although men might act compassionately, economic self-interest generally won out, and the same gentleman whose gates were open to strangers and who willed ten pounds to the local almshouse might beat his slaves and keep his bond servants on a starvation diet. The social gospel was more viable in the North. John Winthrop set the standard when he told the Bay colonists "if thy brother be in want and thou canst help him, thou needst not make doubt, what thou shouldst doe; if thou louest God thou must help him." William Penn preached a similar lesson to Quakers, "The best recreation is to do good;" and Cotton Mather, though he referred to the Indians as "unkennell'd wolves" and deprecated the efforts of John Eliot in translating the Bible into the Algonquian language, instructed his congregation to devote themselves to "a perpetual endeavor to do good" among their own. One of the earliest private welfare organizations in North America was the Scots' Charitable Society, founded in 1657 by twenty-seven Boston Scotsmen for the care of needy Scots. In New York a French Huguenot, Elias Neau, gave up his business in order to devote time to educating Negro and Indian slaves. His neighbors thought he was insane.

One of the more curious facts of social life in the colonies was that although there were many lawsuits there were very few lawyers. The settlers had a distrust of them that dated back to the Middle Ages, when the average man was illiterate and could easily be hoodwinked by a legal document. Many of the first American settlers, although not highly educated, could read and write, and therefore preferred to compose their own wills and handle their

Pocahontas, dressed as a planter's wife

own lawsuits and legal proceedings. In fact, there was a widespread feeling that a lawyer was little better than a usurer. Nathaniel Ward's "Bodie of Liberties," drawn up in 1641 for the governing of the Bay colony, specified that no man should take money for representing another in court. Although that law was repealed in 1648, the feeling that prompted it remained. John Hull, Samuel Sewall's father-in-law, said that the law was like a lottery— "great charge, little benefit." In Virginia, in 1658, all lawyers were ordered out of the colony. Not until 1680 were they readmitted—and then under strict surveillance.

Since the law was such a despised profession, no gentleman went into it. Samuel Sewall was called Judge and often acted as one, but his legal training consisted in having read Edward Coke's *Reports*. Most gentlemen knew a smattering of law, in order to look out for their own interests; but there were no law schools in America until the late eighteenth century. In 1700 New York had seven lawyers, only three of whom had any legal training. Of the others, one was a former glover, one was a dancing master, and two were previous tenants of English gaols.

Nor was the seventeenth-century approach to crime and punishment far removed from the medieval. Some still believed that the body of a murdered person would bleed afresh when touched by the murderer; and that a guilty person would float if thrown into water, while an innocent one would sink. But one advance made in the New World was in the reduction of the number of capital crimes. In England a man might be hanged for any of over three hundred offenses. The Puritans reduced that number to fifteen, including witchcraft, murder, treason, blasphemy, rape, adultery, perjury endangering life, kidnapping, bestiality, and sodomy (all mentioned as capital crimes in the Bible). Under William Penn's "Great Law" the death penalty was imposed only for murder. Ward's "Bodie of Liberties" stipulated that a wife was not to be struck by her husband unless she hit him first; also that "no man shall exercise any Tirrany or Crueltie towards any bruite Creatures which are usuallie kept for man's use"—the first legislation in American history for the prevention of cruelty to animals.

For crimes not demanding the death penalty—drunkenness, vagrancy, writing censorable books, petty thievery—there was a variety of unpleasant punishments. In early Boston the bilboes (leg irons) were much used; John Winthrop brought some with him. Later, towns had wooden stocks, usually on the common in front of the meetinghouse. Their arms and legs confined, offenders suffered public humiliation for a fixed number of hours, while the townsfolk jeered. In a pillory, the prisoner stood and thrust his head and hands through wooden holes. Sometimes offenders were whipped while in the pillory or had their ears nailed to the wood. Sometimes nostrils were slit, ears cut off, or tongues bored with an awl or hot instrument. Women with bad tempers—"scolds"—were tied to a chair and ducked in the nearest pond. "Riding the wooden horse" meant sitting on the narrow side of a board with weights tied to the feet. This punishment was abandoned in the next century, for it frequently caused permanent injury or death. A "whirligig" was a spinning cage, causing nausea at the least. Or the judge might order a "barrel-shirt" or "drunkard's cloak," requiring the offender to walk around town wearing a barrel—a not particularly painful but certainly humiliating punishment that was used as late as the Civil War. More serious offenders were

Members of the Society of Friends, gathered at Sunday morning meeting, await the "inner voice" of God to speak through one of them. Hats are essential attire.

very often branded with a letter—*I* for incest, *A* for adultery, and the like.

Most Americans raised on Hawthorne's *The Scarlet Letter* suppose that bastard children in Puritan New England were almost unheard-of. Yet, in fact, when the population of Boston stood at 4,000, there were 48 recorded cases of bastardy and 50 of fornication, a not inconsiderable percentage. When, in 1697, the Reverend John Cotton of Plymouth was accused of "Notorious Breaches of the Seventh Commandment," he was not arrested, but instead was asked by a church council to "make an orderly secession from the Church." He went to Charleston, South Carolina, where two years later he contracted yellow fever and died—to no devout New Englander's surprise.

Smuggling, piracy, and trading with pirates was a crime often tacitly condoned in the colonies, because England's colonial policy made it difficult for honest merchants to carry on a profitable trade. The scoff-law attitudes that later contributed to the spirit of revolution had their origins in the seventeenth century. While England was at war, it was not only legitimate but patriotic for colonial ships to prey on the ships of the enemy; but a peace treaty suddenly turned the patriotic colonial into a pirate. So it happened with one John Quelch, who raided Portuguese ships without having heard the news that Portugal had become an ally. Quelch and some of his men were hanged at Boston. Cotton Mather, following the Puritan custom of preaching a public sermon to the condemned, browbeat Quelch for several hours before. The contrite pirate told the assembled to avoid making his mistakes.

Blackbeard, scourge of the Carolinas

The most worldly colony in North America was New York—or New Amsterdam, as it was known until 1664. Its colonists came from a tolerant, prosperous, and politically stable country, and they came because the Dutch West India Company, their sponsor, had the Dutch government's promise to make a patroon of any settler who could found a community of fifty adults in six years' time. The first comers were tough, brave, largely illiterate, and ruthless. They cheated the Indians without compunction and were so greedy about land—even greedier than the Virginians—that later immigration was stifled, leaving upper New York thinly settled long after neighboring Pennsylvania was blossoming into farms. Kiliaen Van Rensselaer, a wealthy merchant and stockholder in the Dutch West India Company, never left Holland, but had agents "buy" seven hundred thousand acres for him. When he had enough tenants to make him a patroon, he required an oath of fealty from them. In return he provided them with various amenities, such as a brandy still and a flag. His son took personal possession of the estate, which comprised Albany and surrounding tracts. Parts of it remained in the family until recently. A poor young Scotsman named Robert Livingston married the daughter of one of the Van Rensselaers and thus obtained a 160,000-acre tract of land on the Hudson. (Livingston prided himself on keeping a retinue of specially selected slaves, each of whom was an African prince or chieftain.) Nearly all these holders of large estates—the Kips, the Roosevelts, the Brevoorts, the Beekmans—were engaged in trade and yet were considered gentlefolk, at least by the people of the colony. What sort of trade was making them so rich, it was sometimes better not to inquire. Known pirates swaggered up and down Broad Street and in and out of respectable offices. After the English took over the colony in 1664, the important Dutch families became members of the royal governor's set and adopted the modes and manners of London rather than of Amsterdam, leaving only their games, their holiday customs of Christmas and New Year's day, and several dozen words to the young American culture.

Except for the short-lived colony of Swedes in Delaware, the first influx of Germans in Pennsylvania under William Penn's hospitable governance, and a handful of titled persons who followed Lord Baltimore to Maryland, the first settlers of the middle colonies were middle- and lower-class English. The way of life was English, and the colonists, because of the primeval wilderness that separated one settlement from the next, were more in touch with England than with each other. Though they might complain of England's politics, religion, and economics, they were loyal Englishmen and the idea of rebellion was still generations in the future. Other colonies might be considered odd, outlandish, deluded, or downright evil, but never England. Yet in spite of themselves, they were growing away from English ways. New words and phrases crept into the colonial vocabulary: an English visitor to Boston remarked disdainfully, "neither days, months, seasons, churches nor inns are known by their English names."

North of the Maryland colony, family units were very close. As in England, Puritans and Quakers were distinguished by their tidy domesticity, their modern concern for the supervision and education of their children. Illegitimate or orphaned children became the town's responsibility and usually were "bound out" when they were old enough to work. Captain Lathrop of Salem and his wife had a houseful of adopted children whom they treated as their own, but that was exceptional. Boys and girls married between the ages of sixteen and twenty; there were very few old maids or bachelors; widows and widowers remarried within months or even weeks of their bereavements. Grandparents and unmarried adult children all lived under the same roof. In the old country married children customarily went to live with in-laws; in the New World there was room enough and opportunity enough for them to set out on their own.

A seventeenth-century colonial house, even among the well-to-do, had one main room, called, as in England, "the hall." Here the cooking and eating took place, spinning wheels whirred, cradles rocked, children performed simple chores (they had not much time to play), and the old people sat in the chimney corner and did whatever they were still capable of doing—carding wool, whittling handles, weaving baskets; no one in these self-dependent households was allowed the luxury of sitting idle. At mealtime, large containers of food were placed on the table, and the family gathered round, the children often standing. The plates, shared by two or more diners each, were either pewter or wooden trenchers; and the ale or beer was passed in a communal tankard. (One ill-mannered Puritan child is said to have called out to a visitor, who was taking a pull at the tankard, "You're using Grandma's place!") Food was eaten with knives, spoons, and fingers. The fork was a rarity. John Winthrop brought one over on the *Arbella* with him, carefully packed in its own case, and for some time it was probably the only fork in North America. Homemade napkins and tablecloths were commonplace.

Larger houses had a parlor, kept for funerals, weddings, and special events. It usually contained a bed for overnight visitors. A really opulent town house had three or four second-story rooms, built to overhang the first story in the traditional English style. These were reached by a precipitous staircase; or perhaps the upper story was simply one unfinished room at the top of a

The pewter nursing bottle above might feed a baby's body; the catechism below fed his Puritan soul.

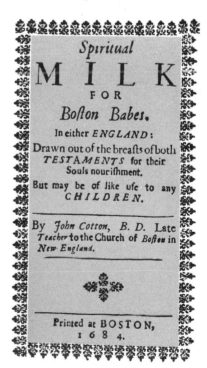

ladder. Cotton Mather had the luxury of a study, where in private he beat his children and prayed, with his mouth "in the dust." (Mather's phraseology is undoubtedly symbolic, not a comment on Mistress Mather's housekeeping.)

Childbearing, though it took place in the home, was one event that was generally conducted in privacy without benefit of friends and family. Colonial obstetrics were still in the Dark Ages, and for reasons of prudery men—even male physicians—were generally kept away from the bedside, leaving midwives of dubious professionalism to take charge. Women were expected to suffer, and only token prescriptions to ease the pain were administered; their efficacy, judging from the ingredients of one such medicament, must have been strictly psychological. The prescription directed, "For Sharpe & Dificult Travel [labor] in Women with child Take a Lock of Vergins haire on any Part of ye head, of half the Age of ye Woman in travill. Cut it very smale to fine Powder or other wise make them dry & make them to powder with the haire, give this with a quarter of a pint of Red Cows milk or for want of it give it in strong ale wort." Seventeenth-century New England's annals are filled with stories of women who died in childbirth and men who of necessity married two and three times.

The Commandment "Honor Thy Father and Thy Mother" was taken so seriously that it was in some colonies a capital crime for a child over sixteen to strike or curse his parent. Parents applied the rod liberally—otherwise some dutiful neighbor would come to warn against the sin of indulgence. Children were treated (and dressed) as diminutive adults. That children did occasionally play is indicated by Boston laws against galloping horses in the streets, where playing children might be run down.

Acceptable adult amusements in New England consisted of ninepins, billiards, shovel board (an ancestor of shuffle board), outdoor sports such as fishing and skating, and convivial drinking bouts. While drunkenness was a sin and a crime, the Puritans must have worked out a fine distinction between drinking heavily and being drunk. They regarded water as unhealthy, and tea, coffee, and chocolate were not yet available. This cleared the way for beer and cider, with rum becoming popular toward the end of the century. Special occasions called for Madeira or canary wine. Inns apparently offered as many mysterious-sounding drinks as one finds listed at a modern cocktail bar: metheglin, calibogus, constantia, kill-devil, rumbullion, Alicante, switchel, mumbo, ebulum.

Golf and ninepins were Dutch games taken over by the English. Backgammon, pool, croquet, and billiards were played throughout the colonies, and cards everywhere but in New England. In Virginia, horse racing was a favorite sport for gentlemen. "The meaner sort" were fined for attempting to race horses, but they were free to amuse themselves with cockfighting, coon hunts, and hunting wild horses. Guy Fawkes Day, November 5, was a colonies-wide holiday. Among the Puritans, Christmas and Easter were studiously ignored, for the reason that they were not mentioned in the Bible as holidays, and also because in medieval and Elizabethan England both had been the occasion for several days of merrymaking and wild goings-on. The festival without scriptural precedence was Thanksgiving, observed in late November or early December as the local authorities saw fit, and then only in New England, until Abraham Lincoln made it a nationwide holiday.

The everlasting labor that was necessary for survival was pleasanter if

Childbirth under a blanket of modesty

neighbors got together to do it, with good food and drink at the end of the job. Few colonists were familiar with the poems of their Anglican contemporary John Donne, but his "no man is an island" fitted both their moral attitude and their condition. The New Englanders' covenant with God was, in a practical sense, a covenant with each other. As villages sprang up farther and farther from the mother town of Boston, the people built them together. A man could not clear a field or build a house without his neighbors to help with log-rolling, stone-piling, stump-pulling, wall-building, roof-raising. Farmers helped each other plow out roads in winter, slaughter livestock, harvest crops, boil maple sugar. The women exchanged help in a myriad of household duties: soapmaking, quilting, making rag carpets, pickling, sausagemaking (the men chopped the meat first with sharp spades), candledipping, cheesemaking, basket-weaving, and goose-plucking, to say nothing of the many steps in preparing wool and flax for the loom. In most townships, only church members were allowed to buy lots, and when they did, the whole town had to agree to the sale. There was common land for cow-pasturing, and it was against the law to fence land so that the village herds could not pass across it. (Possibly this may be the origin of the latter-day American custom, so surprising to Europeans, of unfenced lawns between houses.) Cows fed on Boston Common until 1840, and pigs ran in the streets of New York and Washington until after the Civil War. One cowherd looked after everyone's cows. There were also haywards—men or boys who looked after the community's hayfields and kept the livestock out. A municipal fence viewer saw that fences were kept mended and not built in wrong places. A hog-reeve kept an eye on roaming hogs. (Ralph Waldo Emerson served as Concord's reeve in the 1830's.) In Boston and Salem, everyone took a turn at the watch, even the magistrates. Carrying rattles, they walked the streets by twos and called out the time and weather—a young man, for combat power, and an older one, presumably to keep an eye on the younger one.

But if members of New England towns were close-knit and neighborly, their treatment of strangers was the opposite of "southern hospitality." A stranger walking down the main street of a New England village—even of Boston as late as 1714—was formally "warned out" by the sheriff or tithingman. If he persisted in lingering and had no local friend to speak for him, he was drummed or whipped out of town. When Madam Sarah Knight, a Bostonian, traveled overland to New York in 1704, she was greeted thus by an innkeeper's daughter: "Law for mee—what in the world brings you here at this time a night? I never see a woman on the Rode so Dreadfull late, in all the days of my versall life. Who are You? Where are You going?" Cases are on record where families were forbidden to have relatives from other towns to spend the night, and even those fleeing Indian attack got a cold reception. The reason was a fear that the community might become responsible for them; or that they might spread an epidemic.

Historians regard the end of the seventeenth century as a bad time for the colonies, a time of retardation in learning and culture and a time when spiritual zeal had declined and nothing important had taken its place. John Winthrop's "Citty upon a Hill" was not what he had hoped for, and the crassest materialism flourished. But as far as manners and morals are concerned, the seventeenth century had been a time of transplanting. It was too early to say how the tree would grow; already it was clearly not an English tree.

Heater to slip between sheets

Pewter bedpan for an invalid

31

Parlous Times

*In which our Moral Fiber
comes Unravelled, Scoffers,
Blasphemers, Ale-House
Haunters, and Wig-Merchants
are Abroad in the Land,
& the Devil & the Red Coats
are Finally Expelled

One day in September, 1686, Judge Samuel Sewall took up his pen and entered in his diary the glum notation that Samuel Shrimpton, one of the richest of Boston's merchants, a Captain Lidget, and others "come in a Coach from Roxbury about 9. aclock or past, singing as they come, being inflamed with Drink: At Justice Morgan's they stop and drink Healths, curse, swear, talk profanely and bawdily to the great disturbance of the town and grief of good people. Such highhanded wickedness has hardly been heard of before in Boston."

Although old-school Puritans like Sewall were not ready to admit it, the Bible State was slowly expiring. Its supporters, dwindling in number but still legally in power, passed blue laws that were flaunted, preached jeremiads to dozing congregations, and blamed the merchants for perverting the "City upon a Hill." New England, wailed Francis Higginson's son John, was "originally a plantation of Religion, not a plantation of Trades. Let Merchants and such as are increasing Cent per Cent remember this." Higginson and other clergymen spoke ever less of doctrine, holiness, and grace, and more of "the worldly mindedness, oppression, & hardheartedness feard to be amongst us." But, alas, they found "that we had as good preach to the Heavens and Earth, and direct our discourse to the Walls and Seats and Pillars of the meeting house, and say, Hear, O ye Walls, give ear O ye Seats and Pillars, as to many men in these Churches."

One sign of the times was that the number of "Visible Saints" was declining. Most new immigrants arriving in Boston were not Puritans. Many were not even English. Moreover, children of first-generation Saints were not coming forward to claim the all-important "converting experience." In desperation the magistrates departed from orthodoxy and devised the "Half-Way Covenant," whereby children of Saints might become church members simply by declaring their belief in Calvinist principles. However, without the

ℰ

Keeping colonial America free for godliness required constant vigilance. As seen in
The Progress of Sin, *a stirring text of 1744, Zion was girt by suburbs of sensuality.*

33

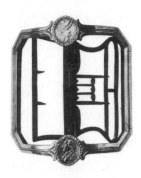

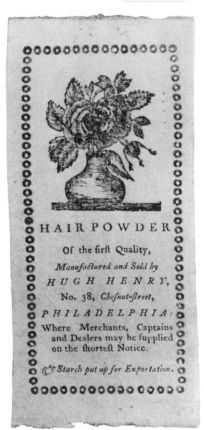

*Gentlemen had a battery of crafts-
men to tend to their needs. Paul
Revere made the shoe buckle above.
The ad below offers wig whitener.*

"experience," they were not allowed to partake of the Lord's Supper nor to vote in parish affairs. Even this was not enough for the new breed of Bostonian. In 1699 some of them founded a new, more liberal Brattle Street Meeting, which would admit any respectable person to membership and baptize any child. Brattle Street also rejected public confessions and allowed the entire congregation a voice in selecting the minister, much to the disapproval of Mather-led conservatives.

Propelled by the law, people still came to meeting twice a week, but instead of wearing homespun and plain broadcloth, they were likely to be tricked out in gold and silver lace, flowered silk, and "China taffeties"—certainly not produced by New England spinning wheels. And many women, especially around Boston, had taken to covering their well-scrubbed faces with make-up, to the consternation of one minister who promised that "at the resurrection of the just there will no such sight be met as the Angels carrying painted Ladies in their arms!" His colleague, Increase Mather, attributed the series of devastating defeats inflicted by the Indians upon the colonists in King Philip's War to a divine protest against such finery and against "monstrous and horrid Perriwigs . . . Borders and False Locks and such like whorish Fashions."

For persons of "the meaner sort," it was a spiritual and civil offense to dress frivolously. The wearing of clothes woven of gold or silver threads was specifically forbidden, and two Newburyport women were arrested in 1653 for wearing silk hoods and scarves, but were discharged when their husbands proved that they were not "mean," each being worth about two hundred pounds. By the end of the century, efforts to legislate against fine clothes were abandoned as hopeless. And although the Massachusetts General Court denounced wigs, even Cotton Mather and members of the Winthrop family were wearing them.

If anything can explain the hysteria over witches that took place in Salem in 1692, it is the utter frustration of those who sincerely believed that New England was on its way to hell. The Mathers and their following reasoned the decline of the Bible State in only one way: the Devil was at large in New England. As an apologia for Salem, it must be remembered that most seventeenth-century people believed in witches. King James I wrote a book on the subject, and a number of executions of witches took place during his reign. Authorities differ as to how many were put to death in Britain and Europe, but it was almost certainly in the thousands, while in New England the total number was thirty-two (and two dogs). Those who watched their beloved Bible State being wrecked by impious "strangers" longed to get Satan by the throat, and in Salem they thought they saw their chance. Even those who, like Judge Sewall, later regretted the executions, did not deny the existence of witches. They only said that probably there had been none in Salem.

The Puritans were nearer the truth when they asserted that education in the New World was in a bad state. "Young men prefer cheap knowledge, easily come by" was their complaint. Though the settlers had been zealous in founding a college to ensure themselves an educated clergy, boys with first-class minds were not attending in sufficient numbers. Those who did go were of too liberal a bent. Reverend Solomon Stoddard's election day sermon for 1703 made the familiar complaint that "places of learning should not be places of riot and pride. Ways of profuseness and prodigality in such a society lay a foundation of a great deal of sorrow. . . . 'Tis not worth the while for persons to be sent to the College to learn to compliment men and court women. They should be sent thither to prepare them for public service." Stoddard and others noted that young men were not seeking training as scientists, lawyers, or teachers. Occasionally, a man like Samuel Sewall or his father-in-law, John Hull, managed to be a Saint, sectarian businessman, and civic leader all at once, pointing out that scriptural justification could be found for making money in Proverbs 22:29. "Seest thou a man diligent in his business? He shall stand before kings." But most young men were preoccupied with bettering themselves in *this* world.

Poor Richard on the perils of borrowing

Such a man was Samuel Shrimpton, whose carousing ignited the wrath of Judge Sewall. The son of a brazier who had made a large fortune as an importer, Shrimpton had "a very stately house . . . with a Brass Kettle atop, to shew [he] was not ashamed of his Original." He owned a fleet in which he shipped fish and lumber to England, and he speculated in the building of new towns in western New England, to the disapproval of the Saints, who did not believe in owning large acreages. Another parvenu was Andrew Belcher, who was first a tavernkeeper, then a master of one of Sewall's ships, and by 1702 was driving around Boston in a coach with a Negro footman. Through hobnobbing with the governor's set, he made important friends and ultimately obtained the lucrative job of provisioning His Majesty's ships when they came to Boston Harbor. His son Jonathan, given a gentleman's education in England and Europe, became governor of Massachusetts and New Hampshire. Jonathan's son followed in his father's footsteps as a colonial administrator, more English than colonial. He spent his young manhood reveling and gaming among the gentlemen-rakes of London, and even became an Anglican.

Divided between crassly materialistic merchants and narrow-minded Puritans, New England at the end of the seventeenth century was barren ground for intellectuals. Among the few was Thomas Brattle, a rich merchant who was also an astronomer. His findings regarding the Great Comet of 1680 were of sufficient worth to be quoted by Newton. Rather pathetically, Brattle wrote, "I am here all alone by myself, without a meet help in my studies." Another was that most complex man, Cotton Mather, who found time between sermons for secular investigations. In his studies he reached some odd scientific conclusions: he sent word to the Royal Society in London that he had observed a flight of pigeons that he felt certain came from "an undiscovered satellite accompanying the earth at a near distance." Mather also postulated that seeds are fertilized by passing through the bodies of birds, and he charged that women who persisted in "multiplied and repeated miscarriages" were blaspheming their sacred duty. Yet it was he who championed the idea of smallpox inoculation, in 1721, when nearly all New England physicians and clergymen opposed it—the physicians on the grounds that it was dangerous and the clergymen that it tampered with the will of God. Cotton Mather, someone has said, backed into modernity.

Conventions of Puritan literature were changing too. The homely, unadorned "plain style" of early sermons had given way to a new prose, some richly adorned with sensuous imagery, some so steeped in metaphysical conceits that it seemed designed to baffle rather than illuminate. The best seller of the day was Michael Wigglesworth's 896-line horror poem, *The Day of Doom.* The first printing, in 1662, immediately sold out, and the work continued to sell steadily for the next two centuries. It dwelt leeringly upon wickedness ("Adulterers and Whoremongers . . . Blasphemers lewd and Swearers shrewd, Scoffers at Purity . . . Witches, Inchanters, & Ale-house-haunters . . . ") while remaining impeccably pious.

The great Puritan decline brought with it a new freedom in sexual matters, which prevailed through the eighteenth century. Sandwiched between debates at Harvard one semester as to "whether the world will be annihilated or refined" and "whether Christ or Hododeus suffer'd" was the question "whether it be Fornication to lye with ones Sweetheart (after Contraction) before Marriage." Nearly all the young debaters were studying for the ministry. Which side won is not recorded, but it is clear from church records of the time that many young lovers did not consider sexual intercourse between engaged people a sin. There were so many seven-months children born in New England towns that few questions were raised about whether or not they had been conceived before their parents' marriage. Some ministers tried to obtain public confessions—from both parties if the couple were still unmarried, from the man only if they were married. But ministers who made such requirements were unpopular. Jonathan Edwards was ousted from his parish in Northampton partly for such meddling and partly because he forbade the young people to read an English sex-thriller called *The Midwife Rightly Instructed.* Sometimes a sign or portent—a fire, epidemic, or earthquake—temporarily packed the churches. A broadside published at Springfield, Massachusetts, in 1728, called attention to a recent "amazing earthquake," and recommended a general reformation before anything worse happened. Cited in particular was the conservatives' "Abhorrence of that notion advanc'd by some that it is no breach of the Seventh Commandment for Persons that have made private Promises, to one another, to have carnal knowledge of one another, altho' not joined in Marriage."

The propriety of bundling, a European legacy, was a subject of controversy throughout the eighteenth century. Bundling was a practical solution to courting in small, crowded houses. A young couple, fully clothed—sometimes the girl was firmly knotted into hers by her mother—had more privacy and comfort lying side by side in a warmly quilted bed than sitting on a hard settle with all the family around them. Besides, it saved fuel and candles. As in most matters, the Bible was searched for precedent and guidance. The following stanzas come from a widely circulated apologia for bundling:

Whether they must be hugg'd or kiss'd when sitting by the fire
Or whether they in bed may lay, which doth the Lord require?
In Genesis no knowledge is of this thing to be got,
Whether young men did bundle then, or whether they did not.
The sacred book says wives they took, it don't say how they courted,
Whether that they in bed did lay, or by the fire sported.
But some do hold in times of old, that those about to wed,
Spent not the night, nor yet the light by fire, or in the bed.
They only meant to say they sent a man to choose a bride,
Isaac did so, but let me know of anyone beside.
Man don't pretend to trust a friend to choose him sheep and cows,
Much less a wife which all his life he doth expect to house.

MARRIAGE.

COURTSHIP.

On reversals suffered in marriage

Isaiah Thomas, editor of the *Massachusetts Spy*, took a less sanguine view:

Young miss, if this your habit be, I'll teach you now yourself to see:
You plead you're honest, modest too, but such a plea will never do;
For how can modesty consist, with shameful practice such as this?
I'll give your answer to the life: You don't undress, like man and wife.
That is your plea, I'll freely own, but who's your bondsman when alone,
That further rules you will not break, and marriage liberties partake?
But you will say that I'm unfair, that some who bundle take more care,
For some we may in truth suppose, bundle in bed with all their clothes,
But bundler's clothes are no defense, unruly horses push the fence.

Mother and child were praised in a tract against bachelors (above). The pin cushion below was a baby gift.

The custom declined as houses became larger and the Franklin stove made rooms easier to heat. The upholstered sofa, which appeared in ordinary households in the latter part of the century, was regarded as nearly as great a danger to morals as bundling.

To be married in church by a clergyman seemed like popery to the Puritans. These very practical people observed that marriage entailed civil obligations—property rights in particular—so they were married at home by a magistrate. Drinking, feasting, and jollity were permissible, however. In the first years of the Bible State, people were allowed buns and cakes only at weddings and funerals. "We were all decently merry two days after the conjugation," wrote a Bostonian in 1713. Several odd customs connected with marriage are worth noting: one was an elaborate practical joke—after the ceremony, the bride would be "stolen" from her husband, who was then obliged to finance a big party in order to get her back. In another, just before the bridal pair joined hands, the bridegroom would make a break for freedom, only to be pursued by the "bridesmen" and dragged back to his place again. According to an ancient English law, a new husband was responsible for his bride's previous debts unless he married her in her shift or chemise on the king's highway. There are several cases on record of this mysterious rule being carried out to the letter. In another case, a more modest but apparently equally indebted bride stood in a closet—presumably in her shift—and joined her hand to that of her bridegroom by extending it through a hole in the door.

Young people in the colonies, North and South, were a little freer than in England to choose their own mates, but they needed the consent of their parents and the bride needed a dowry. If large sums were involved, financial haggling might go on for some time; and if the parents refused consent, their word was usually law. William Byrd II, of Virginia, having forbidden his daughter Evelyn to marry an English baronet who was pursuing her, wrote the suitor, "I fear your circumstances are not flourishing enough to maintain a wife in much splendor that has nothing and just such a fortune as that my daughter will prove if she ventures to marry without my consent"; Evelyn Byrd died in 1736 at the age of thirty, an old maid—or, in the language of the time, "a thornback."

Less docile young women occasionally rebelled against the system, as the columns of the *Royal American Magazine*, a colonial monthly, attest. In their regular feature, "The Directory of Love," letter writers with romantic problems were given a patient hearing. "Nancy Dilemma" wrote to say: "I am a poor unhappy girl, with what the world calls a pretty face and a fine person, but no fortune; and am courted by a young gentleman who has no accomplish-

Boston's "Repository of Instruction"

ment or qualification in my eyes to recommend himself, but an estate of five hundred a year. My parents insist upon my marrying him; and I really think he loves me; but I remonstrate against that, as I never can like him; and besides there is a person of whom I am very fond, and of whose returns I have no reason to complain; but has at the same time so inferior a fortune to the other, that I believe, with industry, we might just make out to live sparingly. Now, as I could wish to marry the first for his money, and the last for the love I have to him, as well as for the sense he is endowed with, which I belive the former is a stranger to: In these cases, what shall I do?"

After deliberation, the *Royal American Magazine* in the person of "Polly Resolute" gave an inspiring answer. "I have presumed to answer you from my being a few years ago in the same predicament that is mentioned in the query. You say, a young gentleman courts you, that has no qualification but five-hundred a year, who your parents want to force upon you, in opposition to your remonstrances. To remedy that oppression, I would direct you in the path which I followed. I conceive parents authority can extend no farther than what may contribute to the happiness of their child: When it is carried beyond that, and apparent, that they are governed by *mercenary* views, and not the *happiness* of their child, it undoubtedly is laudable in any lady, to avoid the yoke that is preparing for her, by making herself happy in the possession of a man, whose affections and endearing behaviour, is far more to be wished for, than five thousand per annum with one she could never love. . . . " Having thus delivered this early declaration for women's rights, Polly Resolute went on to analyze the merits of marrying for love. "You say there is a person of whom you are very fond, and who makes returns to your mind, but is much inferior to the first in point of fortune. The road before you here is very plain: Accept by all means of the one that possesses most *sense* (as I think you observe the latter does) be his fortune ever so small, provided you can live moderately well; for that one qualification with the man you esteem, will establish lasting happiness; while five-hundred a year with a fool (whom you could not but hate) will no time yield one permanent joy or a single agreeable reflection. The enjoyment of riches can be but short, I would advise you, as well as every young lady, to take such steps as may procure *contentment* here; the principal of which is, *to marry the man you love*." By this time, the *Royal American*'s readers must have been deeply involved in the predicament, for its editors thoughtfully provided a postscript to the story: as Nancy Dilemma's parents remained fore-square against her marrying the young man with good sense but no money, the couple eloped to another town. Hearing that the young man's prospects shortly improved and that the "world in general approved," the parents came round, and everyone was thereafter "perfectly happy."

Ambitious parents were probably behind another marriage which was aired in the pages of the *Royal American*. The complainant, describing himself only as "a rich old man of sixty," wrote that some months before, he had married a young lady of eighteen. "The affection she pretended to have for me I find is all vanished, and given to her gay young sparks; and as I am almost crazy about it, pray what shall I do?" Back came a most unsympathetic answer in the next issue: "I am not the least surprised," wrote the lovelorn's advisor. "When the no small odds of sixty and eighteen wed, little happiness can be expected from their union; for youthful madam, instead of being fixed to the husband she wished for, and which her years demanded, finds herself joined to a parcel of dried bones, and a most unsubstantial withered body. . . . Disappointed love after marriage, is the most irreconcilable passion in nature, especially on the woman's side."

Not until later did the ratio of men to women even out, and almost any female, no matter how difficult, was a pearl of considerable price. A woman who willfully remained single was an object of reproach and scorn. Society had no place for her. It was not meet for her to live alone, at least not until she was a very old crone indeed—and in the intimate confines of a colonial household an unattached woman could cause awkward situations. (No doubt for this reason, both Puritans and Anglicans sternly enforced the sexual prohibitions of Mosaic law: marriage or intercourse between in-laws counted as incest. In Connecticut, in-laws who married were punishable by forty lashes plus the wearing of the letter *I* sewn on their clothing.) "Ancient maids" and widows who failed to remarry sometimes kept little shops, did dressmaking, or taught small children their ABC's. Otherwise they made themselves useful around the households of their married relatives.

New England thriftiness is legendary, and one of the originators of the legend was surely Miss Mary Ann Faneuil, housekeeper for her bachelor brother, Peter. Miss Mary used to send her silk dresses to London to be turned and redyed, and on one occasion sent a bundle of "discarded snuffboxes, buckles & Glove Strings" to be sold. Later, the Revolution made even extravagant ladies careful, for English goods were boycotted. Martha Washington made chair covers by unraveling and reknitting her husband's old silk stockings. Abigail Foote, a young Connecticut girl, managed to combine a phenomenal number of household chores with fun. In her diary for 1775 she recorded a day's activities: "Fix'd Gown for Prude Just to clear my teeth— Mend Mother's Riding hood—Ague in my face—Ellen was spark'd last night—Mother spun short thread—Fix'd two Gowns for Welch's girls— Carded tow—spun linen—worked on Cheese Basket—Hatchel'd Flax with Hannah and we did 51 lb a piece—Pleated and ironed—Read a sermon of Dodridges—Spooled a piece—milked the cows—spun linen and did 50 knots—made a broom of Guinea wheat straw—Spun thread to whiten—Went to Mr. Otis's and made them a swinging visit—Set a red Dye—Prude stay'd at home and learned Eve's Dream by heart—Had two scholars from Mrs. Taylor's—I carded two pounds of whole wool and felt Nationly—Spun harness twine—Scoured the Pewter."

Differences in attitudes, manners, and morals between the colonies became even greater as each developed without much communication with its neighbors. Throughout the eighteenth century most colonials died where they had been born, or perhaps made one move. A few wealthy southern families came North, usually to Newport, during the summer in order to escape the hotweather epidemics of typhoid, yellow fever, and cholera. Northerners went South only on business. Most intercolonial journeys were made by sea, along a coast fraught with danger from storms, pirates, and unreliable lighthouses. Benjamin Franklin took twelve days to travel by water from Philadelphia to Boston and counted it a good trip. Overland, the roads improved very gradually. Those who did travel extensively were mostly sailors, itinerant craftsmen, or peddlers. All had become socially acceptable courses for an adventurous young colonial, although some peddlers were so unscrupulous that

A girl's education stressed such household skills as spinning, in the scene from a birth record, above. Ribbon was made with the loom below.

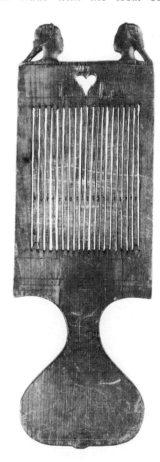

THis is to give Notice to all Perfons in Town and Country, that are Indebted to *Andrew Hay*, Poft-Mafter at *Perth-Amboy*, for the Poftage of Letters, to Pay the fame, or they may expect Trouble; fome having been due near four Years.

Andrew Hay.

The postman above carried mail on credit. As the ad below it says, collecting postage was often hard.

they eventually gave the calling a bad name. Some towns "warned them out," and in the South, where Yankee peddlers invaded the tidewater settlements in small boats, they were regarded by "the better sort" as a nuisance, for they offered temptations to the poor. A peddler's pack was a general store in miniature. Combs, knives, cheap jewelry, thread, essences and spices, cheese, religious books, woodenware, brooms, jews' harps, shawls, laces, broadsides, seeds, tinware, shelf clocks, oysters and fish (packed in kegs and carried in saddlebags), shoelaces, and pins were only a few of the items offered, and in many a wilderness household they became the only "store-bought" possessions. Cobblers, weavers, tailors, candlemakers, cabinet-makers, pewterers, dancing masters, and portrait painters also made the high-road circuit. A portrait painter would spend his winters painting headless torsos, male and female, adult and child, on canvases; come spring he would load the canvases into a wagon and set forth on a quest for clients, whose likenesses he would add to appropriate shoulders. In the North his social standing was low, as was that of a dancing master. In the South, on the other hand, planters' families were eager to imitate the ways of landed English gentry. To dance well and to adorn the walls of one's house with family portraits were two very proper English things to do. Accordingly, the portraitist and the dancing master were sure of a warm welcome.

People whose business took them from place to place were often entrusted with letters, for until the mid-eighteenth century, when Benjamin Franklin became deputy postmaster, His Majesty's Postal Service left much to be desired. Between Philadelphia and the Potomac, for example, a postrider was scheduled to travel eight times a year. But in fact he only did so if he had enough letters to make the trip worthwhile. The cost of postage was very high.

With so little communication, it was a wonder that the thirteen colonies ever united. John Adams said of the First Continental Congress that it consisted of "fifty gentlemen meeting together, all strangers." George Washington labeled all frontiersmen "a parcel of barbarians," and in 1775 remarked that the New Englanders were "an exceeding dirty and nasty people." The Pennsylvania Quakers, with a long memory of seventeenth-century persecutions, disliked New Englanders too, and William Beekman, one of New York's leading merchants, once remarked that "seven-eighths of the people I have credited in New England has proved to me [such] damned ungreatful cheating fellows that I am now almost afraid to trust any man in Connecticut though he be well recommended from others." New Englanders, on the other hand, thought New Yorkers hopelessly immoral, and southerners hypocrites, hiding intemperance, impiety, and barbarous treatment of slaves behind a veneer of fancy manners. The German immigrants in Pennsylvania thought the English Quakers sharp in their dealings and ridiculously soft toward the Indians, while the Quakers feared that the Germans would ruin Pennsylvania with their warlike ways, their foreign language and customs. The first wave of poverty-stricken Irish reached Boston in the early eighteenth century. Very poor and very Roman Catholic, they aroused the immediate dislike of the stranger-wary Bostonians, a prejudice that lasted until the mid-twentieth century. French Huguenots never arrived in such great numbers as to offer a serious threat to any colony, though in terms of manners, artistic taste, and fashionable dress, they became a dominant influence in South Carolina, bringing to the port city of Charleston a touch of gaiety and culture.

(Continued on Page 42)

Albany: 1750

Today's capital of New York, as seen by the Swedish naturalist Peter Kalm. The following observations in his journal often fall short of scientific detachment.

The inhabitants of [Albany] are as a whole all Dutch or of Dutch extraction. . . . Both sexes dress now very nearly like the English. . . . Between themselves they always speak Dutch, so that rarely is an English word heard. They are so to speak permeated with a hatred toward the English, whom they ridicule and slander at every opportunity. This hatred is said to date back to the time when the English took this country away from them. The avarice and selfishness and immeasurable love of money of the inhabitants of Albany are very well known throughout all North America. . . . For this reason nobody comes to this place without the most pressing necessity. . . . I was here obliged to pay for every thing twice, thrice, and four times as dear as in any part of North America . . . and when I wanted to purchase any thing, or be helped in some case or other . . . they either fixed exorbitant prices for their services, or were very backward to assist me. Indians . . . are frequently cheated in disposing of their goods. . . . The merchants . . . are highly pleased when they have given a poor Indian a greater portion of brandy than he can bear, and when they can after that get all his goods for mere trifles. The houses in this town are very neat. . . . on both sides [of the front door] are [porches with] seats, on which, during fair weather, the people spend almost the whole day, especially on those [porches] which are in the shadow of the houses. The people seem to move with the sun and the shade, always keeping in the latter. When the sun is too hot the people disappear. In the evening these seats are covered with people of both sexes; but this is rather troublesome, as those who pass by are obliged to greet every body, unless they will shock the politeness of the inhabitants of this town. It is considered very impolite not to lift your hat and greet everyone. [In their homes] the inhabitants . . . are much more sparing than the English and are stingier with their food. The meat which is served up is often insufficient to satisfy the stomach. . . . They . . . eat cheese . . . not in slices, but scraped . . . which they pretend adds to the good taste. The [punch] bowl does not circulate so freely as amongst the English. They commonly drink very small beer, or pure water. The women (neatly but not lavishly dressed) are perfectly well acquainted with economy; they rise early, go to sleep very late, and are almost over nice and cleanly, in regard to the floor, which is frequently scoured several times in the week. At this time [October] since it was beginning to grow cold, it was customary for the women . . . even maidens, servants and little girls, to put live coals into small iron pans which were in turn placed in a small stool. . . . They placed this . . . under their skirts so that the heat therefrom might go up to the *regiones superiores* and to all parts of the body which the skirts covered. As soon as the coals grew black they were thrown away and replaced. . . . It was almost painful to see all this changing and trouble in order that no part should freeze or fare badly.

New and penniless immigrants supplied the need for servants and apprentices in the northern colonies. A profitable business developed in the port cities: a soul-driver met incoming ships and dickered with the captain for the indentures of the most likely white immigrants aboard. He got a special rate for buying wholesale and made his profit by selling the indentures ashore one by one, literally driving the people through the streets, like a flock of sheep. A typical indenture contract (a document in duplicate with identical notches, or "indents," along the edges) committed the servant to work for four years: "His master's money, goods, or other estate he shall not purloin, embezzle, or waste; at unlawful games he shall not play; taverns and alehouses he shall not frequent; fornication he shall not commit, nor matrimony contract; but in all things shall demean himself as a faithful servant." In return the master promised to provide food, clothing, lodging, and, if necessary, medicine, "and to learn him to read a chapter well in the Bible, if he may be capable of learning it." When the four years were up, he also owed the servant two complete outfits of clothing, one for work and one for church.

The life of the great eighteenth-century landowners in Virginia was so attractive that writers enjoy dwelling upon it: the charming houses filled with English furniture, French wallpaper, Irish crystal, Chinese porcelain; the balls, the hunting parties, the "fish festivals," the excursions in painted launches gliding along quiet rivers; the London-educated gentlemen in perukes and gold-lace coats, dancing minuets with ladies in rustling dresses made of materials with such alluring names as lutestring and paduasoy. The picture has truth in it, but it is slicked up. For one thing, of the white population of Virginia in, say, 1700, the vast majority were small farmers whose lives were a struggle and who were as far removed socially from the gentlemen-planters as peasants from nobles. During the first half of the century, their numbers increased several fold, while the numbers of the aristocracy stood still. In 1765 titled nobility lost control of the government, which they had dominated since 1660. Secondly, the price of tobacco declined steadily throughout the eighteenth century, so that many of the plantation owners were living on credit, and a few of them, alas, on what they managed to embezzle from the government (a scandal uncovered by Patrick Henry in 1766). To make ends meet, some bred and sold slaves as a business, while others had the foresight to invest in townsites. During the eighteenth century there was still a dearth of towns in the South, but several got their start: among them, Baltimore, Frederick, Hagerstown, Savannah, Fredericksburg, and Winchester. William Byrd II divided a portion of his vast property into lots, which eventually became the nucleus of Richmond.

Sometime during the 1740's, the young George Washington prepared himself for his role as a leader of the colony by copying one hundred and ten "Rules of Civility and Decent Behaviour in Company and Conversation." The rules have been traced to a book published in 1595 by French Jesuits, but someone translated and simplified them for young George, and a copy in his boyish script survives. Many of them are still good advice. For example: "If you Cough, Sneeze, Sigh, or Yawn, do it not Loud but Privately; and Speak not in your Yawning, but put Your handkerchief or Hand before your face and turn aside . . . Sleep not when others Speak . . . Spit not in the Fire . . . bedew no mans face with your Spittle, by approaching to near him when you Speak . . . Kill no Vermin as Fleas, lice ticks &c in the Sight of Others . . .

Virtuous George as hatchet man

Jog not the Table or Desk on which Another reads or writes . . . Keep your Nails clean and Short, also your Hands and Teeth Clean yet without Shewing any great Concern for them . . . Reproach none for the Infirmaties of Nature. . . . When a man does all he can though it succeeds not well blame not him that did it."

A shorthand diary kept by William Byrd II reveals the unvarnished details of life in a First Family of Virginia in the early decades of the eighteenth century. We see Byrd presiding at court day, mustering the militia, and riding up to Williamsburg to consult with the governor (and, on occasion, to borrow his coach). From a library of over 3,600 titles, he reads books in Hebrew, Latin, Greek, French, Italian, and Dutch; he eats well (roast beef, crab, duck pie, pickled oysters, chocolate), says his prayers except when he forgets, and enjoys his bottle of canary or port; and he tells us when he quarrels with his wife and when he takes her to bed and gives her "a flourish." All of this makes him sound like *The Compleat Gentleman* and rather endearing besides. Less endearing are such notations on the management of his servants as "Eugene was whipped for running away and had the bit put on him . . . Jenny had run into the river last night but came out again of herself and was severely whipped for it . . . Eugene was whipped for pissing in bed and Jenny for concealing it . . . Eugene pissed abed again for which I made him drink a pint of piss."

Another close view of a great Virginia household is provided by the diary and letters of a young tutor, Philip Fithian, who, in 1774-75, instructed the many children of Robert Carter of Nomini Hall. The plantation, like its neighbors in tidewater country, was similar to a little town, with numerous white artisans, craftsmen, and overseers, besides over five hundred slaves. Fithian mentions that the family was trying to live frugally, due to financial reverses, but where they were cutting down is not clear, except that for patriotic reasons they were now drinking coffee instead of tea. The Carters and their neighbors treated themselves to frequent balls and other festivities, which rather shocked young Fithian, who was studying for the Presbyterian ministry; but he noted it all down with good humor. A ball might last days and include upwards of seventy guests. Those who lived nearby went home to sleep; others slept several in a room, for plantation houses were not as large as we might imagine, considering "southern hospitality." (William Byrd frequently mentions that overnight guests slept in the same bed with him.) There were seventeen children in the Carter family, nine of whom survived infancy, and Nomini Hall had but four rooms on the second floor—one for the parents, one for the girls, and the other two for guests. The boys slept in an outbuilding, along with Mr. Fithian. A white housekeeper seems to have shared the girls' room, and a slave girl slept on the floor, by the door.

At one ball given by a neighbor, festivities began in the afternoon with cards (avoided by Fithian) and conversation. The ladies were served dinner at half past four, followed by the gentlemen. "For Drink there was several sorts of Wine, good Lemon Punch, Toddy, Cyder, Porters, &c." At seven the dancing began. The young divinity student sat in a corner and watched: "first Minuets one Round; second Giggs; third Reels; and last of All Country-Dances; tho' they struck several Marches occasionally—The Music was a French-Horn and two Violins—The Ladies were Dressed Gay, and splendid. . . . But all did not join in the Dance for there were parties in Rooms

Instructions for mounting a horse with dignity are offered in The Modern Riding Master: or Key to the Knowledge of the Horse, *c. 1776.*

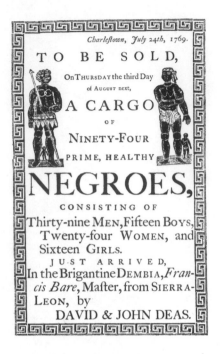

Charleston planters were notified of a 1769 slave auction with the broadside above. The seal below identified an English emancipation society.

made up, some at Cards; some drinking for Pleasure; some toasting the Sons of america: some singing 'Liberty Songs' as they call'd them, in which six, eight, ten or more would put their Heads near together and roar. . . . " Fithian left the ball with Mrs. Carter and the girls at eleven, but reports that next morning eighteen-year-old Benjamin and fifteen-year-old Robert Carter "are yet at the Dance."

Fithian was distressed by the treatment of slaves, who, in the midst of plenty, lived on corn meal and a pound of meat apiece a week and were subjected to cruel punishments. He told of one overseer who invented several "experiments," such as having backs of offending slaves lacerated with a currycomb and salt rubbed in the wounds. Fithian was also shocked to find out that "the slaves in this Colony never are married, their Lords thinking them improper Subjects for so valuable an Institution." Reporting an abortive slave uprising on a neighboring plantation, Fithian concluded, "the ill Treatment which this unhappy part of mankind receives here, would almost justify them in any desperate attempt for gaining that *Civilitie*, & *Plenty* which tho' denied them, is here, commonly bestowed on Horses!" Like Fithian, many southerners were concerned about the increasing numbers of black slaves. Since the early eighteenth century, Negroes had been arriving by the hundreds. Byrd blamed the "foul traders" (many of whom were Yankees) and added, "I am sensible of many bad consequences of multiplying these Ethiopians amongst us. They blow up the pride and ruin the industry of our white people, who seeking a rank of poor creatures below them, detest work for fear it should make them look like slaves. . . . Another unhappy effect of many negroes is the necessity of being severe. Numbers make them insolent and then foul means must do what fair will not." Still, the system was so profitable and made planter life so comfortable that almost no one thought seriously of putting a stop to it.

By Robert Carter's day, some fifty years later, 40 percent of the Virginia population was black. Carter took the very unusual step of manumitting a number of his slaves; but as they were unprepared to cope with life on their own in a hostile white world, those who were freed apparently did not get on well. Carter died before his plan of gradual manumission had gone very far. With the invention of the cotton gin greatly raising the value of slaves, his children never completed their father's plan.

Both at William Byrd's Westover and Carter's Nomini Hall, illness struck often: ague, distemper, the gripes, the bloody flux, the putrid quinsy, and sundry other mysterious and frequently fatal afflictions. Byrd handed out purges and "vomits" with all the assurance of an internist and had "Tom whipped for not telling me he was sick." The most drastic treatment, dreaded by the whole plantation from Byrd himself down to the least slave child, was "an infusion of the bark," probably a crude form of quinine, which deafened and dazed the patient and made him sweat and vomit and almost prefer to die than undergo the cure.

Just as Congregationalism was the established church in Massachusetts, so the Church of England reigned in Virginia. Before the establishment of the College of William and Mary, its ministers had been sent out from England and, regrettably, were apt to be of lesser caliber, for the best minds preferred to stay home where there was a more promising future. The missionary spirit was not strong in the eighteenth century, and although a few dedicated clergymen rode circuit to outlying farms and Indian villages, most settled down near the plantations, where they could enjoy their parishioners' lavish hospitality. Fithian disapprovingly reported the presence of two Anglican clergymen at a ball, adding that although they did not dance, their wives did. On Sundays sermons lasted no more than twenty minutes, and the congregation spent more time gossiping in the churchyard than they did worshiping in their pews. What in New England was called the noonhouse — a house where people might wait for the afternoon service — was known as the Chapel of Ease in Virginia, and by the eighteenth century was not much used because most of the parish skipped the afternoon service. One Anglican clergyman in Maryland is said to have passed a busy life gaming, drinking, dancing, and riding to hounds, and died in bed deliriously shouting "View Halloo!" Unlike the New England clergymen, the social position of southern clergymen was not high. One minister, bent on raising funds to save souls, was told by a wealthy gentleman, "Souls! Damn your souls! Make tobacco!"

Both North and South, when a member of the family died, his funeral was the occasion for another get-together. An English custom demanded that each funeral guest be provided with a black scarf, a pair of black gloves, and a mourning ring — or as many of these things as the bereaved could afford. Beginning in 1721, laws limited such gifts to the six pallbearers and the officiating clergyman. One Boston minister wrote that he had a collection of several hundred pairs of gloves and mourning rings. Judge Sewall noted on the death of John Ive, "I was not at his Funeral. Had Gloves sent me, but the knowledge of his notoriously wicked life made me sick of going . . . and so I staid at home, and by that means lost a Ring. . . . " In August, 1721, he wrote, "Mrs. Frances Webb is buried, who died of the Small Pox. I think this is the first public Funeral without Scarves. . . . " At the time of the Revolution, black mourning clothes were dispensed with, because of the difficulty of importing them, and black arm bands came in.

Death was a more real and matter-of-fact occurrence to colonials than it is to us. People died at home, in small quarters, surrounded by family and friends who came in to "watch." Childbed fever and various infants' diseases made each lying-in a fateful affair. In the country, particularly in the South, bodies were interred in a family burying ground within sight of the house; in towns, the graves were in the churchyard, where the surviving family saw them regularly. A great deal of thought went into the design and inscribing of gravestones, giving local artists and littérateurs a chance to show their talents, and nobody thought it morbid to ornament the stone with a grinning skull or inscribe it with such a verse as,

> *Stranger, pause as you pass by*
> *As you are now, so once was I*
> *As I am now, so you must be*
> *Therefore prepare to follow me*

Samuel Sewall amused himself one Christmas by rearranging the coffins in his family tomb, presumably for the greater comfort of the deceased, though he confessed, "'T was an awfull yet pleasing treat." William Byrd II had his father's grave opened "to see him but he was so wasted there was not anything to be distinguished."

The Great Awakening, the first orgy of moral reform that was to shake

Gift spoon for funeral attendants

America, brought profound changes North and South. Many people had regretted and feared the decline of religion. In the towns Sundays had become a perfunctory ritual, while the rest of the week was dedicated to the pursuit of money and pleasure. On the frontier hundreds of families were without any spiritual guidance, and children were growing up without once having been inside a church. Among those who were actively religious there was not much "love thy neighbor," for although the overwhelming majority of colonials were Protestants, they were divided into sects that despised each other. During the 1720's Benjamin Franklin's older brother James published a paper in Boston that regularly attacked the clergy, and although James was at one point sent to jail when he took on the king's agents as butts of his satire, it was clear that impiety sold newspapers.

Rev. Jonathan Edwards, c. 1750

Benjamin Franklin, a deist himself, believed that humble and uneducated people had "need of the motives of religion to restrain them from vice, to support their virtue, and retain them in practice of it till it become habitual. . . . " But no one could suggest a cure until, during the 1720's, two New Jersey ministers (Theodore Frelinghuysen, of the Dutch Reformed Church, and Gilbert Tennent, a Presbyterian) began to preach in an unprecedented way. throwing aside the intricacies of doctrine and speaking in simple, evangelical terms.

After them, in the 1730's, came Jonathan Edwards, the revival's best-remembered leader. Edwards packed his church at Northampton, Massachusetts, and wherever else he preached by delivering, in a quiet, unhistrionic manner, the most frightening threats of hell-fire and damnation. "The God that holds you over the pit of hell, much as one holds a spider or some loathsome insect over the fire, abhors you, and is dreadfully provoked," he told a fascinated throng. "You are ten thousand times so abominable in his eyes, as the most hateful and venomous serpent. . . . You hang by a slender thread, with the flames of divine wrath flashing about it, and ready every moment to singe it and burn it asunder. . . . If you cry to God to pity you, He will be so far from pitying you in your doleful case, or showing you the least regard or favor, that instead of that, He will only tread you under foot." By such language, Edwards brought about "conversions," which in his view meant embracing one's duty, loving to do what one ought to do. Edwards was a truly intellectual man who couched his sermons in colorful terms in order to reach as many souls as possible.

After him came the Englishman George Whitefield, whose message was similar to Edwards', but who ranted and raved to keep his listeners alert. He was cross-eyed, which probably contributed to the strong effect he had on people, for no one could be sure at whom he was looking. Following one of his sermons, "some were struck pale as Death, others wringing their hands, others lying on the ground, others sinking into the arms of their friends, and most lifting up their eyes toward heaven, and crying out to GOD."

An otherwise unknown Connecticut farmer named Nathan Cole wrote a wonderfully vivid account of what happened when Whitefield came to Middletown:

"Sudden, in the morning about 8 or 9 of the Clock there came a message and said Mr. Whitefield . . . is to preach at Middletown this morning at ten of the Clock, I was in my field at Work, I dropt my tool that I had in my hand and ran home to my wife telling her to make ready quickly . . . then run to the pasture for my horse with all my might; fearing that I shoud be too late; . . . I with my wife soon mounted the horse and went forward as fast as I thought the horse could bear, and when my horse got much out of breath I would get down and put my wife on the Saddle . . . and so I would run untill I was much out of breath . . . all the while fearing we should be too late to hear the Sermon . . . and when we came within about half a mile or a mile of the Road that came down from Hartford . . . to Middletown; on high land I saw before me a cloud or fogg rising . . . but as I came nearer the Road, I heard a noise something like a low rumbling thunder and presently found it was the noise of Horses feet coming down the Road and this Cloud was a Cloud of dust made by the Horses feet . . . and when I came within about 20 rods of the Road, I could see men and horses Sliping along in the Cloud like shadows . . . a steady stream . . . scarcely a horse more than his length behind another, all of a Lather and foam with sweat . . . every horse seemed to go with all his might to carry his rider to hear news from heaven for the saving of Souls. . . ."

Whitefield left thousands of conversions in his wake, but they did not last, and by the mid-1740's the Great Awakening appeared to be over. The main dissenter groups—Congregational, Presbyterian, and Baptist—became further splintered; but at the same time the old intolerance of sect for sect was diminished, and even the word *sect* was replaced by *denomination*. Whitefield himself was an Anglican, but he had been put out of his pulpit in England for undignified ranting and raving. "God help us to forget party names and to become Christians in deed and truth," he said (or more likely, shouted).

As an immediate response to the need for more American-trained ministers, new colleges were started: Princeton by revivalist-minded Presbyterians; Brown by Baptists; Queens College (later Rutgers) by followers of Frelinghuysen, the Dutch Reformist; and Dartmouth, which was at first a school for Indians, by a Whitefield-inspired Congregationalist. Presbyterians and Anglicans shared—sometimes with sharp dissension—King's College (the future Columbia) and the College of Philadelphia (the future University of Pennsylvania). The already existing colleges of Harvard and Yale had always had a Congregationalist bent, while William and Mary was Anglican. All these colleges had two peculiarly American characteristics in common: they were governed by lay trustees of interdenominational persuasion, and the students were not required to embrace the denomination of the college. By the end of the century, only one-fifth of the graduates were becoming ministers. It was the beginning of the unique American system of higher education for more than just the elite.

At Harvard and Yale students were for many years listed in order of their social position; not until 1769 were they listed in alphabetical order. (It is said that at William and Mary there were no written lists at all: everybody *knew* the "young gentlemen" and in what social order they belonged.) Seating in church no longer had class distinction. Except for a few pews in front, reserved for governors, local officials, and prominent elder citizens, it was a matter of first to come, first to rent the pew for the year. (And by the time of the Revolution, men and women were sitting together.)

The anti-intellectual element that was a prime factor in the Great Awakening became rooted in American life. Even an ill wind blows some good, and perhaps if standards had been higher no one would have had the temerity to start new colleges—for there were very few trained professors, and classes were for many years in the hands of young tutors. But from then on, and per-

Boys marched off to school at a tender age, as in the cut from a speller, above. A privileged few went on to colleges like King's (later Columbia), below.

For the Encouragement of Learning, in

King's-College, New-York.

SEVERAL Gentlemen having thought proper to form themselves into a Society, under the Denomination of the Literary Society; the said Society met on the Eleventh of November, 1766, in the Evening; and agreed, each to subscribe the Sum of Three Pounds, yearly, for five Years, to be expended in Premiums, either Medals or Books, at the Option of the Students, in the following Manner;

First Class.

Moral Philosophy, best	£. 6. –. –.
Natural Philosophy, best	6. –. –.
Modern History, best	3. –. –.
Latin Poetry, best	3. –. –.

Second Class.

Geometry and special Geography, best	6. –. –.
Arithmetick and Algebra, best	6. –. –.
Ancient History, best	3. –. –.
English Poetry, best	3. –. –.

Third Class.

Greek, best	4. –. –.
Latin, best	2. –. –.

Fourth Class.

Greek, best	4. –. –.
Latin, best	2. –. –.

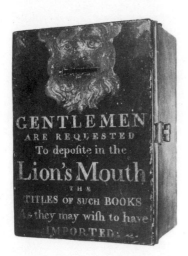

Suggestion box for a library

haps until the Russians put up Sputnik, scholars were apt to be confused with stuffy pedants in the public mind. Waves from Europe's Age of Enlightenment reached our shores, but the idea of reason and scientific curiosity was generally admired only if an immediate practical advantage was apparent. Because Franklin used his knowledge to make a lightning rod, a stove, and the rest, he was adored. But men working in the more mysterious and taboo-ridden areas of medicine, anatomy, geology, astronomy, prehistory, and other learned professions had an uphill road.

The American penchant for clubs and organizations had its beginnings in the eighteenth century. Now that church and the Thursday evening lecture were no longer the center of everyone's life, and in the settled parts of the country work "bees" were no longer essential, there had to be other ways of getting together. James Franklin started the Hell-fire Club in Boston, attracting those who (in the words of an old-line Puritan) dared "vomit up their spiritual milk with scoffs." In Philadelphia James's milder brother Benjamin started the Junto, a discussion group, and much later, in 1769, organized the first scientific club, the American Philosophical Society. Annapolis had a group called the Ancient and Honorable Tuesday Club, "dedicated to raillery." There were several subscription libraries, some of which—in Philadelphia, New York, and Newport—still exist.

After the middle of the century, a large proportion of Americans— whether the new upper class of rich merchants, the old ruling classes of clergymen and plantation owners, or the great masses of farmers, craftsmen, and laborers—found a united cause in their resentment of England's colonial policy. That resentment had been growing for a hundred years or more, ever since Edward Randolph, an emissary of Charles II, had become customs agent in 1678, "Impowered to prevent their Irregular Trade." He made no secret of his opinion that the colonials were an inferior lot—"inconsiderable Mechanicks," and "generally inclined to Sedition." English condescension toward colonials contributed toward the eventual revolt, even though that complaint goes unmentioned in the Declaration of Independence. Gentlemen like the Byrds and Carters and would-be gentlemen like the Shrimptons and Belchers might model themselves on English gentry and send their children to England to complete their education, but the vast majority of colonials had moved up in the world just enough to enjoy more comfortable and self-respecting lives than they could have known in England, and they did not wish to return to a caste system in which they would have had an inferior place.

Having served for nearly two centuries in England's North American wars, they disliked everything that smacked of Redcoat soldiery, too. They felt that they had been discriminated against, passed over for promotion, and given the most unpleasant assignments. When the opportunity arose, the colonial militia elected its own officers, who being themselves amateur soldiers, had little idea of military procedure. The camps were unsanitary, the sentries fell asleep, the men wandered off to shoot game while on the march, and no serious attempt was made to reclaim deserters, who, it was assumed, had some good reason for deserting, such as going home to bring in the hay. "Never to be sure was such a motly Herd," wrote an observer of General Johnson's New York army, "almost every man his own master & a General." Few Englishmen expected these undisciplined troops, who entered the Revolution as colonists, to come home as free and independent Americans.

The Colonial Way

The stern truths of mortality were ever apparent to the colonial American. They occupied the thoughts of young Prudence Punderson, who stitched this somber view of life c. 1770. She sees herself first as a baby being rocked in a cradle, then as a young woman preparing her needlework, finally as the "P.P." occupying the coffin.

The New Breed

JOHANNES DE PEYSTER III, 1694–1789, was the grandson of a Dutch merchant who emigrated to New Amsterdam and became one of its richest burghers. When the British seized the province in 1664, Johannes I reluctantly switched allegiances and tenaciously clung to his Dutch ways. Though offered the mayoralty of New York, he refused because he had not learned English. It was from men like the De Peysters that such words as *boss*, *boor*, and *spook* entered the language. The term *Yankee* (from *Jan Kees*, the Dutch John Doe) was a pejorative epithet describing Connecticut traders, whose ethics reputedly left something to be desired. By the time Johannes III had become mayor of Albany in 1729, most New Yorkers, if not liking the king, at least spoke his English.

NEW-YORK HISTORICAL SOCIETY

RICHARD LEE, d. 1664, progenitor of the renowned Virginia family, claimed aristocratic descent from a certain Launcelot Lee, who distinguished himself at the Battle of Hastings. However, the majority of Virginia planters were self-made "gentlemen," often coming from lowly backgrounds. As one historian observed," 'tis not likely that any man of a plentiful estate should voluntarily abandon a happy certainty to roam after imaginary advantages in a new world." Whether or not Lee's heraldic pretensions were valid, soon after emigrating to the colony about 1641, he acquired vast land holdings, wealth, and recognition as a member of Virginia's ruling class. Superficially, Lee's life resembled that of the English country squire, yet he was not afraid to sully this traditionally idle role by engaging in such mercantile pursuits as the tobacco trade and shipping. He also assumed the social responsibilities befitting his position and served the royal colony at various times as burgess, attorney general, king's councilor, sheriff, and secretary of state.

MUNSEY'S MAGAZINE, MAY, 1896

ROBERT FEKE, c. 1705–c. 1750, a self-taught limner, traveled from Philadelphia to Boston painting prominent citizens. His success was largely attributable to the new worldliness of his subjects.

HENRY WILDER FOOTE COLLECTION

LORD CORNBURY, 1661–1723, was fortunate to be Queen Anne's cousin; she made him governor of New York and, later, of New Jersey. His administration, however, proved so odious to the colonists that he was eventually relieved of the sinecure and arrested for helping himself to public funds. Cornbury's peculiarities included tatting on the front porch of the governor's mansion and strutting around in petticoats with the excuse that he was impersonating his royal relative.

NEW-YORK HISTORICAL SOCIETY

COTTON MATHER, 1663–1728, often remembered as the intolerant Puritan who influenced the outcome of the witchcraft trials, was also one of America's first philanthropists. He donated much of his money and energies to rehabilitating the poor—materially and spiritually. Lest idleness be encouraged, he warned potential do-gooders that "the poor that can't work are objects for your liborality. But the poor that *can* work and *won't*, the best liberality is to *make* them." In addition, Mather charitably took it upon himself to rout the Devil from Massachusetts. In 1703, after the first Mrs. Mather had died, he nearly became prey to "The Great Adversary" when a comely maiden of dubious reputation offered herself as a matrimonial candidate. Renouncing this "fearful Snare," he lamented: "Was ever man more tempted, than the miserable *Mather*!" Lying "prostrate in the dust," the praying and fasting preacher "committed unto . . . Christ, the care of providing [a wife]" and soon was rewarded a "Gentlewoman of Piety and Probity . . . . the most agreeable Consort (all considered) that *America* could have afforded."

JAMES LOGAN, 1674–1751, Quaker statesman and scholar, accompanied William Penn to America in 1699 and was attacked by pirates en route. Legend has it that the pacifist proprietor hid below-decks, while Logan defended the ship. When chastised for his un-Friendly conduct, Logan replied, "I being thy servant, why did thee not order me to come down?" This compromising attitude characterized the man, who

during the next fifty years held such major Pennsylvania offices as mayor of Philadelphia, chief executive, and chief justice. Unlike most Quakers he approved of oath taking: "However unfit were that affirmation for Friends in England, yet here, where such a rotten or insensible generation shelter themselves under the name, there is a necessity for a greater security." He also provided for the colony's protection, as "others are involved." Like his brethren, Logan became rich in trade and land speculation. His mansion, as grand as any Anglican's, housed one of the largest libraries in the colonies. Logan's collection of more than three thousand books was bequeathed to the public at his death.

HISTORICAL SOCIETY OF PENNSYLVANIA

JOHN ELIOT, 1604–1690, succeeded with the Indians where other Saints had failed. The "Apostle" taught red men civility as well as Christianity; to this end he set up Indian villages and published an Algonquian Bible and primer. Finer theological points may have eluded the savages, but the tobacco that Eliot distributed after sermons helped ensure numerous conversions.

HENRY E. HUNTINGTON LIBRARY AND ART GALLERY

PHILLIS WHEATLEY, c. 1753–1784, overcame the barriers of being a slave, a woman, and a poet. Born in Africa, she was educated and later freed by the enlightened Bostonian from whom she took her surname. When she patriotically addressed Washington with the familiar "Thee, first in peace and honours," the flattered general granted the endearing lady a personal interview.

NEW-YORK HISTORICAL SOCIETY

An effective if extralegal way to export a scolding wife is described in this English ballad.

Begged, Borrowed, or Stolen

Of all the commodities Virginia planters ordered from England, women headed the list. The Virginia Company, a purely economic venture, had recruited mostly young bachelors for its first settlements, but realizing that "the Plantation can never flourish till . . . wives and children fix the people on the Soyle," its agents began to advertise for adventurous young women to join the men. Irish colleens were "reddear to goe than men," but English maidens were often loath to part with the amenities of their homeland. In the early 1600's the colonies offered no fine ruffs, no "bums" to pad derrieres, no fabrics in "gooseturd green" or "peease-porrige tawnie," no gowns with décolletages permitting "paps . . . layed forth to mens view," no beauty preparations from apothecary shops, such as Jacobean women, rich and poor, had come to affect. And the lass who spent her formative years practicing at the lute and virginals, setting rhetoric to memory, and learning all manner of busywork skills, would find herself ill-equipped for the strenuous life in America. Despite many imaginative attempts to get them aboard ship—including promises of freedom to migrating felons and numerous instances of kidnapping—women comprised only 10 percent of the population by 1642. Supply would not match demand for two more centuries. In a sellers' market, a girl's housewifely talents were seldom examined. The custom of dowries lapsed, too; a prospective groom, anticipating long-term gains, was prepared to bid financially for his bride's hand when she stepped ashore. It was not uncommon or even unseemly for several men to pool their resources to buy a wench and live in relatively happy promiscuity, for as one disappointed Virginian protested, "the poore men are never the nearer for them they are so well sould."

BRATHWAIT, *ENGLISH GENTLEWOMAN*, 1631. RADIC TIMES HULTON PICTURE LIBRARY

*The gentlewoman who consented to go or who was carried to
America did well to forget the lessons in Richard Brathwait's
manual of deportment. Seventeenth-century life would offer
few opportunities for such virtues as Grace and Gentility.*

Pursuits of Pleasure

In England, one writer noted, hunting and hawking were sports for the rich and "not for every base inferior person, who while they maintain their falconer, and dogs, and hunting nags, their wealth runs away with their hounds, and their fortunes fly away with their hawks." America, however, was virtually one vast game preserve, where middle-class colonists, as in the needlepoint below, derived both food and pleasure from chasing or fishing. Occasionally, problems not unknown today occurred: a New York paper in 1734 reported that a woman in an "Orange Brown Wast-Coat" was mistaken for a fox and shot. Regarding fishing, one Puritan argued: "If I eat fish for Refreshment, I may as well catch them. . . . It's as lawful to delight the Eye as the Palate."

Big Wigs and Crowning Glories

The length of a man's hair was of topmost concern to the founders of the Bay colony. Elders decried the perfumed ringlets of English Cavaliers as "horrid bushes of vanity," and cautioned Puritan youths to crop their curls. As early as 1649, however, beginnings of civil disobedience were in evidence, and the following proclamation was issued: "Forasmuch as the wearing of long hair after the manner of ruffians and barbarous Indians has begun to invade New England . . . we, the magistrates . . . manifest our dislike and detestation against the wearing of such long hair . . . a thing uncivil and unmanly, whereby men doe deforme themselves, and offend sober and modest men, and doe corrupt good manners." Women were likewise censured; after derogating the sex as "apes of Fancy,

ABOVE: METROPOLITAN MUSEUM OF ART. RIGHT: WINTERTHUR

Marie Antionette may have inspired the headdress at left. Silk beauty patches were kept in the box above left. Made from human or horse hair, the wigs above had such names as "Cauliflower" and "Staircase." Before donning them, men were shorn with razors like the one facing.

frizling and curling their hayr," Cotton Mather asked, "Will not the haughty daughters of Zion refrain their pride. . . . Will they lay out their hair, and wear their false locks, their borders and towers like comets about their heads?" New heights of adornment were reached in the eighteenth century. The size of the "bigwig" lacquered to a gentleman's head was in direct proportion to his social pretensions. A lady's crowning glory was often so bouffant that she either had to ride with her head out the window or kneel on the floor of her carriage. Maintaining a coiffure required money and time. Before one Philadelphia fete, "so great was the demand on hairdressers, that many ladies were obliged to have their heads dressed between four and six o'clock in the morning.

WINTERTHUR

The British creator of "Cupid's Tower" (above right) carica-tured the vogue for ridiculous tresses. He dubbed another style "Bunker Hill," where toy sol-diers fought on a hairy battle-field. A hairdresser advertising at right thought credulous New Yorkers would pay his prices.

Me givee de Avertfement to every Body of
NEW-YORK.

DAT me tinkee me fall makee de Marriage, of Avantage, very fo foon : For vy, I borrow de great deal de Money of my very much Friends. I know dis, dat dey makee de big Recommend for me to de von young Lady of de Fortune. Yes, d---m mee my Soale, fhe havee de Houfe, de Horfe, de Cou, de Negre, de all fo much : By Gar, dis be very good, very fine, de Englifh bribee me for ftay vid dem, and givee me de Cafhee for pay my Debt : I dont caree, me gettes de Money, me takee de Vife, and me makee Stay here, in Spite of all de dam Barbare of de Town. Yes, dammee, me avertifee for makee de Vig, cuttee and curlee de Hair, drefee and fhavee de Beard of de Ghentlemans, felle de Pomate, and de Powdre, fo fweet for de Hair, and de Vig, for makee de bon Approach to de Madam-mofelle : For vy, I know dis,----Dat de Englifh ver villing for givee me de greatee de Prife dan dere own Coutrymans, and, be Gar me lettee de Lodg-ment, and keepee de Private Tavern : Me havee de Correfpondance, dat fend mee de very bon Claret ; and me gettee de great deale de Money.---Me havee de Two Wheel Char-riage ; now.---Prefontally, me havee de Four-Wheel Chariotte, and de fine Horfe, for my Vife go vifit all de fine Lady, and makee de Bon Appearance.---For vy I fpeakee dis becaufe I havee de very Grande Friends, and me makee de Grin, and de Ha, ha, ha, at all de Foolifh Tings dam Barbere makee de writte of.

N. B. Me makee all in de Bon Tafte, Ala-mode de Paris ; and me no chargee above three Hundred per Cent. more dan all de Workmans in Town.

Me havee de Prifes fo.

For dreffee de Hair,   £. 0 6 6
For curlee de Hair,   0 4 0
For cuttee de Hair,   0 6 6
For makee de Bag,   0 10 6
For makee de Ramille, de Half de Piftole.
For makee de Toupee,   de Half of de Piftole.
For Von Stick de Pomat.   £. 0 2 6
For Von Bottle de Lavender,   0 4 0
And fo in de Proportion.

NEW YORK GAZETTE: OR, THE WEEKLY POST-BOY, JANUARY 5, 1756, NEW YORK PUBLIC LIBRARY, RARE BOOK DIVISION

ARTHUR

NEW YORK HISTORICAL SOCIETY

The children in the 1768 portrait above are distant cousins of Sarah Rapalje, the first Dutch girl born in America. How far the family has progressed from those rigorous years is told in the silks and smirks which this generation wears.

Wooden tops like those above enter-tained children in all the colonies. The lad on the tile plays with a hoop, but most New Amsterdam boys pre-ferred bows, arrows, and war whoops.

Sparing the Rod

Foreigners had long criticized the Dutch for being terribly permissive parents. As William Bradford put it, the "great licentiousness of youth" in Holland influenced the Pilgrims to go to America. In Dutch New Amsterdam adult authority was even more lax. Instead of being cowed into submission, as in New England, or drilled into miniature models of decorum, as in the South, little Manhattanites had relative carte blanche to amuse themselves in a veritable "fun city." Boys and girls customarily joined mixed groups, to which they belonged until marriage. These companies had fine times (*hunky-dory*, as the Dutch said) bowling on the green, playing versions of golf and croquet, and going on unchaperoned jaunts to the country—purportedly to pick wild strawberries, but more likely to sow wild oats. During the winter, there were such sports introduced from the homeland as ice skating and sledding. New York children were more fortunate than their contemporaries in Albany, whose activities were curtailed by a 1713 decree: "Whereas ye children of ye sd city do very unorderly to ye shame and scandall of their parents ryde down ye hills in ye streets . . . with small and great slees . . . by which accidents may come [it] may be lawful for any Constable . . . to take . . . and break any slee . . . in pieces." On birthdays or holidays members entertained the gang at parties such as "waffle

frolics." Grownups were cordially uninvited and apparently had no choice but to abandon their homes to the pint-sized revelers. After games of *Tick-tack*, a type of backgammon, and much gorging, the uninhibited celebrants would kiss one another in extended farewells. Though parents encouraged a modicum of filial obedience, it was often observed in the breach. A token of disrespect was shown by putting thumb to nose and wriggling one's fingers. In a manner similar to today's rebellious youth, Dutch boys flouted authority; there was much "cutting of *hoekies*" from school, and night watchmen were heckled with cries of "Indians!" Most children did behave on or about December 6, when a visit from jolly Sint Klaas was eagerly anticipated. According to Washington Irving's whimsical rendition of history, "in the sylvan days of New Amsterdam," its patron saint "would often make his appearance . . . of a holiday afternoon, riding jollily among the tree-tops, or over the roofs of the houses . . . drawing forth magnificent presents from his breeches pockets, and dropping them down the chimneys of his favorites. Whereas, in these degenerate days of iron and brass, he never . . . visits us, save one night in the year, when he rattles down the chimneys of the descendants of patriarchs, confining his presents merely to the children, in token of the degeneracy of the parents."

Punishments were cruel: at a Boston tea party of sorts (above) a culprit is tarred and feathered; the woman at right is about to be immersed. However, the man in the stocks fiddles away his time.

The Rule of Law

According to John Winthrop's doleful commentary on the state of affairs in Boston, "As people increased, so sin abounded." The Puritans had envisioned a theocratic utopia, but experience soon proved that God's law had to be supplemented with man-made statutes. In addition to a criminal code, the overseers of souls enacted blue laws (named either for the blue Puritan emblem or for the blue paper in which they were bound) to regulate morals. Among things never to be done on Sunday were running, walking in a garden, cooking, making a bed, sweeping, or shaving. Such trivial transgressions brought stern measures. One man, returning from a three-year voyage, embraced his wife on his doorstep and was thrown in the stocks. Another, admitting that he was uninspired by a minister's sermon, was whipped. If caught in the act of adultery, a man and woman were "Scourged . . . unless it appear that one party was meerly surprized, and consented not." For serious acts of violence, law enforcers found it cheaper to have a malefactor pay his debt publicly and immediately—to deter potential wrongdoers and to save prison costs. Sometimes the punishment fitted the crime, as in restitution for stolen goods, but more often justice was meted out with un-Christian severity and a vengeance unbefitting even the Almighty. Having ears cut off, holes bored in tongues, noses slit, and being branded with irons were common penalties. In the colonies, where labor was scarce, there were fewer capital offenses than in England, whose population was kept in check by a commensurate number of executions. When they did occur, death sentences were attended by much publicity. Broadsides were circulated with particulars of the crime, and some were set to verse, one rhyming the confession of a rapist: "I seiz'd the advantage of the dark'ning hour, (And savage brutes by night their prey devour) This little child, eleven years of age, Then fell a victim to my brutal rage." Sermons were delivered to the condemned at the gallows, and the supposedly penitent addressee would then enjoin the spectators to avoid the wages of sin. Though the last words of one felon were "I pray God that I may be a warning to you all, and . . . the last that shall ever suffer, after this manner," records show that not everybody profited by his example.

A few LINES on
Magnus Mode, Richard Hodges & J. Newington Clark.
Who are Sentenc'd to stand one Hour in the
Pillory at Charlestown;
To have one of their EARS cut off, and to be Whipped 20 Stripes at the public Whipping-Post, for making and passing Counterfeit DOLLARS, &c.

BEHOLD the villains rais'd on high !
(The *Post* they've got attracts the eye :)
Both Jews and Gentiles all appear
To see them stand exalted here ;
Both rich and poor, both young and old,
The dirty slut, the common scold :
What multitudes do them surround,
Many as bad as can be found.
And to encrease their sad disgrace,
Throw rotten eggs into their face,
And pelt them sore with dirt and stones,
Nay, if they could wou'd break their bones.
Their malice to such height arise,
Who knows but they'll put out their eyes :
But pray consider what you do
While thus expos'd to public view.
Justice has often done its part,
And made the guilty rebels smart ;
But they went on did still rebel,
And seem'd to storm the gates of hell.
To no good counsel would they hear ;
But now each one must loose an EAR,

And they although against their will
Are forc'd to chew this bitter pill ;
And this day brings the villains hence
To suffer for their late offence ;
They on th' Pillory stand in view :
A warning sirs to me and you !
The drunkards song, the harlots scorn,
Reproach of some as yet unborn.
But now the *Post* they're forc'd to hug,
But loath to take that nauseous drug
Which brings the blood from out their veins,
And marks their back with purple stains.
    From their disgrace, now warning take,
And never do your ruin make
By stealing, or unlawful ways ;
(If you would live out all your days)
But keep secure from Theft and Pride ;
Strive to have virtue on your side.
Despise the harlot's flattering airs,
And hate her ways, avoid her snares ;
Keep clear from Sin of every kind,
And then you'll have true peace of Mind.

Public participation in the punishment of criminals was enthusiastic, as reported in this Massachusetts broadside.

So complicated were the steps of "Sir Fopling's Aires," danced c. 1710, that some couples preferred to sit it out.

Terpsichorean Temptations

Biblical sanctions for mixed dancing did not prevent Increase Mather from taking steps to ban it from Boston. His *Arrow against Profane and Promiscuous Dancing* of 1684 pointed out that the "question is not, whether all *Dancing* be in it self sinful. It is granted, that Pyrrhical or Polemical Saltation: i.e. when men vault in their Armour, to shew their strength and activity, may be of use. Nor is the question, whether a sober and grave *Dancing* of Men with Men, or of Women with Women, be not allowable." The minister's barb was aimed only at *"Gynecandrical Dancing . . . commonly called Mixt,"* for fear that unmarried couples who yielded to terpsichorean temptation would doubtless yield to others.

Southerners, however, did not consider dancing an inducement to sin — indeed it was a mandatory grace and marked the civilized man. Large plantations often had their own dancing masters, ballrooms, and orchestras comprised of indentured servants. The belle of a Virginia assembly could cut the proper figures of a minuet and manage the informal footwork of an English country dance, like the one above, where taking a pinch of snuff, patting one's head, and hopping "carelessly" were required. Another rustic favorite, the "Sir Roger de Coverley," a dance in which two lines of couples stepped to a lively beat, proved to be so popular in the colonies that it was renamed the Virginia Reel.

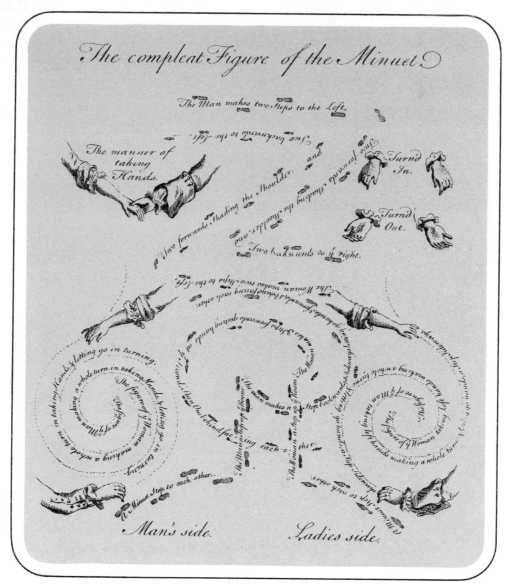

The compleat Figure of the Minuet

Man's side.   Ladies side.

To earn his keep, a dancing master not only gave ballroom instruction, but also inculcated basics of etiquette and posture in tender young minds. Though discipline was often unwarranted, the teacher who "struck two . . . young Misses for a fault . . . in the presence of the Mother of one of them" shocked an observer. The minuet could also be learned from manuals like that illustrated above and below.

ABOVE AND BELOW: BICKHAM, *AN EASY INTRODUCTION TO DANCING*, 1738, NEW YORK PUBLIC LIBRARY, DANCE COLLECTION

Stone immortalized old soldiers like Major Hide.

Nearer Their God

Even the sturdiest Puritan held a tenuous grip on life, and that was apt to be snuffed out quite suddenly by an Indian attack, storm, famine, or epidemic. Only faith in the justice of heaven enabled settlers to accept death's terrifying reality. The community of the dead occupied a prominent place in every New England village. Throughout the churchyard, graves of rich and poor intermingled democratically; family plots were rare (though a husband might be buried with his wife); and no ornamental shrubbery concealed the tombstones. Epitaphs embellished with grinning skulls, grim reapers, and emptying hourglasses contained specifics about the deceased and moral messages to inform or warn passersby. One short route from cradle to grave was skeptically pondered: "What did the Little hasty Sojournr find so forbidding & disgustful in our upper World to occasion its precipitant exit?" An ironic act of God hastened a youth's departure: entering church, he was felled by a bell clapper. A faulty inoculation released another soul: "The means Employed his life to save, Hurried Him Headlong to the Grave." Epitaphs also paid simple tributes: a slave had virtues "Without which Kings are but slaves"; a minister "Came into Wilderness, And left it a fruitful field."

Stephen Fisk is depicted at left in the costume of other eighteenth-century earthlings — a frock coat and wig. However, the sprouting wheat indicates that his soul has indeed moved on to kingdom come.

By 1775, the date of the grave below, stonecarvers replaced symbolic motifs with likenesses of the deceased. A stern-faced Reverend Nathaniel Rogers from Ipswich, Massachusetts, glares out to admonish his less pious descendants.

As the headstones below attest, old age was seldom a cause of death. Katherine Bartlet's demise at the age of thirty-one perhaps resulted from childbirth. "A clap of thunder" severed "lifes thrads" of a slightly older Marcy Halle. Moses Willard's untimely death was caused by Indians. Cupids, hearts, and winged skulls commemorate the death of three Dunsmoor tots

Fun and Profit

COLLECTION OF EDGAR WILLIAM AND BERNICE CHRYSLER GARBISCH

Eighteenth-century children were introduced to "the Devil's play-things" at an early age. Playing cards were often imprinted with "Moral and diverting histories" to disguise their entertainment value; and dominoes, as long as no money was wagered, were sanctioned. In the 1775 portrait above by an anonymous New Jersey artist, a girl lines up her ivory "bones" in anticipation of her partner's arrival.

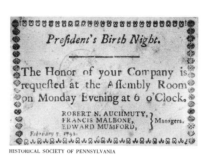

HISTORICAL SOCIETY OF PENNSYLVANIA

George Washington's birthday suitably honored in 1792

Taking their cue from James I, who floated the Virginia Company on the proceeds of a 1612 lottery, the colonists became inveterate gamblers. Coming to America was in itself a calculated risk, and settlers before long bet on everything from horses to gamecocks. The pious admonition that he who is "a Cully to a Gaming Table, may as well be one to a Harlot," was ignored, and southern gentlemen waged fortunes, plantations, and even servants at cards. Striking both young and old, the disease had no known cure: one man was shocked to find his aged aunt gathered with her "Partners round a Table playing Cards at that Vulgar game fit only for the meanest gamblers, 'All Fours'"; William Byrd vowed to lose no more than fifty shillings at a crack, but a few months later confessed he "played at dice and lost almost £10." Clandestine games of chance also took place in New England—often at backroom billiards tables in taverns. When, as self-appointed vice warden, Samuel Sewall raided a bout, he was duly rewarded with "A Pack of Cards . . . strawed over my foreyard, which, tis supposed, some might throw there to mock me." In particular turmoil because of the Biblical precedent for drawing lots, Cotton Mather's conscience admitted their use only "in weighty cases," when God was presumably "sitting in Judgment." Whether he would have considered the lotteries benefiting Harvard, Yale, Dartmouth, and Columbia "weighty cases" remains a matter of conjecture. By the late 1700's gambling seemed a permanent evil. Games of whist and loo enlivened tea parties of the rich, and plain-backed cards were pressed into service as invitations to balls or as tickets to college lectures. Professional sharpers conned the poor at thimblerig, the precursor of today's shell game, as well as at cards. One biddy, apparently luckless at gambling and love, proposed a raffle in which widows and those "in the unnatural state of virginity" would be offered as prizes. In descending order of desirability, she listed "Beauties, Pretty Girls, Agreeables, Good Card Players, Misses of General Accomplishment, Friskies, and Special Breeders."

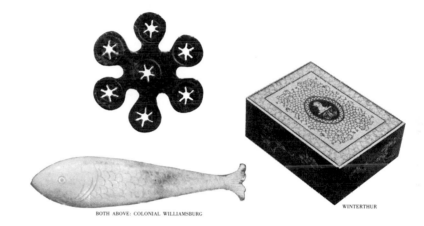

BOTH ABOVE: COLONIAL WILLIAMSBURG
WINTERTHUR

Counters and a fancy storage box for the game of loo

MARYLAND HISTORICAL SOCIETY

Several hustlers of 1797 matching skills at billiards

COLONIAL WILLIAMSBURG

Inlaid wood scoreboard for cribbage

A	In *Adam's* Fall / We Sinned all.
B	Thy Life to Mend / This *Book* Attend.
C	The *Cat* doth play / And after flay.
D	A *Dog* will bite / A Thief at night.
E	An *Eagles* flight / Is out of fight.
F	The Idle *Fool* / Is whipt at School.
G	As runs the *Glafs* / Mans life doth pafs.
H	My *Book* and *Heart* / Shall never part.
J	*Job* feels the Rod / Yet bleffes GOD.
K	Our *KING* the good / No man of blood.
L	The *Lion* bold / The *Lamb* doth hold.
M	The *Moon* gives light / In time of night.
N	*Nightingales* fing / In Time of Spring.
O	The *Royal Oak* / it was the Tree / That fav'd His / Royal Majeftie.
P	*Peter* denies / His Lord and cries.
Q	Queen *Efther* comes / in Royal State / To Save the JEWS / from difmal Fate.
R	*Rachel* doth mourn / For her firft born.
S	*Samuel* anoints / Whom God appoints.
T	*Time* cuts down all / Both great and fmall.
U	*Uriah's* beauteous Wife / Made *David* feek his / Life.
W	*Whales* in the Sea / God's Voice obey.
X	*Xerxes* the great did / die, / And fo muft you & I.
Y	*Youth* forward flips / Death foonest nips.
Z	*Zacheus* he / Did climb the Tree / His Lord to fee.

A reader warned, "Idleness breeds ignorance."

FREE LIBRARY OF PHILADELPHIA

Operation Headstart

The Puritan child, much like his modern counterpart, was forced to attend school, whether or not he absorbed the instruction he received. Massachusetts' early laws for public education were motivated by the desire to prepare youths for serving church or state, keep would-be idlers off the streets, and thwart "that old deluder, Satan," by enabling children to read the Scriptures. Training of "infant scholars" began at home, for parents were advised that "babes are flexible and easily bowed." Though Joseph Sewall toddled off to lessons at a prodigious two years and eight months, elementary education for slower learners commenced by the age of five. New England schoolmasters practiced the democratic if somewhat chaotic custom of moving the class to different parts of town during the year so that each child might at some point live nearby. Believing that intellectual initiative led to heresy, colonial masters commonly used the doctrinaire *New England Primer* to inculcate by rote the ABC's, the catechism, the Lord's Prayer, and moral precepts. A supplementary text, Eleazer Moody's *School of Good Manners*, attempted to mold proper little Puritans with such dicta as "Stand not wriggling with thy body hither and thither, but steady and upright," and "When thou blowest thy nose, let thy handkerchief be used." The birch rod maintained classroom discipline, and there was little worry about its stunting personality growth. "Better whipped than damned" justified the correction.

Illustrated rhymes accompany the alphabet in the New England Primer *at left.*

NEW ENGLAND PRIMER, 1727, NEW YORK PUBLIC LIBRARY, RARE BOOK DIVISION

When the colonial child excelled at studies and behaved in a suitably priggish manner, he was awarded a trophy like the silver-luster cup at left.

COLLECTION OF MARIE B. O'HILL

FREE LIBRARY OF PHILADELPHIA

A hornbook, like the one above, was the first text in the arduous process of learning to read. The wooden paddle was originally covered with a transparent sheet of horn to protect the lesson underneath from dirty fingers. The frontispiece from a 1710 speller at right portrays an idealized student-teacher relationship. Here, a scholar who minds his p's and q's catches the fruits of knowledge.

JOHNSON, *OLD-TIME SCHOOLS AND SCHOOL-BOOKS*, 1904

Hearts and Flowers

When William Penn peopled his newly chartered lands in Pennsylvania, he looked for dependable family folk. In addition to welcoming his English Quaker brethren, he sent a special invitation to the Mennonites and other pious Protestant sects of German-speaking farmers and artisans in the Rhine valley. The "Pennsylvania Dutch," as they came to be called, brought their homely traditions intact to the Lehigh and Susquehanna valleys. By 1750 they comprised a third of the colony's population, for as Dr. Benjamin Rush marveled, "No dread of poverty or distrust of Providence [inhibits them] from an increasing family. . . . Upon the birth of a [child] they exult in the gift

70

of a plowman or waggoner . . . a spinster or a milkmaid to the family." Like their German ancestors, the Mennonites had a passion for orderliness and thoroughness, and every personal event from birth to death was recorded. The plate opposite is a souvenir of courtship in 1793. It bears the legend "God hath created all the beautiful maidens. They are for the potter, but not for the priests." Above, another young man's medium is the valentine. The framed paper cutout confesses in characteristic *Fraktur Schriften* (a form of Gothic lettering kept alive in folk art) that to live and not possess is harder than stone and to love and not possess the addressee is hardest of all.

A Nation of Joiners

Scottish immigrant Hamilton suddenly ended his active role in the Tuesday Club. As a friend lamented, "poor Hamilton is gone—not dead, but married." On these pages the doctor caricatures himself, as well as the progressive breakdown of decorum at meetings.

During the "Grand Ceremony of the Capation," a newcomer is solemnly initiated. The mysterious rites are similar to goings-on at modern fraternities.

Minutes are formally read to comrades assembled, like Arthurian knights, at a round table. Their motto reads "Long may the members stand, and still maintain their badge of hand in hand."

Members turn to serious business.   *Clashing opinions end in a brawl.*   *Swords mediate where reason fails.*

Most colonists accepted democracy in small doses. Liberty and equality were tolerable in the government, market place, or even at home, but when it came to fraternizing, lines were drawn. By the 1740's "knots of men rightly sorted" were forming clubs as asylums from the common man, not to mention wives. Though some professed lofty aims, others, like Annapolis' Tuesday Club, were frankly dedicated to good times. As its founder-secretary, Dr. Hamilton, put it, the club was "designed for humor, and . . . a sort of farcical Drama of Mock Majesty." Bylaws which limited "vittles" to one dish per meeting and ordered the bar closed at eleven were rarely enforced. As for anyone mentioning politics, "no answer shall be given thereto, but . . . the society shall laugh at the Member offending in order to divert the discourse." Pennsylvania's Fishing Company of the State of Schuylkill outranked all other colonial clubs in exclusiveness—vacancies occurred only when members died. Snobbishness also expressed regional prejudices. New Yorkers established the St. Nicholas Society in 1835 for "Combating the social influence of New England." Ironically, the joining impulse was not a prerogative of the upper classes. The Freemasons attracted the commoner sort with secret rituals, pompous titles, and exotic costumes. At first, Masons were "continually complimented with Snow Balls and Dirt." However, when outstanding men like Ben Franklin and George Washington joined, the brotherhood gained acceptance.

Differences are forgotten, and a united fellowship marches forth in the "Grand Anniversary Celebration."

73

The Road to Ruin

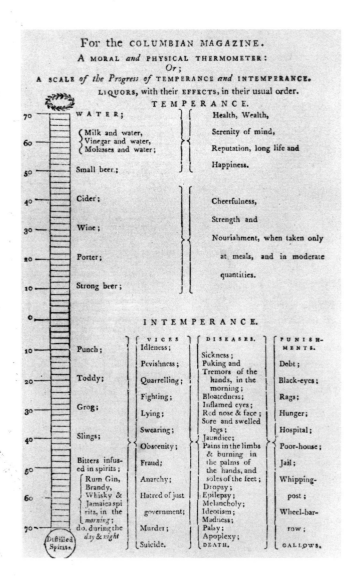

For the COLUMBIAN MAGAZINE.

A MORAL *and* PHYSICAL THERMOMETER:
Or;

A SCALE *of the Progress of* TEMPERANCE *and* INTEMPERANCE.

LIQUORS, with their EFFECTS, in their usual order.

TEMPERANCE.

70	WATER;	Health, Wealth,
60	Milk and water, Vinegar and water, Molasses and water;	Serenity of mind, Reputation, long life and
50	Small beer;	Happiness.
40	Cider;	Cheerfulness,
30	Wine;	Strength and
		Nourishment, when taken only
20	Porter;	at meals, and in moderate
		quantities.
10	Strong beer;	

INTEMPERANCE.

	VICES.	DISEASES.	PUNISHMENTS.
Punch;	Idleness;	Sickness;	
	Pevishness;	Puking and Tremors of the hands, in the morning;	Debt;
Toddy;	Quarrelling;	Bloatedness;	Black-eyes;
	Fighting;	Inflamed eyes; Red nose & face;	Rags;
Grog;	Lying;	Sore and swelled legs;	Hunger;
	Swearing;	Jaundice;	Hospital;
Slings;	Obscenity;	Pains in the limbs & burning in the palms of the hands, and soles of the feet;	Poor-house;
Bitters infused in spirits;	Fraud;		Jail;
Rum Gin, Brandy, Whisky & Jamaica spirits, in the *morning*;	Anarchy;	Dropsy;	Whipping-
	Hatred of just government;	Epilepsy; Melancholy; Ideotism; Madness;	post;
do. during the day & night	Murder;	Palsy; Apoplexy;	Wheel-bar- row;
Distilled Spirits.	Suicide.	DEATH.	GALLOWS.

For the lusty Englishman, no matter what his religious persuasion, drinking alcoholic beverages was an inalienable right. Even the stern-minded Puritans on the *Arbella* carried along quantities of beer and cider to fortify themselves for an otherwise bleak life in New England. During the voyage America's drinking problems may have been anticipated when John Winthrop discovered some unworthy Saint surreptitiously tapping the beer barrel under the guise of fixing a leak. New Amsterdam, which reputedly had more taverns than churches and where, in 1638, one house in four sold rum or beer, was the first urban center to be concerned about excessive drinking. Heavy tippling was also common in the South, where even the clergy, "being given to many vices not agreeable to their coats," were notorious sots. And by 1712 the bottle was thought to be luring so many New Englanders to spiritual degradation, that Increase Mather wailed, "Is not that worse than brutish Sin of Drunkenness becoming a prevailing Iniquity all over the Countrey? How has Wine and Cyder, but most of all Rum, Debauched Multitudes of People, Young and Old?" People continued to debauch—until the temperance movements of the next century—and to match skills, as with the puzzle jug above, awarding sixpence to anyone who could quaff without spilling.

According to Dr. Benjamin Rush's thermometer at left, anything from water to "strong beer" abetted good living; when alcoholic content rose, morals fell. In a more sober work, the doctor diagnosed the stages and consequences of drunkenness.

The "Prodigal Son," a compendium of New Testament sins, was a favorite subject of folk artists.

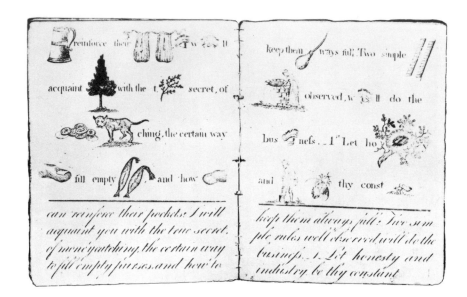

Dollars and Sense

Benjamin Franklin put himself in a position to be listened to by Americans. He demonstrated to an anti-intellectual young nation that the mind could be more than an ostentatious ornament. His interpretation of the Puritan code was that he who serves man best, serves God best. Franklin served and made it pay. He not only distinguished himself as a scientist, philosopher, and statesman, but he achieved the American dream—financial independence at the age of forty-two. To aid his countrymen who aspired to this goal, he offered scores of maxims which have become an indelible part of the national folklore. Most of his memorable sayings—some original, some adapted from European writers—appeared in various issues of *Poor Richard's Almanack*, which Franklin wrote under the pseudonym of Richard Saunders. The *Almanack*, a compendium of humor, practical lore, and "scraps from the table of wisdom," appeared in 1732 and was a great and lasting success, selling some ten thousand copies annually for twenty-five years. Poor Richard's followers learned to trust no one but themselves, and to be careful about even that. With no offense

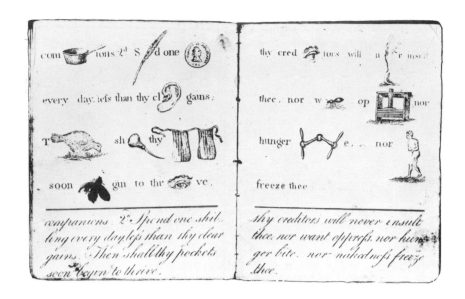

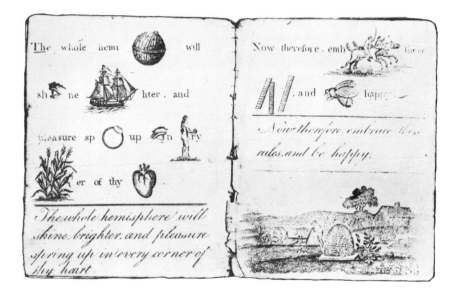

meant to the Almighty, Poor Richard advised, "In the affairs of this world men are saved, not by faith, but by the want of it." Sloth emerged as the deadliest of the earner's sins. "He that lives on hope will die fasting." "Industry need not wish." Benjamin Franklin was one of the founding fathers of an ethic that was neither crass nor dishonest, but the fruit of sound reasoning and hard work. "A life of leisure and a life of laziness are two things," said Poor Richard. But labor alone was not a source of riches. "A man may keep his nose all his life to the grindstone and die not worth a groat at last." "Fools make feasts and wise men eat them." Poor Richard's suggestions, simple as they sounded, were painfully antithetical to human nature. "We may give advice, but we cannot give conduct," Poor Richard reminded his readers. Those who heeded, succeeded. Lest Franklin's own essay on frugality, "The Way to Wealth," prove too long and theoretical for young minds, *The Art of Making Money Plenty* (above) was published c. 1810. With simple word games, the little book told "the moneyless how they can reinforce their pockets."

As late as 1840, when this plate was manufactured, Franklin's durable advice to "keep thy shop and thy shop will keep thee" was still prodding Americans to try harder.

COLLECTION OF MARIE D. O'NEILL

Arms and Men

LIBRARY OF CONGRESS

By His EXCELLENCY

WILLIAM SHIRLEY, Esq;

Captain-General and Governour in Chief in and over the Province
of the Massachusetts-Bay in New-England.

To John Bench Gould

SIR,

AS you have receiv'd Beating-Orders from Me to enlist Men into His Majesty's Service for the Expedition intended,

In the Management of that Trust, I give you the following Directions;

1. You are to enlist no Person under the Age of eighteen Years, nor above Forty-five Years.

2. You are to enlist none but able-bodied effective Men, free from all bodily Ails, and of perfect Limbs.

3. You are to enlist no Roman-Catholick, nor any under five Feet two Inches high without their Shoes.

4. You are to assure such Persons as shall enlist, That they shall enter into Pay ~~~~~~~~~~~~~~~~~~~~~~~~~ upon their first general Rendezvous

5. That they shall at the Day of their Enlistment receive a good Blanket ~~~~~~

6. That their Pay will be Twenty-six Shillings and eight Pence, per Month, lawful Money, during their Service ~~~~~~~~~~~~~~~~~~~~~

7. That they shall be exempt from all Impresses for Three Years next after their Discharge.

8. To such of them as shall be provided with sufficient Arms at their first Muster, they shall be allowed a Dollar over and above their Wages, and full Recompence for such of their Arms as shall be inevitably lost or spoiled.

9. You are to enlist no Person but such as you can be answerable for that they are fit for Service; and whom you have good Reason to think will not desert the Service.

10. You are before your delivering the Blanket allowed, or any other Bounty that may be allowed by this Government to any Person, cause the second and sixth Sections of War to be read to them, and have them also sworn before, and their Enlisting attested by, a Justice of the Peace.

Given under my Hand at Boston, the Seventeenth Day of April 1755, in the Twenty-Eighth Year of His Majesty's Reign.

Thos Hutchinson
by Gov. Shirley's Order

LEFT: MUSEUM OF THE CITY OF NEW YORK

Maneuvers of splendidly arrayed regiments in George Ropes's 1808 painting above were reported "highly gratifying" to the Salem spectators. Antimilitary types made these gaudy parades the subjects of ridicule, as exemplified by the hawk-nosed officer above left. Boston's draft regulations of 1755 (left) exclude "Roman-Catholicks" and men "under five Feet two Inches."

ESSEX INSTITUTE, SALEM

Foreseeing that the Promised Land might not welcome them with hosannas, the Puritans brought along "arms, ammunition, and great artillery." Indians proved a very real threat, and colonists soon became proficient musketeers, joined militias, and drilled on Training or Muster Days. (Massachusetts' penalty for evading enlistment was death. Quakers, Moravians, and others who morally objected to any form of fighting—even self-defense—were labeled cowards.) Though dangers decreased, Training Days continued as pretexts for social gatherings. As Sarah Kemble Knight described New Haven's 1704 festivities: "The Youth divert them-

selves by Shooting at the Target . . . where hee that hitts neerest the white has some yards of Red Ribbin presented him . . . he is Led away in Triumph, with great applause, as the winners of the Olympiack Games." After the Revolution, Americans liked to think that nonprofessional "minutemen" and "embattled farmers" had won the war. To the new nation a permanent standing army meant tyranny, and as a safeguard, the Second Amendment provided: "A well regulated Militia, being necessary to the security of a free State, the right of the people to keep and bear Arms, shall not be infringed." Its application is still being argued.

79

Home Rule

In which Columbia's Sons & Daughters rejoice in Independence; Gentlemen are Chosen as Leaders; and French Modes, Camp Meetings, and Good Works become Republican Fashion

Perhaps the least worry of the Revolutionists had been the problem of how Americans were to conduct themselves socially when they were free of the English. Yet once peace had come, the new nation was in the position of a young bride suddenly faced with housekeeping and entertaining. How should the President be addressed? His Highness? His Magistracy? His Supremacy? His Supreme Mightiness? All of these were suggested, and there were even those who wanted George Washington crowned as King George the First. John Adams thought "His Elective Majesty" would be nice, and that members of the presidential staff should have impressive-sounding titles as well—that the presidential cook, for instance, should be "Steward of the Household." It was Adams' opinion that the masses needed and enjoyed official pomp and circumstance. Other members of the government thought that the United States should be as unlike the mother country as possible and that, in a republic, simplicity had a majesty of its own. One senator remarked that while "His High Mightiness" might be suitable for a robust man like George Washington, a short, puny president would make such a title ludicrous. In the end, "Mr. President" won out, and although Martha Washington was called Lady Washington, her successors were all known as plain Mrs. As for titles among the rank and file, there was some talk of adopting the appellations "Citizen" and "Citizeness," as the French Revolutionists had called themselves, but the Jacobin craze went out of favor before anything came of that idea.

The Society of the Cincinnati, composed of former Revolutionary officers and presided over by George Washington, attracted heavy criticism for the reason that membership was hereditary and was transmitted to eldest sons in each succeeding generation. Both hereditary honor and primogeniture were deplored by most Americans. Benjamin Franklin thought the officers should be allowed their "little badge and ribband" while they lived, "and

&

In the small New England town of 1800 the paths of righteousness between church and home were still well-trodden, as this central panel from an appliqué quilt shows.

let the distinction die with those who have merited it." After some reflection, Washington also objected to the hereditary clause, but even his prestige was not enough to change the rules. Today there are some 2,400 members.

The first and second Presidents observed considerable ceremony in their official entertainments. One of Washington's first policy decisions had been directed at the matter of presidential entertaining, for no sooner had he been installed at his New York headquarters than he discovered that his dinner table "was considered as a public one, and every person who could get introduced, conceived that he had a *right* to be invited to it." The President was treated, he said, no better than a maitre d'hôtel. Then there were the levees, formal afternoon receptions held after the fashion of the European royal courts. Washington foresaw that he would have little time for the office of the Presidency if he did not put a stop to the rounds of party-making. He polled John Adams, Alexander Hamilton, and several other leaders on the problem and, after some deliberation, decided on "that line of conduct which combined public advantage with private convenience," namely, that he would continue to hold open house two afternoons a week, but that he would close the dining room to casual visitors, and most emphatically, that he would accept no invitations to make official visits outside the President's House. Martha Washington later confessed that she sometimes felt "more like a state prisoner than anything else," but the alternatives were far worse.

John Adams and his wife, Abigail, the first family to occupy the executive mansion in Washington, continued the custom of the levee, receiving on a dais, acknowledging guests with a slight bow. (The handshake was inaugurated with Jefferson.) Adams had often been at the English court during his term as ambassador there. He knew how royalty behaved and followed suit—not from any personal snobbery but because he believed his position called for it.

What made him fit for this role? The President must be an aristocrat, not necessarily the sort who came from a hereditary ruling class, but a man educated to his responsibilities. Adams was explicit: a gentleman was one of "those who have received a liberal education, an ordinary degree of erudition in liberal arts and sciences, whether by birth they be descended from magistrates and officers of government, or from husbandmen, merchants, mechanics, or laborers; or whether they be rich or poor." A gentleman in politics was, according to Adams, an aristocrat.

Some of his contemporaries were so rude as to question Adams' own right to the position of gentleman. Senator William Maclay of Pennsylvania remarked, "A little learning is a dangerous thing ('tis said). May not the same be said of breeding?" And he went on to accuse Adams of "believing that good manners consists entirely on punctilios [and] stiffened airs, [while] excluding good humor, affability of conversation, and accommodation of temper and sentiment as qualities too vulgar for a gentleman." Another contemporary said that Adams "cannot dance, drink, game, flatter, promise, dress, swear with the gentlemen, and talk small talk and flirt with the ladies; in short, he has none of the essential arts or ornaments which constitute a courtier."

Thomas Jefferson, on the other hand, although he was equally well acquainted with the formal etiquette which directed Adams, seemed to delight in ignoring it, especially whenever he was entertaining His Britannic Majesty's envoy, Anthony Merry. When Merry came to present his diplomatic credentials, wearing full court dress, Jefferson received him in "an old brown

Portrait of Washington in Mason's regalia

coat, red waist coat, old corduroy small clothes [breeches] much soiled, woolen hose and slippers without heels." Jefferson had installed a round table in the state dining room, so that no one might be seated "above" anyone else, and on one occasion further appalled Mr. Merry by strolling into dinner with Dolley Madison on his arm instead of the ranking guest, Mrs. Merry. The envoy made this outrage the subject of a dispatch, advising London that "the excess of the democratic ferment in this people is conspicuously evinced by the dregs having got up to the top." Another dispatch, during the second Jefferson administration, reported sourly that at a New Year's Day reception, Mr. Jefferson gave the diplomatic corps no more than a bow, but held a long conversation with a party of Osage Indians.

"If in his manner he was simple, affable and unceremonious," wrote Mrs. Margaret Bayard Smith, an arbiter of social life in the Capital and one of Jefferson's admirers, "it was not because he was ignorant of, but because he despised the conventional and artificial usages of courts and fashionable life. His simplicity never degenerated into vulgarity, nor his affability into familiarity. . . . At his usual dinner parties the company seldom or ever exceeded fourteen, including himself and his secretary. The invitations were not given promiscuously, or as has been done of late years, alphabetically, but his guests were generally selected in reference to their tastes, habits and suitability in all respects, which attention had a wonderful effect in making his parties more agreeable, than dinner parties usually are. . . . At Mr. Jefferson's table the conversation was general; every guest was entertained and interested in whatever topic was discussed. To each an opportunity was offered for the exercise of his coloquial powers and the stream of conversation thus enriched by such various contributions flowed on full, free and animated; of course he took the lead and gave the tone, with a *tact* so true and discriminating that he seldom missed his aim, which was to draw forth the talents and information of each and all of his guests and to place every one in an advantageous light and by being pleased with themselves . . . please others."

Jefferson's successor, James Madison, had no such social gifts, but fortunately his wife did. Dolley Madison, according to Mrs. Smith, united "to all the elegance and polish of fashion, the unadulterated simplicity, frankness, warmth, and friendliness of her native character." Under her regime the President's House continued to be a place where the best American manners could be found. Even so, curious behavior was observable among visitors. At one of Jefferson's dinners, a manufacturer from Beverly, Massachusetts, took it upon himself to fascinate the guests by producing specimens of bed-ticking and wadding for ladies' cloaks. And when Mrs. Madison, at one of her receptions, paused to say a friendly word to a young man who was trying to balance a cup of coffee, he became so confused that he dropped the saucer and put the cup in his pocket. The tactful Dolley pretended not to notice, asked him how his mother was and whether he was enjoying Washington, and later sent a servant to bring him a fresh cup of coffee.

As new states to the west joined the Union, they sent representatives to Washington who had never been in a city before. Mrs. Smith wrote her sister of being "very much diverted" by a visit from two backwoods senators. When she observed them peering at the piano, she asked her daughter Susan to play for them. "I believe it was the first time they had seen or heard such a thing. They looked and looked, felt all over the outside, peeped in where it

Dolley Madison, who set a standard for White House entertaining, poses for a portrait, above. Below, performers at a musicale are seen in a contemporary silhouette.

was open, and seemed so curious to know how the sound was produced, or whence it came, that I begged Susan to open the lid and to display the internal machinery. Never did I see children more delighted. 'Dear me,' said the judge, 'how pretty those white and red things jump up and down, dear me what a parcel of wires, strange that a harp with a thousand strings should keep in tune so long.' 'Pray,' said the other senator, 'have you any rule to play musick?' We tried to explain how the keys were the representatives of the notes, they did not seem to comprehend, supposing all Susan's sweet melody was drawn by chance or random from this strange thing." Mrs. Smith added shrewdly, "Do not think now these good men are fools, far from it, they are very sensible men and useful citizens, but they have lived in the back woods, thats all."

Most foreign observers were less willing than Mrs. Smith to forgive unorthodox manners. Perhaps the chief cause of offense was the prevalent American habit of spitting tobacco juice. When Lord Chesterfield's *Letters to his Son* were especially edited for American consumption, a "Chapter Addressed to Americans" inveighed against this "ungentlemanly and abominable habit. . . . A person . . . guilty of so unpardonable a violation of decorum, and outrage against the decencies of polished life, should be excluded from the parlour, and allowed to approach no nearer than the hall-door steps." But in spite of such strongly worded injunctions, and in spite of the widely publicized denunciations from such visitors as Mrs. Trollope, Harriet Martineau, and Charles Dickens, Americans continued to spit, and they spat all the way through the nineteenth century and well into the twentieth. They spat on the elegant carpets of the new de luxe hotels; they spat in drawing-rooms, at the theater, and out the window. Ladies on the decks of steamboats were hard put to it to keep their skirts free of the brown slime underfoot. An etiquette book on "Clerical Manners," published in 1827, advised clergymen to avoid spitting in church (anywhere else was apparently alright). The marble halls of Congress were stained a walnut brown with tobacco juice. Each congressman and senator had his own spittoon (he still does), but frequently missed it. That all this spitting was acceptable to the general public is suggested by the following poetical work entitled "Mrs. Trollope and the Spitters," which appeared in a New York newspaper of 1832, shortly after Mrs. Trollope's American memoirs were published:

> *Mrs. Trollope is commendably bitter*
> *Against the filthy American spitter,*
> *For spitting his juice all about;*
> *While the English they (for so it is writ)*
> *Disgustingly in their handkerchiefs spit —*
> *Thus leaving a case of some doubt,*
> *Which, gentle reader, I beg you will sit on*
> *And fairly judge 'tween the Yankee and Briton;*
> *So render your verdict I pray:*
> *Whether, to weigh its merits to a tittle,*
> *You think it better to POCKET the spittle,*
> *Or freely to spit it away?*

Ladies neither smoked nor chewed, although some women of the more rustic areas of the frontier — Mrs. Andrew Jackson, for instance — smoked a

"Lounger" from an 1852 issue of Yankee Notions; *his object, a fancy spittoon.*

corncob pipe. Snuff-taking was acceptable in all circles. Dolley Madison was addicted to it, even though it must have caused a permanent yellow stain under her pretty nose. Another and less socially acceptable habit was called dipping, in which a bit of splayed stick was dipped into snuff and used to rub the teeth. "A knott of young ladies will assemble in a room as though it were a tea party and lock themselves in, and dip for hours," reported Mrs. Anne Royall, on her visit to Raleigh. "I have seen little girls walking in the streets, with their lips besmeared with snuff and saliva, which rendered them objects of disgust, and it evidently distends the mouth."

When the Monroes succeeded the Madisons, and Elizabeth Monroe announced that she would make no social calls, it became clear that there would be no continuity in White House etiquette—each presidential family would set its own style. The Monroes went through eight stately, withdrawn years. The John Quincy Adamses, in the view of the sometimes hypercritical Mrs. Smith, were marked by a "silent, repulsive, haughty reserve." John Quincy used to complain that his mother's dictum of "children should be seen and not heard" had ruined him for the social graces. He had no Chesterfieldian guiles, and he also lacked the common touch—although he sometimes made rather poignant efforts to attain it. Once, at a family wedding held in the White House, Adams was actually observed to dance a Virginia reel. He was the first President to wear pantaloons (before 1815 they had been worn only by the lower classes) instead of knee breeches, and at the ceremonial to mark the beginning of work on the Chesapeake and Ohio Canal, he took off his coat and wielded the first shovel.

Washington and its leaders had none of the impact on national manners and etiquette that the capitals of Europe had had on their countries. It was too small and too isolated a city, and its social leaders, many of them transient, arrived from various corners of the country with preconceived convictions as to what manners ought to be. New England ladies were shocked to find their compatriots from the South using "pearl," a type of face-powder, and rouge, "with as much sangfroid as putting on their bonnets." And when a Boston lady inquired of Mrs. Henry Clay if she was not distressed by her husband's playing cards, Mrs. Clay replied, "Oh! dear, no! He 'most always wins." Southerners sniffed that northerners tended to be dull and graceless.

Benefitting from the anti-British feelings that survived the American Revolution, Frenchmen and their French manners were making inroads into American life. Politics, theater, literature, conversation, all were showing marked French influence. Some new words were taken into the language, especially when American speech offered no equivalent: "bon ton" for elegance; "soiree" for a particularly elegant evening reception; "soigné" for a well-turned-out costume, which was very likely to be of French inspiration anyway. As Washington Irving reported, even the conservative colonial tastes of the North led by the English-born milliner Mrs. Toole were under French siege, for "Madame Bouchard, an intrepid little woman, fresh from the headquarters of fashion and folly, has burst like a second Bonaparte upon the fashionable world. . . . [American] ladies have begun to arrange themselves under the banner of one or the other of these heroines of the needle, and everything portends open war. . . ."

Irving also took note of the many French émigrés earning their way as dancing masters. Watching an assembly from the side lines, he observed,

Series of illustrations from Le Blanc's Art of Tying the Cravat

Removing the hat

Bowing slightly

Extending the hand

Steps to "Elegance of Manners," 1810

"Frenchmen, dead or alive, are born dancers. . . . A Frenchman passes at least three-fifths of his time between the heavens and the earth, and partakes eminently of the nature of a gossamer or soap-bubble. One of these jack-o'-lantern heroes, in taking a figure, which neither Euclid nor Pythagoras himself could demonstrate, unfortunately wound himself—I mean his feet—his better part—into a lady's cobweb muslin robe; but perceiving it at the instant, he set himself a-spinning the other way, like a top, unraveled his step, without omitting one angle or curve, and extricated himself without breaking a thread of the lady's dress! He then sprung up like a sturgeon, crossed his feet four times, and finished this wonderful evolution by quivering his left leg, as a cat does her paw when she has accidentally dipped it in water. No man . . . who was not a Frenchman, or a mountebank, could have done the like."

It was a Frenchman who also brought America its first society divorce. Though the day of the title-hunting heiress had not yet dawned, the Baltimore belle Betsy Patterson had pursued and married Napoleon's brother, Prince Jerome, only to have her imperial brother-in-law order them to the divorce courts of France. Divorce had been possible since the very first settlements in America, but it was still rare among all classes. The Bonaparte fiasco was followed shortly by the divorce of Thomas Law, of Washington, and his wife, a granddaughter of Martha Washington. To do so, he had to establish residence in Vermont, that being one of the few states where a divorce was available on grounds of incompatibility. For many years the Law divorce and the Bonaparte divorce were the only such instances in the world of American "bon ton."

Marriages were easier to make than to break. From earliest colonial times, a female had been a highly valued creature—in short supply and absolutely essential to the progress of the country. Parents, once the sole arbiters of her future, played a diminishing role, at least as matchmakers. She grew up with a sense of power and independence that never ceased to astonish foreign visitors. "A very remarkable custom in the United States gives girls the freedom to choose a husband according to their fancy," wrote an Austrian observer. And her fancy was often guided by the most whimsical rules. *A New Academy of Compliments*, a compendium of pre-Freudian analysis published in 1795, guided readers in the mysteries of "moles in all parts of the body," and what they told about the object of one's affections: "A mole on the nose signifies speedy and often marriages, and the party to be fruitful in children. . . . A mole on or near the private parts, promises ability in duty, vigorous in love, and successful in many children. . . . " The author offered lovers a quick course in dream interpretation as well. "To dream of fire, denotes anger. . . . To dream you put a gold ring on your finger signifies speedy marriage. . . . To dream another kisses you, signifies barrenness, or disappointment."

Bundling was old-fashioned now, but a girl might go sleighing or buggy-riding with a young man without comment from Mrs. Grundy. Only a thorough-going blackguard would take liberties with an unchaperoned female. "Universal indignation and the marks of infamy will catch up with . . . a villainous seducer," wrote the émigré Moreau de Saint-Méry. "No matter to what point he might flee, so long as that point is in the United States . . . he will never be able to obtain any kind of a post, even that of a watchman. . . . A maiden trusts herself to the restraint of her lover. . . . Each day they are left alone. Since the young lady must wait for her servant, who leaves the house as soon as night has arrived and cannot be persuaded to return until eleven-thirty or midnight, her only protection is her suitor. Her father, her mother, her entire family have gone to bed. The suitor and his mistress remain alone; and sometimes, when the servant returns, she finds them asleep and the candle out, such is the frigidity of love in this country!"

As in colonial times, the hazards of premarital sex were partly circumvented by early marriage. A girl was marriageable at fourteen. Moreau de Saint-Méry noted "thousands of beauties between fourteen and eighteen," but added that most of the women were "dried up at twenty-three, old at thirty-five, decrepit at forty or fifty. . . . Girls generally hold on to their lovers, at least unless urgent causes force him to leave. In that case, they will choose a second."

The Frenchman was troubled by a certain cold and passionless air of calculation among American young ladies. "Without emotion enough to alter the expression they will engage for hours in that which ought not to be tolerated except in the grip of an irresistible ecstasy." (One cannot but wonder how this eighteenth-century Dr. Kinsey went about his research.) Another characteristic of American women appears to have been prudishness—or as more sympathetic observers would have it, delicacy. Saint-Méry noted that women would object to hearing "certain words," but he suspected that "the extent to which that scruple is observed discloses rather an excess of knowledge than of ignorance. . . . American women also have a false modesty," he went on, "that makes them unwilling to discuss, even with their husbands, bodily ailments that may become serious. That is the source of so many bad teeth, of stomach troubles and of poor skins. Americans divide the whole body into two parts: from the top to the waist is the stomach; from there to the bottom, the limbs. Imagine then the difficulties of a doctor who must guess from these rudimentary identifications the nature and the seat of an illness. The slightest contact is forbidden and the ill woman will, even at the risk of death, not make the vagueness more specific."

Perhaps it was this same fear of doing anything improper that led ladies traveling alone to frown and scowl at gentlemen whom they did not know, while at the same time expecting them to give up their seats in the stagecoach, carry their luggage, and pick up their handkerchiefs. A European visitor, writing some years later than Moreau de Saint-Méry, was amazed by the deference shown American women ("a sort of limitless respect and a boundless submission"), and also by the coldness and stiffness with which the ladies responded. "Even after having been introduced according to the rules, the stranger hardly dares the first time to speak with a woman for more than a few moments. He is always watched; an extended conversation would certainly lead to whispering. The more beautiful and more graceful the ladies, the more they are the butts of gossip, a circumstance which deprives them of charm in mixed company, makes them cold, or at least embarrassed." Mrs. Trollope describes some girls she saw on a Hudson River steamboat, who, having rudely appropriated the best seats, sat looking "like hedgehogs, with every quill raised." Mrs. Trollope, something of a prude herself, expressed the hope that well-bred American women ("the instances are rare, but they are to be found") might "speedily become the reformers of all the grossness and ignorance. . . . " Perhaps it was the heavy responsibility of this mission that caused women to refuse to hear "certain words," and to behave like hedgehogs toward strangers. Mrs. Trollope saw little indication of change.

Pas de deux *essayed by a stylish pair*

In the South a young girl of good family was more carefree, less educated, and perhaps more sheltered and innocent than her sisters in the North and West. But after marriage, her responsibilities were tremendous. Besides being wife and mother, she was doctor, nurse, seamstress, teacher, housekeeper, and manager of a huge household staff. The plantation way of life was a matriarchy. The southern planter was prone to abdicate his responsibilities as "master" to his wife or mother and live by a code of manners as peculiar as his "peculiar institution."

In New Orleans a young bachelor frequently took a mistress from among the quadroons, mulatto women known for their beauty, charm, education, and decorum. A quadroon who was faithful in her affections was not considered a prostitute. A young white man courted her under the surveillance of her mother. If he became her lover, she used his name and expected that she and any children she might bear him would be provided for. When he married, he presumably left his mistress. Sometimes he would send a quadroon daughter to France, where with a good dowry, she had a chance of marrying into respectable French circles. In other parts of the South interracial sex was not so open, but the number of upper-class white men who acknowledged mulatto children leads us to suppose that the practice was not uncommon. Mary Chesnut, wife of a wealthy South Carolina planter, wrote in her diary, "Any lady is ready to tell you who is the father of all the mulatto children in everybody's household but her own. Those, she seems to think, drop from the clouds." Perhaps in an effort to atone for his peccadillos, the southern gentleman put his lady on the highest pedestal in history. Her virtue, purity, and innocence were straight out of the Garden of Eden. She, of course, was expected to stay aloft on the narrow confines of her pedestal and smile, whether she liked it there or not.

Novelist Harriet Beecher Stowe

Doing the family mending chores

While the South barricaded itself in a closed society and frontiersmen were working out a new society of their own, the country people of New England went on living much as they always had, grouped around a town whose life centered in the church. Harriet Beecher Stowe described it in *Oldtown Folks*, a novel set in one of these towns, in the period of the early Republic: "High and low, good and bad, refined and illiterate, barbarian and civilized, negro and white, the old meetinghouse united us all on one day of the week, and its solemn services formed an insensible but strong bond of neighborhood charity. . . . The man or woman cannot utterly sink who on every seventh day is obliged to appear in decent apparel, and to join with all the standing and respectability of the community in a united act of worship. . . . The minister and his wife were considered the temporal and spiritual superiors of everybody in the parish." But in a more subtle way, there had been a momentous change from the pre-Revolutionary years, which Mrs. Stowe deftly describes: "Our minister was one of those cold, clear-cut, polished crystals that are formed in the cooling-down of society, after it has been melted and purified by a great enthusiasm. Nobody can read Dr. Cotton Mather's biography of the first ministers of Massachusetts, without feeling that they were men whose whole souls were in a state of fusion . . . [while those of the later generations were] mostly scholarly, quiet men, of calm and philosophic temperament, who . . . came to regard the spiritual struggles and conflicts, the wrestlings and tears, the fastings and temptations of their ancestors with a secret scepticism—to dwell on moralities, virtues, and decorums, rather than on those soul-stirring spiritual mysteries which still stood forth unquestioned and uncontradicted in their confessions of faith."

In the long-settled regions of the South, religion was even less a matter of import. A New Englander visiting Virginia in 1818 wrote, "too few regard the sabbath, except as a holiday; or wherein to begin or end a journey. In some places, toward Norfolk, shops are kept open, only the buyer may walk round to the side door, to evade the law. . . . The ancient Episcopal churches which once were so predominant, are mostly in a state of dilapidation. The rank reeds rustle round their doors; the fox looks out at their windows. . . . "

However, on the frontier the first five years of the new century were marked by a sweeping religious upsurge that became known as the Great Revival. In the tradition of Edwards and Whitefield sixty years earlier, preachers traveled from place to place warning in lurid language of approaching hell fire and damnation. Methodists predominated, with a sprinkling of Baptists and Presbyterians. Sometimes as many as twenty thousand people gathered from a hundred-mile radius, camping in the woods in family groups from a Friday to a Tuesday, and listening to sermons morning, noon, and night. Each meeting reached a crescendo of excitement, at which point hysteria generally broke out and the congregation was prone to twitch, jerk, leap, shout, sob, and emit an eerie sound called the holy laugh. Those who believed themselves repentant came forward and fell on their knees. Those who were inclined in that direction but had not made up their minds went and sat in a special place called the anxious bench, hoping for further intimations of salvation. While relays of preachers took charge of the mass meetings, others held small, more personal meetings in tents.

The Great Revival simmered down after its first explosive glory, and frontier sinners sinned again, but still camp meetings continued. For some they brought religious consolation; for others perhaps nothing more than a break in the monotony of hardworking lives and a chance to meet new people. The revivalists of Kentucky and Tennessee have had their twentieth-century descendants in Billy Sunday and Aimee Semple McPherson, and today in Billy Graham and the leaders of Moral Rearmament.

But if the day had passed when shared religion was the guiding factor in the lives of whole communities, the day of wide-ranging philanthropy, reform, and good works was dawning. The Pennsylvania Quakers had always been ahead of the rest of the country in this respect, having started, in the eighteenth century, the first city almshouse, the first hospital (with a special section for "twenty-five lunatics"), and the first penitentiary. Pennsylvania was the first state to eliminate such punishments as the stocks and the whipping post, and the first to abolish capital punishment except for treason and murder in the first degree. In regard to slavery, Pennsylvania was first with a program of gradual emancipation and with an Abolition Society. In 1789 a "society for the free instruction of orderly Blacks and People of Color" was formed at Philadelphia. In the South a number of slaveowners who deplored the institution, but could see no remedy for it other than to ship all Negroes back to Africa, formed the American Colonization Society in 1817. Such eminent southerners as Bushrod Washington, Henry Clay, and John Randolph were charter members.

Nearly all other reform movements of the early Republic were initiated in the more populous regions of the North. (The southern champion of slavery

Going to Sunday service in Missouri, 1820

George Fitzhugh remarked that this was not surprising—the North was in need of reform.) To mention a few groups, there was the Society for the Prevention of Pauperism, the Society for the Relief of Poor Widows with Small Children, the Association for the Relief of Respectable, Aged, Indigent Females, several Magdalen societies concerned with prostitution, and a Society for Alleviating the Miseries of Public Prisons.

In order to keep homeless children out of the crowded almshouses, the Orphan Asylum Society of the City of New York was founded in 1806, the first in the United States. In Washington Dolley Madison was the first directress of the Washington Female Orphan Asylum, where good orphans were rewarded on visitors' day by being allowed to dress in pure white instead of the regular uniform, and bad ones were condemned to wear a tag bearing the word *BAD*. Orphan girls were bound out to families at an early age, and usually spent their lives as servants. Orphan boys were apprenticed at various working-class skills. Child adoption, except among the nonprocreating Shakers (who took in orphans to keep their ranks filled), was undreamed of. Most people could not help believing that the poor were poor through some fault in their make-up and that this fault was "in the blood."

By the 1820's children rich and poor were being sent to Sunday school. The practice was begun in England as an educational charity for factory children and was copied by American factory owners. The original intent was to teach reading and writing, using the Bible as text. But gradually Sunday school became a way for children to escape the long church sermons in exchange for lessons in scriptural history and doctrine that were taught to them on a level they could understand.

The temperance movement, which was eventually to have more supporters than any other reform, was stimulated partly by humanitarian, partly by religious, and partly by democratic idealism. It started modestly enough in 1808 in Saratoga, New York, when a group of men agreed to abstain from rum, whiskey, gin, and wine except at public dinners, when apparently the etiquette of toasting took precedence. Within a few years, societies and committees of correspondence had cropped up throughout the Republic. For some, like the group in New Jersey whose members agreed to drink no more than a pint of applejack daily, the word *temperance* was not to signify total abstinence until the 1830's. Only those signing the pledge with a capital *T* for *Total* beside their name (hence the expression "teetotaler") meant to go that far. The Methodist Church, which was one of the strongest forces behind the movement, enjoined its ministers not to distill or sell liquor, either.

America was clearly a nation of joiners, and if the society they joined had a lofty purpose, so much the better. Noah Webster, who was concerned lest such a new country be lacking in patriotism, proposed an "Association of American Patriots for the Purpose of Forming a National Character." He wrote textbooks that extolled American superiority. Our land was God's country and we were his chosen people, said Webster echoing the Puritans. The Fourth of July became the most important holiday in the year. A people inured to long sermons did not object to three-hour-long patriotic speeches, particularly when preceded by picnics and followed by fireworks. The day might also include footraces, horse racing, ninepins, bowls, quoits, or even a balloon ascension. Washington had not permitted celebrations of his birthday while he was alive, but a few years after his death, February 22 became

(Continued on Page 92)

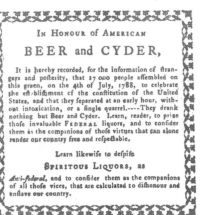

Philadelphia temperance broadside

Philadelphia: 1798

The City of Brotherly Love, as it appeared to Moreau de Saint-Méry, a French émigré. The following summarizes his acute, if somewhat cynical, observations.

Philadelphia is the most beautiful city of the United States. The houses . . . more than nine thousand in number . . . have a gloomy appearance because of the bricks of which they are built. Only a few . . . deviate from the regulation shape and size. . . . A custom that might be termed extravagant is that of washing doors, sidewalks and window ledges every Wednesday and Saturday morning. . . . This lunacy exposes the passers-by to the danger of breaking their necks; and . . . falls on the sidewalk are not rare. The true character of Americans is mirrored in their homes. They always have broken windowpanes, doors without locks; and leaks are common to every attic. Decoration of the houses is only to be found in the rooms which a visitor is likely to see . . . for everything that is normally out of sight is very ugly and very little cared for. Even in Philadelphia . . . America's outstanding city, everything is for sale, provided the owner is offered a tempting price. He will part with his house, his carriage, his horse, his dog—anything at all. American women are pretty, and those of Philadelphia are prettiest of all. . . . Philadelphia has thousands of them between the ages of fourteen and eighteen. . . . They are markedly extravagant in their purchase of ribbons, shoes and negligees of lawn and muslin and have a habit, which they think is stylish, of letting the men pay for what they buy in the shops, and of forgetting to pay them back. All the colored

women . . . dress well Sunday, and wear chignons of white people's false hair. . . . Negresses wear pale pink. The Quakers, who are numerous in Philadelphia, are becoming fewer, because many Quaker children leave the faith. I repeat that morals in this city . . . are not pure, although they pretend to be virtuous. When a Quakeress feels lecherous impulses, she notifies her husband of it, and does her best to make him share her torment. Quaker youths are frequent visitors in the houses of ill fame. . . . The daughters of Quakers are extremely imprudent, and frequently get into trouble. Bastards are extremely common. It is to the influence and the number of Quakers . . . that one must attribute the melancholy customs of this city, which has less society than most places. However . . . Philadelphia has public establishments, to wit: 33 churches; 3 markets; 22 cemeteries (But I am not attracted by the frequency with which children go to these cemeteries to play, thus trampling upon the ashes of those who gave them life.); 35 taverns; 1 City Tavern where merchants gather . . . to find out about market prices, to learn about ship movements . . . and to hear the news; 2 theaters—the actors are of a bearable mediocrity. . . . The performance is boisterous, and the interludes are even indecent. It is not unusual to hear such words as Goddamn, Bastard, Rascal, Son of a Bitch. Women turn their backs to the performance during the interludes; a library and museum.

Young chauvinists getting into step, c. 1825

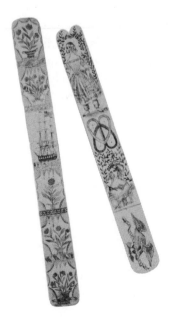

Scrimshaw corset stays

another important holiday, with more flag-waving and patriotic speeches. Uncle Sam, though not yet in striped pants and starry waistcoat, became a familiar folk figure. "Yankee Doodle" was an unofficial national anthem until Francis Scott Key came along with his more lofty-minded "Bombardment of Fort McHenry," or "Star-Spangled Banner," in 1814.

Foreign visitors found American nationalism irritating. Stephen Decatur's famous toast, "Our country . . . may she always be in the right; but our country, right or wrong," was the noisy theme everywhere. A German traveler, writing in 1800, observed that the plots of American plays centered around liberty rather than love and marriage, "and the development is marked by the warmest patriotism." A French Royalist émigré remarked that "the dominant character of Americans is arrogance carried to an extreme. . . . Since it is not pleasant to tell people that which will offend them, I hide my ideas as much as possible. But they will find you out simply from the failure to go the full length they desire in exaggerated praise. In any case, nature has not made me capable of calling a frog a bull, no matter how it blows itself up." And De Tocqueville, despite his frequently sympathetic view of the country, reported that "nothing is more embarrassing in ordinary social intercourse than the irritable patriotism of the Americans."

Sectionalism continued to be a potent danger. John Calhoun, though an ardent champion of states' rights, was nonetheless concerned about separatism. At the end of the War of 1812, he advocated building roads and canals to "bind the Republic together." Since the seventeenth century, land commerce had been carried on by pack trains, single-file processions of stunted horses, each carrying up to two hundred pounds of goods—furs and hides or country produce for the towns, hardware and other store-bought treasures for the backwoods. The packers objected strenuously when the government decreed the building of wider and better roads, but the more enterprising of them invested in Conestoga wagons and draught horses (a four- or six-horse team could pull two tons) and learned to become drivers.

The first regular passenger lines began before the Revolution and ran between New York and Philadelphia. By 1812 there was more travel between these two cities than anywhere else in the country. The fastest service made the trip in about fifteen hours, stopping only to refresh horses and riders. The stagecoach held seven passengers, paying ten dollars each. Slower and cheaper stages stopped at Trenton or Bridgeton, New Jersey, for the night. Food and lodging cost extra: $87\frac{1}{2}$ cents for a bed, $62\frac{1}{2}$ cents for breakfast, and 75 cents for dinner and alcoholic table drink.

On less civilized routes, the going was rougher. Any road wide enough for a wheeled vehicle was called a turnpike, though it might be clogged with rocks and tree stumps, and turn to pure mud in wet weather. Going around corners, the passengers were requested to lean to the left or right in the hope of keeping the coach from overturning. If it bogged down in mud, the gentlemen passengers got out and tried to pry it loose with fence rails. Streams often had to be crossed without the amenities of ferries or bridges, and from time to time the stage was swept away and the passengers drowned.

As soon as steamboats were in general use, travelers used them wherever possible, for provided they did not blow up, they were faster and more comfortable. A stagecoach journey from New York to Albany in 1815 took three days, while the steamboat made it in twenty-four hours. Travelers to Boston were apt to take a Long Island Sound steamboat as far as New Haven (eighteen hours), and then, to avoid the open ocean, continue by stage via Hartford, Pomfret, and Dedham, ending at the Exchange Coffee House in Boston on the fourth night after leaving New York.

The man who owned a stagecoach line was also likely to own one or more of the inns along its route. An inn, in the heyday of the stagecoach, was one of the most lively, heterogeneous, and interesting places in America. The taproom, where local people gathered round the fire to drink, play cards, and exchange news, also served as a hotel lobby. Here travelers made arrangements for accommodations and signed the register, which, being kept behind the bar, was called the bar book. Here they left their boots to be cleaned, took a pair of slippers and a candle, both provided by the management, and went upstairs to sleep in a bed that not infrequently contained fleas, bedbugs, or a total stranger as bedfellow. In an upper room, called the long room, where the floor was built on shallow-arch trusses to make it springy for dancing, there was usually something going on in the evening, whether a dance, a party caucus, a lecture, or a play put on by a traveling troupe of actors.

The social position of the innkeeper was one of consequence, a fact that baffled foreign visitors. His daughters helped wait on table and make beds, but they were young ladies, definitely not for pinching. One traveling Frenchman found the landlord's daughter "genteel and well educated, who played the piano very well." At a Connecticut inn, he noted that "the tables are served by a young girl, respectable and pretty, by an amiable mother . . . or by men who have that air of dignity which the idea of equality inspires and who are not ignoble and base like most of our own tavern keepers."

Mrs. Trollope was not interested in whether or not the chambermaid could play the piano, and she objected strenuously to American inns except those in the South. "I am very far from intending to advocate the system of slavery," said she. "I conceive it to be essentially wrong; but so far as my observation has extended, I think its influence is far less injurious to the manners and morals of the people than the fallacious ideas of equality, which are so fondly cherished by the working classes of the white population in America." In Cincinnati Mrs. Trollope and her party were ejected from a lodginghouse by its owner because they did not wish to take tea with the other lodgers. "'Madam, I must tell you, that I cannot accommodate you on these terms; we have no family tea-drinkings here, and you must live either with me [and] my wife, or not at all in my house.'" Mrs. Trollope, as "a sort of apologistic hint," replied that she and her friends were strangers and unaccustomed to the manners of the country; not to be placated, the patriotic landlord retorted briskly, "Our manners are very good manners, and we don't wish any changes from England."

"It is a part of the American character to consider nothing as desperate; to surmount every difficulty by resolution and contrivance," wrote Thomas Jefferson in 1787. "Remote from all other aid, we are obliged to invent and to execute; to find means within ourselves and not to lean on others." These words were addressed to his little daughter Patsy, to urge her to greater efforts in translating Livy; but they perfectly describe that famous quality, Yankee ingenuity. By the end of the Revolution, new fortunes had been made (in supplying the Continental Army, in privateering, in acquiring at low sums the property of departing Tories), and now that Americans were free of

Inns were often named after local heroes, as these signboards show.

English restraint, there were boundless opportunities for the shrewd, the industrious, and the imaginative.

New Englanders, whose rocky soil was unpromising (although one of its rocks, granite, was made into monuments and tombstones from Maine to New Orleans), turned toward the sea and the world. Salem merchants made their town famous as a trading post for peppercorns; fishermen of New Bedford and Nantucket sailed to the ends of the oceans in pursuit of the whale; coffee, sugar, and cotton were picked up on one side of the world and delivered on the other. Yankee captains skippered ships to China loaded with ginseng, an herb without value in America but prized as a medicine and aphrodisiac by the Chinese, and brought them back filled with tea, silks, and porcelain. In 1805 a 21-year-old Bostonian named Frederic Tudor hit upon the idea of cutting ice in the ponds of New England, packing it in sawdust, and shipping it to the West Indies. On the cover of his diary, he wrote, "He who gives back at the first repulse and without striking the second blow despairs of success, has never been, is not, and never will be a hero in war, love, or business." Tudor practiced what he preached, for it took him fifteen years to devise a successful way of preserving the ice, to establish monopolies, and to bring about a reputation for his product in the hot countries of the world.

Businessman is an American word, and it began to supercede the word *merchant* after men like Tudor had expanded the old-fashioned functions of a merchant to include those of a promoter, an entrepreneur, a financier, an innovator, an advertising man, and (if he succeeded) a social leader. Between 1787 and 1815, businessmen brought the cotton textile industry into being in New England. In the British Isles, industrialization created a class of factory workers. But in America most able-bodied unskilled men either worked on farms or had other, more ambitious plans for themselves, and so the mill-owners had to turn to women and children for a labor force. In the rustic villages of the Blackstone River valley, near Providence, where the first cotton mills were established, farmers were willing to spare their children from farm work for the sake of a wage of fifty cents a week plus keep; and teen-age unmarried girls enjoyed a few years' escape from farm and household drudgery and a chance to earn up to $3.00 a week. A thrifty girl could save all but $1.25, that portion going to room and board. When the millowners built "company houses," whole families were attracted to the mill towns.

Davy Crockett, while he was serving as a congressman from Tennessee, between 1827 and 1835, visited Lowell, Massachusetts, and saw "a mile of gals" —more than five thousand female factory workers. He reported that they seemed cheerful and healthy, though he "could not help observing that they kept the prettiest inside and put the homely ones on the outside rows." The girls lived in boardinghouses, six to a room, watched over by chaperons provided by the millowners. As the girls worked a thirteen-hour day, they had little time to get into mischief; but for those with strength left in the evenings, two-hour lectures of an improving nature were provided.

Crockett, on his tour of New England, was impressed with Yankee hospitality—"more than they generally get credit for." And he added, "I wish all who read [my] book, and who never were there, would take a trip among them. If they don't learn how to make money, they will know how to use it; and if they don't learn industry, they will see how comfortable every body can be that turns their hands to some employment."

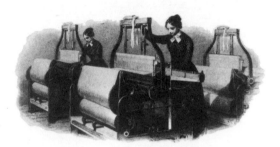

Mill girls at their weaving machines

Shipping notice in an 1817 journal

LINE OF AMERICAN PACKETS
BETWEEN N. YORK & LIVERPOOL.

IN order to furnish frequent and regular conveyances for GOODS and PASSENGERS, the subscribers have undertaken to establish a line of vessels between NEW-YORK and LIVERPOOL, to sail from each place on a certain day in every month throughout the year.

The following vessels, each about four hundred tons burthen, have been fitted out for this purpose:

Ship AMITY, John Stanton, master,
" COURIER, Wm. Bowne, "
" PACIFIC, Jno. Williams, "
" JAMES MONROE, —— "

And it is the intention of the owners that one of these vessels shall sail from New-York on the 5th, and one from Liverpool on the 1st of every month.

These ships have all been built in New-York, of the best materials, and are coppered and copper fastened. They are known to be remarkably fast sailers, and their accommodations for passengers are uncommonly extensive and commodious. They are all nearly new except the Pacific; she has been some years in the trade, but has been recently thoroughly examined, and is found to be perfectly sound in every respect.

The commanders of them are all men of great experience and activity; and they will do all in their power to render these Packets eligible conveyances for passengers. It is also thought, that the regularity of their times of sailing, and the excellent condition in which they deliver their cargoes, will make them very desirable opportunities for the conveyance of goods.

It is intended that this establishment shall commence by the departure of the JAMES MONROE, from NEW-YORK on the 5th. and the COURIER from LIVERPOOL on the 1st, of First Month (January) next; and one of the vessels will sail at the same periods from each place in every succeeding month.

ISAAC WRIGHT & SON,
FRANCIS THOMPSON,
BENJAMIN MARSHALL,
JEREMIAH THOMPSON.

10mo24

Thomas Jefferson had also been impressed with northerners' acumen. He once drew up a list of notable regional differences.

In the North they are:	In the South they are:
cool	fiery
sober	voluptuary
laborious	indolent
independent	unsteady
jealous of their own liberties, and just to those of others	zealous for their own liberties, but trampling on those of others
interested	generous
chicaning	candid
superstitious and hypocritical in their religion	without attachment or pretensions to any religion but that of the heart

Pistols used in the Burr-Hamilton duel

Like all generalizations, these were open to many exceptions. Nevertheless, there was no doubt that the two parts of the country were strikingly different, and paradoxically, were becoming more so, despite the growing strength of the political Union. In the South there were almost no businessmen in the New England sense of the word. The pinnacle of society was reserved for southern gentlemen, rich in land, possessions, courtly manners, and charm, but poor when it came to ready cash and commercial experience. Their business affairs were managed by factors, who lived in the seaboard cities—Charleston, Norfolk, and Savannah—and who sold the produce of the plantations, which after the invention of the cotton gin, was principally cotton. The formula of selling cotton in order to buy more slaves and then using the slaves to plant still more cotton worked so well that during the sixty years before the Civil War neither factor nor planter wanted to try anything new.

The colonial prejudice against lawyers was unchanged in the South. A gentleman considered his word of honor binding, and business was conducted with a bare minimum of paper work. Broken contracts and libel were matters not for law courts but for the field of honor. In the North, where dueling had never been frequent, the duel between Aaron Burr and Alexander Hamilton in 1804 aroused such public distress that the custom died out completely. Duels were illegal everywhere in the country, but in the South unwritten law usually took precedence over written ones. Since duels were fought outside the law, there are no reliable statistics on their number. But that there were many is attested to by the scores of prominent men who had dueling scars (including Andrew Jackson and Henry Clay); the number of tombstones bearing the words "killed on the field of honor"; and the fact that a book called *The Code of Honor, or Rules for the Government of Principals and Seconds in Duelling*, written by a governor of South Carolina, was reprinted regularly until as late as 1858.

Immigrants from Europe avoided the South, put off by the lack of industry and the competition from slave labor. The poorer whites farmed or kept shops, with little hope of changing their status. Between the planter and other whites (with the sole exception of his traveling representative, or factor) there was a social gulf, mitigated only slightly by the fact that there were often genealogical ties between them.

Thus, while the rest of the country went forward into the adventurous 1830's with an equally adventurous willingness to change manners and behavior, the South settled more deeply into its own way of life—a way that worked for decades by virtue of its very immobility.

Vol. 2.] "GO AHEAD!!" [No. 3.

THE CROCKETT ALMANAC 1841.

MANNING DEL. HARTWELL SC.

Tussel with a Bear. See page 9.

Containing Adventures, Exploits, Sprees & Scrapes in the West, & Life and Manners in the Backwoods.

Nashville, Tennessee. Published by Ben Harding.

The Common Manners

꒒

*In which the Locofocos
toss the Aristocratic
Rascals out of Office and
declare for Frontier
Manliness, Democratic
Delicacy, Hard Cider and
Harder Work for All*

"We have become the most careless, reckless, headlong people on the face of the earth. 'Go ahead' is our maxim and password. . . ." So wrote the New York gentleman-diarist Philip Hone, in the mid-1830's. He was referring specifically to the frequent explosions of Hudson River steamboats and the fiendish compulsion of their captains to engage in races. But "Go Ahead" was indeed the maxim of the Jacksonian era: Go Ahead in business; Go Ahead to the frontier; Go Ahead in new inventions, new reform movements, new amusements, new theories of child rearing, new manners, new moral and social standards.

Only conservatives like Mr. Hone, who had made a large fortune before 1820 and now wished to take no chances with it, resisted the Go-Ahead mania. Hone hated Andrew Jackson just as conservative businessmen a century later hated Franklin D. Roosevelt. He loathed not only Jackson's politics, but his manners and morals as well. He thought the man a violent ruffian, citing as an example Jackson's duel in 1806 with a man who had slandered Mrs. Jackson. Jackson (so the story went) had worn loose clothing so that his opponent could not easily aim for the heart, and had let his adversary fire first. Then, wounded in the ribs but still on his feet, Jackson had very deliberately taken aim and killed the slanderer, afterward boasting, "I left the villain wallowing in his blood." Hone considered dueling immoral, but thought that Jackson had been guilty of something even worse, a duel lacking in propriety.

In Hone's world, violent and unlawful behavior seemed to be on the increase. "There is an awful tendency toward insubordination and contempt of the laws," he noted, "and there is reason to apprehend that good order and morality will ere long be overcome by intemperance and violence." Hearing of riots in Baltimore, he wrote, "My poor country, what is to be the issue of

꒒

Davy Crockett, whose real life was a model of derring-do, became in death the comic-book symbol of the frontier hero: boastful, optimistic, manly. Here he tames a bear.

the violence of the people . . . ?" He disapproved of abolition because it caused riots. The South should be left alone to take care of its own affairs. Abolition, he said, was "a new enemy to the peace of mankind." He was equally disturbed by news of lynchings—"remedies worse than the disease." In New York at that time, abolitionists were not the only target of mob violence. There were anti-Irish riots, anti-German riots, anti-Negro riots, anti-Catholic riots, and even anti-actor riots—on one occasion an English actor who was rumored to have spoken disparagingly of the United States escaped just as a mob arrived at the Bowery Theatre prepared to tear him apart.

Hone shared the patriotic fervor of the mob, if not its violence. Born in 1780, he cherished the anti-English sentiments that had been common in his youth, and was shocked because upper-class New Yorkers were beginning to bring back from trips abroad "the foppery of foreign manners and the bad taste of anti-Americanism." Returning from a European sojourn himself, he observed, "The English swarm so on the Continent. They are generally vulgar people, without taste, and with their pockets well filled, and the French and Swiss do love so dearly to handle their money that the market is spoiled for us Americans, who can better appreciate the value of the articles offered."

During his lifetime—he died in 1851—Hone watched New York's population grow from 20,000 to more than 500,000. He enjoyed the enormous profits to be had in real estate, noting that "the whole of New York is rebuilt about once in ten years," with Broadway, ever expanding commercially, looking like "the ruins occasioned by an earthquake." The increasing wealth of his social set made it possible for New York to have an opera and to build mansions with painted ceilings, gilded moldings, splendid mirrors, and "curtains in the latest Parisian taste." On the other hand, he worried about the huge numbers of foreign riffraff that swarmed from stinking immigrant ships into lower Manhattan. From 1835 until the Civil War the annual invasion only twice dropped below 50,000. Between 1830 and 1840, half a million had arrived. In 1832 Hone wrote, "The boast that our country is the asylum for the oppressed in other parts of the world is very philanthropic and sentimental, but I fear that we shall, before long, derive little comfort from being made the almshouse and place of refuge for the poor of other countries."

He was not alone in his misgivings. The anti-foreigner, anti-Catholic movement that would become the "Know-Nothing" party was born during the 1830's, and although most of its members were indeed know-nothings, some were intelligent, educated citizens who sincerely believed in a Papist-Imperialist conspiracy to take over the United States. In 1835 the painter-inventor Samuel F. B. Morse published a pamphlet to warn his compatriots of the danger: "Up! up! I beseech you," he wrote. "Awake! To your posts! Let the tocsin sound from Maine to Louisiana!" The incoming immigrants, he believed, were in the pay of the Holy Roman Emperor and were organized by the Jesuits. Recommending strict immigration laws, he warned that such measures would be called "religious bigotry, and illiberality, and religious persecution, and other popular catchwords, to deceive the unreflecting ear."

The Irish, though white and more or less English-speaking, seemed a strange and undesirable breed to all "nativists," like Morse. They were by far the largest single group arriving in these years, and the working classes, whose jobs they threatened, especially feared and disliked them. They were

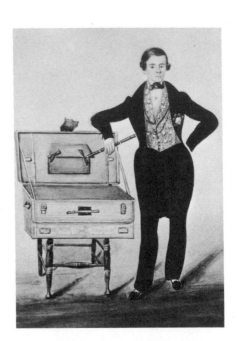

Concert flutist, painted by J. E. Levie

so ready to do dangerous work for low pay, and so able to live under the most crowded and unsanitary conditions. To thrifty, Puritanical, anti-Catholic Yankees, they were dissolute, superstitious, rowdy, and shiftless. "Our Celtic fellow citizens are almost as remote from us in temperament and constitution as the Chinese," commented the New York aristocrat George Templeton Strong. He wrote in his diary of "a strange, weird, painful scene" at the site of excavations for new houses on Fourth Avenue. "Seeing a crowd on the corner, I stopped. . . . The earth had caved in a few minutes before and crushed the breath out of a pair of ill-starred Celtic laborers. They had just been dragged, or dug, out and lay white and stark on the ground where they had been working, ten or twelve feet below the level of the street. . . . Fifteen or twenty Irish women . . . were 'keening'; all together were raising a wild, unearthly cry, half shriek and half song, wailing as a score of daylight Banshees, clapping their hands and gesticulating passionately. Now and then one of them would throw herself down on one of the corpses, or wipe some trace of defilement from the face of the dead man with her apron, slowly and carefully, then resume her lament. It was an uncanny sound to hear, quite new to me. . . ."

A prominent Hartford clergyman, Horace Bushnell, offered the comforting prediction that vice among the Irish would soon "penetrate the whole stock and begin to hurry them off. . . . It is not true, as many suppose, that they become an integral part of our nation to any considerable extent. They become extinct. It is very seldom that their children born in this country live to mature age. Intemperance and poor living sweep them away, both old and young together. If you will glance over the catalogues of our colleges and legislatures, the advertisements of merchants and mechanics, you will almost never find an Irish name among them, which shows you at least that they do not rise to any rank among us. At the same time if you will search the catalogues of alms-houses, and prisons, and potter's field, there you will find their names in thick order."

Despite the absence of a welcome mat, the Irish continued to arrive in large numbers. So did Germans, and people from Great Britain. To succeed, an immigrant needed rugged good health, a disposition that combined caution with a willingness to adapt to new circumstances, and an almost fanatic will to work and "go ahead." The weak easily succumbed to disease aboard ship or in the miserable harborside slums; the unambitious were bowled over in the race toward success; the gullible were fleeced by a wicked race of "immigrant runners," who, under pretense of being helpful, stole luggage, sold invalid railroad tickets, and lured young girls into houses of "ill repute." Between the two major groups of immigrants, Irish and German, there was rivalry and hatred. A German on the streets of New York might be beaten up by Irish thugs just for looking like "a damn Dutchman," and Germans joined nativist white Americans in bloody anti-Irish riots in New York and Philadelphia. But all got together whenever feeling ran high against Negroes and abolitionists, for everyone feared the economic competition of freed slaves.

The Erie Canal labor force included thousands of "Paddies," who left their bones there, the victims of smallpox and cholera epidemics or ill-timed gunpowder blasts. After the canal was opened in 1825, hundreds of boatloads of new citizens traveled along it, bound for Ohio, Michigan, Indiana, and points westward. The slow, horse-drawn canal barges were not as dangerous as steamboats or transatlantic immigrant ships, the chief hazard being that of

The Irishman above has just arrived in America. The Fraktur *hymn sheet below belongs to a German settler of Pennsylvania.*

decapitation while passing under a low bridge. But they were unsanitary and crowded. Bedbugs and lice were inescapable. Filthy blankets were handed out at night for use in narrow, three-tiered bunks. During the days, the blankets were stored in a heap in the middle of the floor. All accommodations were alike, and the passengers suffered, in true democratic fashion, equally. Because the barge owners competed for passengers, the rates were low — sometimes as little as $2\frac{1}{2}$ cents a mile, with meals.

But the real revolution in American travel came with the railroad. In 1830 there were only a few experimental miles of track; at the end of the decade, trains were no longer an experiment, but a way of life. In the face of vast distances and inadequate capital, only that American trait of recklessness that had so alarmed Mr. Hone made railroads succeed. "Flying is dangerous," wrote Hone. "I never open a newspaper that does not contain some account of disasters and loss of life on railroads. . . . By and by we shall have balloons and pass over to Europe between sun and sun. Oh, for the good old days of heavy post-coaches and speed at the rate of six miles an hour!" A visiting Englishman who wanted to catch a certain train was advised by his American host to await it a few miles beyond the station. "Why? Is that a regular stop?" asked the visitor. "No," replied the American. "But most always there's an accident there." For years, the American rail accident rate remained much higher than the European, but there was no lack of business because of it. The cautionary saying "slow and steady wins the race" had no currency in Go-Ahead America.

As the railroads lengthened their flimsy lines farther into the West, ambitious visionaries began to plan towns and cities where only wilderness existed. Some of these were never more than names, or after a few years became ghost towns; others by wise promotion or by apparent sheer luck grew into large cities: Chicago, Little Rock, Milwaukee, and Grand Rapids were among many that expanded during the 1830's. Every city had its boosters back East — public relations men, they would be called today. In the Halls of Congress, legislators praised the towns they represented, or hoped to represent, filling up pages of the Congressional Record throughout the nineteenth century. As a random example, here is a Minnesota congressman extolling Duluth:

"If gentlemen will examine the map they will find the town of Duluth exists in the centre of a series of concentric circles. . . . I see it is represented on this map as situated exactly half-way between the latitudes of Paris and Venice, so that gentlemen who have inhaled the exhilarating airs of the one or basked in the golden sunlight of the other, may see at a glance that Duluth must be a place of untold delights — a terrestrial Paradise, fanned by the balmy zephyrs of an eternal spring, clothed in the gorgeous sheen of ever-blooming flowers, and vocal with the silver melodies of nature's choicest songsters."

As often as not, these heavens on earth failed to live up to expectations. The pseudonymous Major Walter Wilkey wrote of his *Western Emigration* in 1839. Having sold the family farm in Maine, he set off with his wife, three children, a black servant named Caesar, and a dog. Somewhere in Michigan they came upon a log hut with a shingle out front grandly proclaiming Hotel. Rousing the proprietor, Wilkey asked directions to Edensburgh City, in which he had bought property sight-unseen, only to be told that the city consisted of two living and six dead citizens and a real-estate swindler's map.

Early New York railway car, c. 1832

Exposé of "The Land of Promise"

"Here we were, in a peck of trouble, sure enough! my Mooseboro Farm gone—irrevocably gone!—more than eleven hundred miles from a single acquaintance (with the exception of my family) and with but one week's provision on hand, or the most distant prospect of obtaining any—and with but just thirteen shillings and sixpence half-penny in my pocket!—my wife sick, dejected and discouraged! the boys disappointed and mortified!—my horse lame and wind-broken!—old Ceaze fretful and saucy!—and *Watch* (the dog) with a leg broken by the wolves half starved and snapping at swarms of bloodthirsty musquetoes!—nor was this all, my 'Farm of 300 acres, producing 400 bushels to an acre!' had been either swallowed up by an earthquake, or in some other way had unaccountably disappeared, and could no where be found! in such a predicament [did we find ourselves] on the first day of [our] arrival in 'Edensburgh!' "

Manners at a Yankee hotel in the 1850's

The French traveler Michael Chevalier described how real estate speculators in the Pennsylvania coal regions vied "in tracing out the plan of whole cities. I have seen detailed plans, with straight streets and fine public squares scrupulously provided for, of cities which do not actually consist of a single street, of towns which hardly contain three houses. This frenzy gave birth, however, to one town of three thousand inhabitants, Pottsville, to ten or twelve railroads, great and small, to several canals, basins, and mining explorations that have proved fairly successful.... First rises a huge hotel with a wooden colonnade, a real barracks in which all activity, rising, breakfasting, dining, and supping, are regulated by the sound of a bell with military precision, uniformity, and rapidity, the hotel-keeper being, as a matter of course, a general or at least a colonel of the militia. The barroom is at once the exchange where hundreds of bargains are made under the influence of a glass of whiskey or gin, the clubroom which resounds with political debate, and the theater of preparations for civil and military elections. At about the same time a post office is established. In the early stages the hotel-keeper commonly acts as postmaster. As soon as there are any dwelling houses built, a church or meetinghouse is erected at the charge of the growing community; then follow a schoolhouse and a printing press with a newspaper, and soon after appears a bank, to complete the threefold representation of religion, learning, and industry." Tree stumps, four or five feet high, were left standing between the hastily constructed buildings, and a short distance away was "primitive forest inhabited by bears and rattlesnakes."

For a brief period in such towns, social life was nearly classless. On the western frontier, what mattered supremely was not who a man was but what he could do. "Rank and birth, as assets, could not be carried to a poorer market than America," remarked a foreign visitor. Pioneer farm life was a repetition of colonial farm life: everyone worked hard and helped another. Yet no sooner did a town spring up along a railroad or a railroad come to a town than the tracks acquired a "right" and a "wrong" side. Mark Twain, describing Hannibal, Missouri, in the 1830's, wrote: "Everybody knew everybody, and was affable to everybody, and nobody put on any visible airs; yet the class lines were quite clearly drawn and the familiar social life of each class was restricted to that class. It was a little democracy which was full of liberty, equality, and Fourth of July, and sincerely so, too; yet you perceived that the aristocratic taint was there. It was there, and nobody found fault with the fact, or ever stopped to reflect that its presence was an incon-

President Martin Van Buren

sistency. . . . My mother, with her large nature and liberal sympathies, was not intended for an aristocrat, yet through her breeding she was one."

To be an aristocrat was a fine thing; to give one's self airs was not. During the first half of the century, the national memory of class-proud, high-living Tory families, who patronized the colonials, was still strong, and simple Republican manners were the right ones. The Presidents from Washington to Monroe were all aristocrats of eighteenth-century America—bred to graceful manners and well-appointed households, yet, because they were imbued with the principles of the Revolution, determined to avoid hauteur and ostentation. John Quincy Adams, as we have seen, was socially ill at ease, a condition that may have come about through being born too late to be an eighteenth-century gentleman and too soon to feel comfortable with men of the people, like Andrew Jackson. Martin Van Buren, a tavernkeeper's son whose tastes ran to luxury, campaigned for Jackson in 1828, criticizing Adams for his lack of workingman's calluses. Succeeding Jackson in the White House in 1836, Van Buren apparently forgot that the people had put him there and that they expected him to behave like one of them. His tastes got the better of him, and during the 1840 campaign the Whigs had a field day contrasting his dandified ways with the rugged, frontier ones of their candidate, William Henry Harrison. (Although Harrison came from a First Family of Virginia and lived in gracious if not lavish style, the campaign symbols assigned him were a log cabin and a jug of hard cider.)

In Congress, in April, 1840, a Pennsylvania Whig named Charles Ogle filled thirty-two pages of the Congressional Record with a gleeful and unrestrained attack on Van Buren, "the royal incumbent of the Presidential palace." Having compared the President to Caesar and Queen Elizabeth, Ogle proceeded with gusto to review recent bills handed Congress for furnishing and repairing the White House. ". . . let us enter his palace, and survey its spacious courts, its gorgeous banqueting halls, its sumptuous drawing rooms, its glittering and dazzling saloons, with all their magnificent and sumptuous array of gold and silver, crimson and orange, blue and violet, screens of Ionic columns, marble mantels, with Italian black and gold fronts, gilt eagle cornices, rich cut glass and gilt chandeliers . . . French bronze gilt lamps with crystal globes."

It appeared that the President had redecorated every room in the White House and had spent far more than an 1837 congressional appropriation of twenty thousand dollars earmarked for furniture. "I am disposed to believe, Mr. Chairman," Mr. Ogle went on, "that the present occupant of the palace is not a 'real genuine' locofoco, hard-handed democrat. . . . Why, sir, he loves tassels, rosettes, and girlish finery almost as much as a real 'Bank Whig' loves 'hard cider'. . . . I would . . . inquire whether 'silk tassels and rosettes' are considered household furniture in the legitimate democratic meaning of the word? . . . Are 'silk tassels and rosettes' hereafter to be written down, deemed, and taken in the same category with frying pans, oaken chests, chaff-bags, and crout tubs? This would be too bad for a Christian country."

Speeches were very long in those days, and Mr. Ogle had only just begun. Van Buren, he now revealed, had spent $11,191.32 on "table furniture," including a French sterling silver plate and gilt dessert set bought from a Russian nobleman, eight tambour-doored food servers, and twelve sweetmeat compotes. "Mr. Chairman, don't you think that one of your plain republican

(Continued on Page 104)

Boston:1833

Thomas Hamilton, a Scotsman, published his view of Men and Manners in America *in 1833, but his assessment of Boston and Yankees holds a perennial validity.*

A traveller has no sooner time to look about him in Boston, than he receives the conviction that he is thrown among a population of a character differing in much from that of the other cities of the Union. . . . He will immediately remark that the lines of the forehead are more deeply indented; that there is more hardness of feature; . . . and that the countenance altogether is of a graver and more meditative cast. Observe him in every different situation; . . . and you will set him down as of God's creatures the least liable to be influenced by circumstances appealing to the heart or imagination. His faculties are always sharp; his feelings are obtuse. Nature, in framing a Yankee, seems to have given him double brains, and half heart. Their puritan descent has stamped a character on [them] which nearly two centuries have done little to efface. In no other part of the globe, not even in Scotland, is morality at so high a premium. If to form a just estimate of ourselves and others, be the test of knowledge, the New Englander is the most ignorant of mankind. . . . After all, he is not absolutely the ninth wonder of the world. Mammon has no more zealous worshipper than your true Yankee. He views the world but as one vast exchange, on which he is impelled, . . . to over-reach his neighbors if he can. The thought of business is never absent from his mind. To him there is no enjoyment without traffic. He travels snail-like, with his shop or his counting-house on his back. . . . The only respite he enjoys from the consideration of his own affairs, is the time he is pleased to bestow on prying into yours. . . . Having directed the attention of the reader to some of the more prominent defects of the New England character, it is only justice to add, that in Boston at least, there exists a circle almost entirely exempt from them. This is composed of the first-rate merchants and lawyers, leavened by a small sprinkling of the clergy. . . . Of the ladies of Boston I did not see much. . . . Unfortunately it is still less the fashion, than at New York, to enliven the dinner-table with their presence. . . . These fair New Englanders partake of the endemic gravity of expression, which sits well on them, because it is natural. . . . Though the New York ladies charge them with being *dowdyish* in dress, I am not sure that their taste in this respect is not purer, as it certainly is more simple, than that of their fair accusers. They talk well and gracefully of novels and poetry. . . . The taste for reading . . . [renders] both families and individuals less dependent on society. A strong aristocratic feeling is apparent in the families of older standing. It is the custom on every Sunday evening for the different branches of a family to assemble at the house of one or other of its members. This generally produces a very social and agreeable party, and though a stranger, I was sometimes hospitably permitted to join the circle. . . . Having passed nearly three weeks . . . I quitted Boston, with sentiments of deep gratitude for a kindness, which, from the hour of my arrival, to that of my departure, had continued unbroken.

'suckers' would feel 'kinder queer like' to be placed at the President's table, before these democratic 'tambours with three stages' and 'compotiers on feet'? . . . I have no doubt that some of my constituents would much rather face the grizzly bear, in the Appalachian mountains, than sit down before these tambours with three stages and compotiers on feet for five consecutive hours—the period usually required by Kings and democratic Presidents to masticate a state dinner. . . . What, sir, will the honest locofoco say to Mr. Van Buren for spending the People's cash on FOREIGN FANNY KEMBLE GREEN FINGER CUPS, in which to wash his pretty, tapering, soft, white, lily fingers, after dining on fricandeau de veau and omelette soufflé? How will the friends of temperance—the real tetotallers—relish the foreign 'CUT WINE COOLERS' and the 'BARREL-SHAPE FLUTE DECANTERS WITH CONE STOPPERS'?"

Ogle went on to castigate Van Buren for wearing jewels, laces, and Eau de Cologne, for using the people's money for billiard tables, and for sleeping late in the morning. "It was but a few days ago that an honest countryman, on his way to the fishing landings, after breakfast, having some curiosity to behold the magnificent 'East Room,' with its gorgeous drapery and brilliant mirrors, rang the bell at the great entrance door of the palace, and forthwith the spruce English porter in attendance, came to the door, and seeing that only 'one of the people,' 'on foot,' was there, slammed it in his face, after saying, 'You had better come [later in the day]; the President's rooms are not open for visitors till ten in the morning.' Whereupon the plain farmer turned on his heel, with this cutting rebuke: 'I'm thinking the President's House will be open BEFORE DAY on the 4th of March next for EVERYbody; for OLD TIP is a mighty early riser, and was never caught napping—and doesn't allow serfs to be insolent to freemen.'" This was the way the wind blew in Washington, and Van Buren was easily bowled over by it before that man of the people, "Old Tip," William Henry Harrison.

Perhaps if Van Buren had had a wife, he might have got off easier. Women were allowed luxuries that would have been condemned as dandified in men. In most cases, it was women who put up the social barriers, doing it almost unconsciously and for a complexity of reasons. First, a frontierswoman often suffered real hardship before gaining a comfortable, secure new home. She might have plowed the fields, slept among rattlesnakes, fended off Indians, or borne a child in a covered wagon. All the time she had dreamed of presiding over a genteel parlor, with a marble-topped table in the center and lace curtains at the windows; and in that parlor there would be no spitting, no feet on the table, no rolled-up sleeves or greasy aprons. Secondly, a woman on the frontier was a scarce article and therefore received a double dose of that sentimental reverence from men that had so irritated Mrs. Trollope. In a book on prairie life, a frontierswoman—or should we say frontierslady—stated the case as many a hard-bitten western husband or pining bachelor no doubt wanted to hear it: "The home, holiest and purest nursery of what is good in the heart, springs up everywhere before woman. In town and country, canyon and ravine, on mountain and in valley, the sacred temple rises at the bidding of this true missionary of love and purity. . . ."

The words *purity, innocence, modesty, refinement, piety,* and, above all, *delicacy* were bound up together as attributes of a lady. "Let her lay aside delicacy, and her influence over our sex is gone," warned the author of a *Discourse on Female Influence.* "On you, ladies, depends, in a most important

Anti-Van Buren political parade, 1836

degree, the destiny of our country. . . . Yours it is to decide, under God, whether we shall be a nation of refined and high minded Christians, or whether, rejecting the civilities of life, and throwing off the restraints of morality and piety, we shall become a fierce race of semi-barbarians, before whom neither order, nor honor, nor chastity can stand." Another friend of the fair sex burbled: "As the constantly-dripping water melts and perforates the hardest rock, so the influence of women, constantly operating upon and influencing the mind of a man, eventually takes entire possession of those parts of his nature which are most susceptible of pure and high feelings."

If this constantly-dripping-water routine got on the nerves of the rock-headed American male, he seldom complained, although the widely read author N. P. Willis once hinted that perhaps a little discrimination was called for: "In honoring, and leaving in unstigmatized respect, a soured and hypocritical old maid, for instance, who does a hundred wrongs in a year that are worse in the eye of Heaven than theft . . . because she is 'a woman,' do we not virtually disparage those of the sex whom we profess to honor? Is there no selection to be made among females, by the general laws of male estimation? Are we, like bulls, horses, dogs, and fowls, to have no preference of honor, for one female over another?" But Willis also asserted flatly that in America "*the female sex* is (collectively, and all qualities taken into account) *superior to the male*. . . . It is the women who read . . . who regulate the style of living, dispense hospitalities, exclusively manage society, control clergymen and churches, regulate the schemes of benevolence, patronize and influence the Arts, and pronounce upon Operas and foreign novelties . . . who exercise the ultimate control over the Press—they being the real constituency of every journal that gets to the fireside, or that is conducted with any pretension to principle."

Any young woman who took seriously her obligations to influence the mind of man, direct the country's destiny, control clergymen, pronounce upon operas, and so on, welcomed all the help and advice she could get, which is one reason why the 1830's saw a rash of books on etiquette and morality. Representative of the tone of the times, yet also filled with refreshing common sense, is *The Young Lady's Friend*, by Mrs. John Farrar, the wife of a Harvard professor. As might be expected, "delicacy" is one of Mrs. Farrar's favorite words, but she is anxious that her readers discern between *true* delicacy and *false* delicacy. In the latter category she puts swallowing food without properly chewing it, out of a misguided notion that chewing is unladylike; leaving food on the plate, in order to show a refined appetite; and refusing to speak to a physician of bodily functions. "The real indelicacy," she says, "is in that state of embarrassment and difficulty which some feel in mentioning such things where it is necessary and proper to do it."

Mrs. Farrar's advice on home nursing reminds us that for all their delicacy, women of that day coped with situations in which a modern woman would dial Emergency-Ambulance. Rarely did anyone but the very poor go to hospitals, and only the alone and friendless would hire one of those dubious characters called nurses—women whose untrained ministrations were often more harmful than no care at all. Consequently, the women of the family took complete care of their sick. "If you have been with persons who were foolish enough to feel any disgust at leeches," says Mrs. Farrar briskly, "do not be infected by their folly; but reason yourself into a more rational state of mind.

For frontier women like the amazon above, there was little time for revery. Even so, she probably had at least one etiquette book tucked away, and perhaps the volume of gentle poetry below.

Robin's Alive

Blindman's Buff

Battledore and Shuttlecock

Games from An American Girl's Book, *1831*

Look at them as a curious piece of mechanism; remember that although their office is an unpleasant one to our imagination, it is their proper calling and that when they come to us from the apothecary, they are perfectly clean though slippery to the touch. Their ornamental stripes should recommend them even to the eye, and their valuable services to our feelings. . . . To make them take hold in the very spot required, you have only to take a piece of blotting-paper and cut small holes in it where you wish them to bite; lay this over the place, and put the leeches on the paper. Not liking the surface of the paper, they readily take hold of the skin, where it appears through the holes, and much trouble is thus saved. When they are filled, they will let go their hold, and you have only to put them on a deep plate, and sprinkle a little salt on their heads, and they will clear themselves of blood; then wash them in water with the chill off, and put them away in clean cold water. . . . In most cases, the blood soon ceases to flow; when the bleeding is too great, and you wish to stop it, a little lint will sometimes suffice, or the nap off a hat. . . . Roll up a little cotton, or lint, or hat fur into a very small and hard ball . . . which is to be pushed . . . directly into the hole made by the leech."

Mrs. Farrar knew nothing of asepsis—Joseph Lister's discoveries were still three decades away—but she did favor such sensible health measures as bathing and exercise. "Some persons avoid the use of soap as pernicious to the skin," she said; but she believed its use far less pernicious than its omission and urged that the sick be washed in soap and water rather than vinegar and rum, as apparently was usual. To maintain good health, a girl should sponge-bathe each morning in tepid or cold water, dry herself with a rough towel, and daily play such games as quoits, archery, battledore, skipping rope, and something called the Graces, a game of catch played with hoops and sticks and a measure of gracefulness. "Look back upon your childhood, and see how many of your early schoolmates are numbered with the dead," Mrs. Farrar wrote, "how many have grown up pale and feeble, how many are habitual invalids."

Unfortunately for sensible Mrs. Farrar, healthy, athletic girls were not in fashion, perhaps because of the heroines of Sir Walter Scott and Alfred Tennyson, who were apt to be slender and pale and to faint easily. The eighteenth-century custom of tight lacing had returned, after the relatively uncorseted freedom of Empire styles. Mrs. Farrar thought the clothes of the 1830's more modest, and rejoiced at the disappearance of "dresses only a yard and a half wide at bottom . . . so that it was difficult for a lady to step across a gutter, or into a carriage, without a great exposure of silken hose." But she disapproved of the tight-fitting corsets that were coming back into fashion. She was not alone in warning of their effects. Doctors charged that the high rate of mortality from consumption was attributable to tight lacing, which constricted the lungs and prevented the blood from circulating properly. The bones, too, were pushed out of shape, one shoulder becoming higher than the other and the spine crooked. It appears to have been the common custom of mothers to put their daughters into stays at an early age and to make them sit for hours strapped to a board so as to acquire a straight back. "The human figure, in a word, [is] not shaped like a wasp," said a writer in *Chambers Miscellany of Useful and Entertaining Knowledge.* "In one instance a mother violently beat her daughter to make her submit to this process of compression. The girl's health was ruined and she became a habitual dram-drinker."

As for the desire of the female to show off her figure, the writer goes on to say, "there is a limit which, we believe, cannot be exceeded without immediate detriment to public morals, and positive offence to delicacy. There was a time when a mode of dressing to display every personal charm was peculiar to an unfortunate class of beings, regarded as lost to all the modesty and dignity of the sex; but it is a melancholy truth, that this distinction between the lost and the reputable no longer exists in our great cities, where leaders of fashion . . . are most remarkable for the solicitude with which they prepare their lovely persons to be gazed at and admired, in all their proportions, by the passing crowd! . . . It has an immediate influence in lowering the sex in the estimation of men, since it lessens their reverence for beings they would otherwise always look upon with deep respect; and surely the fair sex have not yet to learn, that modest reserve and retiring delicacy are among the most potent auxiliaries of their charms."

A woman had to rely heavily on modest reserve and retiring delicacy to get what she wanted, for before the law she had almost no rights at all, being classified with children, Negroes, the insane, and the criminal. In espousing causes of philanthropy and reform she was considered to be in her province; after all, N. P. Willis had said that she should "regulate the schemes of benevolence." The trouble was that once involved in causes, she tended to want to run them, and that meant holding office and addressing meetings, even "promiscuous" gatherings of men and women together! The hue and cry against such unseeming "female exhibitions in publick" gave some of the ladies another cause to work for—that of women's rights. Not until the 1840's was there an organized women's rights movement, but the seed of it was planted in the Delicate Thirties.

Patented baby jumper

Other unprecedented social changes began in the 1830's due to a rash of new inventions, some important, others petty, but all reaching into the daily lives of Americans. Balloon-frame construction, a type of prefabrication, made housebuilding much cheaper and quicker than ever before. And it was not uncommon to see one of these light but sturdy houses being trundled along a road on a low, flat cart—from one end of a town to another and even from town to town. Machinery for making lace, carpets, hats, and shoes was invented, bringing these household articles within reach of all but the very poor. High-heeled shoes came in during the late thirties, as did the collar button. India rubber was in use for overshoes and raincloaks; in the next decade Charles Goodyear would discover and patent a way of vulcanizing it. The first mechanical reapers and steel plows appeared in the thirties; also the first poured concrete. Yankee clippers became the fastest sailing ships afloat. (Nathaniel Bowditch, a Salem-bred mathematician and astronomer, had already made the art of navigation an exact science.) Samuel Colt was experimenting with Eli Whitney's ideas of interchangeable parts for manufactured goods and developing his own revolving six-cylinder pistol. Bedsprings first appeared in 1830, although not for years did they generally replace the old-fashioned wire or rope webbing by which mattresses were supported. Farmers, during this decade, were introduced to chemical fertilizer and to improved methods of draining swamps in order to create farmland. The appearance of lawnmowers, about 1840, enabled the well-to-do to maintain wide, rolling lawns without maintaining an army of gardeners to clip them by hand. Ether was first used for surgery in 1842; most people thought its use

Tête-à-tête in a city boardinghouse

immoral. Regular ice deliveries enabled the housewife to market less often — or, rather, enabled her husband to market less often, for it was usually he who took care of this chore unless she had servants to carry the bundles for her.

The new inventions not only changed everyday life for the general public, but opened up new ways by which a man could better his lot. Many fortunes were founded during this decade and others consolidated and multiplied. *The Wealth and Biography of the Wealthy Citizens of the City of New York*, published in 1844, listed hundreds of men who were worth several hundred thousand dollars, and a few worth over a million; the French term *millionaire* was introduced to Americans by a journalist in 1843 while writing an obituary for Pierre Lorillard, manufacturer of snuff and tobacco. Even the average, middle-class American suddenly found himself more prosperous than ever before, with money for luxuries and leisure to enjoy them. Business, said a foreign observer, was a passion with the Americans; it was not the means, but the very meaning of existence.

Husbands did not expect their wives to understand business, and "it occurs but too often that a lady who believes herself to be in affluent circumstances is suddenly informed by her husband that they must give up housekeeping because they cannot afford it." During the pre-Civil War generation, it was common for married couples, even with several children, to live in a hotel or boardinghouse instead of keeping house. For one thing, it was cheaper; for another, it was easier for the wife, especially if she was still a teen-ager and unaccustomed to doing housework or managing servants. And of course, American families were constantly on the move.

Americans used the word *hotel* loosely. It had been added to the American language in the 1790's, no doubt inspired by the talk of French émigrés, as a designation of an inn of more than usual pretension. America's first hotel opened in New York in 1795. It had seventy-three rooms, but except for its size was no more elaborate than an ordinary inn. The other port cities soon acquired similar establishments. Boston's Exchange Coffee House was seven stories high, an infant skyscraper. The Tremont House, built in the late 1820's to replace the Exchange, which had burned down, was the first American hotel that was grand other than in size. Among its innovations were separate tables in the dining hall, a reading room, eight flush toilets (all on the ground floor, as the miracle of indoor plumbing did not yet include propelling water upstairs), and locks on the bedroom doors. A city boardinghouse offered no such comforts. With cramped quarters, no plumbing, no closets, primitive heating, and rudimentary sanitary arrangements belowstairs, life must have been an ordeal.

Since it would have been unsuitable for a wife with any notion of being a lady to become gainfully employed, there was little for her to do all day. Such wives were "generally very ignorant and full of the strangest affectations and pretentions," wrote Mrs. Bodichon, an English observer. "The young ladies, especially, reminded me of certain women I have seen in Seraglios, whose whole time was taken up in dressing and painting their faces." As time went on, the pernicious effects of such idleness among "the mothers of men" came in for a good deal of comment in the press. The suggestion was made more than once that these idle, thoughtless creatures were becoming parasites, and ought to be employed "to save their souls from the devil, and to save their husbands, too, from that 'everlasting grind' in which American men live."

To the average American male, still burdened with vestiges of a Puritan conscience, leisure was a suspect thing. He stayed at his "everlasting grind" because he was afraid of being criticized if caught with his hands folded. When the first resorts came into being, therefore, they called themselves health spas, for if one were sick one might be excused for not working. Saratoga Springs began to attract "patients" in the last half of the eighteenth century. Washington Irving, describing the first decades of the spa's popularity, wrote, "It originally meant nothing more than a relief from pain and sickness; and the patient . . . called it a pleasure when he threw by his crutches, and danced away from them with renovated spirits, and limbs jocund with vigor." All this changed (for the worse in Irving's judgment) when *fashion* entered on the scene. "This, of course, awakens a spirit of noble emulation between the eastern, middle, and southern states; and every lady hereupon finding herself charged in a manner with the whole weight of her country's dignity and style, dresses and dashes, and sparkles, without mercy, at her competitors from other parts of the Union. . . . The lady of a southern planter will lay out the whole annual produce of a rice plantation in silver and gold muslins, lace veils, and new liveries; carry a hogshead of tobacco on her head, and trail a bale of sea-island cotton at her heels; while a lady of Boston or Salem will wrap herself up in the net proceeds of a cargo of whale oil, and tie on her hat with a quintal of codfish."

By the mid-thirties, improved turnpikes and rail lines enabled families to come to Saratoga from hundreds of miles away. The principal hotels, the Congress House and the United States, could accommodate two thousand guests, and there were many humbler boardinghouses. Social climbers who had studied their etiquette books and knew that they must not rinse out their mouths from their finger bowls nor drink from them nor spit into them, had a much better chance at resorts of being accepted by the socially arrived than they had in their home towns. If their manners were good, who was to know that they had but recently lived over the family sausage making concern? One etiquette book cautioned that it was ill-mannered to mention a friend's occupation if you ran into him at a resort. "How are you, Bates, old fellow? Pork a bit slow in summer, eh?" was not rated a genteel conversational gambit.

Newly rich westerners made Saratoga Springs a point of pilgrimage, as did thousands of southerners (an estimated fifty thousand annually) until unpleasant feeling before the Civil War drove most of them to patronize such southern resorts as White Sulphur Springs, in Virginia, instead. "All the world is here," wrote Philip Hone from Saratoga in 1839, "politicians and dandies; cabinet ministers and ministers of the gospel; office-holders and office-seekers; humbuggers and humbugged; fortune-hunters and hunters of woodcock; anxious mothers and lovely daughters; the ruddy cheek mantling with saucy health, and the flickering lamp almost extinguished beneath the rude breath of dissipation." (Hone, even in his personal diary, wrote in the style of the day, unable to resist a touch of sentimentality and a hint of moral lesson.)

Except for a Saturday evening ball and an occasional week-night "hop," life at Saratoga Springs was not what we would account exciting. Everyone rose early and made a fetish of drinking the waters. After that, there was little to do but eat three heavy meals, promenade, or perhaps make an "excursion" by carriage into the surrounding countryside. The young people flirted, the ladies sat on the piazzas, and the gentlemen gambled, drank, and loafed in the

Artists made health spas an endless subject of satire: above, addicts sip mineral waters; below, a bachelor offers himself to the highest bidder.

barrooms. Barroom etiquette required that each patron stand the others to a round of drinks at least once a session; also that when offered such a treat, one must drink it down straight and not toy with it as if one did not like it. Small wonder, then, that topers regularly emerged from saloons on a considerably less even keel than when they entered them. Horse racing was not introduced at the spa until 1863, and there were no active sports. Croquet was yet unknown on this side of the Atlantic, and the young people of the thirties would be grandparents before they would ever see a female brandish a tennis racket. Philip Hone quit the scene, calling it "a crowd of queer strangers, dragging out a tiresome day of artificial enjoyment."

But at the seaside resorts—such as Newport, Nahant, Rockaway, Long Branch, and Cape May—there was a daring new sport: promiscuous bathing. As early as the 1790's there had been "bathing machines" on American beaches, wherein a female, attended by a female, could be wheeled into the surf unseen by masculine eyes. But now the more daring ladies and gentlemen were dispensing with bathing machines and running into the waves hand in hand. They were, of course, covered from head to toe with all-concealing garments; bathing suits were not invented until the 1870's, and people made do with odd combinations of their normal daily attire. However, one newspaperman wrote of having observed "cunning little blue-veined feet twinkling in the shallow water."

Thus swimming might be called both an active and a spectator sport. Earlier, in colonial America, most sports had been competitive, with the young men of the village challenging one another at quoits, wrestling and shooting matches, or foot races. Many city dwellers of the 1830's had once lived in the country, and they missed the spontaneous life of the village green. If they could no longer participate in competitions themselves, the next best thing was to watch others do so. Spectator sports began to take on importance in the lives of city people, rich and poor. Of the fans, most were rowdies, ne'er-do-wells, and idlers, but respectable gentlemen also swelled the throng. Although straitlaced people disapproved of spectator sports because they almost always involved gambling, thousands turned out to watch (and bet on) horse races, sailing and rowing regattas, and foot races. In 1835 Philip Hone was one of some twenty-five thousand spectators watching a foot race in which a purse of a thousand dollars had been offered to any man who could run ten miles in less than an hour.

Other amusements of the 1830's, besides the old-fashioned ones of visiting, hunting and shooting, sleighing, skating, and dancing, were seeing waxwork shows, freaks, menageries, and acrobats (the ingredients that would in future form a circus), dioramas, and the theater. After overcoming a Puritanical prejudice against playgoing, together with an anti-English prejudice—most of the stars and best-known plays were English—Americans took to the theater with enthusiasm. New York's principal theaters held from twenty-five hundred to four thousand people—more than many movie theaters today. Prices were low, and the patrons came from all walks of life, but chiefly from among the humble. Even the best of theaters presented hardships that no twentieth-century theatergoer would brave: they were so cold in winter that patrons kept their hats and coats on; they were stuffy and hot in summer, smelly, teeming with vermin (including rats bold enough to venture out during performances), and equipped with hard, backless benches in the pit and crowded,

A traveling acrobatic troupe, as advertised in an early broadside

110

unupholstered seats in the boxes. Neither candles, oil, nor gas provided really satisfactory lighting, and the fire hazard was appalling. The last drama to take place at many a nineteenth-century theater was a three-alarm fire.

The manners of the audience startled foreigners and would no doubt startle us. In the pit there was constant commotion—eating, drinking, arguing that sometimes led to fistfights, and unrestrained comment on the play, either by applause and huzzas, or by groans, hisses, and hurled objects such as rotten fruit. Mrs. Trollope said she saw a man vomit in the pit at a moment when one of the actors on stage was playing a doctor. "I expect my services are wanted elsewhere," the actor remarked cheerfully, and everyone shrieked with merriment. The top gallery was reserved for Negroes, toughs, and low-class prostitutes; the third row of boxes went to the more successful courtesans. (At the Tremont Theatre in sedate Boston, they only had to scurry across a catwalk from the connecting brothel to get to their seats.) Even in the boxes where the "bon ton" sat, there were gentlemen who put their feet on the railing. Spitting, of course, was ceaseless. Shakespeare was played often, although sometimes with the omission of certain passages that were "inconsistent with modern delicacy." Negroes were not allowed to see *Othello*.

Taking a turn at the polka, c. 1844

Ladies and gentlemen of Philip Hone's social level braved the crudities of New York's theaters to see Shakespeare, and they also supported an opera company, although Hone feared it would not succeed (it did not). But Hone, his family and friends, most enjoyed private dinner parties and evenings of quadrilles. He went on alternate Thursdays to the Book Club to sup, talk, and drink wine. "I don't exactly understand why this is called a Book Club," he remarked, "for the book of subscriptions to the expenses is, I suspect, the only one in the library." He was one of the founders of the Union Club, "a great resource for bachelors and men 'about town.'"

Dancing, despite the croaking of the moralistic, was extremely popular from Boston to the farthest frontier camp. Waltzing was introduced to this country in the first decades of the nineteenth century. In 1827 John Tyler, the future President, wrote to his daughter that the waltz was a "dance which you have never seen and which I do not desire to see you dance." For a man to press the waist of a woman not his wife, that was the worst of it. And besides, the whole ballroom enjoyed a show of ankles and even more as the lady whisked over the floor, while her partner, if he were tall enough, had a bird's-eye view down her décolletage. Lest the gentleman be carried away by this closeness, he was expected to wear gloves or, in the extreme, to put a handkerchief between his palm and the lady's waist, with no squeezing allowed. Nevertheless, the waltz, once in, never went out, and it was followed a few years later by the polka and then by the galop. They were all performed at a furious pace and seemed to the older generation to be well in keeping with this reckless age of steamboat racing and thundering, sixteen-mile-an-hour locomotives. Catharine Beecher, one of the Reverend Lyman Beecher's illustrious progeny and the author of numerous books examining the woman's role, wishfully thought that dancing was "fast leaving this (refined) rank of society," and suggested calisthenics instead.

The influential *Godey's Lady's Book* helped make round dances respectable by printing directions for dance steps, piano music for waltzes, and alluring pictures of ball gowns suitable for waltzing parties. Mrs. Sarah Josepha Hale, the magazine's editor, saw to it that dancing was taught in a young ladies' school she ran on the side, and it was also in the curriculum at Emma Willard's Female Seminary, in Troy, New York. Mary Lyon, at her Mount Holyoke Seminary for young ladies, devised a system of calisthenics meant to promote gracefulness, but warned that "care should be taken that the exercise does not become like dancing in the impression it makes on the observers." Dr. William Ellery Channing, the eminent clergyman, thought dancing was dangerous to health because of late hours, crowded ballrooms, and diaphanous clothing, but in an address to the Massachusetts Temperance Society he suggested that families might dance together for "exercise and exhilaration," and that the working classes were better off dancing than drinking.

Negro dancing was watched with amusement but not imitated except by white men in blackface—"Jim Crow" (Thomas "Daddy" Rice) and the Virginia Minstrels, led by Daniel Emmett, were among the first. New Yorkers congregated at the Bowery Theatre to be entertained by the raucous, burnt-cork humor of the Virginia Minstrels, who billed themselves as "The novel, grotesque, original and surpassingly melodious Ethiopian Band entitled the Virginia Minstrels, being an exclusively minstrel entertainment combining banjo, violin, bone castanets and the tambourine, and entirely exempt from . . . vulgarities and other objectionable features. . . ." Theatergoers in most cities were soon enjoying shows by such groups as the Congo Minstrels, the Ethiopian Serenaders, the Sable Harmonists, and Christy's Minstrels. The acts drew great crowds and started a vogue for blackface dancers and comedians.

Halfway between amusement and serious study was the pseudoscience of phrenology, which was in vogue during the thirties and forties. A European doctor, J. K. Spurzheim, who made a lecture tour of the United States in 1832, was its earliest exponent here. His theory, to state it briefly, was that the qualities of a man's character could be determined by an examination of the outside of his skull. A strongly marked trait was evidenced by a bump. An amateur could not make the diagnosis, however, for the interplay of traits and bumps required protracted study. Spurzheim was endorsed by many respected American medical men, and the country was soon well supplied with phrenologists who charged up to a dollar for a private reading. Women debated as to whether it was "delicate" to submit to this sort of examination, but most decided that it was. Among confirmed believers in phrenology were such respected figures as Henry Ward Beecher, Horace Mann, and Nicholas Biddle. At the height of the vogue, prospective servants and even prospective spouses were sometimes asked to take phrenological tests.

Hypnosis also became widely known at the same period, but most people thought of it as nothing more than a parlor game. It seems strange that phrenology became so popular, since the Jacksonian American was for the most part a skeptical fellow, interested chiefly in things he could see and understand and, preferably, make money on. One disenchanted European visitor wrote that "America worships two idols": money and women. There was much truth in what he said (and the 1830's were to set the tone for the next four or five decades), but it was not the whole truth and nothing but the truth. The American was more complex than foreigners believed. As phrenologists said, he had some very interesting bumps in his skull. A wit added:

Know well thy skull, and note its hilly lumps:
The proper study of mankind is bumps.

T. D. Rice, creator of "Jim Crow"

The
Young
Republic

William Sidney Mount, in painting The Rustic Dance, 1830, *rejected the stilted art conventions of his day to portray rural Americans the way they really were — somewhat less than heroic. The party, probably set in his father's Long Island tavern, is just beginning, and Mount's bashful young men and handkerchief-twisting girls seem destined to get together before the frolic ends.*

A Fool's Paradise

Sentimental histories to the contrary, the little red schoolhouse of the young Republic was inhospitable to both student and teacher. Though some Americans shared John Adams' conviction that a child was better off never born than uneducated, a strain of democratic anti-intellectualism had overtaken the land. Many town schools had closed during the Revolution, and except for small land grants in the Northwest Territory, the federal government took no interest in the matter. In most New England states tax-supported district schools taught children the rudiments, but the more rigorous training once offered in Latin grammar schools was no longer to be found except in private academies. Noncompulsory

public education in the middle states was provided at charity schools, to which the proud were reluctant to send their offspring. The masses fared still worse in the South. Everywhere girls were for many years excluded from school, and when finally admitted, they attended for shorter terms, generally during the summer when the boys were off. The typical one-room schoolhouse, holding up to eighty pupils, was usually located on some valueless piece of land near the district's center or at a crossroads, with the road as playground. Underpaid masters taught from insufficient texts by means of rote memorization. It would take the guidance of Horace Mann and his disciples to set things right after 1838.

In Thomas Birch's views of pedagogy, c. 1806, a schoolmarm (left) must learn to suffer fools, disorder, and furtive tardiness. The schoolmaster above, wizened though he is, commands exemplary obedience, showing the value of mule rule.

CONNECTICUT HISTORICAL SOCIETY

Matthew Talcott's writing sheet (right) is typically filled in with sentiments to warm a schoolmaster's heart. Though Matthew professes that virtue is its own reward, his parents will probably sweeten his efforts with a few coins. The 1793 specimen sheet is edged with engravings of respectable trades.

The Polite Penman

Mastering the second "R" was mandatory for the well-bred citizen of the new Republic. During the era in which Noah Webster standardized American spelling, calligraphers attempted to develop a national style of penmanship. John Jenkins' round hand—a repetition of heavy lines on downstrokes of the pen—might have prevailed but for the zealous efforts of Platt Spencer, who promised that mastery of fine-line Spencerian had moral and monetary rewards. A businessman's reputation, he said, depended upon the legibility of his records; female sensibilities were best shown in his diminutive "Ladies' Hand." Those lacking in equivalent epistolary talents could seek guidance in books offering everything from RSVP's to this lugubrious condolence: "Dear . . . . : I sympathize with you in your grief for the loss of your pretty dog. Poor thing! I little thought when I was playing with him yesterday that he would be dead to-day. I trust, however, you will soon be able to repair your loss by a successor as faithful and engaging, but not so unfortunate as he. Yours affectionately, . . ."

METROPOLITAN MUSEUM OF ART, GIFT OF MRS. DARWIN MORSE, 1963

At left, the versatility of the newfangled steel nib, introduced c. 1830, is demonstrated with flourish. Below, in the frontispiece to John Jenkins' Art of Writing, 1813, one of America's earliest guides, a young lady of impeccable posture and penmanship exercises the recommended round hand.

In the diagram from Benjamin Franklin Foster's 1832 manual below, the reader is shown how "free, rapid writing [can] be effected by the combined movements of the arm, hand, and fingers." After a week's practice, he could discontinue finger binding.

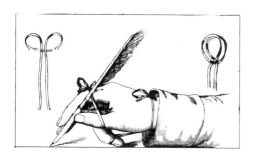

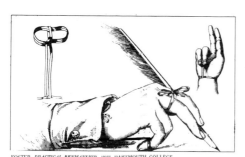

FOSTER, *PRACTICAL PENMANSHIP*, 1832, DARTMOUTH COLLEGE

JENKINS, *ART OF WRITING*, 1813

If you would win a Pen of Gold Learn first of all your Pen to hold.

To Write with ease & Elegance,

is a most Useful, Polite and

Necessary Accomplishment

For all Young

Gentlemen & Ladies.

By diligence & care Your Writing will be fair

Arts and Crafts

If idle hands were the Devil's helpers, unorganized leisure was a thing to be abhorred. Even before a little girl learned her alphabet, she was set to making samplers displaying pretty messages and intricate stitchwork. By the time she had become a young lady, she had probably added quilting and embroidery to her repertoire, and if she lived in a city, she might even have learned to do "pieces"—allegories on death, patriotism, and morality were favored—at a painting academy. With the nation relatively peaceful, there was time and place for learning all manner of "female arts" to beautify the hearts and households of America. Ladies were cautioned, however, not to let their minds lapse into "vague reverie (some persons dignify it with the name of thought, or meditation)" while their hands worked, for "that slothful state will enervate every faculty." The author of these remarks went on in *The Young Lady's Friend*, 1838, to recommend memorizing poetry or listening to the lessons of a younger sibling at the same time. Such discipline, she argued, would sharpen the intellect and train the future housewife to use time economically—talents sure to please God and husband.

Eunice Pinney's 1813 memorial water color for her child (opposite) employs traditional symbols of mourning—the sorrowful family, the weeping willow, and the tomb. The demurely clad "Marimaid" above, painted by Mary Ann Willson, c. 1820, is joyfully unfunctional. Below, students learn to draw in one of the dozens of academies that flourished after the Revolution.

COLLECTION OF EMILY CRANE CHADBOURNE, MUSEUM OF THE CITY OF NEW YORK

The Culture Boom

When the Continental Congress of 1774 decreed that government should "encourage frugality, economy, and industry . . . and discountenance and discourage . . . shews, plays, and other expensive diversions," it was making a late, futile effort at Puritan censorship. The discouraging of native literary efforts had only surrendered an important medium of public instruction to the English, whose intellectual and social contamination was far more to be feared. Within fifteen years, Brother Jonathans would be seeing themselves depicted in plays and novels set against American backgrounds, expounding American moral themes. Royall Tyler's *The Contrast* ("A Moral Lecture in five parts," as billed in stuffy Boston) was hailed in 1787 as the first successful comedy to be produced. Against the foolish posturings of Dimple, "a flippant, palid, polite beau, who devotes the morning to his toilet, reads a few pages of Chesterfield's letters, and then minces out," it set the "probity, virtue, and honour" of soldier-patriot Manly, with results that were certain to please the pit. Early efforts at fiction were also Anglophobic. Charles Brockden Brown, the first to make writing his profession, decried the "puerile superstitions and exploded manners, the Gothic castles and chimeras hitherto usually employed," endorsed Indians and frontiersmen as more suitable subjects, and then went on to write sensational tales of religious obsession (*Wieland*), anarchy (*Ormond*), and sleepwalking (*Edgar Huntly*) for an eager, culture-hungry public.

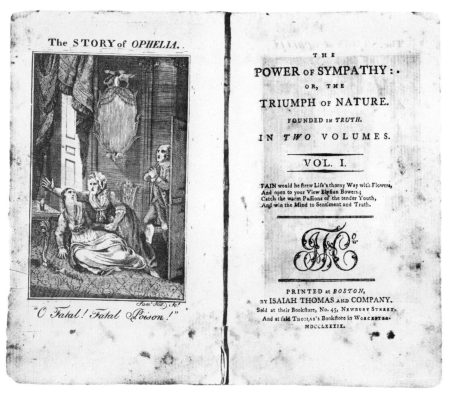

Like many "handkerchief novels" that would follow, William Hill Brown's 1789 best seller (above) directed itself to the ladies, promising in this case "To Expose the fatal CONSEQUENCES OF SEDUCTION" with a tearful tale of incest, infidelity, and suicide. The painting opposite shows New York's elegant 2,500-seat Park Theatre, as seen by John Searle in 1822.

Though a dancing master and serious actor, John Durang also played to the pits. Since the masses loved to see misfits, he here poses as a "Dwarf Metamorphosed." How he achieved this is unrecorded.

HISTORICAL SOCIETY OF YORK COUNTY

Knowing that at least some of the people could be fooled all the time, entrepreneurs of the late 1700's sought to capitalize on public gullibility. Years of spartan living under Puritanism had made the common man quite willing to accept any entertainment, believable or not, provided, as an ad ran, the "deceptions are completely executed, and exhibitions . . . interesting or agreeable." At first, itinerant fakes and freaks toured New England towns, and evidently were often booted out by official guardians of public morality before showtime. One, John Childs, who proposed to fly off a Boston churchtop, was informed by town spokesmen that "as the performances led many People from their Business, he is forbid flying any more in the Town." Mrs. Dugee, the "Female Samson," fared better, and enthralled crowds watched six men balance on her ma-

Something for Everyone

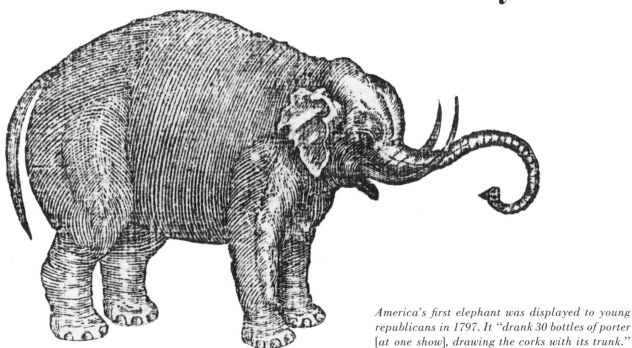

America's first elephant was displayed to young republicans in 1797. It "drank 30 bottles of porter [at one show], drawing the corks with its trunk."

NEW-YORK HISTORICAL SOCIETY

tronly breast while she was stretched out between two chairs. Gradually, curiosities, living as well as dead, found homes in museums. Rembrandt Peale's Baltimore "gallery of art" also contained mastodon bones. When the greatest showman on earth, Phineas T. Barnum, took over New York's American Museum in 1841, he touted his "chaste scenic entertainments" as strictly educational and moral, so as to attract the pious. Unlike the sinful theater, Barnum's show was staged in a "lecture-room," and each act or "service" described in jargon worthy of a minister. Under the same roof were some half-million wonders including Biblical waxwork figures, a bearded lady, guaranteed real, and a dog-run knitting machine. Visitors could also follow a sign marked TO THE EGRESS—presumably an animal rarity. It led the suckers to the street.

The 1804 New-York Gazette *advertises a card shark (left) that can "perform several curious experiments." In the same paper, the midget above offers the public a variety show for a dollar admission.*

BOTH: *NEW YORK GAZETTE & GENERAL ADVERTISER,* APRIL 25, 1804, NEW-YORK HISTORICAL SOCIETY

Daniel Lambert, Boston Museum's "wonderful production of Nature," c. 1820, goes in for some light weight-lifting to maintain his ten-foot girth.

NEW-YORK HISTORICAL SOCIETY

Where the Action Was

This "Yearly Market, or publick fare," was held in the borough of York on June 9, 1801. While parents tend to business, a tambourine player, a fiddler, and a man with hoop and bell entertain the children.

When Thomas McKean defeated James Ross in the gubernatorial election of 1800, a "Publick Feast" was given on the York Common. As the men work up an appetite by parading, the womenfolk toil with dinner.

The American farmer, unlike the European peasant, often led a lonely existence. His large holdings not only kept him working long hours, but also kept him isolated from society other than his family. Since colonial times, election days and market fairs had proved effective antidotes for this syndrome of the six-day work week. Such affairs were also favorite subjects of Lewis Miller, a carpenter of York, Pennsylvania, who in these sketches depicted his German neighbors at play in the early 1800's. These convivial settlers welcomed the opportunity to pack produce and children in the Conestoga wagon, go to town, and make a day of it. As illustrated, farmers in broad-brimmed hats and frauen in their Sunday best watched rival regiments march, listened to fifes and drums, purchased "store-bought" goods from vendors, and banqueted on the public grounds. The day often terminated with dancing and a

trip to the local tavern; the latter practice, as Miller reported, became such a "common nuisance" that York's "Privilege of a Stated Yearly Market" was rescinded in 1816. Besides parades and celebrations, Miller also chronicled the everyday life of York. No event, however insignificant, eluded his halting English or more eloquent paintbrush, whether it was the installation of "hydran water," a pumpkin grown by Christian Lehman "as large as a barrel," or a domestic squabble in which a certain Jacob ordered his wife to "boil me some eggs," and upon her refusal "threw a dish full of broken eggs on her head." Shortly before his death, the artist reminisced in his peculiar English: "All of this Pictures . . . I search and examin them. They are true Sketches, I myself being there upon the places and Spot and put down what happened. . . . I SEE ALL IS VANITY IN THIS KNOWING WORLD."

Living Made Easy

To prevent his pockets from being picked, if indeed he has any, the man above has securely fastened his possessions to the brim of his hat, thus also obviating the necessity of holding anything. Upon slight pressure from the wearer, the top hat rotates and presents him with his scent box, monocle, hearing apparatus, bifocals, and cigar, which untouched by human hands, appears to have been miraculously lit. Fortunately, his nose extends far enough to sample the snuff.

A "wine helper," "nut cracker," and "body fanner" facilitate easy summertime living.

An umbrella, mufflers, and safety

With a chronic manpower shortage plaguing the new nation, the resilient American turned to "the mechanic in his soul" to devise substitutes for manual labor. By 1830 mechanization had given the common man an unprecedented amount of leisure. He spent this inventing new gadgets to further increase his free time for puttering around still more. To De Tocqueville it seemed that the curious goal of democracy was "to enlarge a dwelling, to be always making life more comfortable and convenient, to avoid trouble, and to satisfy the smallest wants without effort and almost without cost." The Patent Office was flooded with novel products—some practical, others purely ridiculous. A sewing machine was guaranteed never to be "troubled with beaux, nor with aching shoulders, nor with mumps, nor mopes." A clumsy ancestor of the adjustable chair was suspended from the ceiling, but promised comfortable seating—a rarity in 1838. Convertible furniture was designed to save space in middle-class homes: rocking chairs turned into cradles; tables folded into beds; and in perhaps the most grotesque mating of all, a piano opened into a complete boudoir with bed, bureau, washbasin, two closets, pitcher, towels, et cetera. "It has been found," claimed the inventor, "that this addition to a piano-forte does not in the least impair its qualities as a musical instrument." Like the proud owners of today's gizmo-filled shrines, people thought new gadgets would answer life's tiny dilemmas. The erroneous belief was satirized as early as 1832 in these drawings.

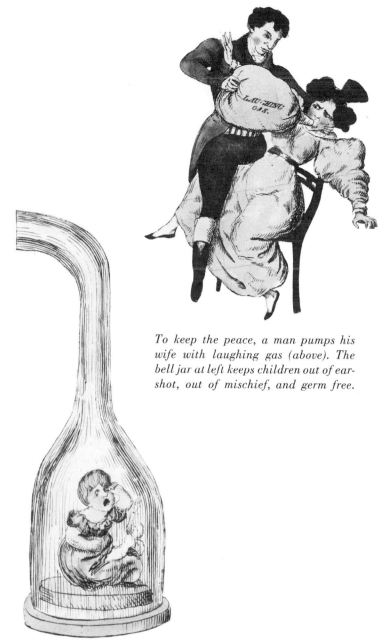

To keep the peace, a man pumps his wife with laughing gas (above). The bell jar at left keeps children out of earshot, out of mischief, and germ free.

bindings protect a timid horseman.

A special magnifying glass makes a lark resemble a capon, but not taste like one.

CAROLINA ART ASSOCIATION, GIBBES ART GALLERY

In summer the Charleston aristocrat left his slaves suffering in malarial fields and retreated to his town house. Thomas Middleton, planter and artist, renders a typical 1827 scene at left, where a chamber ensemble listens more to clinking glasses than to "strains of their own music."

According to antebellum romanticists, the old plantation was a veritable Elysium where spiritual-singing slaves took a few hours exercise in the fields to aid digestion. Since benign masters provided for their needs, the carefree darkies otherwise amused themselves hunting 'possum, attending horse races, and "whirling in the giddy mazes of the dance with their buxom Dulcineas, each seeming to vie with the other in dancing the most. . . . What luxury of motion, what looks—breathing and sighs! What oglings, exclamations and enjoyment!" Holidays gave new arrivals an opportunity to preserve their African customs. In the South Carolina scene at right, gaily turbaned participants at what is probably a wedding prepare to jump over a cane (a holdover from tribal ceremony), while musicians keep time on a drum and a type of banjo. Unfortunately, the crueler sort of planter did much to discredit these glowing descriptions. He could prohibit all recreation. At whim, he might forbid a black woman to marry, force on her a series of mates until she proved fertile, or take her as a concubine. And children, of whatever paternity, belonged to the planter, who disposed of them as he saw fit. Whippings and worse kept the chattel in line, and there were always bloodhounds to retrieve runaways. Slaveowners did not like to see the truth; instead, they preferred to go on defending the moral rectitude of their "peculiar institution" and believing that their bondsmen would continue to "live and work in freedom . . . governed alone by the law of duty and love, and where all succeeds excellently."

The Feudal Society

ABBY ALDRICH ROCKEFELLER FOLK ART COLLECTION

Dids
and
Didn'ts

GOD'S REVENGE

AGAINST

ADULTERY,

AWFULLY EXEMPLIFIED IN THE FOLLOWING CASES

OF

AMERICAN CRIM. CON.

I. THE ACCOMPLISHED DR. THEODORE WILSON, (DELAWARE,) WHO FOR SEDUCING
MRS. NANCY WILEY, HAD HIS BRAINS BLOWN OUT
BY HER HUSBAND.

II. THE ELEGANT JAMES O'NEALE, ESQ. (NORTH CAROLINA,) WHO FOR SEDUCING
THE BEAUTIFUL MISS MATILDA L'ESTRANGE, WAS KILLED
BY HER BROTHER.

BY MASON L. WEEMS,

AUTHOR OF THE LIFE OF WASHINGTON.

THIRD EDITION.

◆

PHILADELPHIA.

PRINTED FOR THE AUTHOR—PRICE 25 CENTS.

1818.

BRIGGS & CO. PRINTERS.

Though George Washington could never tell a lie, Mason Locke Weems could, if it furthered larger moral truths. The cherry tree episode and other immortal inaccuracies written by Weems in 1806, were meant to show that "every youth may become a Washington" by following the hero's illustrious example: his "unparalleled rise & elevation were owing to his Great Virtues, His Veneration for the Deity . . . His Magnanimity, His Industry, His Temperance & Sobriety, His Justice &c. &c." When the erstwhile parson was relieved of his Maryland parish for unbefitting conduct—abolitionist views, concern for the poor, love of merriment, and authorship of a pamphlet on sexual aberrations—he took to the road, vending virtue as well as books. Between New York and Savannah, showman Weems captivated rural audiences with a witty sermon or an impersonation of a drunkard "quite capsized," and afterward hawked his wares. He often relied on George Washington's endorsement of his moral tracts as a sort of seal of approval. *Hymen's Recruiting Sergeant: or the New Matrimonial Tat-too* for bachelors pointed out that man cannot live in bed alone. His *God's Revenge* series on adultery, drinking, murder, gambling, and dueling, encompassed Sin with plenty of lurid detail. Concerning the last subject, illustrated above, the good parson warned, "Never fight *duels*. Nine times in ten the memory of the murdered drives the murderer to the bottle."

The title page at left and the illustrations on these pages were taken from some of Parson Weems's moral tracts, which usually sold for twenty-five cents apiece and by the cartload.

A depraved murderer drowning his wife

A drunkard ending up moneyless and miserable

The gambler floored by his losses

An adulterer receiving just deserts by having "his brains blown out"

Seduced and Abandoned

Crimes of passion, kindled where high and low life meet, have always captured the public imagination. Their fascination is that they often reveal widespread but tacit practices that the upper crust would sooner disown. In the 1830's New Yorkers were stunned by the Robinson-Jewett case. The murder occurred in the City Hotel—one of Manhattan's "most splendid establishments devoted to infamous intercourse." There nineteen-year-old Richard Robinson made a bloody end of his young mistress, Ellen Jewett, and of his illicit affair. But his inept attempt to remove one spot from his character only produced a larger, more indelible stain, just as the unfortunate Ellen's past had always dogged her. Maneuvers to cover up a boarding school seduction—unforgivable by any standards of her day—only plunged her deeper into the morass of hard-core prostitution. The Massachusetts girl struck off for New York to make a fresh start, but the anonymity she sought was no help when it came to finding a job. Unskilled and penniless, no young maiden would have had a chance, and Ellen fell back with uncommon speed upon her known assets. She was, as a reporter for the New York *Herald* wrote, "one of the most beautiful of her degraded caste. . . . She has seduced by her beauty and blandishments more young men than any known in the Police Records. She was a remarkable character and has come to a remarkable end." Like many of his townsmen, the reporter sym-

At midnight on April 10, 1836, Richard Robinson felled Ellen Jewett with three hatchet blows, motivated by fear that she might reveal their relationship to his society sweetheart. The loathsome deed inspired these first tabloid lithographs.

pathized with the girl. Robinson's cool and disinterested conduct when he was confronted with the crime showed him to be a "villain of too black a die for mortal," said the papers, but he was "very well and highly connected," and he was acquitted. Because his guilt was so clearly established in the public eye, he became known as "the Croat Unhung." In a parting speech with overtones reminiscent of Ellen's own life he said: "It is enough that I am charged with crime. To be suspected is to be damned. Who can live in ignominy? I will go to the rising empire of Texas, where the brand of Cain is honorable." The "sensation in this city never before felt or known" was soon forgotten by fickle New Yorkers. There would be others.

The jury's preposterous verdict of "not guilty" spared Richard Robinson's life, but not his good reputation.

Despite a fire which Robinson set, he failed to conceal his crime—the smoke was detected and the villain identified by his unconsumed cape. The conflagration succeeded only in flushing several fashionable young men from adjoining rooms.

133

MUSEUM OF ART, RHODE ISLAND SCHOOL OF DESIGN

Ring-tailed Roarers

Born in a whirlwind and "weaned on panther's milk," the backwoodsman leaped, fought, and roared his way into the hearts of his countrymen. For all except eastern intellectuals, who considered anybody from west of the Alleghenies scum, the buckskin-clad braggart became an ideal of manhood. After 1830 awareness and pride in a national lore began to dawn, and even country courtrooms, noted for their extrajudicial proceedings, buzzed with tales of the frontiersman's exploits. He excelled at contests where gouging an opponent's eyes was common practice. He supposedly could "outrun, outjump, outshoot, throw down, drag out, and lick" any adversary. His lingo was as flabbergasting as his antics; he was "puckerstoppled" when embarrassed, and "peedoodled" at the sight of a deer. Other of his inventions—"go the whole hog" and "kick the bucket"—still enrich American speech. In spinning tall tales, no one outdid Tennesseean Davy Crockett, the epitome of the folk hero, who described himself as "shaggy as a bear, wolfish about the head, and could grin like a hyena until the bark would curl off a gum log." Plumb full of fantasy and uproarious adventures, Crockett yarns and the like were even appropriated by Yankees. Adapting the backwoods character to fit their dry, understated brand of humor, they produced peddler Sam Slick, "cast iron all over, and pieced with rock."

Informality prevails in A. Wighe's "Rural Court Scene" of 1849 where time out is taken for catching up on the news, swapping tall tales, and, doubtless, swigging corn likker. Between trials, defendants might even join the prosecution, jurors, and judges at a nearby tavern for cards or tenpins.

135

BOTH RIGHT: *FAMILY MAGAZINE*, 1834–35, VOL. I

An 1834 issue of Family Magazine *recommended these forms of climbing, running, and vaulting as regenerative to flabby gents.*

The warm-up recommended before attempting the above exercises was to "hop and strike the lower part of the back with the feet."

The Body Beautiful

METROPOLITAN MUSEUM OF ART, EDWARD W. C. ARNOLD COLLECTION OF NEW YORK PRINTS, MAPS AND PICTURES, BEQUEST OF EDWARD W. C. ARNOLD, 1954

Observing that young women were wont to take their sole exercise in dancing, Catharine Beecher retorted that such recreation exposed frail young things to "damps and miasms" and did little for grace or manners; it was better to pursue "Calisthenics . . . a much more perfect system." An 1832 issue of Casket *agreed, telling readers how to construct the swing above (wrap the bar in velvet to protect the hands) and how to exercise gracefully upon it.*

In the first decades of the nineteenth century, America's streams and rivers were still delightful places in which to swim. A naked John Quincy Adams, leaving his presidential finery on the river bank, regularly plied the Potomac. New Yorkers, as in William Chappel's painting c. 1810 below, dipped in the East River at the foot of Stuyvesant Street.

Physical fitness was one concern that never nagged the founding fathers. Every colonist engaged in strenuous activity, whether it was raising barns, crops, or children. By the nineteenth century, urban living had become quite sedentary, and Oliver Wendell Holmes lamented that lack of exercise was turning the nation's youth into "a pale, pasty-faced, narrow chested, spindle-shanked, dwarfed race." To toughen the flabby American fiber, health enthusiasts built gymnasiums and advocated vigorous workouts on parallel bars, ropes, wooden horses, and rings. Women kept in trim mainly with household tasks, but they occasionally went in for milder rhythmic exercises like calisthenics. Walking was popular among both sexes (like the more recent jogging craze), and by the 1830's professional "peds" sporting their own colors drew large crowds in marathon races. Americans did not readily take to water despite the early efforts of Benjamin Franklin to promote swimming: "After having swum for an hour . . . one sleeps cool the whole night. . . . It is certain that much swimming is a means of stopping diarrhoea and even of producing a constipation." Around 1830, however, people flocked to swimming lessons, public baths, and seaside resorts. Coeducational aquatics were allowed on the grounds that it was dangerous for the weaker sex to plunge unescorted into the surf. Though the couples were always fully clothed, this did not discourage one body cultist who observed "hundreds of bathers, clad in garments of every shape and color . . . gaily disporting before me. . . . The blooming girl, the matronized yet blushing maiden, the dignified mama, were all playing, dancing, romping and shouting. . . . I noticed several ladies of admirable shapes. . . . Oh! ye happy waves, what a blissful destiny is yours, when you can enclasp and kiss such lovely forms."

137

Treeing the Devil

Camp revival meetings of the early 1800's offered simple frontier folk outlets for pent-up emotions, and something to look forward to besides lonely days in log cabins. To backwoods people, salvation for an elect few as preached by highfalutin eastern Calvinists was undemocratic; frontier preachers maintained that any repentant soul could enter heaven. Crowds would respond with cries of "Amen," "Yes, Lord," "Jesus," and barking noises that were said to "tree the Devil." As emotions rose and inhibitions fell, participants might tear off their clothes, hug and kiss one another, and fall to the ground (which had providentially been strewn with straw). Trances and convulsive spasms were a sure sign that God was wrestling with the sinner. As recorded by a fellow Kentuckian, a girl "was struck down, fell stiff, heer hand and arm also become cold as Death, heer fingers cramp'd, recov'd heer speech in 2 hours, was haled home on a sled, continues in a state of dispare which has lasted 3 weekes." An infidel onlooker was seized with "the jerks," snapped his neck, and died cussing. The Great Revival introduced religion to a frontier that was "hair-hung" over hell. One minister who participated in Kentucky's moral make-over reported in 1803 that "drunkards, profane swearers, liars, quarrelsome persons, et cetera, are remarkably reformed. . . . Some neighborhoods, noted for their vicious and profligate manners are now as much noted for their piety and good order." Other results of camp meetings were less publicized: some people went "almost as much to meet each other as to attend upon the means of grace"; backsliders were reconverted at each meeting; and couples, interpreting "love thy neighbor" literally, took to the woods around the camp and were reputed to have "begot more souls than were saved."

"Barefoot and bare-headed, with flowing hair, they step solemnly into the river, while a choir sings," wrote a European of American baptisms like the one above. Here a woman is immersed in the chilly Hudson River. All hell breaks loose at the camp meeting depicted in the 1839 water color opposite. The preacher's ranting causes the guilt-ridden to roll in the aisles.

138

MRS TROLLOP'S

QUICK STEP.

A New Tune on an old Subject.

Composed and Dedicated,

To all the Trollops.

By Nimrod Fish Music Bachelor.

To be had at all the principle Music Stores.

Entered according to Act of Congress by Michael Williams
A.D. 1837 in the Clerks Office of the Dist. Court of U.S. for
South Dist. of New York.

Nº 124 Leonard Street

Cursed with a name that invited punning, the unpopular Mrs. Trollope was depicted in numerous unflattering roles. No lyrics were needed to explain that the subject of this tune, her girls, and their male companion, plied a dubious trade.

LIBRARY OF CONGRESS

Trollope vs. The People

"They marry young. [You never] meet with young women in that delightful period between childhood and marriage."

After a three and a half year ordeal in the United States, Frances Trollope returned to England in 1831 and published her *Domestic Manners of the Americans*, for which her friend August Hervieu executed the water colors at right. Though a London best seller, the book made blood boil on this side of the Atlantic and was dubbed "Lies of an English Lady." Mrs. Trollope's visit unfortunately occurred at a time of patriotic fervor when the new nation was especially paranoiac about foreign criticism; Americans could be hospitable to commentators who shared their enthusiasms for "the noble experiment"—Alexis de Tocqueville and Harriet Martineau among them—but they hated being regarded by missionary types as a race of friendly savages with rather curious customs. Mrs. Trollope became the butt of national satire and scathing attack. What piqued Americans most of all was that this self-claimed mentor of manners often practiced them in the breach, and she was lambasted in return for such vulgar habits as dangling her legs over theater balconies. Admittedly opinionated, she provided candid descriptions of her travels, whether to backwoods communities where colonels picked their teeth with pocketknives, or to cities like Cincinnati. At the latter such rigid rules of decorum prevailed that "whatever may be the talents of the persons who meet together in society, the very shape, form, and arrangement of the meeting is sufficient to paralyze conversation. The women invariably herd together at one part of the room, and the men at the other." Thirty years later, Anthony Trollope added to his mother's list of criticisms, caustically writing about spoiled children, swindlers, and the "dirty mass of battered wirework, which [a woman] calls her crinoline, and which adds as much to her grace . . . as a log of wood does to a donkey, when tied to the animal's leg."

"I never saw any people who . . . live so much without amusements as the Cincinnatians. . . . They have no dinner parties."

"The gentlemen spit, talk of elections. . . . The ladies look at each other's dresses till they know every pin by heart."

The Glorious Fourth

Not until 1826, with a half century of national existence and two victories over Britain under their belts, did Americans join in a unified celebration of the Fourth of July. The day had previously witnessed Federalists and Antifederalists pitted against each other in partisan celebrations that degenerated into brawling and even murder. The date was long and rightly challenged, for neither America's first formal declaration of independence nor the signing of Jefferson's Declaration occurred on July 4. The error was irrevocably fixed, however, when both Thomas Jefferson and John Adams happened to die on that date. Once established, the holiday became synonymous with patriotic speechifying, touting community development, and re-explaining the national purpose. The following excerpt is from Charleston statesman Hugh Legaré's Independence Day oration of 1823, in the heartfelt if exsufflicate style that typified these addresses: "It is the proud distinction of Americans . . . that in the race of moral improvement . . . we have outstripped every competitor and have carried our institutions, 'in the sober certainty of waking bliss,' to a higher pitch of perfection than ever warmed the dreams of enthusiasm or the speculations of the theorist. It is that a whole continent has been set apart, as if it were holy ground, for the cultivation of pure truth. . . ."

The people of Weymouth Landing, Massachusetts, wind up a day of parades and orations with outdoor games and dining on the village common in Susan Merrett's painting (c. 1845) of the traditional Independence Day picnic.

ART INSTITUTE OF CHICAGO

The Inner Sanctum

*In which the Victorian Age
is in Full Flower,
Delicate Sensibilities
do battle with Sense, &
Good Manners become More
Useful than Good Morals*

When Andrew Jackson lived in the White House, he kept it filled with small grandnieces and grandnephews. Except at formal dinners, the children sat at table with the President, and he always served them first, saying that "they have better appetites and less patience." He was also apt to have them present when cabinet officers conferred with him. "The children are too loud occasionally in their play," wrote a visitor. "The President inclines his ear closer to the Secretary, and waves his pipe, absently, but with an exquisite smiling tenderness toward the noisy group. . . ." Even when, at a Christmas party, the children snatched up the decorations — snowballs of starch-coated cotton — and began throwing them about the East Room, the old gentleman's good temper did not waiver.

Obviously, somewhere between Andrew Jackson and Cotton Mather, American notions of child rearing had changed drastically. American children were now readily distinguishable from their cousins in the Old World — being as different, some foreign observers might have said, as poison ivy from English ivy. One visitor from London wrote, "to see sensible people smile with secret admiration at the spirited exhibition of rebellious will on the part of their offspring excites in an English mind a sense of lurking danger." An American etiquette book put the matter even more bluntly: nowadays "American children . . . inspire terror rather than love in the breasts of strangers and all persons who seek quiet and like order. . . . [George Washington] we venture to say, never spoke of his mother as 'the old woman.'" A few foreigners admitted, however, that they were impressed by the self-reliance and resourcefulness of these surprising children.

In truth, the American Revolution had revolutionized more than the political system in America. In breaking away from the unkind parent, England,

In a busy nation even courting was sometimes accomplished on the run and often in full view of parents and siblings. This Currier & Ives couple is managing nicely.

thoughtful Americans had taken time out to scrutinize their own behavior as parents. Some began to wonder whether the old ideas of ruling children by the rod might not be as unfair as King George's tea tax. Perhaps a child was something other than a pint-sized and unprincipled adult. Perhaps he was not even born bad. Perhaps he might be better helped by kindly guidance than by a trip to the woodshed. American intellectuals, such as Dr. Benjamin Rush, imported Rousseau's ideas of natural goodness and transmitted them through the land; and as the generations rolled by, they were embraced by people who had never heard of Rousseau. Children were very important in the new Republic, for it needed more citizens and infant mortality was high. Small wonder that the little ones who survived childbirth, cholera infantum, and the killer diseases of childhood should be objects of respectful attention.

In the theological state of the Puritans, the prime concern had been to save the child from the Devil. But in the Republic, if a citizen remarked that a child was "full of the Devil," it would be in a tolerant, half-amused manner. Jonathan Edwards' decree that bad children were "young vipers and infinitely more hateful than vipers" no longer carried any weight. Among quantities of new books on child nurture, only a few strove to maintain the old-fashioned standards. "Break their wills betimes," said one. "Begin this work before they can run alone, before they can speak plainly, or speak at all. . . . break their wills if you would not damn the child." But most took the opposite view: "Why need a child's will be broken?" asked an exponent of the new school. "He will have use for it all. . . . Train a child to self-control, so that his will may be his strong point, but do not break his will."

At the heart of the new attitude was the idea that parents were largely responsible for the way their children turned out—that children were not "born that way." And as society headed toward industrialization and the fathers of families were often gone from home all day, the duty of raising children fell heavily on the mothers. "George Washington had a mother who made him a good boy," declared the author of *Homes of Our Country*. "The *mother* of Washington is entitled to a nation's gratitude. *She* taught her boy the principles of obedience, and moral courage, and virtue."

As for fathers, *Homes of Our Country* gave them a stern talking-to: "A sad house is that in which the father's seat is vacant; a sadder house is that in which the father has vacated his influence and left the children fatherless even whilst he lives. . . . There is plenty of womanish manhood in the world to-day, but the lack of the father element testifies the neglect of the father's influence. . . . Where is your son to-night, father? Where does he spend his evenings?" (A notice that flashes across TV screens from time to time in some American cities echoes that long-ago warning: PARENTS—DO YOU KNOW WHERE YOUR CHILDREN ARE? IT IS TEN P.M.)

When the average American girl began her maternal career she was less than twenty and had had an extremely sketchy education. If she could read and write well she was unusual, at least during the first half of the century. She could work simple sums, but all higher learning, beginning with long division, was regarded as "man's education." In 1829 the fact that a girl had mastered geometry caused a public furor. Girls were shielded from geography because it might disturb their faith in Genesis; from higher mathematics because that complex subject might overtax their naturally weak brains; from medicine because it was "indelicate." These attitudes persisted through most

One of the precocious boys above essays a pinch of snuff, while the other adjusts his monocle. The rattan baby carriage below was offered in an 1892 trade catalog.

of the century. "The idea of giving woman a man's education is too ridiculous to appear credible," wrote a college president in 1855.

How, then, were the mothers of America expected to turn out housefuls of little George Washingtons? By teaching them manners and morals from the earliest possible age. "Civility is not only an essential of high success," said *Homes of Our Country*, "but . . . almost a fortune of itself. . . . he who has this quality in perfection, though a blockhead, is almost sure to get on where, without it, even men of high ability fail. . . . Manners, in fact, are minor morals, and a rude man is generally assumed to be a bad man." Nathaniel Hawthorne, shy and socially inept all his life, endorsed that point of view: "God may forgive sins, but awkwardness has no forgiveness in heaven or earth." Etiquette books of the early Republic had generally preferred the Christian gentleman to the fine gentleman, but now both Hawthorne and the author of *Homes* seemed to echo Chesterfield's dictum of the previous century: "You had better return a dropped fan genteelly than give a thousand pounds awkwardly. . . ."

Engraving from a manual for ladies

Even etiquette writers agreed that no book could replace a mother's teaching. Oliver Wendell Holmes thought that it took three generations to polish a gentleman for American society. Holmes rose from a quiet Yankee family of scholars and clergymen to the top levels of Boston society. It was he who coined the phrase "Boston Brahmins," and he believed this "caste" was the result of Darwinian natural selection. "If aptitudes for the acquisition of knowledge can be bred into a family as the qualities the sportsman wants in his dog are developed in pointers and setters, we know what we may expect of a descendant of one of the Academic Races." Still, he believed in what he called Nature's Republicanism. "The last born nobleman I have seen . . . was pulling a rope that was fastened to a Maine schooner loaded with lumber." By "felicitous crosses," such a person might attain the level of a Brahmin. He did not think it likely, however, and "*other things being equal, in most relations of life, I prefer a man of family.*" Holmes's definition of a gentleman was a man who, though "not trying to be a gentleman," fulfilled all the requirements by instinct. He must be distinguished by "Good dressing, quiet ways, low tones of voice," and should "have nothing in [his] dress or furniture so fine that [he] cannot afford to spoil it and get another like it, yet . . . preserve the harmonies, throughout [his] person and dwelling."

James Russell Lowell, born to the Brahmin caste, thought that a good university education could produce "not a conventional gentleman, but a man of culture, a man of intellectual resource, a man of public spirit, a man of refinement. . . ." Ralph Waldo Emerson wrote that the marks of a gentleman are "so precise that it is at once felt if an individual lack the masonic sign. . . ." The word *gentleman*, he said, "denotes good-nature or benevolence: manhood first, and then gentleness." Like Holmes, he believed that there had to be an inborn capacity for culture. "'Take a thorn bush,' said the emir Abdel-Kader, 'and sprinkle it for a whole year with water; — it will yield nothing but thorns. Take a date-tree, leave it without culture, and it will always produce dates. Nobility is the date-tree and the Arab populace is a bush of thorns.'"

However, if the sale of etiquette books was any indication, most Americans firmly believed that a thorn bush could become a date tree. Between 1830 and 1860, more than a hundred etiquette books were published, many of which were best sellers. Most of them were written by and for women, who presumably conveyed their contents to their husbands and to the little sons and daughters at their knees. Like modern how-to books, all were written in a brisk, optimistic tone, seeming to promise results or double-your-money-back.

A good education, which Holmes and his fellow New Englanders considered essential for the gentleman, was not easy to come by. New England led the country in free education, but even there it was not compulsory and schools were in session only a few months of the year. Good elementary teachers were difficult to find. The factory town of Lowell was one of the first to accept women teachers. In 1829 Lowell schoolmarms earned $2.25 a week, plus room and board—only thirty-five cents a week more than the mill girls. Teachers everywhere were paid only during the school year, and the people who served were generally on their way to something else—a young man earning money for future education or to set himself up in business; a young woman hoping for a husband or engaged to a sweetheart who had gone west to seek his fortune. Or perhaps a poor old lady would keep body and soul together by teaching small children in a kind of haphazard nursery school and first grade. By the post-Civil War years, most teachers were women, who, it was found, worked harder for less pay than most men.

Though a child was lucky if he acquired a good education, he was even luckier if he grew up healthy. His best bet was to have a naturally robust constitution so that no doctor or apothecary need ever be consulted and his mother would have no occasion to look in one of the many household manuals that prescribed home remedies. Many physicians practiced without medical degrees. Apothecaries needed no licenses, and when, in the 1840's, it was suggested that some governmental control of lethal drugs and their prescription might be wise, the idea was dismissed in Congress as unconstitutional and a violation of civil liberties. Some recipes for home remedies were harmless, others were in the nature of desperate gambles. Consider, for instance, "*To Kill Worms in Children.* Take sage, boil it with milk to a good tea, turn it to whey with alum or vinegar, and give the whey to the child, if the worms are not knotted in the stomach, and it will be a sure cure. If the worms are knotted in the stomach, it will kill the child."

Many mothers declined to breast feed their babies, finding the practice "indelicate." Children who survived the ordeal of being farmed out to a wet nurse or being raised on unpasteurized milk soon found themselves faced with a further unpleasantness: uncomfortable and restrictive clothing. Until the end of the eighteenth century, children had always been dressed like small adults. Then, following Directoire and Napoleonic fashions in France, little girls wore their hair short and the hems of their dresses above the ankles, while little boys were put into pantaloons instead of knee breeches. But when ladies' fashions changed again, c. 1830, to wide skirts and compressed waists, both boys and girls were put into pantalettes, stays, ruffs of starched cambric, and high-buttoned boots. Little girls followed their mothers' fashions through the eras of the petticoat, the hoop skirt, and bustle; their brothers had a better time of it, dressed in sailor costumes or trousers and jackets like their fathers, until the 1880's, when Mrs. Frances Hodgson Burnett wrote *Little Lord Fauntleroy* and a generation of protesting little boys were subjected to wine-red velvet suits with white lace collars.

Children of the poor wore no confining clothing, but they suffered in other ways. Often they went to work at an age when modern children start first

Geography lesson, as administered in 1844

grade, putting in twelve or fourteen hours a day in mines, factories, or on farms. A ten-year-old could make seventy-five cents a week in the Norwich mills. The scale rose about ten cents with each year of maturity. Some states attempted to put the brakes on child labor with compulsory education laws in the 1840's, but they were not enforced.

But rich or poor, whether tending a spinning machine or rolling a hoop, children were early imbued with the American compulsion to "go ahead." "All those who're idle in their youth Will suffer when they're old," warned a child's primer. "Improve your time. When you play do it because God gives you leave." Little girls were given samplers to make and daily stints of sewing to get through. If a boy's father was scholarly, he set his son to doing lessons; if a workingman, he set him to chores. Either way, time for play was limited. As the century advanced, more toys were on the market, but still, writers on child nurture, such as Catharine Beecher, thought that children should occupy themselves with useful amusements: cultivating flowers and fruits; learning to sing and to play the piano; collecting shells and other scientific specimens. Boys should learn to make wheelbarrows, carts, sleds, and other useful objects; girls should sew. They might also walk, ride, and visit, and (presumably, if they had absolutely nothing else to do) play games and laugh.

The Victorian code preached by people like Miss Beecher had developed years in advance of young Queen Victoria's ascent to the English throne in 1837; and that American combination of latent Puritanism with extreme modesty, delicacy, purity, and squeamishness that came to be labeled Victorianism made a strong brew indeed. Many a proper family of the 1840's must have been embarrassed when ancient grandparents, survivors of a coarser age, referred to "chicken legs" and "chicken breasts" instead of "dark meat" and "white meat"; "underpants" instead of "white-sewing" (the word *lingerie* came in around 1860); "body" instead of "shape"; "hips" instead of "nether portions"; "coffin" instead of "casket"; "underdrawers" instead of "unmentionables." The English traveler Captain Marryat reports of having visited a household in which miniature pantalettes covered the stark nudity of piano limbs. But, for all their delicacy, Victorian Americans did not hesitate to use such phraseology as Lunatic Asylum, Home for Incurables, Home for Incorrigibles, Home for the Aged, and Poor Farm — all of which were to be given euphemisms by twentieth-century Americans.

Along with the struggle toward gentlemanly and ladylike manners and exalted morals came a determined striving for culture. In colonial days, reading, for the vast majority, had been limited to the Bible, newspapers, and almanacs. The first thirty years of the Republic produced very little in the way of American literature. "Who reads an American book?" remarked one English critic — superciliously but justifiably. Ralph Waldo Emerson, speaking of Massachusetts, said that between 1790 and 1820 "there was not a book, a speech, a conversation or a thought in the State." Then, in the 1820's, James Fenimore Cooper, Washington Irving, and William Cullen Bryant became widely read — even in England. In the thirties, technological improvements in printing and papermaking, together with the reprehensible practice of pirating foreign works, made the American public conversant with classics such as *Pilgrim's Progress* and *Robinson Crusoe*, as well as the latest works of Scott and Dickens. McGuffey's *Eclectic Readers*, first published in the thirties and studied by three generations of children from coast to coast, opened the stu-

Infant's pinafore

Knitted drawers

Embroidered bib

Basket for baby food

Patterns from Harper's Bazar, *1886*

Louis Godey's monthly magazine promised its women readers "one blaze of beauty throughout." Sentimental stories, pretty pictures, and high fashions like the headdress, c. 1850, above, were regular features.

dents' eyes to the world of good poetry and prose as they learned to read.

Not only were books and magazines easier to produce, but people had more money and leisure to spend on them. Thousands of Americans began to write; hundreds saw their work in print, whether in books, newspapers, magazines, pamphlets, or tracts. Dozens made their living by the pen. Among the magazines, of which four or five thousand were started but had short lives, *Godey's Lady's Book* was the front-runner with a circulation of 150,000 on the eve of the Civil War. Louis Godey, the publisher, and his literary editor, Mrs. Sarah Josepha Hale, caught the spirit of the antebellum years, which, possibly because the facts of life at that time were unbearably harsh if faced head on, were years of sentimentality. The Indians were being decimated, differences over slavery and economic interests were clearly going to bring about the dissolution of the Union, politics had become so corrupt that it was often hard to find honest men who were willing to run for office, the legality and wisdom of the Mexican War was questionable, and many native-born Americans felt threatened by the oncoming rush of immigrants.

Godey's Lady's Book turned its back on all these disagreeable subjects. Month after month, year after year, it offered a blancmange mixture of directions for fancywork, the words and music of new dances, and short stories that were either about domestic tempests in teapots or were set in the olden days in the manner of Sir Walter Scott. For the armchair traveler, there were exciting but never hair-raising accounts of missionary journeys in Africa or antiquarian pokings-around in Egypt. Poems, more than likely, were concerned with death and translation to heaven. *Godey's* frequently offered house plans—for a Gothic cottage, perhaps, or an Italianate villa—or gave directions for remodeling one's embarrassingly old-fashioned Greek revival house or crude old seventeenth-century colonial in the newest architectural style. Expensive hand-colored engravings graced each issue, showing several ladies and little girls dressed in the latest fashions. There were directions for pronouncing French phrases, for making wax fruit, for drawing a rabbit, for making a velvet inkstand cover in the shape of a teapot, and for removing water spots from black crepe veils. There were jokes: "Would you not love to gaze on Niagara forever? Oh no—I shouldn't like to have a cataract always in my eye."

Godey's subscribers received a free engraving every year as a premium. One year it was "The Deathbed of the Reverend John Wesley," another, "General Taylor and Old Whitey" (General Taylor was President Zachary Taylor and Old Whitey was his horse). To distribute the likeness of a president was as close as *Godey's* came to politics—unless we assume that a cape called the Hungarian Circle was inspired by the visit to the United States of the Hungarian patriot Kossuth. "Politics are not for the drawing-room," Mrs. Hale told her readers firmly. In April, 1861, as guns opened fire on Fort Sumter, *Godey's* subscribers were enjoying a pleasant, drowsy tale of domestic life on a plantation; humming a new song, "My Baby's Shoe," a mother's song, affecting enough to draw tears from every eye; and following directions for making a penwiper in the shape of a butterfly.

By 1860, with slightly less than half the population accounted literate, American booksellers had a potential market of 15,300,000 readers. By far the most popular kind of book was the how-to manual. Books on manners and morals were usually among the top best sellers, but any manual that explained how to do something was sure of an audience—how to sail a ship, how to carve gravestones, how to build a locomotive, how to raise silkworms, in fact how to accomplish anything an enterprising American might take it into his head to do. The next great category comprised religious books (other than the Bible, which of course was a steady best seller) and paper-bound tracts, distributed at low prices, or given free to those who could not pay, under the auspices of the American Tract Society. Over 12,000,000 copies were produced in 1855 alone. Hundreds of door-to-door salesmen who were also missionaries carried the tracts far and wide, from the slums of New York to the farthest frontier camp, while the home office shipped them to missions overseas, to the army and navy, to American Indians, and to merchant seamen. The message was Protestant (and patently anti-Catholic). Some tracts were couched in the language of sermons, others masqueraded as "pleasing and delightful" fiction. More printed words flowed from the press of the American Tract Society than from any other source during the antebellum years.

Like waltzing and theatergoing, novel-reading became an American predilection in spite of frantic objection by moralists. A breakthrough was scored when Miss Catharine Beecher, in 1843, declared in favor of novels provided they had a moral message. No novel of the period would surpass her sister's *Uncle Tom's Cabin* in its moral influence. Reading aloud was a favorite form of nineteenth-century family togetherness, and the prime authors were Scott, Dickens, Cooper, and Thackeray. Dickens' popularity even survived the publication of his *American Notes*, in which he affronted our extremely touchy national pride with harsh comments on our manners and morals, particularly southern ones. (Southern book reviewers ignored him as much as possible, or praised him grudgingly, but southern families went right on reading him.)

The forties and fifties produced some popular American poets—Longfellow, Lowell, Holmes, Whittier, and Mrs. Lydia H. Sigourney, who published over sixty volumes of poetry and prose, and collected more laurels and more money than any woman poet of her century. When "the Sweet Singer of Hartford" died in 1865, *Godey's* wrote, "A polished stone of our American temple of social, literary and religious life has fallen. . . ." Yet today not a line of her verse and scarcely her name is remembered. Like *Godey's*, her success came from an ability to tell her generation what they wanted to hear—much sentiment, no controversy, and a preoccupation with lugubrious death scenes that has today the cloying and slightly sickening effect of a roomful of oversweet flowers.

On the level of TV serials was a raft of novels by "scribbling women" (as Nathaniel Hawthorne called all lady novelists). The heroines wept continually, but nothing happened that could not be read aloud in any family parlor, and things came out alright in the end, except for a few harrowing deaths by expendable characters. All along the way, the paths were strewn with clear-cut messages about truth and beauty. Not for family consumption were the works of George Lippard. They sold by the thousands. Gothic novels full of gruesome scenes, bloodshed, rape, and naked women, they dwelt on the sins of the rich and the innocence of the poor. Lippard's stories have their descendants in today's tabloid newspapers, and the author thrived on the threats that regularly came his way, traveling about his native Philadelphia "wrapped in an ample cloak, and carrying a sword cane to repel assaults." For the semiliterate, the *National Police Gazette*, founded in 1845,

Traveling salesman, drawn in 1846

told lurid stories with the help of explicit pictures. It survived until 1932, when it was killed by a combination of the Depression and the invasion by ladies of barbershops (where men had always been able to read it in peace).

Dime novels, or "story papers," found a wide market throughout the nineteenth century among boys and girls, who bought them on the sly and read them in the attic or outhouse. According to Anthony Comstock, author in 1883 of *Traps for the Young*, story papers bred "vulgarity, profanity, loose ideas of life, impurity of thought and deed." This Goliath among Victorian vice wardens continued, "They render the imagination unclean, destroy domestic peace, desolate homes, cheapen woman's virtue, and make foul-mouthed bullies, cheats, vagabonds, thieves, desperadoes, and libertines." During the 1830's, some daily newspapers began to sell for a penny and to cater to the public interest in crime. More reputable were the two-cent papers. Weeklies, such as *The Saturday Evening Post* and *The New York Ledger*, went in for serial fiction, essays, history, and true tales of travel.

But there were more ways to acquire culture and to show that one had acquired it than through the written word. An elegant handwriting was greatly admired, particularly that taught by Platt Rogers Spencer, who was a sort of Johnny Appleseed of calligraphy. Spencer was born in New York State in 1800 and went to Ohio in 1810 with his family. From boyhood he seems to have been fascinated with handwriting. Too poor to buy paper, he practiced on snowbanks and on the sandy beaches of Lake Erie. By the time he was twenty, he had developed a distinctive hand, one that lent itself to embellishment, shading, and feathery flourishes, the inspiration for which, he said, had been the waves, the grass, and the vines of his Ohio childhood. He made a career of going from place to place teaching penmanship. Five of his sons and a nephew later helped perpetuate the fame of "a fine, Spencerian hand."

The old Puritan suspicion of music finally disappeared for good during the prosperous forties and fifties, probably because of the sudden availability of pianos and other musical instruments and because of the presence of several first-class musicians. Lowell Mason of Boston composed hymns and introduced choirs and organs to Protestant churches and, furthermore, encouraged the congregation to join in. By the 1850's, Sunday service was often musically pleasing, with the old painful lining-out of psalms eliminated except in very remote or change-resistant meetinghouses. Jenny Lind and a brilliant Norwegian violinist named Ole Bull opened American ears to serious concert music. Grand opera was introduced into the United States as early as 1825 (recruited by one of New York's few rich Irishmen, Dominick Lynch, himself an accomplished singer). Some of Jenny Lind's songs, such as "The Last Rose of Summer" and "The Bird Song," sounded deceptively easy, and the sheet music sold like wildfire to Main Street songbirds all over the country. So did the works of Stephen Foster. "'Old Folks at Home' is on everybody's tongue," reported a music journal in 1852. "Pianos and guitars groan with it, night and day; sentimental young ladies sing it; sentimental young gentlemen warble it in midnight serenades; volatile young 'bucks' hum it in the midst of their business and pleasures; . . . all the bands play it; . . . the 'singing stars' carol it on the theatrical boards, and at concerts; the chambermaid sweeps and dusts to the measured cadence of *Old Folks at Home*." Like the most popular literature of the time, Foster's songs were sentimental, sweetly melancholy, morally pristine, and unlikely to offend anyone.

Instruments like the violin so proudly displayed above, could be ordered by mail. Sears, Roebuck's "Grand Concert Violin; genuine Stradivarius model" sold for $9.30. The 1890's Talking Machine below was also from Sears.

Musical instruments were almost as common in American homes as TV sets are today. Most expensive and most desirable was a piano. A cheap one cost as much as $300, but even so, by 1860 one in every fifteen hundred citizens owned a new piano. Production—totaling some $5,000,000—was mostly in eastern factories, but a few were starting up here and there all the way to California. Jonas Chickering, of Boston, was the leading manufacturer, with a German immigrant, Henry Steinway, offering serious competition. Families that could not afford a piano settled for a melodeon, or reed organ, which could be had for about $100. The guitar business was also thriving, and of course sheet music was in demand for all these instruments as well as for *a capella* singing. But the piano was the great status symbol.

In the year 1840, for every hundred students in primary school there were only ten in high school and one in college. (All schools were private, except a few primary schools.) For the many adults who felt their education had been sketchy, something more was needed. In 1826 Josiah Holbrook, a lecturer in the natural sciences, founded the first American lyceum in Millbury, Massachusetts. He had three objectives: to establish a library and museum of the natural sciences in every town of every state; to improve school education in these subjects; and to provide lectures and discussion groups for adults. Within eight years, the number of lyceum branches had increased to three thousand; by the end of the thirties the word *lyceum* had come to signify a local organization devoted to arranging lectures on any subject for adults. Emerson and Thoreau organized and lectured at the Concord branch; Hawthorne was secretary of the branch at Salem; in every town, the most intellectual citizens took an interest. The standard fee was "fifty dollars and meals," from which custom came the popular acronym of the FAME lectures, but on the small-town circuit even someone of Emerson's reputation might receive only ten dollars. To make it pay, he often used the occasion to try out a new idea before publishing it in polished form as an essay. The modest payments attracted many other dedicated men who enjoyed dispensing knowledge or had an important message to convey. Abolitionists, temperance men, political leaders, and even women, who had their first opportunities to speak in public, were heard on lyceum platforms. The sizable minority of folk who wished to inform themselves on controversial matters flocked to halls all over America. During the winter of 1837–38, for example, the Boston Lyceum held twenty-six lectures, with a total attendance of thirteen thousand people.

Mrs. Farrar, in *The Young Lady's Friend*, gave her readers a few tips on lyceum etiquette. "Never run, jump, scream, scramble, and push, in order to get a good seat." The lyceum "affords opportunity for learning to respect strangers, and to behave courteously and delicately to all." It is well to remember "that all, who attend lectures together, meet on terms of perfect equality." Don't whisper; don't go in late and expect people to relinquish the best seats for you; don't wear a tall headdress; don't keep seats; don't handle the specimens or displays passed around; don't step on people's dresses going downstairs; take copious notes, and make a study of the subject.

After the Civil War, lecture fees rose, and the booking-agent business became a profitable new enterprise. Henry Ward Beecher was first paid $500 a lecture, and later $1,000. Henry M. Stanley, fresh back from Darkest Africa, delivered a series of a hundred lectures for $100,000. Some lectures were not

"Home, Sweet Home" hits a sour note.

exactly cultural—for instance, Ann Eliza Young, number 19 among the Mrs. Brigham Youngs and the only one to get a divorce, delivered an eyebrow-raising exposé of life among plural wives. By the end of the century, as one of the lyceum's original boosters remarked, it was "no longer the New England conscience bound on a voyage to convert the world." However, lyceums lasted into the 1920's, when they finally succumbed to competition from radio, moving pictures, automobiles, and Chautauqua.

In the summer of 1874, at Lake Chautauqua, New York, a group of Sunday-school teachers convened for religious lectures. From that came the Chautauqua movement, a cross between the camp revival and the lyceum. It grew until forty thousand people were coming each summer to the lake to study not only religion but politics, economics, science, and literature. The speakers were eminent. Theodore Roosevelt appeared five times. In its wake it left *The Chautauquan* magazine, memberships in the Chautauquan Literary and Scientific Circle (a four-year program of selected works for more than a hundred thousand readers), and a host of other community endeavors for young and old. The name Chautauqua was later borrowed by groups of speakers who traveled from place to place, set up tents, and provided folksy but informative lectures—a sort of cultural traveling circus. To borrow from Edith Wharton, the followers of Chautauqua were people who liked to "pursue Culture in bands, as though it were dangerous to meet alone." In small middle-western towns, where businessmen ruled and professors were thought of as absent-minded or worse, perhaps culture *was* dangerous to confront alone. At any rate, the Chautauqua circuit filled a social and intellectual need. The summer sessions at Lake Chautauqua are still being attended by thousands.

In the late eighteenth century, John Adams had said, "I must study politics and war that my sons may have liberty to study mathematics and philosophy, geography, natural history and naval architecture, navigation, commerce, and agriculture, in order to give their children a right to study painting, poetry, music, architecture, statuary, tapestry and porcelain." In Adams' day, most people of creative bent became in their spare time carpenters and house-builders, carved figureheads and weathervanes, or, if they were women, designed quilt patterns, dresses, bonnets, needlework, and embroideries. Ladies of the early Republic took to embellishing their houses with homemade bas-reliefs in wax, silhouettes, and *memento mori* painted in water colors or on glass. But the idea of making a living in the fine arts was approached very cautiously. Of the few professionally trained American painters before 1840, nearly all lived abroad for long periods of their lives. There was a Puritanical doubt in the public mind as to whether paintings came under the heading of "Amusement" or "Culture." Panoramas of the Mississippi or of other natural wonders—painted on a half mile of canvas and unwound across a stage—had been shown at fairs or theaters for twenty-five cents admission fee—one Saratoga impresario collected $20,000 in a six-week appearance; clearly, they were amusement. But when Frederick Edwin Church's heroic painting of Niagara Falls was exhibited at the same admission fee, and *The New York Times* listed it under "Amusements," there were those who claimed indignantly that it was not intended to amuse. Church later proved that he was not to be taken lightly by asking and getting up to $10,000 for his Hudson River landscapes; and when he built an extravagant pleasure dome, "Olana," near Hudson, New York, thousands of people who saw it from the decks of passing steamboats

Erastus Palmer, Albany sculptor, pauses to admire his emerging work. T. H. Matteson recorded the moment in a painting, detail above.

had an uneasy feeling that perhaps art was as serious and profitable an enterprise as hardware and dry goods.

But for an artist to make money there had to be a market, and in 1838 a New Yorker named Herring opened the Apollo Art Gallery, with a brilliant scheme. Following a plan that had already proven successful in Scotland, Herring sold five-dollar yearly subscriptions to the "Apollo Association." Each subscriber received an engraving, plus a lottery ticket that entitled him to a chance on a painting by an American artist. The money from subscriptions was used to buy the paintings. The idea of getting something for nothing appealed to Americans as much as it had to Scotsmen. For the next twelve years this cultural gambling game—which became known as the American Art Union—acquired thousands of members all over the country. In 1849, the peak year, more than $100,000 was paid out to American artists, most of whom, ten years before, would have had to make their living some other way. If no American Michelangelos were turned up, the Art Union did perform an important service to American art, primarily by convincing the public that paintings did not have to come from across the Atlantic in order to be art, and that an Adirondack could prove as noble a subject as an Alp. Artists were urged to avoid imitation of European art, past or present: to paint American subjects, especially those appealing to "national feeling"; and to scrupulously observe the proprieties ("Let this ever be the motto of American art, inscribed in golden characters upon a snow-white scroll, 'Truth and Purity.'"). Four out of every five pictures bought by the Union were landscapes, and verdant, placid ones at that. Snow scenes, no matter how peaceful, were not bought—and rarely painted—until the late 1850's. The experience of colonial and frontier struggles with untamed nature was still too close to make anyone want to share a parlor with it. In addition to the traditional portraits, figure paintings included romantic and religious allegories by such men as Washington Allston, pseudo-historical scenes like Emanuel Leutze's "Washington Crossing the Delaware," and—perhaps most popular—genre scenes by William Sydney Mount and George Caleb Bingham, and dozens of others, showing realistic American country people, types everyone knew, and for whom migrants to the city felt a fervent nostalgia.

The Art Union fell on evil times. Tight money and the competition of many other attractions caused the membership to drop; and in 1852 a suit was brought against it on the grounds that the lottery was unconstitutional. After a long court fight, the verdict went against the Union, and without its lottery the fun was over. But the scheme had changed American taste. Thousands of "large and costly Original Engravings" adorned parlors the country over, and the lucky few who had won paintings were the envy of their towns. Art was culture; art was something of value; art was a status symbol.

Engravings were too expensive for humble people, but chromos (ranging in price from $7.50 to $12) could be saved up for, and almost anyone could hope to own a lithograph by one of the Kellogg brothers or Currier & Ives (from fifteen cents, for one the size of a modern snapshot, to $3, for a folio print, eighteen by twenty-seven inches). Bucolic scenes went very well, as might have been expected; but so did Currier & Ives's representations of catastrophes—the wreck of the steamboat *Lexington*, for example, or a hotel fire on Broadway—scenes that would never have found a place at the genteel Art Union.

Taste is a mirror of manners and morals, and nothing mirrors the manners

Lithographs depicting patriotic subjects were guaranteed best sellers. The boy posed with the panache of a Rebel general above, and the gent sashed with bunting below, were both issued by Currier & Ives.

and morals of the antebellum years better than the public reaction to the three most famous sculptures of that time: Clark Mills's equestrian statue of Andrew Jackson; Horatio Greenough's "George Washington"; and Hiram Powers' "Greek Slave." The first was received with almost universal pleasure. Jackson was portrayed realistically, down to every buttonhole: and by a clever balancing trick, Mills had managed to show the horse rearing back on two legs. If it looked more like a nursery toy than a real war horse, that was unimportant. People looked at it and marveled that it stayed put while waving its forefeet in the air. That was American Know-How for you. Congress was so pleased that it added an extra $20,000 to Mills's $12,000 contract.

Greenough chose to model Washington in the guise of a Roman god, seated and half draped. The head was definitely a portrait of Washington, even to the familiar hair arrangement. As for the body—naked down to the navel and with naked feet thrust into sandals—who could tell if that was Washington's? And who could be so indelicate as to want to know? Philip Hone's remarks after viewing the statue (commissioned by Congress and costing a whopping $21,000) probably sum up the national reaction: "It looks like a great herculean warrior—like *Venus of the Bath*. . . . Washington was too prudent and careful of his health to expose himself thus in a climate so uncertain as ours, to say nothing of the indecency of such an exposure—a subject on which he was known to be exceedingly fastidious." Symbolism could be carried just so far: it was all very well to portray the Father of His Country as a Roman god; but to remove his shirt was overdoing it. The mammoth statue stood exposed for years on the east Capitol grounds, and—possibly so it would not catch cold—was finally moved to the Smithsonian Institution.

The nude body was not only considered indecent in the United States of that day, it was scarcely to be mentioned, let alone be placed on public view. But curiously enough, Hiram Powers removed every stitch of clothing from his "Greek Slave" and got away with it. Powers was a Vermont-boy-made-good (among his first professional assignments was painting scenes of hell-fire for a diorama in his adopted city of Cincinnati). For years he studied abroad, but he did not forget the American popular taste; and before his "Greek Slave" was exhibited he was careful to explain that the young lady was not exposed in *person* but in *spirit*.

Accepting this rather mystifying explanation, the public came to see versions of the statue by the thousands. Some museums had a "ladies' hour," when women could view the statue without the blush-producing presence of gentlemen. In Cincinnati her honor was protected by a calico blouse and flannel drawers reaching to the ankles. It should be noted that a museum in that day was not primarily a repository of art objects, but of oddities and rarities, usually of a scientific nature: dinosaur bones, stuffed birds, Indian relics, or a pickled two-headed lamb. Dioramas, showing an erupting volcano, for example, or the Burning of Moscow, were also found at museums, and so were live attractions—magicians, freaks, trained animals. Museums did not settle down to their present-day sobriety as repositories of art or science until the last decades of the nineteenth century.

How did Powers get away with it? Several explanations have been offered: first of all, the girl was manacled. Her clothes were on a pedestal right behind her, and one assumed she would have put them on if she could. A crucifix dangling from her chains identified her as a Christian. A Turkish captive, she

(Continued on Page 158)

Queen Victoria, c. 1880

Natchez: 1835

The Mississippi port, viewed when "cotton was king." In these excerpts, a Yankee, Joseph Ingraham, paints a not entirely romantic picture of the Old South.

Natchez is the centre of a circle which extends many miles around it . . . and daily attracts all within its influence. Thus families, who reside several leagues apart, meet together, like inhabitants of one city. The ladies come in their carriages "to shop," the gentlemen, on horseback, to do business. Cotton and negroes are the constant theme—the ever harped upon, never worn out subject of conversation among all classes. A plantation well stocked with hands, is the *ne plus ultra* of every man's ambition. . . . Young men who come . . . "to make money," soon catch the mania, and nothing less than a broad plantation, waving with the snow white cotton bolls, can fill their mental vision. . . . Hence, the few professional men of long or eminent standing. The cliff or bluff, upon which Natchez stands . . . rises abruptly. At the foot . . . are long straggling lines of wooden buildings. This part of the town is not properly Natchez—and strangers passing up and down the river, who have had the opportunity of seeing only this place, have, without dreaming of the beautiful city over their heads, gone on their way, with impressions very inaccurate and unfavourable. "Natchez under the Hill" as it has been aptly named . . . for many years . . . has been the nucleus of vice upon the Mississippi. Though now on the high way of reform, there is still enough of the cloven-hoof visible, to enable the stranger to recognise that its former reputation was well earned. The principal street . . . is lined on either side with . . . gambling houses, brothels, and bar-rooms. . . . The low, broken, half-sunken side-walks . . . blocked up with fashionably-dressed young men, smoking or lounging, tawdrily arrayed, highly rouged females, sailors . . . negroes . . . pigs, dogs, and dirty children. In "Natchez under the Hill," the Sabbath, as a day of rest and public worship, is not observed according to the strictest letter of the old "blue laws." On that day the stores are kept open and generally filled with boatmen and negroes. With the latter this day is a short jubilee, and . . . they make the most of it—condensing the occupation and the jollity of seven days into one. (It is customary for planters . . . to give their slaves a small piece of land to cultivate for their own use. . . . They have the Sabbath given them as a holiday, when they are permitted to . . . come into town to dispose of their produce, and lay in their own little luxuries and private stores.) The numerous drinking shops . . . are, on that day, as much . . . if not more than on other days, filled with a motley assemblage of black, white, and yellow, drinking and carousing. Here may always be heard the sound of the violin, the clink of silver upon the roulette and faro-tables, and the language of profanity and lewdness; and the revellers, so far from being interrupted by the intervention of the Sabbath, actually distinguish it by a closer and more persevering devotion to their unhallowed pursuits and amusements of all sorts and descriptions.

was herself a Greek (a noble people because of their revolution against the Turks and because of having thought of democracy). Furthermore, everyone knew that Greeks, ancient ones, at least, had been in the habit of making undraped statuary, so hers was a kind of innocence by association. Lastly, there was something unreal about her—she looked boneless, and her breasts were unnaturally far apart. She was definitely cold marble, not warm, living, breathing flesh; there was no danger that she might start walking around, causing trouble.

Sculpture for everyman was produced in the plaster groups of John Rogers; from the sixties to the nineties, very few middle-class homes were without at least one. Each group was about sixteen inches high and showed a typical American scene, with a touch of humor or pathos. "The Slave Auction" was sold to hundreds of abolitionists, but that did not prevent southern buyers from hankering after "The Checker Players" or "Neighboring Pews." The price was between $6 and $25, depending on the number of figures, and businesslike Mr. Rogers shipped each one with instructions for mending.

As producer of art for the masses, sculptor John Rogers had no peer. Typical of his work are the sentimental engagement scene above and the anecdotal slave school group below.

There were no professional interior decorators until the twentieth century, but after the Civil War and especially at the time of the Centennial Exhibition at Philadelphia in 1876, books about household taste found a wide audience. The Victorian housewife was eager to read what the Joneses had in their house in order that she might keep up with them. "Provided that there is room enough to move about without walking over the furniture, there is hardly likely to be too much in a room," wrote one adviser. The sparsely furnished interiors of earlier days now connoted everything that Americans were seeking to escape—poverty, making-do, and a struggle with the primitive frontier. *Horror vacui* was the theme of High-Victorian rooms, as well as of High-Victorian architecture and ladies' fashions. One coolheaded commentator warned, "Never have anything in your house that you do not know to be useful or believe to be beautiful." But there were now so many beautiful, useful things—why not have as many as one could possibly acquire?

The Centennial Exhibition brimmed over with the fascinating results of industry's marriage with art. Mrs. M.E.W. Sherwood, a prolific writer on taste and etiquette, announced that "like a Fairy's wand" the Exhibition had banished bad taste from the homes of America, demonstrating that there was no end to the tasks machines could perform; they could print fabric, stamp leather, plate silver, cut glass, weave carpets, turn furniture, tat lace. The author of a book called *The House Beautiful* commented that there had never been so many books on the subject of houses beautiful. They were written, he said, so that "on a matter which concerns everybody, everybody may know what is the latest word." Thus the how-to books moved confidently into a much more difficult field than that of how to make a wheelbarrow—even more difficult than that of how to tip a hat. They now proposed to enter millions of American parlors and, no matter who lived in them, rearrange and adorn them according to "elevated taste." And who was to decide what taste was elevated? Charles Perkins, president of the Boston Art Club, advised deferring to "men of cultivated artistic feelings" when it came to such matters, just as one turned to jurists on points of law and theologians on theology.

Most Americans did so without urging. They loved conformity. The Puritan idea of doing things in groups had spread wherever Yankees migrated, and to differ from one's neighbors in any area of behavior was regarded as eccentric if not positively immoral. "Togetherness" was expected. Even to fence one's property was generally considered an unfriendly act. The antebellum landscape architect Andrew Jackson Downing, whom Mr. Perkins would undoubtedly have included on his list of men of cultivated artistic feelings, believed that "cooperation, kindness, and regard for all" should lead people not to fence. Downing wanted Americans to live in parklike surroundings, and fences interfered with the vista. Forty years later, a leading etiquette and how-to book called *Hill's Manual* upheld his views. Fences, said *Hill's*, are put up by those who expect trouble from their neighbors; they prevent acquaintance with neighbors and make a resident "careless of his obligations toward others, and consequently . . . a less worthy citizen." Unfenced houses, *Hill's* went on, are evidence of a higher civilization. In an "elegant park with winding pathways," neighbors can congregate. "All delight in the scene and all are made better by it. . . . While the resident could be coarse and selfish in his own little lot, he is now thrown upon his good behavior as he mingles with others on the beautiful grounds."

Downing, the father of the American suburb, died in a steamboat accident in 1852 and did not live to see the completion of the first experiment in suburban living, Llewellyn Park, in West Orange, New Jersey. As far as shrubbery and vistas were concerned, Llewellyn Park would surely have been Downing's idea of Eden, but, unfortunately, even as in Eden, the Devil took up residence. There was scandalous talk about atheists and unorthodox marriage ceremonies, and a case of a young woman buried in the park "with only a shroud between her body and Mother Earth." Conformity soon closed in, the free spirits were asked to move, and Llewellyn Park settled down in respectability.

Downing's concept of planned suburbs reflected a new American need: a longing to escape from the tensions of the cities and of business. Now that Nature was no longer to be feared, people wanted to enjoy her gentler side. Trees were beautiful when they did not have to be felled; grass and flowers were beautiful when there was plenty of cheap Irish labor available to take care of them. Downing used "the colors of nature"—russet, gray, rose, or yellow—to paint his houses, instead of the traditional white, which made a house stand out sharply from its surroundings.

In the cities, pangs were suddenly felt for the rapidly receding countryside, and in 1857 New York began to lay out Central Park so that its citizens need not travel miles in order to skate, sled, or row. Flowers were first sold on New York streets in the 1850's; before that, the notion of paying for flowers would have seemed preposterous. Sentimental ladies pressed flowers in books, and etiquette manuals wrote of the language of flowers: "The gentleman presents a Red Rose—'I love you.' The lady admits a partial reciprocation of the sentiment by returning a Purple Pansy—'You occupy my thoughts.' The gentleman presses his suit still further by an Everlasting Pea. . . . The lady replies by a Daisy, in which she says—'I will think of it.' The gentleman, in his enthusiasm, plucks and presents a Shepherd's Purse—'I offer you my all.'" A young man had to be careful what flowers he sent.

An America where flowers had to be bought and people paid thousands of dollars for a painting of an oak tree was worlds away from the simple place where flowers were wild and oak trees merely a challenge to the woodsman. Nature was now harnessed to culture, and so were the American people.

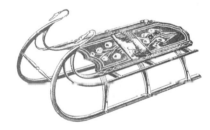

The child's coaster, top, and the horse-drawn sled above were offered in a trade catalog of the 1880's.

Golden Moments

ℰ

*In which the Genteel
Generations pass with
measured gait Life's many
Milestones from the Cradle
to the Grave, & the
Nation adopts its Calendar
of Patriotic Holidays*

The restlessness and rootlessness of nineteenth-century Americans was often noted and deplored by foreign observers. Americans themselves were aware of the phenomenon, but saw it as necessary to their growing prosperity and enterprise. "Home is where you hang your hat" and "Home is where the heart is" were popular sayings. "Love of country rather than love of home characterizes the American people," was the judgment of *Gems of Deportment*, an etiquette book published in 1881. Nevertheless, home was an ideal even when not a reality, as the immense popularity of the song "Home, Sweet Home" attests. Of the significant moments of life, from birth to death, most were passed at home, and especially the first and the last. The custom of coming into the world and going out of it by way of a hospital was not usual until the 1920's.

By the time of the Civil War, even the most "delicate"-minded woman preferred a doctor rather than a midwife to attend her lying-in. The moment of delivery was deeply private. The baby's father paced the hall outside the matrimonial bedroom. Children of the household went to stay with relatives or friends, to be told later that the new arrival had been brought by the doctor in a bottle. Pregnant women did not even mention that a baby was expected. Writing of the 1890's in Boston, Marian Lawrence Peabody tells us that when a silver wedding party was planned for her parents, "it was obvious" that her mother was expecting another baby, but neither she (a young woman in her early twenties) nor anyone else dreamed of asking when it was due. "Such things were never mentioned and never had been. I imagine this was usual in those days but it certainly was hard on the children and made for many embarrassments and misunderstandings and worries. Only one person — a schoolmate — had ever spoken of such a personal affair to me and I was so shocked I never spoke to her again if I could help it." The baby arrived just three days after the party, presumably to nearly everyone's surprise.

ℰ

The wayward husband, sneaking home with shoes in hand at 3 A.M., and the wounded wife play time-honored roles in this satiric lithograph by Haskell & Allen, c. 1871.

Golden youth, sketched by Winslow Homer

Nineteenth-century etiquette books were admirably thorough. They stood ready with first-aid etiquette not only for novices in society but for inexperienced businessmen as well. Only two areas of life were consistently side-stepped: sex and pregnancy. Nor were any hints dropped by novelists, who usually managed to waft their characters magically from wedding day to baby's first tooth. There were no baby showers, of course, nor were presents offered before a child was born. One reason for the taboo was the prevailing squeamishness about sex; another and sounder reason was the high mortality of mothers and newborn infants. It was a time for prayer, hope, and silence. Once a baby was born, however, the manners books were ready to take over. "Fashionable mammas . . . should remember that in our harsh climate maternity is beset by much feebleness as to nerves in both mother and child," warned Mrs. M. E. W. Sherwood, an editor of *Harper's Bazar* and the Emily Post of her day, in *Manners and Social Usages* (1884). "Therefore a long seclusion in the nursery is advised before the dangerous period of entertaining one's friends begins." Mid-Victorian America, sentimental about its colonial forebears, revived the Puritan custom of regaling the first callers received by the new mother with a drink known as caudle. It consisted of oatmeal gruel, boiled for hours with raisins and spices and mixed with Madeira or rum. Callers waited a month or six weeks before paying their respects, by which time a colonial mother would have been back hoeing the turnips or stirring a kettle of soap. Says Mrs. Sherwood, "Mamma receives her friends in a tea gown or some pretty convalescent wrap, very often made of velvet or plush . . . elaborately trimmed with cascades of lace down the front. The baby is, of course, shown, but not much handled."

Godparents were to be selected from among responsible people who should be prepared to watch over the religious education of the child and guide him to adulthood. A little present was expected from each godparent—"a silver cup or porringer, knife, fork and spoon, silver basin, coral tooth-cutter, or coral and bells, were the former gifts," Mrs. Sherwood tells us, "but, nowadays, we hear of one wealthy godfather who left a check for $100,000 in the baby's cradle; and it is not unusual for those who can do so to make some very valuable investment for the child." Baptism was usually performed in a church, followed by a party at home and presentation of gifts. "Old-fashioned people give the baby some salt and an egg for good luck, and are particular that he should be carried up-stairs before he is carried down, and that when he goes out first he shall be carried to the house of some near and dear relatives."

"We always name our children, or we are apt to, for some dear friend," Mrs. Sherwood continues. In colonial times, as we have seen, names from the Old Testament were favored. In the early nineteenth century, child naming followed the fashion for classical references, and many a tot learned to answer to Cornelia, Lydia, or Cassandra, Homer, Orestes, or Junius Brutus. The popularity of Scott, Tennyson, and other romantics riveted public attention on such names as Rowena, Percival, Maude, Quentin. Among the humble especially, there was a taste for naming babies after famous men—George Washington, Andrew Jackson, Ulysses Grant. Beginning with the Civil War, many a southern baby acquired the middle name of Lee, and was called by both first and middle name as if the two were one—Sumter Lee, Mary Lee, and so on. The fashion of naming for a friend, mentioned by Mrs. Sherwood, was largely out of favor by the turn of the century—perhaps too many friend-

162

ships had failed, leaving a child with a no-longer-cherished name—and the country became addicted to invented names, sometimes combining names of parents: Mary and David, for instance, might produce Mayvida. Southwesterners, particularly, admired contrived names: Bevelene, Bytha, Zazzelle, Moneer, and of course, the well-known Ima, daughter of former Governor Hogg of Texas. The custom of writing "2nd," "3rd," et cetera after a boy's name became popular in early-nineteenth-century America. By late Victorian times, "Jr." was preferred to designate a son who bore the same name as his father, while "2nd" meant someone who bore the same name as his grandfather or uncle. The use of Roman numerals after a boy's name was a later development, popular on these shores. Through all the name fashions, Mary and John have remained the most common choices.

Holidays stood out as the "golden moments," especially for children and working people. A child's life was embedded in routine, while a laborer toiled up to sixteen hours a day, six days a week. Sundays were not for frivolity. Therefore, when holidays came, they were enjoyed with typical American energy. *Hill's Manual* suggested forming committees that would help extract every moment of pleasure from the holiday. Such committees "should be especially noticeable for the absence of all formality—jollity and mirth reigning supreme. If another committee is appointed outside of the executive, let it be a committee on *fun*." The committee's duties might include arranging a public ball on Washington's Birthday, mass picnics or steamboat excursions on the Fourth of July, and parades and bands on almost every holiday except Christmas. The public still had a surprising appetite for patriotic speeches, although Americans had lost some of their strident chauvinism.

The national attitude toward the English was ambivalent. Visiting royalty was received with enthusiasm and even awe, but the mollycoddle lord was a stock comic character on the stage, and Americans still bridled at real or fancied condescensions from across the water. Even *Town Topics*, a magazine that circulated among the fashionable, liked making fun of the English—and of Americans who aped them. A chat between two dandies was reported:

"Were you at the wedding bweakfast of the Lawrence's, Geawge?"

"Haw. I should wathaw think I wa-as."

"Chawming, I heah."

"Pawfectly intwesting, deah boy. Bay Jawve! You might have fawncied you were in England don't chew know."

By mid-century, Christmas was being celebrated by most Americans with a Christmas tree and presents. The tree was lit with candles. Santa Claus was a nationwide figure, although in some localities he arrived on Christmas Eve and in others on Christmas morning. A turkey dinner on the great day was expected everywhere. (*Hill's* had a toast to suggest for the festive table: "To Christmas hospitality, and the ladies who make it delightful by their *mincing* ways.") "There are some difficulties in giving a Christmas dinner in a large city," remarks Mrs. Sherwood, "as nearly all the waiters are sure to be drunk, and the cook has also, perhaps, been at the frumenty."

On New Year's Day in New York and in other large cities where New York's manners were a standard for the fashionable set, the old Dutch custom of visiting was carried out as a social ritual. The ladies stayed at home and received, dispensing punch, oysters, and a medley of other treats. The gentlemen, wrapped in cloaks and braving any sort of weather, made a tireless round

Printed cotton cutout of Santa

Love Preserved—an 1851 valentine

of calls. In the early part of the century, a New York gentleman could complete his list in an afternoon. By the Victorian era, the number of calls gentlemen were expected to make had grown so large that some had to finish their rounds the next day. It was taxing work. More than one etiquette book warned against the hazard of lingering over too many punch bowls and ending up a social liability. Besieged hostesses complained that "indifferent strangers" often drifted in with one's friends. St. Valentine's Day, though not an official holiday, provided titillation to young people. The first commercial valentines appeared in the 1830's. Between that time and the Civil War, St. Valentine's Day rated next to Christmas in terms of pleasure and excitement.

The tradition of sunrise services on Easter was brought to America by Moravians in 1741. The Easter rabbit also came from Germany, while the egg as a symbol of Easter and the Resurrection is as old as Christianity. Children in Washington first rolled Easter eggs at the suggestion of Dolley Madison, who asked to have the Capitol grounds turned over to local youngsters. During Rutherford B. Hayes's administration, the Capitol groundskeepers complained that egg rolling spoiled the lawns, whereupon Mrs. Hayes invited the children to the White House. Perhaps because of the Puritans, May Day had not become a festival for adults in this country, though young lovers might "go a-Maying" in the countryside. Victorian children made May baskets, filled them with flowers and small presents, and left them at one another's doors. Memorial Day may owe its origin to women of Columbus, Mississippi, who, in 1866, took flowers to the graves of both Confederate and Union dead. Their act, in that time of bitterness, touched hearts both North and South; and in 1882 May 30 was set aside as a day for honoring the American war dead. Labor Day did not become a nationwide holiday until 1894, though a few states had marked the day for several years. Lincoln's Birthday was declared a legal holiday in Illinois in 1892. By 1909, the hundredth anniversary of his birth, it was observed in all but sixteen states. Most Halloween customs were brought by the Irish, but "Trick or Treat" is a twentieth-century development. Thanksgiving was first proclaimed a national holiday in 1863, when Abraham Lincoln called upon citizens of the Union to give thanks for the victory at Gettysburg. Gradually it became more a day of massive meals than of actual thanksgiving.

First Communion and Confirmation were important social occasions in America only among Catholics—perhaps because of deep-seated Puritan prejudice against anything that looked like religious fuss. Children's birthdays were usually observed about as they are today.

For a small percentage of American boys, there were the golden moments of college life. The average age of entering freshmen was seventeen, though boys as young as fourteen were readily admitted if they could pass the examinations. Edward Everett Hale, later to become one of New England's leading Unitarian ministers, was a wide-eyed boy of thirteen when he was sent up from Boston Latin School to make application. "The examination was to last from six in the morning to seven in the evening on [the first] day, and from six till two on the next day; and with the exception of an hour for dinner we were kept in the various recitation rooms all the time." This grinding schedule, he wrote later, was supposed to give prospective students a taste of college life.

Greek-letter fraternities began at Union and Hamilton colleges in the twenties and thirties; by 1840 the idea had proved so popular that there were chapters at most eastern colleges. They filled a social need, for college administrations backed away from the lighter side of life. Founded for religious reasons, most colleges believed in teaching morals, not manners, and frowned on fraternities, fearing lest they develop an antireligious bent. Mark Hopkins, president of Williams College, grumbled, "They create class and factions, and put men socially in regard to each other into an artificial and false position." However, he admitted that "one object of some of the Societies here is the cultivation of manners, and so far they have improved."

Organized college sports did not develop as fast as might be supposed, due to the same Puritan distrust of anything that looked like fun. At Harvard in 1826, a German instructor set up bars, trapezes, and flying rings, but they were not popular. Most of the college turned out for a cross-country run, led by the German, but were stopped by an outraged property owner before reaching the finish line. Reverend Hale thought the inactivity of students stemmed from "utter ignorance that there was any connection between body and mind worth notice," an ignorance not likely to be altered until the senior year, when students were obliged to attend lectures on "the art of preserving health" by a member of the Harvard medical faculty. "The joke was that we did not go till our constitutions were destroyed." At Brown, President Francis Wayland joined his students for a swing on newly installed gymnasium equipment, but even that did not suffice to popularize gymnastics. Most students came from farms and equated physical exercise with productive labor; such activity, therefore, seemed to them a foolish way to pass the time. Until the 1850's, when intercollegiate competition was introduced and the gymnasium movement was at last accepted, most students were content with skating and impromptu games of football, cricket, bowling, and "bat and ball." At Harvard they swam in the Charles and walked amid the pretty surroundings of Cambridge. When a gymnasium was built at Amherst in the 1860's, it bore the inscription "Keep thyself pure: the body is the temple of the Holy Ghost" — thus providing a Puritan excuse for what some thought of as self-indulgence.

The Boston theater was out of bounds to Harvard undergraduates during the first four decades of the nineteenth century, and students were required to spend the Sabbath eve quietly in their rooms. During the week, classes were held every other hour, from 6 A.M. to 4 P.M., so that college life would necessarily remain centered on the campus.

Student riots were far from rare. At Harvard, one fracas began like this (according to a college poet):

> *Nathan threw a piece of bread.*
> *And hit Abijah on the head.*
> *The wrathful Freshman, in a trice,*
> *Sent back another bigger slice;*
> *Which, being butter'd pretty well,*
> *Made greasy work where'er it fell.*
> *And thus arose a fearful battle;*
> *The coffee-cups and saucers rattle;*
> *The bread-bowls fly at woful rate,*
> *And break many a learned pate. . . .*

Before "the Bread and Butter Riot" subsided, four sophomores, one of them the future president of South Carolina College, were suspended. A

The freshman

The sophomore

The junior

Views by J. N. Mead, Harvard Class of '51

165

second rumpus, this time in their behalf, resulted in suspension of several more students, among them Ralph Waldo Emerson. In the 1830's there was an extended period of student disorder, brought about by the unpopular administration of President Josiah Quincy. Quincy thought it his job "to make the College a nursery of high-minded, high-principled, well-taught, well-conducted, well-bred gentlemen." Some of the student body objected to being in any kind of nursery, and in the spring of 1834 there were window smashings, bonfires in Harvard Yard, and other riotous behavior, leading to the dismissal of all sophomores for the year. Quincy compounded his unpopularity by violating an ancient canon of academic freedom—he invited civil authorities to prosecute the offenders. Not before the "black flag of rebellion" had been raised by the remaining students, more property damaged, and more boys dismissed was peace restored.

By the middle of the nineteenth century the trend at all colleges was toward more relaxed discipline. As with children, so with young men: they were no longer regarded as full of natural evil which must be crushed by severity, but as malleable souls that would respond to reason and kindness. "The chief concern," said the president of Union College in 1854, "has been to teach the young men to bring themselves under the rule of inward principle rather than of outward fear and restraint." Reverend Hale, summing up the benefits of his college career, said, "we acquainted ourselves with friends from all parts of the United States; we got broader views of politics and society than those we had picked up at home; and we certainly left college willing to do our duty. . . . At the moment when one receives a piece of parchment . . . his boyhood may be said to end and his manhood to begin."

But the number of young men who spent four years at college was very small—in 1870 there were only eight thousand graduating in a total population of over thirty-eight million. Most college men were headed for the professions. If a boy was going into business, he was generally believed to be better off as a clerk or salesman, learning from the ground up, than acquiring theoretical notions at college. In *Letters from a Self-made Merchant to His Son* (1903), George Horace Lorimer, editor of *The Saturday Evening Post*, satirized a common view toward the college graduate in business: "Got him in a bank, but while he knew more about the history of banking than the president, and more about political economy than the board of directors, he couldn't learn the difference between a fiver that the Government turned out and one that was run off on a hand press in a Halsted Street basement. Got him a job on a paper, but while he knew six different languages and all the facts about the Arctic regions, and the history of dancing from the days of Old Adam down to those of Old Nick, he couldn't write up a satisfactory account of the Ice-Men's Ball. Could prove that two and two made four by trigonometry and geometry, but couldn't learn to keep books; was thick as thieves with all the high-toned poets, but couldn't write a good, snappy, merchantable streetcar ad. . . . The last I heard of him he was writing articles on Why Young Men Fail and making a success of it, because failing was the one subject on which he was practical."

In the year 1870 the number of women to graduate from college was 1,378. By 1900 the figure had risen to 5,237, but was still so small as to make college women almost freakish. Coeducation was less popular in the East than in the West, where women had, from the earliest days, been more readily

Gibson Boy scoring for Yale

accepted by men as equals and working partners. Most Victorian Americans, however, shared the views expressed by one clergyman: "Must we crowd education on our daughters, and for the sake of having them 'intellectual,' make them puny, nervous, and their whole earthly existence a struggle between life and death?" The usual path for a young woman, therefore, was to write *finis* to her studies when in her mid-teens, and then to spend a few precious years of flirting and being courted.

The etiquette of courting, Victorian style, was more restrictive than in earlier times. No more cozy buggy riding or sleighing alone with a young man. No more close sitting on the parlor sofa after the family had gone to bed. Mrs. Farrar's *Young Lady's Friend*, written in the late thirties, had presaged the change. She had thought that mothers or sisters should be present when a young girl received a gentleman caller. Young people would thus be saved "from extremes that they would themselves condemn, in a cooler moment." She quoted Mrs. Sigourney's rule for insuring propriety: "Converse always with your female friends, as if a gentleman were of the party, and with young men, as if your female companions were present." She advised young girls to remember that it was for eternity they were preparing, and therefore, they should not take up all their thoughts with love and marriage. "Never join in any rude plays, that will subject you to being kissed or handled in any way by gentlemen. Do not suffer your hand to be held or squeezed, without showing that it displeases you by instantly withdrawing it. If a finger is put out to touch a chain that is round your neck, or a breast-pin that you are wearing, draw back, and take it off for inspection. Accept not unnecessary assistance in putting on cloaks, shawls, over-shoes, or anything of the sort. Be not lifted in and out of carriages, on or off a horse; sit not with another in a place that is too narrow; read not out of the same book; let not your eagerness to see anything induce you to place your head close to another person's." Thus could a young lady, ever on guard against familiarities, avoid "that desecration of the person, which has too often led to vice."

Forty or fifty years later, etiquette books agreed that young girls must be "matronized" on all occasions, but apparently there were still unchaperoned couples, particularly in the country, for Mrs. Sherwood and her colleagues found it necessary to rebuke them. Mrs. Sherwood attacked the "liberty permitted to engaged couples in rural neighborhoods, where the young girl is allowed to go on a journey at her lover's expense. A girl's natural protectors should know better than to allow this. They know that her purity is her chief attraction to man, and that a certain coyness and virginal freshness are the dowry she should bring her future husband. Suppose that this engagement is broken off. How will she be accepted by another lover after having enjoyed the hospitality of the first? . . . This evil of excessive liberty and of the loose etiquette of our young people cannot be rooted out by laws. It must begin at the hearth-stone. Family life must be reformed; young ladies must be brought up with greater strictness. The bloom of innocence should not be brushed off by careless hands. If a mother leaves her daughter matronless, to receive attentions without her dignified presence, she opens the door to an unworthy man, who may mean marriage or not. He may be a most unsuitable husband even if he *does* mean marriage. If he takes the young lady about, paying for her cab hire, her theatre tickets, and her journeyings, and then drops her, whom have they to thank but themselves that

"Hug Me Closer, George," by Currier & Ives

her bloom is brushed off, that her character suffers, that she is made ridiculous, and marries some one whom she does not love, for a home.

"Men, as they look back on their own varied experience, are apt to remember with great respect the women who were cold and distant. They love the fruit which hung the highest, the flower which was guarded, and which did not grow under their feet in the highway. . . ."

The gentleman letter writer

Young ladies who took this sort of advice to heart were understandably ill at ease, but the manuals scolded about that as well. "A want of perfect self-possession," says *The Illustrated Manners Book* (1855), causes "an affected tittering or an hysterical 'he! he!' which fills the pauses of all their sentences. You will hear a very nice, pretty girl running on in this absurd fashion: 'Good morning, he! he! Charming morning, isn't it? he! he! he! Where have you been this ever so long? he! he! he! . . . Poor Mrs. Thompson! what a sad misfortune that was! he! he! he!' etc." Another arbiter of deportment begs young readers not to "jiggle" nervously, as though they were strung like marionettes. It seems a wonder, under these circumstances, that suitors ever had the courage or even the wish to propose. Etiquette books stood ready to help them do so by letter, in case a personal confrontation seemed too agonizing. Sample letters for a young man and woman went as follows:

"Dear, dear Clara: You cannot be indifferent to the fact that I have long devotedly loved you; and at the hour of parting, I feel that I cannot go without telling you my heart, and asking you if I may not have your love in return. And now, while I am asking, will you not take me and my heart, and in turn allow me to be your protector through life? . . ."

"Sir: the attentions which you have so long and so assiduously shown to me have not escaped my notice. . . . I admit the truth, that pleased and flattered by such attentions, I fondly endeavored to persuade myself that attachment toward me had formed itself in your breast. . . .

"On consulting my parents, I find that they do not object to your proposal; therefore, I have only this to add—may we still entertain the same regard which we have hitherto cherished for each other, until it shall ripen into that affection which wedlock shall sanction, and which lapse of time will not allow to fade. Believe me to be, Yours, sincerely attached."

This young woman naturally consulted her parents, for the etiquette books had warned her that she was not a practical judge of character. According to *Homes of our Country*, she must watch out for male idleness, extravagance, a bad temper, and bad morals; avoid the proud, the censorious, the revengeful, the teller of *double-entendre* jokes, and all men more stupid than she. In addition, she must "avoid as . . . a plague-spot the companionship of the scoffer at religion" and should be suspicious of any man who delayed marrying unless he planned to be a soldier or a missionary first. "There are few men who are bachelors for good and manly reasons."

In the South, young ladies never had as much freedom as their northern counterparts. A northerner visiting there in 1804 said, "Gentlemen cannot visit young ladies often unless they declare themselves as intended suitors . . . . Young ladies do not dare to ride out or appear abroad with young gentlemen. . . ." In 1840 the situation was the same: "No set of girls in Christendom were watched with more vigilant eyes. . . ." And in antebellum Washington, "As for a buggy alone, perish the thought!" A northern woman who worked as a governess in the South wrote, "In the North the young lady is left alone with her beaux and pa and ma retire. In the South it is deemed indecorous for them to be left alone . . . and the mother or some member of the family is always in the room; and if none of these, a female slave is seated on the rug at the door. . . . I was told by a married gentleman, a few days since, that his wife never took his arm till she took it to be led to church on her wedding day; and that he never had an opportunity of kissing her but twice while he was addressing her (they were six months engaged!) and in both cases by means of a strategem he resorted to of drugging a peach with laudanum which he gave to the attending servant, and thereby put her into a sound sleep."

In the North, engaged couples were often allowed more freedom than courting couples, even after the advent of chaperons. Etiquette books deplored it, however. Writing in 1904, Margaret E. Sangster warned against long engagements, for they led to a couple's reaching "the end of the matters about which they can talk. . . . They spend long evenings in each other's company, and often the man sees only the girl, her parents and her family avoiding the parlor as if it held some fearful danger, and the man lingers late, far too late. No engaged couple are sensible to meet night after night, and stay side by side till eleven or twelve o'clock, exchanging the caressing demonstrations that custom, in some localities, permits to the betrothed."

There must have been a sigh of relief in a girl's family when the wedding day finally arrived. The wedding ceremony was usually performed at home before the Civil War, more often at church thereafter—again, an influence from abroad. A wedding breakfast followed, in the bride's home if possible. If they were married at home, the happy pair took their vows beneath a floral bell or a floral umbrella or in a grotto of flowers built in a bay window. Mrs. Sherwood was not quite sure that she liked some of the "latest freaks in floral fashion"—a bower of tall ferns, meeting over the heads of bride and groom, or a house of roses. She feared that they suggested a bathhouse or a confessional.

A "stylish wedding" described in a manners book of the fifties called for two bridesmaids, simply dressed in white. A bride of the eighties might have as many as eight bridesmaids, dressed in pastel colors, plus a couple of little flower girls in Kate Greenaway dresses. The bride's attire in both cases was all white, with a white lace veil and few jewels. The author of the fifties book found it necessary to add, "We hope and believe that the frolics which were once customary at weddings, have become obsolete—the deep and riotous drinking, from which the bridegroom had to be carried to bed; the games and jests, often indecent; the general kissing of the bride, a distasteful and even disgusting practice; the ceremonies of bedding the couple, which may have been all well enough in the 'good old times' we read about, but which are utterly inconsistent with our present ideas of refinement." Books of the later decades did not even choose to recall such vulgarities.

The groom and his ushers embellished their frock coats with enormous boutonnieres of lilies of the valley, gardenias, or stephanotis, and white flowers also ornamented the ears of the horses and the coats of the coachman and footmen. At a summer wedding one type of flower might furnish the motif for the decorations—daisies or roses, for instance. For an autumn bride, Mrs. Sherwood suggests that several "earnest and unselfish girl friends" get together and sew autumn leaves on a piece of coarse fabric, forming a picture

The elegant bachelor above lacks nothing in life—but a wife. The bride below has just made her match.

of a pair of lovers, Romeo and Juliet or Abelard and Héloïse, for example.

To the question, "Who should be asked to a wedding?" Mrs. Sherwood replies decidedly, "All your visiting list, or none." Little advice is offered concerning the wedding journey, except to warn against an "outward display of tenderness. Such exhibitions in the cars or in public places as one often sees, of the bride laying her head on her husband's shoulder, holding hands, or kissing, are at once vulgar and indecent." After the wedding journey, the bridal pair announced that they were ready to receive friends by sending out "at home" cards. Anyone who previously knew either the bride or the groom and who failed to receive a card had to assume that his friendship was no longer desired.

The change from the illusions of a Victorian girlhood to the realities of kitchen, bedroom, and nursery must have been less than golden for myriads of young women, but few questioned or complained. According to a French observer of the eighties, the contrast was striking. The unmarried girl, he said, was "independent as independent can be, but very pure . . . flirts all the season with this one or that one, and dismisses him at the close in favor of another; goes out alone, travels alone. When the fancy strikes her, she travels with a gentleman friend or walks anywhere with him; puts boundless confidence in him; conjugal intimacy seems to exist between them; she lets him tell what he feels, talk of love from morning till night, but she never gives him permission to kiss so much as her hand. . . . After marriage she is a mother annually; is alone all day; hears at night nothing except discussions about patent machinery, unexplosive petroleum, chemical manures. She will then let her daughters enjoy the liberty she used without grave abuse."

Mother-in-law in a frontal assault

Such standards seem to have remained stabile for at least three generations, until the moral upheaval that followed the First World War. *Home Life in America*, published in 1910, echoes the judgments of earlier writers, commenting that the American girl marries the man of her own choosing but is untouched by passionate, romantic love. "Some cause, possibly climatic, has certainly reduced the intensity of sex-emotion. . . . Perhaps the independence of girlhood makes for a certain hardness instead of a strength of character; perhaps living on the surface of their impractical superficial existence before marriage has precluded any deeper appreciation of emotion, and makes the selection of a life-partner more of a cotillion feature than the cataclysmic decision with which she is credited."

Despite the fact that families moved often and young people left the nest early—or perhaps because of it—family life was deeply reverenced. The immense popularity of Louisa M. Alcott's *Little Women* owed much to its vivid presentation of a close-knit, loving family. Novels and short stories of family life were very popular, as was the royal Mother of the Age at Windsor, with her nine children and widening circle of grandchildren. A story in *Godey's Lady's Book* for April, 1845, epitomized the Victorian standard of domesticity, and might have been written any time, anywhere, in Victorian America: "A quiet, gentle, wifely creature was Lucy Torrington; pretty and pleasing, devoted to her husband and child, and as happy, after three years of married life, as the trouble of looking after servants and the anxiety about baby's tooth-cutting would allow. Her husband, an easy, good-humoured, pleasant fellow, was doing what is usually termed 'an excellent business.' He was very domestic, never dined out, staid home in the evenings, and read the newspaper and the last novel, played a little on the flute as an accompaniment to Lucy's somewhat infrequent PIANISMS (a new word, gentle reader,) and, on the whole, was a sort of pattern husband, as things go."

William Dean Howells called a happy marriage a "long life of holidays." For many it doubtless was; but everyone could make a holiday of a wedding anniversary. Doting couples like the Torringtons were wont to make their anniversaries occasions for elaborate parties. The first to be celebrated was the wooden anniversary, the fifth one. Ever-helpful *Hill's Manual* had a toast to suggest: "And may all the children be *chips of the old block*." Suitable presents might be furniture, wooden baskets filled with flowers, or "watercolors framed in wood-carvings in bog oak." The tin anniversary after ten years and the crystal after fifteen gave guests no special problem in regard to gifts—tin pans were always welcome for the kitchen, and cut crystal was a Victorian delight. The crystal and silver anniversaries—the latter marking twenty-five years of marriage—were thought particularly important, and very often the bride wore her wedding dress and the whole ceremony was lovingly re-enacted, complete with all surviving ushers and bridesmaids. If these were unavailable, the couple's children filled in. A crystal wedding is described in the popular Victorian children's series *Dotty Dimple*. Dotty, aged about six, acted as bridesmaid. "Mrs. Parlin was to wear the same dove-colored silk and bridal veil . . . and Mr. Parlin the same coat and white vest, though they were decidedly out of fashion by this time. . . . The same clergyman officiated now who had married Mr. and Mrs. Parlin fifteen years before; and after he had married them over again, he made a speech which caused Dotty to cry a little. . . ."

"The twentieth anniversary of one's wedding is never celebrated," announces Mrs. Sherwood. "It is considered very unlucky to do so. The Scotch think one or the other will die within the year if the twentieth anniversary is even alluded to." But the twenty-fifth anniversary might be as grand as one could afford. Mrs. Sherwood suggested invitations printed in silver and the sending of silver gifts engraved with a monogram and love knot. If held in the morning (any time up to five o'clock was "morning" in the Victorian social world), "the hostess should take care not to be too splendid." But an evening celebration permitted any amount of splendor. "In savage communities [the wife] would dig the earth, wait upon her lord, and stand behind him while he eats; in the modern silver wedding he helps her to fried oysters and champagne, and stands while she sits." For those celebrating their golden wedding anniversary, gifts "must be somewhat circumscribed," says Mrs. Sherwood, alluding in her ladylike way to the expense. "Some delicate-minded people," she goes on, "cause a line to be printed on their invitations, 'No presents received.'" For decorations, Mrs. Sherwood suggests golden roses, autumn leaves, sheaves of ripe corn, a marriage bell made of ripe wheat, and of course, a houseful of descendants. This was the most golden of all possible golden moments.

Funerals can hardly be classified as golden moments, but for Victorian Americans they were at least as important as christenings and weddings and were surrounded by strict etiquette. In this respect, Victorians were like Puritans, who set great store by the number of mourners who followed the corpse to the graveside and by the quality and amount of food and drink offered afterward. Victorians adorned the hearse with plumes, from two to

Suitable wedding and anniversary gifts offered by Reed & Barton c. 1885 included the lidded butter dish above and the combination napkin ring-candlestick below.

171

seven or eight. Passersby counted them, for they indicated the financial status of the deceased. Any congressman who died in Washington was entitled to a state funeral that included an impressive array of carriages — even though most of them might roll along empty for lack of mourners. The funeral procession of a prominent citizen usually included bands from various fraternal orders, the local fire company, or organization of Civil War veterans. As the authors of *The History of American Funeral Directing* put it, "The bereaved felt they had an obligation to insure that the funeral provided the fullest measure of respect for the dead; and in a time when the measure of things was becoming increasingly worldly they were likely to translate this respect into material objects and display."

However, there was a subtle difference between the colonial and the Victorian views of death. The colonials had been matter of fact about it. In the 1740's, George Whitefield, the apostle of the Great Revival, composed a lengthy hymn to be sung at his funeral. It began:

> *Ah! Lovely appearance of death,*
> *No sight upon earth is so fair;*
> *Not all the gay pageants that breathe,*
> *Can with a dead body compare.*

Death poems of the first half of the nineteenth century were less bluntly necrophilic, but usually could not resist lingering for a verse or two on the subject of the clay-colored corpse, decay, worms, and dust. Poets professional and amateur seem to have seized pen in hand whenever a friend or relative died. Mrs. Sigourney must have turned out hundreds of elegiac works — "The Holy Dead," "The Tomb," and so on. Seeking an explanation for the high mortality of the young, many people came to the conclusion that the good die young and that therefore an early death was desirable. Evidence of ill health in the complexion of young girls was termed "an interesting pallor." Robust and rosy-cheeked young people were suspected of being rather too earthly. Children's books, far from sparing their readers from what must have seemed a terrifying reality, dwelt on the subject in detail. Mary Pilkington, one of the more prolific antebellum writers, assured little girls "'Tis virtue makes an early grave." Elsewhere she comforted boys with an example "calculated to impress the youthful mind with an admiration of virtuous Principles." Her model youth was:

> *Struck by stern death's unerring dart when every virtue bloomed,*
> *When rich perfection graced his brest then was his heart entombed.*

Nor were children spared any of the grisly details of death. One nursery offering of the 1820's went like this:

THE CHILD:
> *Tell me, mamma, if I must die one day as little baby died,*
> *And look so very pale and lie down in the pit-hole by its side.*

THE MOTHER:
> *'Tis true, my love, that you must die; the God who made you says you must.*
> *And every one of us shall lie like the dear baby in the dust.*
> *These hands and feet and busy head shall waste and crumble quite away;*
> *But though your body shall be dead, there is a part which can't decay.*

(Continued on Page 174)

Bereaved before their loved one's picture

Washington: 1857

The Capital, as described by an anonymous citizen. In these excerpts from his book, it is seen that knowing protocol and succeeding in politics were related.

There is no place in the United States where less attention is paid to mere money than at the seat of government; and the millionaire, whose magnificent equipage attracts attention in the commercial cities, is surprised at the little influence he exercises here. No one is elevated in [this] society by his residence. . . . It is no unusual thing to find a Senator, whose lofty talents and gifted eloquence are the theme of every tongue, plainly lodged with his family at furnished apartments. Hence, in Washington the tone of society is more elevated, freer from restraint, and consequently more agreeable, than in most of the other cities. It is quite common in Washington to make visits by card. Ordinarily, the lady of the family or her daughters drive to the houses of their acquaintances . . . and drop their cards without leaving their carriage. When [a visitor] has gained admission, he should never . . . throw off the garb of ceremony, even in the apartment of the most familiar friend. Guests to evening parties are expected to assemble between nine and ten o'clock. It is not unusual for persons coming from the country to find themselves in an awkward position by going to the house of their entertainer before this time. Once . . . an exceedingly plain-mannered . . . wife of a member of Congress . . . received an invitation to an evening party . . . and . . . complied with it by visiting the house at six. . . . She was received with kindness, but an embarrassment which she could not fail to mark, and, after the assemblage of the guests, was glad to escape, deeply mortified at her error. If any accident occurs [at a party] it should pass unnoticed, especially by the entertainer. A lady who had suddenly sprang into affluence gave a large party to her friends in her new house. During the evening a servant . . . overturned a large quantity of ice-cream. . . . This was too much for the good lady's philosophy, who exclaimed, "There goes the ice-cream over my new Turkey carpet," and fell to the task of removing it with her own hands, infinitely to the amusement of her guests and the mortification of her friends. Each of the members of the Cabinet, once or twice during the season . . . give a grand fête, rather celebrated for the number of guests than any thing else. Invitations to these fêtes are given to hundreds of persons with whom the entertainer has no personal acquaintance. These parties, like the public levées of the President, are intended to be in keeping with the peculiar character of our institutions; and it is remarkable what order and decorum prevail at both, notwithstanding the absence of all force except the self respect of the guests present. Every citizen of the United States who visits Washington considers that he has a claim to visit the Chief Magistrate of the Union; and he is accordingly presented to him, and, after *shaking hands* and conversing for a few moments, retires, delighted with the suavity of the President, and elevated in his own estimation. It is easier to gain an interview with the President of the United States than with the most insignificant, petty noble in a monarchy.

But as the century progressed, less was said about the crumbling hands and feet, more about the "part which can't decay." The Puritan settlers' favorite gravestone decoration, death's heads, had been largely supplanted in the eighteenth century by cherubs blowing trumps of doom; now in the nineteenth century, lambs and weeping angels came into favor, along with such epitaphs as these, suggested by *Hill's Manual:* "All Is Well," "Gone Home," "Absent, Not Dead," and "Over In the Summer Land." A Puritan would have thought them all blasphemous lies.

A ladies' magazine called *Casket*, briefly popular during the 1830's, would have had to change its name, had it survived into the sixties, for by that time the word *casket* no longer connoted a pretty repository for jewels or love letters. The wedge-shaped coffin, in use since medieval times, had been replaced by a rectangular box which gradually became known as a casket — "in order to obviate in some degree the disagreeable sensation produced by a coffin." By the time of the Philadelphia Centennial of 1876, the casket business was of such importance that Stein Patent Burial Casket Works, the leader in the field, had its own exhibit at the fair. Stein had made his name by creating the casket in which James Gordon Bennett, the celebrated editor of the New York *Herald,* was laid to rest, in June of 1872. A reporter from the New York *Sun* described it in awe-struck detail: "The casket . . . is remarkable for its elegance. It is nearly square, and made of a species of wood said to be more durable than any metal. The side of the panels are covered with the most costly Lyons velvet. The handles, of which they are eight, are of solid silver. They represent two hands grasping a rod about eight inches long. The lid is in two parts, or panels, and made of French crystal plate glass. Two panels of Lyons velvet are made so as to cover the glass when required. The lid is hung on heavy silver hinges, and is secured by two heavy locks. The entire casket is surrounded by a massive moulding of silver, forming a framework which will survive the lapse of ages. The inside is upholstered with white satin, silk, and Venetian lace, heavy silken tassels dropping from each corner." Among other devices intended to mitigate the "harsh realities of the grave" were artificial grass covering the gravesite, canopies to shield casket and mourners from inclement weather, and the custom of leaving the casket on top of the ground, not to be buried until the mourners had departed. Cremation, associated with pagan Rome, was virtually unheard of before the 1870's. During the last quarter of the century less than 1 percent of the dead were cremated.

Not until after mid-century were the unhappy duties of preparing the deceased for burial taken from the hands of "delicate" females and assumed by "undertakers of funerals." Up to the early part of the nineteenth century, an undertaker was someone who made coffins; usually he was also a cabinet-maker and upholsterer. The women of the departed's family, aided perhaps by a professional midwife or nurse, washed the corpse and wrapped it in cerements (cloth soaked in wax, pitch, or alum, supposed to delay decomposition). Family and neighbors gathered for a wake. Even if death took place away from home, the body was brought there. Undertaking parlors did not exist before the 1880's and were not much used for funerals until well into this century. The family chose a casket from a catalog that showed a considerable variety of styles, colors, and materials — a change indeed from the days when everyone got a plain board coffin. In small towns neighbors came

The dear departed were often photographed one last time before burial. The daguerreotype below even includes the casket.

spontaneously to "see the corpse," even before it could be laid in a casket, and to bring condolences for the family, as well as cakes, pies, and hot dinners. After the services, neighbors cleaned and tidied the house. If the body was to be embalmed the undertaker brought his equipment to the house. (Embalming fluids were invented in the early sixties, but for years many people objected to their use on moral grounds as a mutilation of the body.)

Detail from a New Hampshire undertaker's ad

Before the days of embalming, the possibility of premature burial was real enough. According to one story, the mother of Robert E. Lee was subject to catatonic trances and during one of them was pronounced dead. The earth was being shoveled on her coffin when the sexton heard feeble cries and knocking from within. The coffin was opened and Mrs. Lee discovered alive. She survived for several years thereafter. In 1883, in Brooklyn, a body awaiting burial in a receiving vault was found out of the coffin, hair disheveled, and the face contorted with horror and despair. The terrible mistake happened often enough to prompt the invention of several devices to permit a prematurely buried person to call for help. A coffin approved by the Patent Office included a bell to be mounted above ground with a long cord running down to the captive's hand. One gentleman on record was buried with an elaborate system of ventilators and a speaking tube that emerged above ground like a periscope.

By American tradition, it was a matter of good manners and neighborliness to attend funerals, even of people who may have been only slight acquaintances. Describing Ohio in its frontier days, one memoirist wrote, "when anyone died, a boy was sent on horseback from house to house to tell the sad tidings. On the day of the funeral, all the men and women in the country round laid aside their work, however important, and attended it. Rough wagons, with boards across for seats, perhaps with a chair for some old grandmother, formed the procession, followed often by men on horseback with their wives behind them. They had no hearse and the best wagon of the settlement held the coffin, and a homespun blanket answered for a pall. . . . I have never seen anything that seemed to me so solemn as those wagons winding through the forests and over rough roads to the half-cleared graveyard of that new country."

Small-town funerals were simpler than city ones, and because of the participation of neighbors, even to the digging and filling of the grave, they were more heart-rending and, psychiatrists might say, more conducive to emotional release. The wake, the funeral, and the grave-filling were to a small American community what the Wailing Wall was to Israel. The Sunday following the funeral, the deceased was eulogized from the pulpit and the bereaved family had to stand up as their names were mentioned.

Fashionable city funerals were sedate and elaborate. The high Victorian age borrowed the European custom of draping the house inside and out with black and purple crape and of dressing the maids in black-ribboned uniforms and the menservants in plain black livery with weeds on their hats. The family carriage might also be lined in black. Protestant funeral services were usually held at home; toward the end of the century, in a church. In either case, there was a strong preference for an open coffin, despite objections from the clergy, who wished to stress the spiritual rather than the temporal. If the deceased's social circle was large, it was permissible to place a death notice in the newspapers, giving brief details of the funeral and the name of the pas-

Funereal floral decoration, 1877

tor who would deliver the eulogy. A memorial poem might accompany the notice, the whole to be printed in suitably somber gothic type. The sending of flowers to a funeral became customary during the last half of the century; old-fashioned people opposed this innovation on the grounds that flowers were pagan, extravagant, and ostentatious. Nevertheless, flowers were in vogue. At the funeral of the Reverend Henry Ward Beecher, in 1887, held in the Brooklyn church where he had preached, the pulpit, chandeliers, gas brackets, Bible stand, and pillars were smothered in roses, lilies, carnations, and azaleas, while the walls, ceiling, and church facade were swathed in ropes of smilax and evergreens. Near the Bible stand was a large pillow of white flowers, monogrammed with the letter *B* in pink roses. Such displays became commonplace, even among the poorer classes, then dwindled with the rising cost of flowers.

A widow was to wear "deep mourning," including a heavy crape veil long enough to cover the entire person, for one year and then "lighten" it by wearing black silk instead of black crape. For one year there was to be no formal visiting and no semblance of gaiety in the household. Cards and writing paper were to be bordered in black, but handkerchiefs with four-inch black borders "may well be deprecated. . . . Jet ornaments alone should be worn for months, unless diamonds set as mementoes are used." A widower wore a black suit and a mourning band on his hat during deep mourning. He might go into society sooner than a widow. Servants also marked the death of the master or mistress for a period of six months to a year. Anyone coming to offer condolences was expected to wear suitably somber clothing.

The colonial dead had been buried beside their fellow townsmen in churchyards or in family graveyards at the back of farms. But by the turn of the nineteenth century, churchyards were becoming crowded and fears were being voiced that burials in the midst of communities might interfere with sanitation. Furthermore, a quiet family plot, removed and private, seemed a more restful place to spend eternity than in a churchyard, hemmed in by former neighbors, walked over by strangers, and with the raucous sounds of the street nearby. New Haven, in 1796, was the first city to set about removing graves from the center of town and to establish a new cemetery divided into family plots. There were those who insisted that being buried near a church would improve their chances on Resurrection Day. "This apprehension has been perceived by common sense to be groundless and ridiculous," was the crisp judgment of Timothy Dwight, president of Yale. New Haven's New Burying Ground became the prototype for cemeteries all over America and later in England. It was divided into rectangular spaces of prescribed size. Carriageways wound among them, the grass was clipped and rolled, and willows and poplars softened the landscape. The cemetery was a private, profit-making corporation and sold plots to individual families.

Mount Auburn Cemetery, begun in 1831 in Cambridge, Massachusetts, was the next of the new cemeteries. It too was laid out in family plots, but the landscaping was much more elaborate than that of the New Burying Ground. It sought to retain the look of a beautiful woodland, with artful plantings of shrubbery and man-made ponds dotted here and there. Throughout the nineteenth century it was a favorite picnic spot of Bostonians, and was widely imitated in other parts of the country. Romantic, bucolic, yet strictly regulated and immaculate, it epitomized the taste and manners of the age.

Victorian
Vicissitudes

Swearing by such treacly truths as the motto above, middle-class Victorians traversed life's rocky road with few backwards glances, secure in the belief that a proper education, a well-corseted wife, a tight roof, and a job with advancement were God's greatest gifts. Affirmations, in the form of pretty lithographs like this Currier & Ives, decorated parlor walls.

Bringing Up Baby

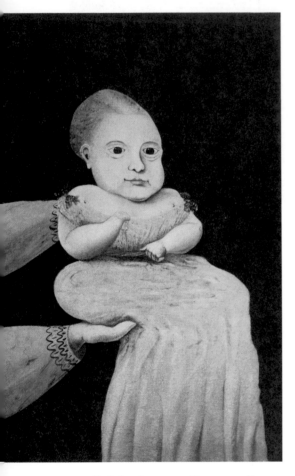

Toilet training was regarded as a moral victory on the side of cleanliness and order and theoretically was completed before the toddler stage. But, all too often, development was halted prematurely. This youngster died at one year eight months.

NEW YORK STATE HISTORICAL ASSOCIATION, GUNN COLLECTION

A four year old was told to select from several objects symbolizing future callings. Choice of a silver knife meant gentlemanly ambitions; a purse, business; or fruit, farming. If dice were picked, adults emphasized that four was not the age of reason.

JAMES ABBE, JR., COLLECTION

Baby's first spanking usually occurred on the family four-poster, amid piles of clean linen and buckets of steaming water. Nary a word had been breathed about mother's confinement, and brothers and sisters were surprised with a "heaven sent" sibling. The infant of 1825 was portrayed as "a plot of ground in which weeds will spring up the more abundantly, the less good seed we sow in it." Careful cultivation of the bud commenced immediately after birth.

NEW YORK STATE HISTORICAL ASSOCIATION

178

*Furnishing dolly with life's neces-
sities was considered the "most innocent amusement for tender youth,
and the most agreeable to their future employ." Though Emma Clark's
sophisticated lady doll hardly evoked
maternal instincts, other five year
olds had homemade rag or wooden
babies which were very lovable.*

ABBY ALDRICH ROCKEFELLER FOLK ART COLLECTION

*The tunic, starched frill, and pantalettes
for a boy of six doubtless inhibited play.
One enlightened doctor said such restraint
was "as unnatural as it would be to confine the deer in the midst of the forest."*

NEW YORK STATE HISTORICAL ASSOCIATION, GUNN COLLECTION

*Phoebe Drake's parents, of a more sensi-
ble ilk, attired their daughter in a simple Empire dress, unencumbered with
stays or hoops. Eight-year-old lasses
helped with household tasks, and were
probably already knitting stockings to
fill pillowcase hope chests. Since sweet-
meats were thought to vitiate children's
morals and appetites, the fruits on the
table as well as candy were forbidden.*

MUSEUM OF FINE ARTS, BOSTON, M. AND M. KAROLIK COLLECTION

179

Hitching rides on the hay wagon was a dividend of the harvest. The hand driving these horses is too busy to chaperon, and a sudden lurch may bring bashful youngsters together.

HARPER'S WEEKLY, AUGUST 29, 1874

Carrying on a tradition that dated back to the Puritans, farmers often marked Christmas with a turkey shoot, a chance to match skills and win a holiday bird. In the engraving at left, the prize has been carried off, but the contest continues with a wooden target. At the husking bee below, a swain who has found a red ear of corn attempts to collect the customary reward—a kiss.

BOTH: BETTMANN ARCHIVE

The farm had its heyday in the mid-1800's when most of the nation's rugged individuals aimed only to work their own land. As the Hoosier in James Whitcomb Riley's poem put it, "I tell you what I'd ruther do—Ef I only had my ruthers,—I'd ruther work when I wanted to Than be bossed 'round by others." According to the idyll-minded, city slickers might have their genteel veneers and stratified society, but country folk offered genuine hospitality and an openness of manners characterized by backslapping, calling strangers by their first names, and accepting people at face value. Even the hardest farm chores were mitigated with recreation. "Bees" buzzed with gossip, but houses and barns were raised and the corn husked. After the work, there might be a square dance or taffy pull, in which swains literally got "stuck on" their favorite girl. Those who romanticized the rural life did not focus on the sixteen-hour working day, the hand-to-mouth existence eked out of rocky eastern soil, or the loneliness of the western prairie, where, rumors to the contrary, pigs did *not* waddle up to be slaughtered, nor did wheat fields instantly produce grain. By the 1870's the farmer was out of the mainstream—less idealized than previously, and often caricatured as an uncouth "hayseed" or "rube." He has been beset by uneven times ever since.

Home On the Grange

The Finishing Touch

Before the public school movement gained momentum, around the middle of the nineteenth century, society's attitude toward women's education, specifically the male attitude, was that women were being spared rather than denied enlightenment. Learning beyond the three R's seemed neither fitting nor necessary for America's ideal female. Not only would it be an indelicate encroachment on male ground, but it was deemed that studying rendered young ladies "puny and nervous." Whatever private education upper-class girls did receive, laced with "accomplishments" such as music and dancing, was tailored to produce engaging dinner partners rather than scholars. Prompted by a mixture of true conviction and financial need, Emma Willard made the first effective start in establishing a broader curriculum. In 1814 she opened a seminary in Middlebury, Vermont; but New York's educational prospects looked more favorable, and she soon petitioned that state for financial aid. Rebuffed by the legislature, Mrs. Willard was invited by the citizens of Troy to bring her girls and her advanced ideas to their city, and in 1821 the Troy Female Seminary was formed. The schoolmistress's argument hinged on the premise that learning would aid and improve women where they were strong, as wives and mothers, and correct them where they were weak, teaching them to act on reason rather than on "fashion and caprice." She warned men, "our national guardians," that women's heads were best filled with "moral and intellectual pleasures . . . rather than . . . the extrinsic frivolities of dress, furniture, and equipage." Her plan of study was broken down into four departments: Religious and Moral, Literary, Domestic, and Ornamental—the charm school training of old. As feared, women were soon setting their sights higher, and in 1837 Mount Holyoke was opened as the first women's college, and Oberlin, already unorthodox, went coeducational.

COLLECTION OF EDGAR WILLIAM AND BERNICE CHRYSLER GARBISCH

Their training in the arts of southern womanhood complete, a graduating class of Virginia maidens in the anonymous painting above wriggle expectantly on the threshold of life while one classmate reads the valedictory address and another receives a wreath of honor.

183

Originally a philanthropic venture to teach reading to underprivileged English children, the Sunday school movement in early-nineteenth-century America catered to both rich and poor, young and old, and was primarily concerned with religious instruction. In a rare ecumenical display, Protestant groups organized the Sunday School Union in 1824 to provide lessons for classrooms throughout the United States and to spread the Word to frontier regions via reams of printed matter. Publications were usually glutinous mixtures of morality and "applied Christianity," and children would save their pennies for information on "Punctuality and Exactness, Obedience, and Improvement." Though angelic moppets carried handkerchiefs printed with "Where do children love to go, When the wint'ry tempests blow, What is it attracts them so? 'Tis the Sabbath school," Tom Sawyer's irreverent attitude more accurately described red-blooded American youth.

A lad apprehended for intemperate behavior

An ingrate making cruel sport of another's misfortune

A slothful daydreamer reprimanded for keeping late hours

Golden Rule Days

At the weekly ordeal "that Tom hated with his whole heart," an hour and a half of infernal boredom was generally enlivened by Tom's "cutting boys, pulling hair, [and] making faces." As in other Sabbath schools, colored tickets were awarded to youngsters who memorized passages from the Scriptures—ten yellow tickets could be traded for a spanking new Bible. Such a prize obviously did not enthrall Tom, but his "entire being had for many a day longed for the glory and the éclat that came with it." By bartering his supply of fishhooks, marbles, and licorice, he obtained the requisite number of tickets. "It was the most stunning surprise of the decade. . . . The prize was delivered to Tom with as much effusion as the superintendent could pump up under the circumstances; but it lacked somewhat of the true gush . . . it was simply preposterous that *this* boy has warehoused 2,000 sheaves of Wisdom on his premises—a dozen would strain his capacity."

A charitable lass leading a blind lady to safety

A wage earner receiving an enthusiastic welcome home

The closely knit family departing for church on the Sabbath

The engravings on these pages come from Picture Lessons, Illustrating Moral Truth, c. 1850. They supposedly demonstrate to impressionable youth virtues of temperance, an early bedtime, and domestic tranquillity, and arouse compassion for the "suffering and distressed." Naturally, the Sabbath is important: "What can be more pleasant than a family—parents and children—on their way, with cheerful but serious thoughts to the sanctuary of God."

ALL: HISTORICAL SOCIETY OF PENNSYLVANIA

THE CORCORAN GALLERY OF ART

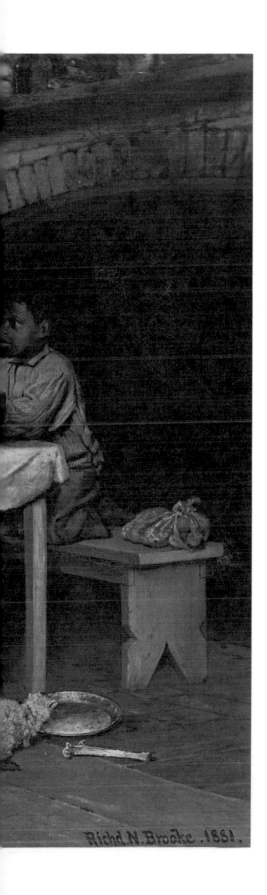

By the very nature of American slavery, Negroes had been made men without country, community, family, or tribal faith. Deprived of all the familiar institutions, they embraced Christianity, making Afro-American churches the pre-eminent social, moral, and educational force in their harsh lives. Though northern Negroes had established a black church in Philadelphia as early as 1787, the white man's religion was withheld from southern slaves for several decades longer. Reluctantly, planters decided to transmit the gospel—under strict supervision—in the belief that they would be discharging their duty to God while teaching blacks Christian humility, the better to bear servitude. Pandora's box was open: Negro preachers, though semiliterate and only casually schooled in Methodist or Baptist practices, soon became powerful leaders, uniting their flocks and channeling the spirit of rebellion. (Nat Turner, who led an uprising of some seventy slaves in 1831, was a part-time Baptist preacher acting on divine inspiration, as he later testified.) Following emancipation, the churches turned much of their energy to putting the Negro family in order. Those former slaves who had managed to maintain some semblance of family union, usually without benefit of clergy, might be persuaded to take wedding vows and settle down as sharecroppers on or near the plantation where they had grown up. But where antebellum ties had been loose, where men had been forced to live separate from mates and children, it proved far more difficult to impose Christian ideas of marriage: thousands of men, freed from their bonds, were not about to take on new ones when better opportunities and a world of promises beckoned in far-off cities. Consequently, many Negro families became matriarchal. In addition, there was more public support for the education of girls than boys; the white community wanted the "mammies" who tended their children to have some training, and the blacks, of necessity, put boys to work as soon as they were old enough. Writing in 1896 of this inequity in *The College of Life . . . A Manual of Self-Improvement for the Colored Race,* Reverend Henry Northrop told black parents, "it is not hard to see that more attention is being paid to the training of girls today. . . . No argument is offered against [girls], but a prayer and petition [is offered] in the interest of the education of the boy, that he may be fitted to worthily represent his race when necessity demands." Postbellum white society, fearful of the Negro, saw to it that "necessity" would not call for some years.

Making the rounds of the parish was one of the chief duties of the small-town minister. The call usually included dinner, for the coins in Sunday's collection plate provided a scant living, and a good meal was always welcome. In "A Pastoral Visit," of 1881 (left), white Virginian Richard N. Brooke offers a sentimentalized look at his neighbors in Warrenton.

187

A landlady serving seconds

The unsociable minder of his own business

Way Stations

Batting practice in the drawing room

A Frenchman airing his political opinions

Disappointment for a finicky eater

A spinster prepared for receiving callers

Were it ever so humble, there was no place like the boardinghouse—home at some point for over 70 percent of Americans. At the worst establishments, inmates who could "tell . . . a new maid by the color of the hairs in the biscuit" reached across table and persons to help themselves at silent, rushed meals. The caliber of fare and guests was quite different at Dr. Oliver Wendell Holmes's lodgings. "I am so well pleased," wrote the breakfast-table auto-crat, "that I intend to remain there, perhaps for years." Prototypical boarders appear here.

A German recalling his homeland

Domestic harmony about to be disrupted

189

The Moving Spirit

Americans have always had a peculiar mania for moving. As one foreigner aptly put it, "The soil itself, or at least the houses, partake of the universal instability." Families eager to hit the road either abandoned their former dwellings, dismantled and shipped them ahead, or took them along in tow. The latter was not without its hazards, and the visiting Charles Dickens nearly became the hit-and-run victim of a house "coming down-hill at a good round trot drawn by some twenty oxen." City folk often had no choice about moving. The first of May to New Yorkers did not mean the traditional spring revels associated with the day, but instead was the time when leases expired, rents for lack of effective controls increased, and people went into the red to remain in their homes or went out into the streets in search of less costly lodgings. One Samuel Woodworth, Esq., writing in 1831, was hard pressed to describe the annual event: "May-Day in New York must be seen, and heard, and felt, and tasted, in order to be known and appreciated . . . . about one-third of a population of two hundred thousand souls change their residence annually." Like a game of musical chairs in which "each must change his place, Uncertain if he get a seat or no," at one point "so many luckless tenants remained without tenements to shelter their families that the common council debated on the propriety of erecting barracks in the Park." With tempers flaring, traffic at a standstill, and trash mounting in the streets, "It will be readily conceived that this general movement must create a great bustle and disturbance. . . . It is certainly a bad system; but it is, perhaps, impossible to devise an adequate remedy."

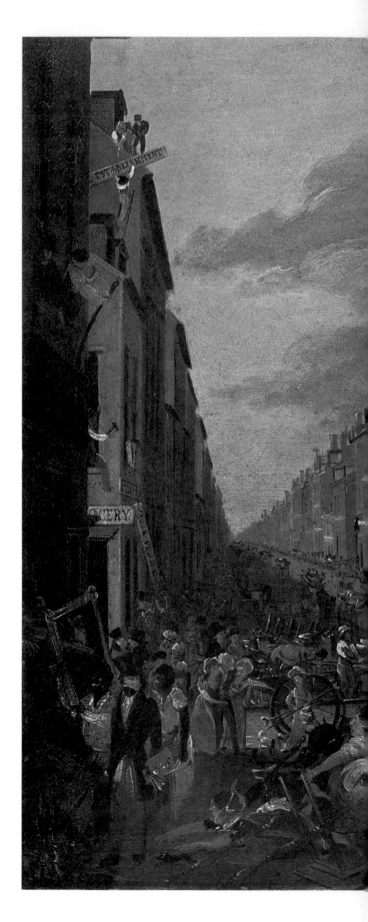

190

COLLECTION OF MR. AND MRS. SCREVEN LORILLARD

New York's annual spring melee, as depicted by an anonymous artist c. 1840, brought a temporary halt to all courtesies and commerce. As one observer remarked, it was not a festival, "for eating on the first of May is entirely out of the question. It is not an amusement, except to landlords."

191

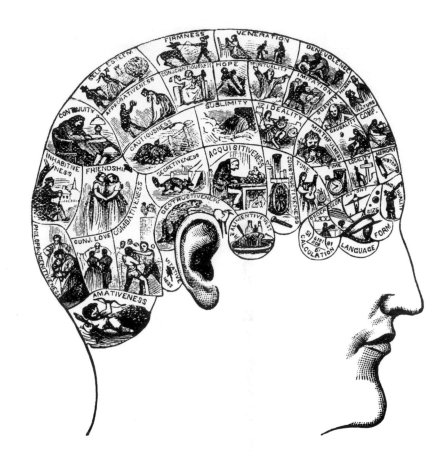

Making Headlines

Telling a person in the 1840's that he ought to have his head examined was not an insult, but a suggestion to consult a phrenologist. Though critics called it fraudulent, the masses, eager for anything new, instructive, and moral, readily accepted the pseudoscience. Its disciples even included eminent eggheads like Henry Ward Beecher and Noah Webster, the latter won over only after his head was swollen with flattery. Phrenology's foremost practitioner and enthusiast, Orson Fowler, lectured throughout America (giving the ladies cut rates for readings), established a school at his New York headquarters, and sold plaster craniums which he noted could double for sculpture, being "very ornamental, deserving a place on the center-table, or mantel." On his topographical chart, reproduced above, some forty "organs" corresponding to mental faculties were localized. Of course, the baser animal drives were relegated to the bottom of the head, while moral traits were suitably situated in large frontal lobes. Whatever their shortcomings, phrenologists paved the way for psychology by emphasizing that bumps — hence, human qualities — were influenced by environment, and were not immutable, God-given characteristics. One man who had a hollow where "Devotion" resided, took up religion, and the spot became a protuberance.

DAVIS, *THE MAGIC STAFF*, 1858

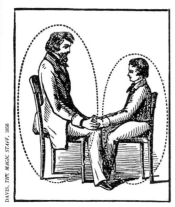

The Ordinary State

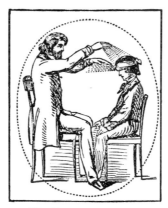

The Psychological State

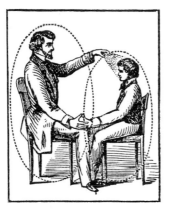

The Somnabulic State

The Superior Condition

At a time when hocus-pocus was more lucrative than the sober pursuit of science, hypnotism, like phrenology, had thousands of adherents. Andrew Jackson Davis, the "Poughkeepsie Seer," shows in the 1858 diagrams above progressive stages in the "magnetic blending of minds," by which he promised to cure an assortment of ills and set the communicant in touch with "Summer-Land." Davis' own conversations with the beyond filled some thirty books.

The hypnotized subject and charlatan professor below illustrated a song sheet of 1843. The popular parody informed the audience, "You'll receive it without any pain sir, You will then close your eyes and learn to tell lies."

James Redfield's Comparative Physiognomy *of 1852, illustrated above, explained the physical and spiritual affinity of men and animals. In the top drawings, the king of the beasts was deemed akin to John Jacob Astor, a gentleman who always had his "lion's share."*

REDFIELD, *COMPARATIVE PHYSIOGNOMY*, 1852

LIBRARY OF CONGRESS

193

Shakers of 1873 dance to "trample sin underfoot" and perhaps to chase away frustrations.

Odd Fellowships

So successful was the Oneida method of birth control, that in 1869 John Noyes introduced scientific breeding as an antidote. The tots in the nursery at right were offspring of couples matched by committee for physical, mental, and spiritual soundness. Public opinion forced the Perfectionists to abandon "stirpiculture" after 1879 and to institute conventional marriages, but the community continued as a manufacturer of silverplate, turning profits over to the workers.

CULVER PICTURES

194

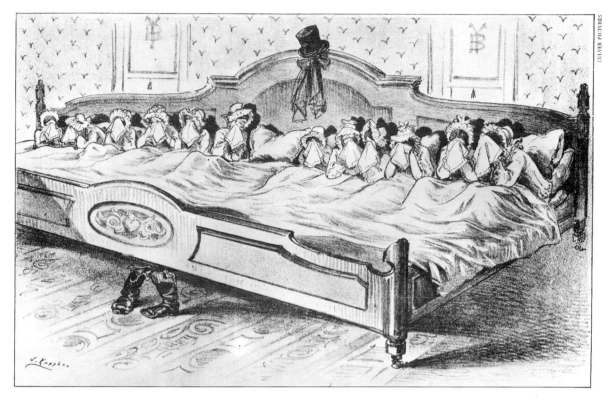

CULVER PICTURES

Brigham Young's death in 1877 inspired this satire, in which twelve weeping widows flank his place of honor.

The traditional one man, one woman alliance was not heaven on earth, despite various Victorian accounts. In Utopian communities of the 1800's, disillusioned Americans inevitably altered the institution of marriage. Polygamy insured Mormons against any domestic shortage and provided numerous little hands to transform the Great Salt Lake Desert. Widely scattered Shaker groups, to the contrary, considered sex the root of sin and led celibate lives. The only intercourse permitted was an occasional evening of chaperoned conversation. Free love, or euphemistically, "complex marriage," was practiced at Oneida, New York. As founder John Humphrey Noyes wrote: "When the will of God is done . . . *there will be no marriage.* The marriage supper . . . is a feast at which *every dish is free to every guest.*" Oneida "dishes" were passed around for the consummation of all "without the jealousy of exclusiveness." Since expending "one's seed . . . merely for the sake of getting rid of it" might result in unplanned pregnancy, Noyes advocated male continence—thus also conserving "virile energy." Women past menopause taught youths the art of *coitus reservatus*, and old men patiently imparted to virgins "the consciousness of having exercised a pure and natural function."

Coming of Age

Thomas Hovenden's companion pieces c. 1890 relive a mother's most heart-rending moments. Home ties are broken with sorrowful farewells (above). When her son comes home with a bride (right), mama knows she has been replaced.

196

KENNEDY GALLERIES, INC.

PHILADELPHIA MUSEUM OF ART

Parting was sweet sorrow, but even dutiful sons of the post-Civil War era generally flew the family coop upon reaching their majority, and sometimes earlier. A reporter for *The Nation* had these words of warning for the old-fashioned patriarch who tried to keep a grown boy under a protective wing: he "straightway finds himself called 'governor,'" and is forced to support a son "clandestinely married to one . . . of his female acquaintances whom common philanthropy will not permit a father-in-law to allow to starve." In a nation where property was equally divided among children, there was little incentive to tend one's share of the farm. Young men with get-up-and-go preferred the big city, still considered an immoral place, but "where they measure men with men." *Our Home*, published in 1889, typifies the maudlin books which comforted mothers at the second severing of the umbilical cord. The lady was assured she would not be forgotten, but "carried into the city on the brow of her son." Her image would tide him over when he "steps out . . . to earn his first morsel of bread with his own hands, and to negotiate independently with the great crafty world." Her example would thwart temptations who "clothe themselves with the livery of beauty . . . sparkle with the gems of wit, and lull to sleep on enticing couches." Succeed or fail, a man could not move home again.

Currier & Ives's 1865 couple, united under God, decorate a civil wedding certificate.

Ties That Bind

When young men's fancies turned to love in Victorian America, engagement and marriage followed as a matter of course. Since pleasure was inextricably allied with duty, the man, dallier or not, who avoided matrimony's burdens was labeled unmanly and was compared to "the wiseacre who secured himself against corns by having his legs amputated." The spinster, whose life was devoted to caring for nieces and nephews, ministering to the needy, or teaching, could console herself that "relatives will rise up in affectionate reverence of [her] hoary hairs, and when consigned to the tomb, they will follow . . . with tears of regret." The unmarried man at death was unwept, unhonored, and unsung. Besides, bachelorhood bred eccentricities—garish attire, unkept whiskers, the "vile habit" of taking snuff, and poor table manners—which only a wife, "the grand wielder of the moral pruning knife," could snip away. Thus, with a sense of resignation, a man allowed himself to be led to the altar. Manuals inundated the wifeshopper with advice: "Regard not the figure, young man; look at the heart: The heart of a woman is sometimes deformed"; even-tempered, sensible, thrifty females who could also serve as general helpmeets were desirable; and hasty marriages—shotgun or those occasioned by love at first sight—were not. A groom, nurtured on romantic fodder, was led to expect a "bride, in the morning of her days; standing on the threshhold of a new existence; crowned like a queen with the virgin coronal, soon to be laid aside." In actuality, timid wives often needed prodding of the sort given by an 1890 manual before adjusting to cohabitation: "When both parties are in good health, and of nearly the same age, one bed chamber if sufficiently roomy may be used without any disadvantage to either. Such an arrangement is also to be commended, because it assures closer companionship, and this develops and sustains mutual affections."

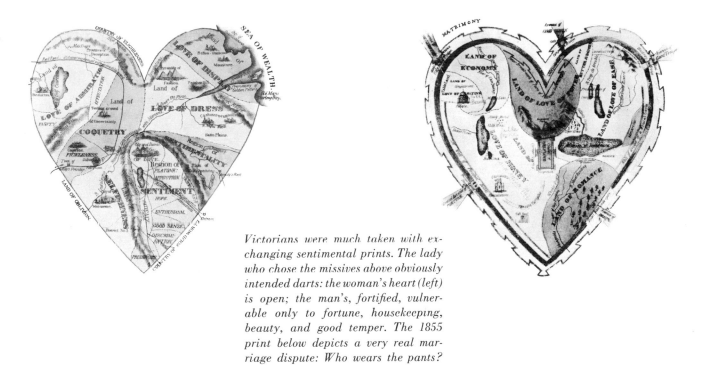

Victorians were much taken with exchanging sentimental prints. The lady who chose the missives above obviously intended darts: the woman's heart (left) is open; the man's, fortified, vulnerable only to fortune, housekeeping, beauty, and good temper. The 1855 print below depicts a very real marriage dispute: Who wears the pants?

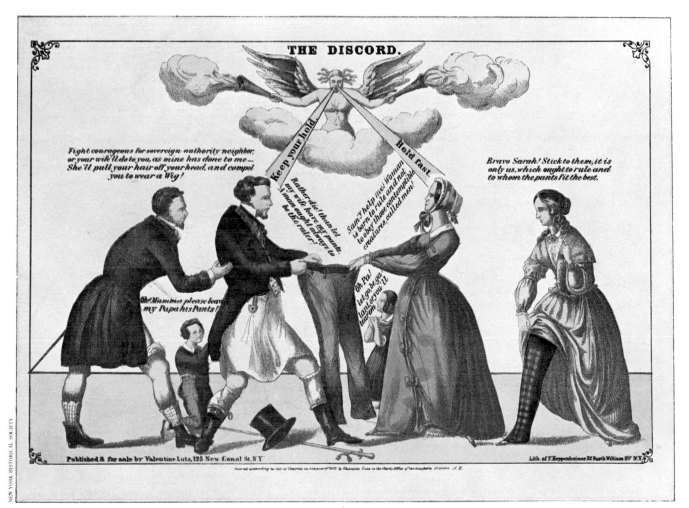

NEW YORK HISTORICAL SOCIETY

A stovepipe hat for the head of the family
KEILLOR COLLECTION

Sentimental Americans began to take their matrimonial milestones seriously in the late 1800's, and manuals of anniversary etiquette soon flooded the market. Many authors did not regard marriage as a "death do us part" affair until the "parties . . . have had sufficient time to discover whether an application for divorce may . . . be deemed necessary by one or the other." They thus discouraged couples from repeating marriage vows at anniversary "weddings" for at least an untarnished twenty-five years. At earlier celebrations, frivolous entertainments were prescribed. A tin decade of con-

Say It With Tin

A comb for marriage snarls
KEILLOR COLLECTION

A lucky shoe for two happy souls
HENRY FORD MUSEUM

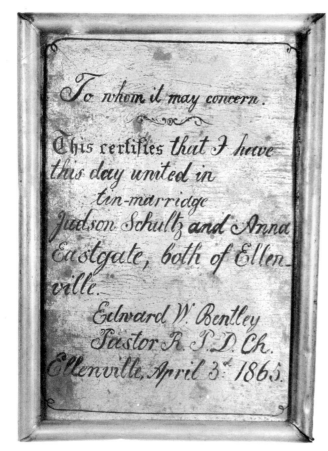

To whom it may concern.

This certifies that I have this day united in tin-marriage Judson Schultz and Anna Eastgate, both of Ellenville.

Edward W. Bentley
Pastor R. S. D. Ch.
Ellenville April 3rd 1865.

Hard facts of a wedding, the second time round
MUSEUM VILLAGE OF SMITH'S CLOVE

Time memorialized in a pocket watch, fob, and chain
KEILLOR COLLECTION

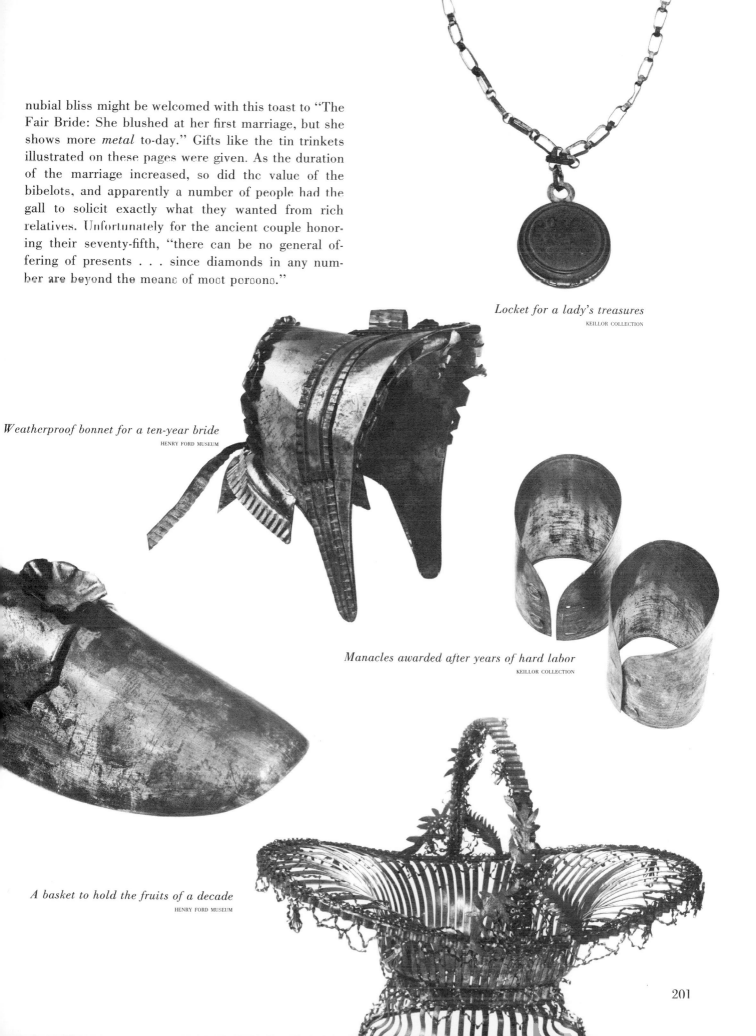

nubial bliss might be welcomed with this toast to "The Fair Bride: She blushed at her first marriage, but she shows more *metal* to-day." Gifts like the tin trinkets illustrated on these pages were given. As the duration of the marriage increased, so did the value of the bibelots, and apparently a number of people had the gall to solicit exactly what they wanted from rich relatives. Unfortunately for the ancient couple honoring their seventy-fifth, "there can be no general offering of presents . . . since diamonds in any number are beyond the means of most persons."

Locket for a lady's treasures
KEILLOR COLLECTION

Weatherproof bonnet for a ten-year bride
HENRY FORD MUSEUM

Manacles awarded after years of hard labor
KEILLOR COLLECTION

A basket to hold the fruits of a decade
HENRY FORD MUSEUM

201

BROWN BROTHERS

Learning In Earnest

A new and militant phase of the perpetual American war on ignorance began in the mid-1800's when adults, often without schooling, zealously sought self-betterment in the form of culture. One of the earliest edifying groups, the YMCA, arrived from England in 1851, and shortly its sister group crusaded to provide working girls with "religious fellowship and instruction . . . acquaintance with the right kind of friends and books, study for culture and self-support." *Harper's Monthly*, warning against squandering resources for mere rest at Newport or Saratoga, touted the "rational recreation" of a

two-week session at New York's Lake Chautauqua, where "the mind wearied by business is turned into new channels of thought; early hours, simple and strengthening food and pure air build up the enervated body." Chautauqua courses ranged from Sunday school teaching to home economics. Biblical historians tried to present the Holy Land in all its former splendor with *tableaux vivants* of daily life in the time of Jesus and a huge outdoor relief map of Palestine molded in sand, which was extremely popular until the wayward feet of a man, groping for his tent in the dark, did irreparable

damage to the Judean mountains and the Dead Sea. Under the neoclassic canopy, people like those above listened to lectures — some inspirational, others interminable. Theater folk were tolerantly allowed to give "readings" and musicales, though the heroine of *Carmen* had to be upgraded to a dairymaid — a tobacco worker was still taboo. When an audience liked a speaker, they honored him with the "Chautauqua salute" by waving handkerchiefs, which one flattered poet compared to "an immense cauldron of pop-corn exploding all over the vast auditorium."

Parlour Pastimes...

PRACTICAL ORCHARD

How can you plant sixteen trees in ten rows, with four trees in each row?

ANSWER

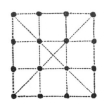

CONUNDRUMS

Why is a pair of skates like an apple?
> They have caused man's fall.

Why is a proud woman like a music book?
> She is full of airs.

Why is a mistaken kiss like an old gun?
> It is a blunderbuss.

Why is the letter D like a sailor?
> It follows the C.

Which has most legs, a horse or no horse?
> No horse has five legs.

REBUS

Ye rebus wits,
Now mind your hits;
For your's the task
My name to unmask:
A fruit we eat,
As sauce to meat:
And with fish too,
That wants a *gout*;
One letter, pray,
Take quite away;
A point of land
You'll understand,

Which sailors dread
Too near their lead,
But when embay'd,
Enjoy its shade:
One more letter
Then unfetter,
The thing that's left,
When thus bereft,
Is worn by all,
Both great and small,
From king and queen
To beggar mean.

ANSWER: Caper, Cape, Cap

THE BALANCED COIN

This engraving represents what seems to be an astounding statement, namely, that a quarter or other piece of money can be made to spin on the point of a needle. To perform this experiment procure a bottle, cork it, and in the cork place a needle. Now take another cork and cut a slit; next place two forks in the cork, as seen in the engraving, and placing the edge of the coin on the needle, it will spin around without falling off. The reason is this, that the weight of the forks, projecting as they do so much below the coin, brings the center of gravity of the arrangement much  below the point of suspension or the point of the needle, and therefore the coin remains perfectly safe and upright above the bottle.

BLOWING THE FEATHER

The players sit in a circle, each taking hold of the edge of a sheet with both hands and holding it up to the chin. A feather is placed on the sheet, and the players are to keep it in motion by blowing it, while one of the company is outside the circle, trying to catch it by reaching out his hands. The quickness with which the position and direction of the feather can be changed by blowing sharply, will make the efforts of the catcher futile for some time. When he finally catches the feather, the person in front of whom the feather is caught must exchange places with him.

ENIGMA

Two brothers, born together: we seldom touch earth, though we go to the ground; though we never eat fodder, buy, sell or barter, we are interested in the corn laws.

ANSWER: A Pair of Feet

LINE DRAWINGS: EVANS, *THE SOCIABLE*, 1858

HOOD'S SARSAPARILLA BOOK OF PARLOR GAMES

Entertaining did not come easily to Victorian Americans. Conversation, gestures, demeanor, were all subject to complicated rules of parlor etiquette, and how to keep everyone amused must have presented problems to the insecure hostess. One sure way to keep the evening afloat was to bring out the games books, which offered the sort of wholesome nonsense described here.

THE FAGOTS

This game consists in forming a circle, the players placing themselves two by two, so that each gent, by holding a lady in front of him, makes what is called a fagot. Players should be of an even number. The circle being formed, two persons are chosen, the one to chase the other. When the person pursued does not wish to be overtaken (which would oblige him to take the place of the pursuer), he places himself in front of any one of the fagots he chooses, but within the circle, so that this fagot is then composed of three persons, one of whom is thus forced outside the circle and must run to avoid being caught. If caught, he takes the place of the pursuer, who in his turn, starts off, or if he prefers, obliges a new player to run like the former one by placing himself before the fagot. It is this which gives life to the game, provided the players have a fair share of spirit and agility.

I LOVE MY LOVE

A pretty game and a prime favorite with country lads and lasses. The leader commences by saying, "I love my love with an *A* because he is Ambitious, because his name is Augustus, and because he lives in Albany. I will give him an Amethyst, feed him on Apple-tarts, and make him a bouquet of Anemones." The next player takes the letter *B* and so on to *Z*.

FLORAL CHARADES

1. A traveling carriage and a body of people
2. Four-fifths of a fop, a vowel, and a fierce animal
3. A wild animal and a gauntlet
4. A domestic animal and a child's dress
5. A measure in poetry and a vowel
6. A farm product and a drinking vessel
7. A make-believe stone

ANSWERS: 1 Carnation; 2 Dandelion; 3 Foxglove; 4 Cowslip; 5 Peony; 6 Buttercup; 7 Shamrock

THE GRASPING LANDLORD

A certain landlord had eight apple trees around his mansion; around these trees eight houses of his tenants; and around these houses ten pear trees. Suppose he wants to have all the pear trees to himself and allot to each tenant one of his apple trees instead. How must he construct a fence or hedge to accomplish it?

ANSWER

A Mating Game

Courting couples often preferred more pacific diversions. Those games that required but two players and allowed time out for meaningful silences were the best. "The Mansion of Happiness," opposite, was the first of dozens of Yankee board games to appear, and it answered the need admirably. Billed in 1843 as "Instructive, Moral and Entertaining Amusement," it was the invention of a clergyman's daughter, and it managed to compress in sixty-seven spaces all the known vices and virtues of the day. The object of the game is to wend one's way, with a minimum of setbacks, toward the goal of happiness, learning along the way "A moral fit t'improve the mind." Spinning the teetotum above, each person advances his playing piece the number of spaces corresponding to the topmost number on the dial when it comes to rest. A player who lands on PIETY, HONESTY, PRUDENCE, CHASTITY, or one of the other wellsprings of virtue, may advance six places further. But, warn the rules, "Whoever possesses AUDACITY, CRUELTY, IMMODESTY, or INGRATITUDE, must return to his former situation till his turn comes to spin again, and not even think of Happiness, *much less partake of it!*" A PERJURER goes direct to THE PILLORY, A DRUNKARD to THE STOCKS, A ROBBER to PRISON for two turns. Even when the goal is near and one has reached the SEAT OF EXPECTATION, dangers lurk: one can still fall from grace on the SUMMIT OF DISSIPATION (presumably the path of those who rejoice in too early victory), and be sent back to RUIN. The first player to reach THE MANSION OF HAPPINESS, where chaste maidens dance to the heavenly sounds of harp and tambourine, is proclaimed the deserving winner. The loser must pay a forfeit—most probably a kiss.

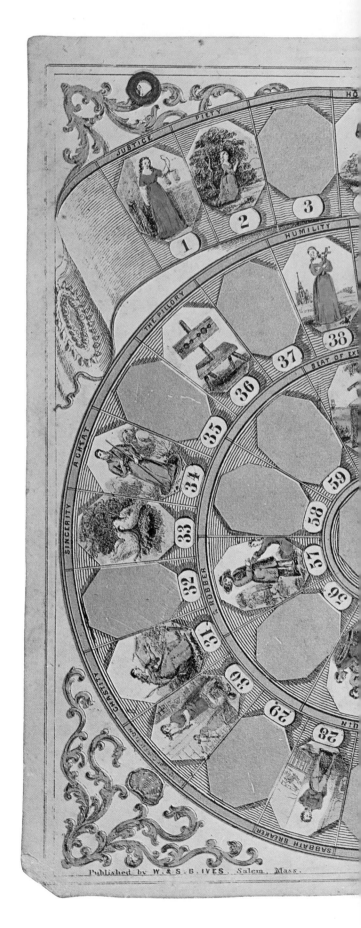

Published by W. & S. B. IVES, Salem, Mass.

206

The Public Sector

❦

*In which the Daily
Protocol of Victorian Life
is Explored & the Rules
governing Calling, Traveling,
Entertaining, & other Patterns
of Public Behavior are told*

"There is no man who can so easily and so naturally become in all points a Gentleman, a Knight, without fear and without reproach, as a true American Republican." Thus spoke the nineteenth-century historian James Parton, out of the infinite confidence and national vanity that characterized the age. But a contemporary etiquette book added gloomily, after quoting Mr. Parton's dictum, "Without perfect self-control you are constantly liable to do something amiss." Etiquette for special occasions, such as weddings or funerals, was not hard for the would-be gentleman to master; it could be looked up and followed like a recipe. In William Dean Howells' *The Rise of Silas Lapham*, several etiquette books were consulted by the unsophisticated Laphams before they attended an important dinner party. But the real grind was being well-bred all day long—knowing when to bow and when to extend the hand, how to dance the figures in a german, what to do with hat and cane while paying a call. Doing such things properly made the difference between the Republican Knight and the hapless clod who did everything wrong. A woman's path was even thornier, for society often forgave an awkward male but never an awkward female. One etiquette book pointed out the unfairness of it all—that men might spit and chew, that they might swear and fight, while women must remain cheerful and smiling; and that men might "groan and bellow" when they had a toothache, while women were expected to "bear it in silence and decorum." The author's point was not that women should also spit and chew, swear and fight, groan and bellow, but that men should stop.

With the onward march of industrialization, Americans became more class-conscious than ever before. Poverty-stricken immigrants formed a new bottom crust to society, automatically elevating all others except Negroes. A caste system developed, but unlike any other in the world it was a caste system

❦

Though the ladies in this detail of William Paxton's "Tea Leaves" appear to be relaxed, hostess and caller perform a ritual according to rules as rigid as court protocol.

in which it was possible, even expected, that people (again excepting Negroes) should move up within one generation. All that was needed was money, determination, and an earnest desire to conform and to be respectable. "In America, that noble, free new country," wrote the Englishwoman Mrs. L. S. Bodichon in 1859, "it is grievous to see the old snobbish idea of 'respectability' eating at society." As Queen Victoria controlled manners and morals of England, so did the imperious female control those in America.

Let us trace a day in the life of an American family in the year 1885. They live in a city west of the Hudson and east of the Mississippi, so that their standards are those of the East, modified by those of the West. Their name — as becomes characters in a book on manners and morals — is Upward. Henry Upward, paterfamilias, is the son of a plain New Hampshire farmer. In the early sixties Henry left the farm and came to work for his uncle, a piano manufacturer. The piano business is booming, and Henry, now forty, bids fair to become a leader in his city. His wife and debutante daughter would like that and urge him daily to pay more attention to the rules of etiquette.

Leaving his house one bright spring morning after breakfasting on oatmeal, lamb chops, hot biscuits, marmalade, an omelette, stewed potatoes, baked beans, and coffee with heavy cream, Henry Upward sets off on foot in the direction of the streetcar line. (He recently acquired a carriage, a coachman, and a matched pair of bays, but his wife will be wanting them later in the day for making calls.) While Henry awaits the streetcar, along comes Mrs. Reverse, a neighbor. He waits for her to acknowledge his presence by a slight bow of her head; then he takes off his hat. Handshaking is not usual, except among good friends. Mrs. Reverse is a widow who runs a boardinghouse. Her late husband, as it happens, was once richer than Upward is now, but he lost his fortune in the Panic of '73; thus Mrs. Reverse is not on the Upwards' visiting list, and her daughter, who works as a typist, is not invited to young Madge Upward's social gatherings.

Bon ton advertised for the smart gentleman in the spring and summer of 1886

Aboard the trolley, the gentlemen give their seats to the females. In the last ten years, Henry has noted with vexation, there have been more and more of them, bound for employment as typists, telephone girls, typesetters, bookkeepers, nurses, librarians, and social workers, as well as schoolteachers, factory workers, and domestics. Clinging to a strap with one hand, Henry reads the morning paper. There are headlines about a musicale given the night before last at the mansion of the Goldmores. The floral decorations, the food and drink, the guest list, and the costumes of the ladies are reported in unctuous detail, and Henry is gratified to read that the presence of the Upwards was reported. "Mrs. Henry L. Upward was charming in fawn silk, set off by a magnificent rope of oriental pearls." If this keeps up (and if Henry can recover from paying for the pearls), the Upwards will soon be among the city's social elite.

Meantime, at home, Mrs. Upward has received a telephone call from a friend who wants to read her this same newspaper account. The Upwards are among the country's small but rapidly growing number of telephone subscribers. In 1880 there had been only 50,000 telephones in the country — one for every 923 people; now, in 1885, the number of sets has risen to more than 100,000, and there is so much interest in the new invention that chapters devoted to telephone etiquette are being inserted in all the most up-to-date social handbooks. Effie Upward listens attentively as the newspaper account is shouted into her ear, and she is delighted on realizing that she is mentioned. "How dreadful!" she shrieks. "Has one no privacy?" But she and her friend do not chat over the telephone, as their granddaughters will. It is hard to hear, other subscribers and the operator may be listening in, and besides, too many household tasks await them, in spite of the fact that each woman has two servants to help her.

Effie now turns back the sleeves of her lacy peignoir and takes the best china into the pantry, where she washes it herself. Katy, the housemaid, has laid out a dish rag and some soap, but is considered too clumsy to take care of the Limoges. She has already cleared the heavily laden breakfast table of the silver and humbler crockery and washed them, while the cook was managing pots and pans in the kitchen. Katy has been at work since about 6 A.M. She has unlocked the front door and opened the parlor blinds and dining-room windows, has washed the front steps and sidewalk, polished the bellpull, and tidied the doormats. She has removed the ashes from the library fireplace and laid a fresh fire (since the Upwards put in a hot-air furnace a few years ago, time spent tending fires is shortened by as much as an hour). She then gathered up the boots and shoes from the bedroom doors, brushed and blacked them, and put them back by the doors. After that, she performed her own toilet, put on her cap and apron, brushed up the dining room, and set the table. It was then her business to arouse the family and wait on table.

Bridey, the cook, arose even earlier than Katy, in time to sweep the halls, take in the empty garbage barrels, make a fire in the range, receive the milkman, iceman, and breadman, and prepare the Upwards' tremendous breakfast. The family being a small one, Bridey's life should be easier than that of many cooks; but the Upwards have been entertaining a good deal of late, and urging Bridey to greater efforts — dishes with fancy French names and dinners of as many as ten courses. Extra waiters are hired for such occasions, but Bridey is thinking of giving notice, while her mistress, tired of the gloomy atmosphere in the kitchen and embarrassed by a recent disastrous attempt at *filets de boeuf Beaumaire*, dreams of replacing her with a French chef and a scullery maid. A French chef, however, commands as much as $100 a month, while even the best Irish cook may be had for $12 a month (an evening a week and every other Sunday afternoon off). A good many more pianos must be sold before the Upwards will be ready for a chef.

Unlike many women of her time, Effie Upward knows how to cook and sew. She owes this to an old-fashioned mother who thought all girls should know how, even if they had "help." She now goes into the kitchen and stirs up a blancmange and some little tea cakes. Then Katy tells her that the seamstress, who comes regularly once a week, has arrived and is ready for a fitting of Effie's new carriage dress. Effie has never liked sewing and has taught her daughter Madge nothing but fancywork.

Grandma Upward is distressed by this and by the rest of Madge's accomplishments: reading French novels, playing the piano and guitar, dancing, playing tennis and croquet, and painting Japanese figures on china vases. Last summer, Madge and her mother went to Cape May, New Jersey, and Madge appeared on the public beach in one of the new bathing costumes. The society magazine *Town Topics* has been dwelling at length on the "saturnalia of moist lewdness" coming about on New Jersey beaches. It seems that bathing suits are respectable enough when dry, but when wet, lead to "a riot of personal

The lady above accompanied an ad for the newfangled telephone. The "desk set" below was made in 1892.

license between the sexes which leaves nothing to the imagination that could be left in open day." The editor pursued the point further with the following bit of jollity:

"At Narragansett: 'Hello, Jones, who'd have thought to see you here, while there is a ballet on the stage in New York yet?'

"'Ssh, old man. We've got a better ballet down on the beach every day, and it's free.'"

Nevertheless, Effie knows from the newspapers that the Vanderbilt girls appear at Newport's Bailey's Beach in bathing suits, so it must be *de rigueur*, particularly since Madge, like the Vanderbilt girls, is always chaperoned. Chaperoning is another of those European customs that have been brought back and adopted by manners-conscious American travelers. Effie and Henry Upward have not yet traveled, but they are impressed by foreign ways, particularly English ones. Effie has read in Mrs. Sherwood's *Manners and Social Usages* that lack of chaperonage "comes of our crude civilization. . . . Until we learn better, we must expect to be laughed at on the Pincian Hill, and we must expect English novelists to paint pictures of us which we resent, and French dramatists to write plays in which we see ourselves held up as savages . . . . Little as we may care for the opinion of foreigners we do not wish our young ladies to appear in their eyes in a false attitude, and one of the first necessities of a proper attitude, one of the first demands of a polished society, is the presence of a chaperon."

William Dean Howells' novel of the period, *A Chance Acquaintance*, turns upon a point of chaperoning: the hero has proposed to a charming young girl, Kitty, whom he has met on a steamer without proper introduction. Kitty has just accepted his proposal when they are surprised by two fashionable ladies from Boston with whom he is acquainted. According to etiquette, he must not present an unchaperoned young woman to them. (The fact that she is unchaperoned suggests that she may be unsuitable for polite society.) His training is so strong that he dares not break it and allows the ladies to engage his attention for half an hour, while Kitty is ignored. Kitty, angry and humiliated, forthwith breaks the engagement and the young man sees "that throughout that ignoble scene she had been the gentle person and he the vulgar one. How could it have happened with a man like him!" But despite Howells' sympathy with Kitty, he makes his point: society is a cruel despot when it comes to manners and morals.

Madge is, therefore, chaperoned wherever she goes, either by her mother or by an "elderly girl" of past thirty who "matronizes" for a small fee (a new line of work for impecunious but well-bred females). If a young man invites Madge to a matinee, the formidable third party is always present, alert for a faltering of masculine rectitude. Gentlemen callers are under the same surveillance. Madge does not like the system, and neither do her grandmothers, who remember days of innocent, unchaperoned merriment back in the 1830's. Grandma Upward lives on a farm, but often comes to visit; and although Effie is too dutiful a daughter-in-law to discourage the visits, the old lady is a source of embarrassment to her with her old-fashioned, countrified ways and her outmoded opinions.

The world has changed dizzyingly since the youth of Grandma Upward, who started housekeeping in 1840. At that time even millionaires' houses were without indoor plumbing and central heating. There were no commercially

Seaside fashions, by Charles Dana Gibson

canned foods or packaged cereals. Gas lighting became usual in city houses during the forties, but oil lamps prevailed in rural areas. Sewing machines were not available to home seamstresses until after the Civil War. Now, in the eighties, electric lights are beginning to be installed in private houses—the Goldmores have them; prudent people, they retain a gaslight system as well. Refrigerator cars, devised in the sixties, have made it possible for fruit, meat, fish, and other perishable food to travel long distances, and better iceboxes have enabled housekeepers to refrigerate food at home. Even window screens are beginning to be available. With these changes, daily living has become more lavish and more complicated, with a correspondingly more demanding etiquette. Effie was brought up on her mother's copy of Mrs. Farrar's etiquette book, but she finds it useless now, hopelessly out of date and written for an age when servants were scarce and people lived simply. Describing how *not* to run a household, Mrs. Farrar wrote, "a ring at the door-bell produces the greatest consternation; the mistress of the house snatches up a broken dish and puts it in the closet, tells one daughter to hide the pitcher that has lost its handle, and another to carry away the odd plates and common spoons. . . . The best dinner-set is often kept in the closet of a spare chamber; so piles of plates and arms full of dishes are seen walking down stairs on company days, and walking up again the day after."

Henry's mother criticizes the Upwards for hiring liveried footmen when they give a dinner party and for having a genealogist look up the family ancestry, hoping to find a coat of arms to have engraved on the Upward writing paper. The old lady believes, with Mrs. Farrar, that "in this privileged land, where we acknowledge no distinctions but what are founded on character and manners, she is a lady, who, to inbred modesty and refinement, adds a scrupulous attention to the rights and feelings of others. . . . Thus we may see a lady sewing for her livelihood and a vulgar woman presiding over a most expensive establishment." She is fond of reminding Effie of the story of how George Washington took off his hat to a Negro slave and when asked why replied that there was no reason for the slave to be more polite than he. Effie means no disrespect either to her mother-in-law or to George Washington, but she does not pass on these precepts to Madge.

Still, a number of Mrs. Farrar's points of etiquette remain valid in 1885. Ladies wear gloves to a dinner party and keep them on until they sit down at table, when they remove them and lay them in their laps beneath their napkins. Anyone so awkward or luckless as to break or spill anything during a meal should delicately ignore it. As an example to be followed, Mrs. Farrar told of "a very accomplished gentleman," who, when carving a tough goose, "had the misfortune to send it entirely out of the dish and into the lap of the lady next to him; on which he very coolly looked her full in the face, and, with admirable gravity and calmness, said, "Ma'am, I will thank you for that goose." Another etiquette writer told of a kindly king who, seeing one of his guests drinking from a finger bowl, did likewise in order to make the guest feel comfortable. Hosts, like the king, had to have "the genius of tact to perceive, and the genius of *finesse* to execute, ease and frankness of manner, a knowledge of the world that nothing can surprise, a calmness of temper that nothing can disturb, and a kindness of disposition that can never be exhausted." As for the hostess, she must keep cool, no matter what enormity is committed by either guests or servants. "No accident must disturb her; no disappointment

Newlyweds admiring their favorite gift

embarrass her. Her precious china and her rare glass, if broken before her eyes, she must seem not to be aware of it." The number and variety of the dishes is about the same as it was forty years or so ago, but they are now passed by waiters, not set on the table to be served by the host. The custom of cutting meat with the fork in the left hand and then transferring the fork to the right before beginning to eat is of mysterious origin. Some say that the Americans adopted it after the Revolution, out of a wish to be different from the English in as many ways as possible. An etiquette book of 1878, by Mrs. H. O. Ward, tells us that "in England, it is considered to be underbred ever to transfer the fork to the right hand." But she makes no judgments of her own as to proper procedure among her countrymen.

Survival of the fittest—dinner-table style

Over the years, mentors of etiquette have written copiously on the subject of dinner-table behavior. "When not engaged in eating," says Mrs. Farrar, "do not let your fingers find employment in playing with any of the table furniture, or in making pellets of bread. If you would be very refined, you must avoid blowing your nose at table, or touching your hair, or adjusting a comb; those are, in some persons' eyes, great offences." *The Behavior Book* of 1853 decrees that "the fashion of wearing black silk mittens at breakfast is now obsolete"; and continues, "While at table, all allusions to dyspepsia, indigestion, or any other disorders of the stomach, are vulgar and disgusting. The word *stomach* should never be uttered at any table, or indeed anywhere else, except to your physician, or in a private conversation with a female friend interested in your health." *The Illustrated Manners Book* (1855) scolds a "vegetarian lady who at a dinner table characterized mince pie as 'chopped corpse and apples'. . . . You will do well not to be talking of dogs when people are eating sausages. . . ." (The name *hot dog*, applied to a frankfurter sausage, was not to be current until 1903.)

"Now all people understand French, or should do so," decrees Mrs. Sherwood. Effie and Henry fear that it is too late for them to learn it, but they have made it high on Madge's agenda. She and several friends have studied with a French tutor since childhood, and can help their parents to distinguish a *vol-au-vent* from a *timbale* (it is in gastronomic realms that French is most obtrusive). A "little dinner of eight," as conceived by Mrs. Sherwood, might be something like this: a soup of sorrel *à l'essence de veau*, lobsters *sauté à la Bonnefoy*, veal cutlets *à la Zingara*, as well as some American favorites. Sherry is served with the soup, Chablis with the lobsters, champagne with the entrees, claret with the cheese and salad, and liqueurs with the coffee. To avoid staggering away from the table (as Silas Lapham did the first time he attended a genteel dinner party), ladies are advised to touch the rim of the glass as a signal to the waiter not to pour; gentlemen should not drain their glasses too quickly. If a toast is offered, Mrs. Ward suggests that "it is sufficient to fasten your eye upon the eye of the one asking you, bow the head slightly, touch the wine to your lips, and again bow before setting down the glass." At the end of the meal, "finger-glasses, with water slightly warmed and perfumed, are preferable to passing a silver basin in which each dips his napkin in turn. . . . The dinner napkin is to be used for wiping the fingers, and never the d'oyley. . . ." Small wonder that Effie longs for well-trained French servants; Bridey has never yet remembered to perfume the finger bowl water, and if she warms it, the guests usually scald their fingers.

Effie's mentor of etiquette, Mrs. Sherwood, is distressed because the modern American working-class girl does not wish to go out to service. Worse still, "English servants lose all their good manners when they come over here, and do not appear at all as they do in London. . . . It is to be feared that the Declaration of Independence is between us and good service." French servants are best, she tells us, but they are expensive and have an irritating way of going back to France. "It is a curious fact that they grow impertinent and do not seem to enjoy the life." Norwegians are good if well trained; Swedes "have every qualification for service excepting this: they will not obey—they are captains." Negroes are "most excellent when good, most objectionable when bad," and "in Chicago, the ladies speak highly of the German servants, if they do not happen to be Nihilists, which is a dreadful possibility." By and large, the Irish are willing, dependable, and good with children, even though likely to "be wanting in head, management, and neatness."

While Effie is busy with the seamstress, Irish Katy has tidied the dining room and made up and cleaned the bedrooms. After that, she cleans the parlor and does some washing (using tub and washboard). It is her duty to answer the doorbell and she has done so several times. But this is an easy day compared with Thursday, which is sweeping day: on Thursdays she sweeps the whole house, shakes the rugs in the back yard, shakes and sweeps down the heavy curtains, and dusts the mirror frames with a long feather duster. (The electric vacuum cleaner will not be invented until 1899, and most of Katy's efforts do nothing but move the dust from one place to another.)

One of the doorbell summonses is a messenger bearing an invitation for the Upwards to attend a "kettledrum" on the coming Saturday. They are already invited to three other kettledrums on that day, but Effie accepts this one as well. A kettledrum is an afternoon gathering of both sexes, old and young. The origin of the name is obscure, but the custom is another British import, enough to recommend it to the socially ambitious, like Effie. Some say that ladies of the regiment in British India originated it, sounding a kettledrum as an announcement; others insist that the word is a combination of *kettle*, meaning that tea will be served, and *drum*, an old-fashioned synonym for party. Coffee, bouillon, and chocolate are also offered, together with little sandwiches and cakes. The more kettledrums one has to hurry off to, the more successful one's social life. Effie decides to wear her new carriage dress and urges the seamstress to greater diligence. It is one of the most sumptuous dresses Effie has yet owned, being made of eighteen yards of garnet-colored crushed velvet imported from Paris.

One of Effie's etiquette books, *Our Deportment*, tells her, "The material for a dress for a drive through the public streets of a city, or along a fashionable drive or park, cannot be too rich. Silks, velvets, and laces, are all appropriate, with rich jewelry and costly furs in cold weather. If the fashion requires it, the carriage dress may be long enough to trail. The light, showily trimmed dresses, which were once displayed in the streets and fashionable promenades, are now only worn in carriages. . . . Morning calls may be made either in walking or carriage dress, provided the latter is justified by the presence of the carriage." Effie is planning a kettledrum of her own next week, as it is an excellent way of acquitting one's social debts at one fell swoop and without the cost of wines or music. Gentlemen come without urging, for they can stop in on their way from downtown without having to change their clothes. For the occasion, Effie is planning to wear a tea gown—a loose-fitting

As shown in an 1858 cookbook, there was a wrong way and a right way to carve, and the young man who failed to know the difference would not be welcome in the best society.

garment with cascades of lace down the front. Some social arbiters frown on the idea of wearing an "undress" in public, but Effie has read in *Harper's Bazar* that the Princess of Wales receives in tea gowns and that is enough for Effie, who is not as slim as she used to be and welcomes an opportunity to ease her corset.

Another ring at the doorbell. Katy brings up a card tray on which repose seven calling cards. Three of them read "James P. Arrived," two read "Mrs. James P. Arrived," and two read "Miss Jane Arrived." (Jane has passed the customary year in society and is now permitted to leave her own cards.) The latter four are bent at the right-hand end. Effie, who owns a copy of *Pasteboard Politeness*, at once understands that Mrs. Arrived and her daughter are here in person to see herself and Madge. Being females, they properly have not sent up cards for Henry; but Mr. Arrived sends cards for the whole family. Since his cards are unbent, it is clear that he has not come in person. Had the right-hand upper corners been turned down, it would have meant that the Arriveds were only paying respects and did not seek to be received; the left-hand upper corners turned down would have signified "congratulations," and the left-hand lower corners, "condolences." A bend of the right-hand lower corners would indicate "P.P.C.," or *Pour Prendre Congé* — the caller is leaving town for an extended period.

Occasions for the use of calling cards are numerous. For example, cards are left if a friend is sick. After a dinner or ball, one must pay a "party call," leaving cards at the hostess' door without necessarily asking to be received in person. Failure to do so may result in never being asked to that house again. Cards must also be left after receiving a first invitation to dine, whether or not one has accepted it; also, to return a first call, even if one does not intend to continue the acquaintance. If a new arrival in town sends a letter of introduction from a mutual friend, the recipient must accompany any first invitation with a card. If one wishes to terminate a friendship it may be accomplished by the simple but significant gesture of enclosing one's card in an envelope and having it delivered.

If the servant at the door says "Not at home" before the cards have been tendered, no offense should be taken; the lady may well be at home, but she is not receiving visitors. It is a common custom to have a regular "At Home" day (from eleven to five with time out for the midday meal), during which a lady sits in her drawing room at a tea table, wearing a best dress, and receives all comers. "It is doubtful," wrote Emily Post in 1922, "if the present generation of New Yorkers knows what a day at home is! But their mothers, at least, remember the time when the fashionable districts were divided into regular sections, wherein on a given day in the week, the whole neighborhood was 'at home.' Friday sounds familiar as the day for Washington Square! And was it Monday for lower Fifth Avenue? At all events, each neighborhood on the day of its own, suggested a local fete. Ladies in visiting dresses with trains and bonnets and nose-veils and tight gloves, holding card cases, tripped demurely into this house, out of that, and again into another; and there were always many broughams and victorias slowly 'exercising' up and down, and very smart footmen standing with maroon or tan or fur rugs over their arms in front of Mrs. Wellborn's house or Mrs. Oldname's, or the big house of Mrs. Toplofty at the corner of Fifth Avenue."

To understand the language of the calling card is essential if one is to get on

(Continued on Page 218)

Calling cards like those above were kept in receivers, often of very ornate design. Ten dollars purchased the gold-plated "Hilarity," below.

New York: 1868

*The best and worst of a northern metropolis, as reported by James D. McCabe, Jr.
The Virginian's views appeared anonymously in* Secrets of the Great City.

The City of New York now extends from the Battery to the Harlem river and Spuyten Duyvil creek, and is built up with great regularity as far as One-hundred and Thirtieth street. . . . The population . . . is over one million of inhabitants. . . . made up from every nation under Heaven. The natives are in the minority. Irishmen, Germans, Jews, Turks, Greeks, Russians, Italians, Spaniards, Mexicans, Portuguese, Scotch, French, Chinese . . . abound. . . . [and] frequently herd together, each class by itself, in distinct parts of the city. . . . It has been well said, that "New York is the best place in the world to take the conceit out of a man". . . . No matter how great or flattering is the local reputation of an individual, he finds upon reaching New York that he is entirely unknown. . . . The people . . . are the most liberal of any in America. . . . Every religious faith, every shade of political opinion, is tolerated and protected. Men concern themselves with their own affairs only. Indeed, this feeling is carried to such an extreme that it has engendered a decided indifference between man and man. . . . Men coming to New York from other parts of the country, seem to think themselves free from all the restraints of morality and religion, and while here commit acts of sin and dissipation . . . they would not dream of indulging in, in their own communities. . . . There are but two classes in the city—the poor and the rich. . . . Only a block and a half back of the most sumptuous parts of Broadway and Fifth Avenue, want and suffering, vice and crime, hold their court. Fine ladies can look down from their high casements upon the squalid dens of their unhappy sisters. . . . Persons who have risen from the ranks . . . look . . . with supreme disdain upon those who are working their way up. They are ashamed of their origin, and you cannot offend one of them more than to hint that you knew him a few years ago as a mechanic, or shop-keeper. It is not difficult to recognize these persons. . . . Their vulgar manners . . . contrast strikingly with the splendor with which they surround themselves. . . . The most wonderful street in the world is Broadway. . . . High and low, rich and poor, pass along these side-walks, at a speed peculiar to New York, and positively bewildering . . . . Vehicles crowd the streets to such an extent that . . . a stranger feels sure . . . [they] cannot be extricated without loss of life or limb. . . . In a few moments, however, he sees a squad of policemen approach, and plunge boldly into the throng. . . . Soon the street is clear again, to be blocked . . . in a similar manner, in less than an hour. At night . . . the lamps of the theatres and concert saloons . . . [and] the long lines of the red, green, and blue lights of the stages, rising and falling with the motion of the vehicles, add a novelty and beauty to the picture. Strains of music or bursts of applause, float out on the night air from the places of amusement, not all of which are reputable. Broadway is a sure cure for the "blues." To persons of means . . . New York's delightful climate, its cosmopolitan . . . character, and the endless variety of its attractions, render it the most delightful home in America.

Ladies' Home Journal, *c. 1900, recommended that every girl include "the indispensable short skirt," above, and the "tailor-made suit," below, in her college wardrobe.*

in society. "The card may well be noted as belonging only to a high order of development," intones Mrs. Sherwood. "No monkey, no 'missing link,' no Zulu, no savage, carries a card. It is the tool of civilization, its 'field-mark and device.'" The author of *Our Deportment* backs her up: "To the unrefined or underbred, the visiting card is but a trifling and insignificant bit of paper; but to the cultured disciple of social law, it conveys a subtle and unmistakable intelligence. . . . The higher the civilization of a community, the more careful it is to preserve the elegance of its social forms. It is quite as easy to express a perfect breeding in the fashionable formalities of cards, as by any other method, and perhaps, indeed, it is the safest herald of an introduction for a stranger. Its texture should be fine, its engraving a plain script, its size neither too small, so that its recipients shall say to themselves, 'A whimsical person,' nor too large to suggest ostentation."

Effie would like to get on with the fitting, but if she directs Katy to say "Not at home" to the Arriveds at this stage, they may never come back; whereas if she receives them now, she will be in the happy position of owing *them* a call. She descends to the parlor where they have been installed by Katy. She makes Madge's apologies (Madge is at a dancing lesson), waves the ladies to seats on the new rosewood sofa, and summons to mind all she has read about how to conduct a conversation. First, she must avoid the five D's: domestics, domiciles, descendants, disease, and dress. She must avoid such phrases as "immensely jolly" and "disgustingly mean." She must not ridicule or satirize. She must avoid scandal and gossip, business, hobbies, religion, and politics. She must display no emotion, nor ask impertinent questions.

Says *Our Deportment*, "Some authorities in etiquette even go so far as to say that *all* questions are strictly tabooed. Thus, if you wished to inquire after the health of the brother of your friend, you would say, 'I hope your brother is well,' not, 'How is your brother's health?'" *Our Deportment* also warns against excessive delicacy. "Do not use the word 'limb' for 'leg.' If legs are really improper, then let us, on no account, mention them. But having found it necessary to mention them, let us by all means give them their appropriate name." Effie also knows that she must not mention prices nor ask about them, must not contradict, interrupt, make puns, monopolize the conversation, nor give unsolicited advice. Fortunately, the ladies remain but fifteen minutes. At the sixteenth minute, guided by instinct, for it would be a breach of etiquette if they look at the watches pinned on their bosoms, they rise and take their departure. Effie hastens to the telephone to tell Henry about this latest triumph, but that miraculous instrument is out of order, as it often is.

Meantime, at the office, Henry has spent a hectic morning, during which he has thought of nothing but pianos. He is devoted to them as deeply as the pork dealer was devoted to pork in George Horace Lorimer's *Letters from a Self-Made Merchant:* "You've got to know your goods from A to Izzard, from snout to tail, on the hoof and in the can. You've got to know 'em like a young mother knows baby talk, and to be as proud of 'em as the young father of a twelve-pound boy, without really thinking that you're stretching it four pounds. . . . You've got to have the scent of a bloodhound for an order and the grip of a bulldog on a customer." Henry leaves the social side of their life to Effie, for whom he has a respect that is something like awe. For her sake, he tries not to go to sleep at evening parties and not to befriend the "wrong" people. Some of his associates at the piano factory are "wrong," and Henry restrains an inclination to go out with them to billiard halls. He adores his daughter Madge, but does not understand her. Madge seems not to appreciate the careful upbringing they have given her. Although she is a pretty girl, attractive to men, she talks about wanting to go to college. She was once even heard to say that she would like to become a doctor, whereupon her mother gave her a story to read in which a young man rejects his sweetheart for that reason: "Do you suppose that I would ever have a wife who had been familiar with all the disgusting details of a dissecting-room? Bah! she would never get rid of it." Both parents would rather see their daughter become a common shopgirl than aim to be a doctor, but they are counting on a grand tour of Europe to put such nonsense out of her head.

Henry decides to lunch at his club today. He has been a member for only a year, and he finds the club one of the pleasantest diversions in his life. For one thing, he can smoke there—Effie has asked him to give up smoking anywhere else, and long ago he gave up spitting. Effie is willing that he smoke at his club and even drink too much there, for he is doing it with the right people. Another important reason Henry likes his club so much is that it is free of women. Within that sanctuary women do not even exist: if, as he sits in a deep leather chair by the window, he sees a lady of his acquaintance passing by, etiquette tells him to ignore her, even if she waves.

To belong to a gentlemen's club has been a mark of social distinction in America ever since the eighteenth century. Henry's fellow members in this one are the city's leading lawyers, physicians, bankers, brokers, and (like himself) wholesale merchants. There are no dentists (still not considered professional men by many), no shopkeepers, and no persons of artistic bent unless they happen to be near relatives of a prominent family, and not always then. Virtually all are persons whose ancestors came from England, Scotland, or the northern countries of Europe. There are one or two Jewish members of long standing, but anti-Semitism is beginning to roll outward from the East Coast and no Jews have been taken in for a number of years. There are no Irish names on the roster, and none of the members is Catholic. In a word, the club is extremely snobbish and makes no bones about it. There are many other clubs and societies in the city, for Americans are indefatigable joiners. Very popular of late are secret orders, with passwords, grips, and cabals; they seem especially to suit people who are lagging behind in the race for social and financial eminence, and they rejoice in pompous titles, such as the Knights and Ladies of the Golden Rule, the American Order of Druids, the Royal Society of Good Fellows, the Prudent Patricians of Pompeii, and the Concatenated Order of Hoo-Hoo.

Henry's club is, as yet, a phenomenon of the city and of the East. In smaller, newer communities, clubs are for joining more than for excluding, and all like-minded respectable white males are eligible for any social, athletic, patriotic, political, or philanthropic organization. Women have their own groups in all the above categories; they also form clubs to advance various branches of the arts—for public opinion does not permit men to take the arts seriously. Effie's mother has joined the Women's Christian Temperance Union, which was founded in 1874 by small-town women, but it does not appeal to Effie, who, though she does not like the taste of alcohol, would hate to give up her friends in the fashionable, cosmopolitan drinking set for the stodgy imbibers of lemonade. Madge interests herself in woman's

Cigars, even the superior 3¢ stogy in this ad, were better smoked outdoors.

rights, thereby embarrassing both her mother and grandmother, who agree with Mrs. Ward: "What do women want with votes, when they hold the sceptre of influence with which they can control even votes, if they wield it aright?"

After Henry has had lunch (which is served with dispatch so that the gentlemen may get back to their offices), he is flattered by an invitation to enjoy a good cigar with George Highup, owner of the city's chief department store. Every word of their talk is sweet to both of them, for they speak of business. Business in America is (to quote Henri Herz, a nineteenth-century French observer) "more than a source of livelihood, it is a veritable ministry." American dedication to the pursuit of the dollar never ceases to amaze foreigners, who ask, *why*, having made money, does not a man retire and enjoy it? "Mr. G. now has a fortune," says Herz, "but continues his business and has not modified his mode of life in any respect. At the height of winter he gets up before sunrise, has a cup of tea, and leaves his sumptuous residence to go to the dingy little rooms in a sort of immense barracks which he calls his office. In this miserable retreat, badly furnished, badly ventilated, and always littered with cases of merchandise, Mr. G. daily carries on his affairs, large and petty, with that calm and righteous spirit characteristic of the Anglo-Saxons. Neither rain, nor snow, nor ice will keep him from his task. When the streets are glassed over to an extent that imperils his limbs, he attaches a little spiked apparatus to the soles of his shoes and somehow gets to his office, as the soldier to his post, the priest to his church."

Commented an observer from Romania, "They kneel before [Mammon], setting their honor aside, day and night, thinking only of amassing wealth, of building palaces." But Englishman George W. Steevens analyzed the situation more thoughtfully: "In a sense . . . the Americans appear to me the most materialistic people in the world. But as for the love of money, I don't think they are down with it any worse than any other people. I still think . . . that it is not the dollars they worship but the faculties that got them. . . . Cut off from the hard-won civilisation of the Old World, and left to struggle by themselves with the forest and the prairie, it was inevitable that the Americans should prize most highly those less highly organised qualities of the mind which insured success in the struggle. The others may come with time. In the meanwhile there is this consolation for those who go down. Failure may be complete, but it is never irredeemable. In Europe a boy goes into a bank; he may hate it, but in the bank he usually remains. In America he will next appear in a newspaper office, then behind a draper's counter, then in Congress, then in bankruptcy, and then in a gold-mine. You never meet the man who has got a good place and don't mean to lose it. No place is good enough for the American's estimate of his own deserts. . . . Nobody is ever done with." The same writer believed that traveling businessmen performed the useful office of holding the country together. "Contact with all parts of the country brings understanding, rubs the edge off prejudice, promotes a candid consideration of the position of others."

Until after the Civil War, most long-distance travelers in America were either migrants or businessmen. About 1870, Americans began to take an interest in touring the more remote parts of their own country. An increasing number of citizens had money for vacation travel; and there was the incentive of visiting relatives in widely separated places. The transcontinental railroad was completed in 1869, and Indians were no longer a menace except in isolated

An 1856 forecast of fashions for the year 3000 satirized the trend toward male foppishness.

and remote areas. Places with sights to be seen, such as Niagara Falls, Washington, and Plymouth, Massachusetts, began to cater to the tourist trade. Bridal couples traveled far and wide; even before the Civil War, Mississippi riverboats were accommodating newlyweds with "honeymoon chambers"—one boat offered twenty-eight. And the mechanics of travel had improved mightily since the early days of train and steamboat, when Mrs. Farrar had found it necessary to write, "No one is fit to travel, who has not acquired enough [self-possession], to refrain from screaming when alarmed." Steamboats still exploded and trains still collided, but not as often. Carriage horses continued to run away ("When I feel the carriage tipping over," said Mrs. Farrar, "I draw myself all up together and make myself as much like a bag of wool as possible."), but roads were gradually improving and the main streets of cities were paved.

As more became known about hygiene, hotels and inns were less likely to be decimated from time to time by typhoid, dysentery, and various unidentified but fatal diseases. "A good traveler will shut her eyes as much as possible to the dirt and bad management of a poor inn," had been Mrs. Farrar's advice in the days before Lister and Pasteur. "She will . . . carefully abstain from mentioning to her companions any discovery of an unpleasant nature, which she may have made, especially in regard to food, as a dish eaten in ignorance may relish well, whilst a word from the more initiated, might turn the whole party against it."

By the 1880's, a lady traveling alone no longer caused raised eyebrows. Hotels even expected it, providing ladies' parlors and ladies' entrances. *Our Social Customs* recommended that an unattended lady traveler should avoid loitering in the halls or standing alone at her bedroom window. Unless invited the lone lady should not play the piano in the hotel parlor nor sing if there were others present; neither should she sing or hum when passing through the halls. *Hill's Manual* conceded, however, that "ladies and gentlemen who are strangers, being thrown into the company of each other for a long journey, need not necessarily refuse to speak to each other."

The pretentious grandeur of hotels and steamboats was an especially American phenomenon; nothing was too good for the traveling citizens of the democracy. Cornelia Adair, a young American traveling with her English husband in 1874, stayed at Chicago's Palmer House and described, in her diary, "what an upholsterer gone mad could do." In one of the public rooms, called the Egyptian Parlor, "sphinxes gazed at us from every direction, and a row of them, varied by a bull or two as a cornice over the windows, which were hung with bright green and red satin curtains, was very imposing. . . . The carpets were beautiful, but Western men had an odious habit of spitting on them, though there were gorgeous spittoons or 'cuspidors' about." Later, journeying through the Far West, the Adairs were struck by the good manners of an Indian chief, who spat into his hand rather than on the carpet, and his left hand at that, not the one he used for shaking. Mr. Adair's "light brown suit of check clothes" apparently seemed more peculiar to Chicagoans than an Egyptian parlor. One person commented that he must be one of Barnum's men, and another remarked, "That there is the uniform at Sing-Sing, I guess."

After the regal Palmer House, a steamer on Lake Superior proved a disappointment. The captain and crew were rude and the food was terrible. When Mr. Adair bought a few eggs and asked the steward to have them cooked, the

The huge size of American hotels—a match for the pyramids, as depicted above—and their clients' habit of cooling heels out the window, below, prompted these satirical views, c. 1865.

221

Hazards of steamboat travel, "not exaggerated," as reported in 1858

answer was, "Wal, I guess you had better go down to the kitchen and cook 'em yourself." A Mississippi steamboat was more comfortable, but the Adairs were alarmed by the nonchalant handling of a cargo of gunpowder; workmen lounged about, smoking, while the hatch of the cargo hold stood open, with sparks from a nearby brazier of coals flying all about. The young couple would have been even more disturbed had they traveled the same route in antebellum days, when the steamboats were unsafe beyond description.

Isabel and Basil March, in Howell's novel *Their Wedding Journey*, rode the Hudson River nightboat with no worse mishap than a collision—the other vessel sank, but there was little damage aboard the nightboat except to etiquette. Running out of her cabin in alarm, Isabel found "a world of dishabille, a world wildly unbuttoned and unlaced, where it was the fashion for ladies to wear their hair down their backs, and to walk about in their stockings, and to speak to each other without introduction." Isabel and Basil enjoyed making fun of the steamboat's lavish appointments. "Good heavens! Isabel, does it take all this to get us plain republicans to Albany in comfort . . . or are we really a nation of princes in disguise?" They were sorry to see "no interval between disgraceful squalor and ludicrous splendor"; the management catered exclusively to the "taste of the richest and most extravagant plebeian amongst us. He, unhappily, minds danger and oppression as little as he minds money, so long as he has a spectacle and a sensation, and it is this ruthless imbecile who will have lace curtains to the steamboat berth into which he gets with his pantaloons on, and out of which he may be blown by an exploding boiler at any moment. . . ."

The breakfast encountered by Isabel and Basil in the Albany railroad station shows that little advance was being made in ordinary American cuisine: they despair over "the peppery and muddy draught which impudently affected to be coffee, the oily slices of fugacious potatoes slipping about in their shallow dish and skillfully evading pursuit, the pieces of beef that simulated steak, the hot, greasy biscuit, steaming evilly up into the face when opened, and then soddening into masses of condensed dyspepsia." The service was equally depressing. The waitress "found their presence so incredible that she would not acknowledge the rattling that Basil was obliged to make on his glass." After a day on the train, the young couple stopped in Rochester, where they made the acquaintance of a traditionally obnoxious being, the American hotel clerk. "He was young, he had a neat mustache and well-brushed hair; jeweled studs sparkled in his shirt-front, and rings on his white hands; a gentle disdain of the travelling public breathed from his person in the mystical odors of Ihlang ihlang. He did not lift his haughty head to look at the wayfarer who meekly wrote his name in the register; he did not answer him when he begged for a cool room." Upstairs, "Basil found that, for his sin in asking for a cool room, the clerk had given them a chamber into which the sun had been shining the whole afternoon; but when his luggage had been put in it seemed useless to protest, and like a true American . . . he shrank from asserting himself." Not until the twentieth century, it appears, did the concept of politeness reach hotel clerks.

The experience of travel made Americans realize how heterogeneous were their fellow countrymen and to what extent customs and etiquette differed from place to place. Small wonder that people like our model family, the Upwards, felt insecure and turned to the long-established manners of England for a dependable example. The Upwards followed the etiquette rules that prevailed in the eastern half of the country, but were bedeviled by confusing exceptions. "Even in Victorian days," Emily Post tells us, "it was proper in Baltimore for a young girl to go to the theater alone with a man, and to have him see her home from a ball was not only permitted but absolutely correct." Yet in neighboring Washington, a young lady went to a ball and returned from it in the family carriage or in a hack, while her young man walked or took the trolley. In some places a maid or a young married woman made an acceptable chaperon; in others nobody would do but a sobersided matron of ripe years. In any event, it was clearly impossible to bring any consistency to the manners of America. The old antagonism toward the mother country still ran deep and was now, in the last quarter of the century, increased by businessmen who resented England's domination of the world markets. The American working classes stubbornly refused to behave like British working classes and stay in their places, or acknowledge that they had any betters. Rich families who wanted liveried footmen around the house had to get them from abroad, as no self-respecting American citizen, no matter how recent, would have been caught dead in a livery. The Englishman James F. Muirhead, author of Baedeker's *United States* (1893) and *The Land of Contrasts* (1898), wrote, "I have hailed with delight the democratic spirit displayed in the greeting of my friend and myself by the porter of a hotel as 'You fellows,' and then had the cup of pleasure dashed from my lips by being told by the same porter that 'the other *gentleman*' would attend to my baggage."

Efforts to achieve instant gentility without education and prolonged contact with "the right people" usually betrayed themselves through language. Upper-class speech was deceptively unaffected, and its practitioners were quick to notice pretentious circumlocutions. Mr. Muirhead was amused to read in a Boston streetcar: "The Board of Health hereby adjudges that the deposit of sputum in streetcars is a public nuisance." But such a sign could never have been written by an upper-class person, who would have said, "No spitting." Nancy Hale wrote a few years ago in *The New Yorker* about a Beacon Street debutante of 1890 who avoided the words "hostess" and "guest," considering them overfancy and preferring instead, "the friend whose house we were at" and "some people who came to call." In proper Boston circles, Miss Hale reports, "what one could *not* say . . . was the euphemistic word, the tearoom word, the word that had an air of 'chewing with your front teeth.' Any word that was refined or dainty or gracious—including those words themselves—was unspeakable."

There must have been a great deal of euphemism in the late nineteenth century, as the etiquette books make a point of denouncing it. They warn against using "retire" for "go to bed," "reside" for "live," "desire" for "want," and "partake of liquid refreshment" for "have something to drink." Other serious offenses were "folks" meaning "family," "visiting with" meaning "talking to," and "home" for "house." For would-be gentlefolk, linguistic pitfalls were far more hazardous and difficult to negotiate than those presented by the calling card, the kettledrum, or the ball. In the West, speech and accent were of less importance. But in the East or South, no parvenu could fool the sharp ears of the elite. Probably because they felt threatened by the oncoming sweep of the newly prosperous, gentlefolk were closing ranks. Snobbery had always been abroad in the land, but now it became rampant.

Device for "theater conversationalists"

THE New Sensation

A LIVELY, ROMANTIC PAPER FOR THE PERIOD

Vol. III.   Ornum & Co., Publishers, Beekman Street, N.Y.   NEW YORK, NOVEMBER 14, 1874.   Single Copies Ten Cents, $1.50 per annum, in advance.   No. 75

Minnie applied the current, and with a howl of pain Claude twisted himself up.

SOMETHING SHOCKING;
OR, A TERRIBLE REVENGE.

BY VAL VERSATILE,

Author of "Barrier of Wood," "Funny and Kate," "Under a Mask," Etc., Etc.

CHAPTER I.
MATTIE AND MINNIE.

"The woman is tricky, ah, well!
The cause of them she may not tell;
Though shocking the revenge she'll take,
'Twas merited—for another's sake."
—HAL HILDEBRAND.

"MINNIE," said Mattie Moore, as she entered the room where her friend Minnie Montford sat, "we will have company this evening."

"Male or she-male?" inquired pretty Minnie, in her careless style.

"Male," returned Mattie. "A genuine male man, and a genuine rascal to boot. Oh! the cruel wretch!"

Minnie looked up from her book and regarded her friend's face quizzically.

"The inconsistency of your proposed action and your last remarks must be apparent to you, my dear," she said. "First you delight me with the idea of having to entertain masculine company, and then horrify me by stigmatizing the coming man. Mattie, my moss rose, tell me what in thunder you really mean."

"It's quite a little story," returned Mattie. "So I'll just arrange myself comfortably and then spit it out. I'll wager that I'll enlist your sympathies by my tale, which I promise you is but too true."

Taboo Topics

*In which Certain Subjects,
unmentionable in the
Victorian Parlour, are
mentioned & Proper Persons
are found to have
Human Needs, Desires
& most of all Frailties*

Victorian Americans limited their polite conversation to noncontroversial topics and the changes in the weather. Even among best friends or between spouses numerous topics were literally unspeakable: sex, prostitution, illegitimate children, birth control, homosexuality, insanity, suicide, underclothes, and all the details of physiology, illness, or hygiene. Nevertheless, beneath the sleek and seemingly upholstered form of every woman was a constricting corset; men and women certainly were cohabiting, for plenty of babies were being born; and the noteworthy rise in the number of bathrooms, once indoor plumbing became readily available, would seem to indicate a need for them.

That birth control was practiced in America from earliest colonial times is shown by a passage in Governor Bradford's *Of Plimoth Plantation*, in which he tells how a young wife of the colony was "overcome" by a certain minister named Lyford, while he was having "private conferences" with her. Says Bradford, "though he satisfied his lust on her, yet he indeaoured to hinder conception." Over two hundred years passed before the next known reference to the subject by an American. This was *Moral Physiology*, a book published in 1830 by Robert Dale Owen, son of the founder of the experimental community of New Harmony, Indiana. Owen took his technical data from an English work on birth control, *Every Woman's Book; or, What Is Love?* An interest in the subject had been spurred by the popularization of the theories of the English economist Thomas Malthus regarding the dire consequences of unchecked population growth.

Anticipating controversy, Owen took the offensive: "Reader! If you belong to the class of prudes or of libertines, I pray you, follow my argument no farther. Stop here. . . . But if you be honest, upright, pure-minded; if you be

If Americans hesitated to discuss Certain Subjects, they were only too delighted to read about them. Magazines, affecting moral indignation, worked a rich lode of sin.

unconscious of unworthy motive or selfish passion; if truth be your ambition, and the welfare of our race your object—then approach with me a subject the most important to man's well-being. . . . 'Honi soit qui mal y pense,' may explain the spirit in which it is undertaken, and in which it ought to be received." He compared, unfavorably, the prudery of American women with the frankness of Europeans: "A French lady of the utmost delicacy and respectability will, in common conversation, say as simply (ay, and as *innocently* whatever the self-righteous prude may aver to the contrary) as she would proffer any common remark about the weather: 'I have three children; my husband and I think that is as many as we can do justice to, and I do not intend to have any more.' Will our sensitive fine ladies blush at the plain good sense and simplicity of such an observation? Let me tell them, the indelicacy is in their own minds, not in the words of the French mother."

Owen set forth his recommendations for birth control. He favored the method of *coitus interruptus.* He also mentioned but did not recommend a vaginal sponge which certain British reformers had been urging upon their own working classes. Owen said that the sponge (which its promoters described as "large as a green walnut, or a small apple," and attached to "a penny ribbon") was unreliable, as was a "covering made of very fine, smooth, and delicately prepared skin" which was good for one time only and cost a dollar. He warned against "solitary vice" as conducive to insanity.

Owen was soon showered with brickbats for *Moral Physiology.* A committee of the Typographical Society wrote to tell him that birth control threatened "inducements and facilities for the prostitution of their daughters, their sisters, and [their] wives." Owen retorted, "Truly, but they pay their wives, their sisters, and their daughters, a poor compliment! . . . For myself, I would withhold from no sister, no daughter, or wife of mine, any ascertained fact whatever. . . . A girl is surely no whit the better for believing, until her marriage night, that children are found among the cabbage leaves in the garden." Despite, or perhaps partly because of, the public indignation it aroused, the book went into repeated editions and was still selling when Robert Owen died, in 1877.

In 1832 a Massachusetts doctor, Charles Knowlton, published *The Fruits of Philosophy,* the first careful and minutely detailed account of contraception since a Greek work of the second century A.D. Some of the spermicides suggested sound alarming (sulphate of zinc, sugar of lead), but vinegar, since proved effective, was high on the list. A vivid commentary on the temperature of American houses before the days of central heat was the advice that a little "spirits" might be added to the solutions to prevent freezing. Knowlton advocated douching because "it costs nearly nothing, . . . requires no sacrifice of enjoyment, . . . it is in the hands of the female, where for good reasons it ought to be; it is harmless . . . as much or even more so than celibacy." Dr. Knowlton cautioned young couples against frequent "connexion," which, he said, might impair mental energies; cause weakness (he estimated that the loss of an ounce of semen was equal to the loss of forty ounces of blood) and diseases; render them irritable, unsociable, and melancholy; and even destroy their affection for each other. He recommended a diet of vegetables and milk for bachelors, and one of meat, turtles, oysters, and red wine for benedicts who craved a spur to lovemaking. Both Owen and Knowlton deplored the lack of research on the subject of contraception, and the fact that almost

Results of taking a gamble: a full house

no one would dare speak of his sexual experiences, even to physicians.

Knowlton found himself facing several court actions as soon as his book appeared. In one, he was sentenced to three months' hard labor. One lawyer accused Knowlton of giving a "complete recipe" for carrying on the trade of prostitution. The *Boston Medical and Surgical Journal* denounced such "unnatural measures," and opined that "the less that is known about [birth control] by the public at large, the better it will be for the morals of the community." At Taunton, where he was heavily fined, one of the jurymen said to him after the trial, "Well, we brought you in guilty—we did not see how we could well get rid of it, still I like your book, and you must let me have one of them." The juror was not alone in wanting a copy. Over the next fifty years, *The Fruits of Philosophy* went through numerous reprintings and revisions in both England and America. By 1881 it had sold 277,000 copies.

Subsequent nineteenth-century writers, whether recommending birth control or attacking it, drew heavily on Owen and Knowlton. In the fifties an Englishman named George Drysdale was among the first to describe a "safe period," but unfortunately, in the light of modern knowledge, the days Drysdale said were safe were unsafe. His suggestions were nevertheless widely followed in this country, as were other birth control nostrums.

Robert Dale Owen

John Humphrey Noyes, leader of the free love community at Oneida, New York, was an advocate of male continence, a method that called for lovemaking—sometimes for an hour or more—without ejaculation. The woman might thereby receive full satisfaction—a rare concept and perhaps possible only in woman-adoring nineteenth century America. Doctors warned that such a method would bring on nervous disease; yet a physician who examined members of the Oneida community in 1877 could find no resulting cases of nervous affliction, and birth records indicate that accidental impregnations by this method were rare. Noyes wrote enthusiastically that *coitus reservatus* would lead to the happy day when "sexual intercourse becomes a method of ordinary conversation and each is married to all." It would become, he said, "a purely social affair, the same in kind with other modes of kindly interchange, differing only by its superior intensity and beauty. . . . Amative intercourse will become one of the 'fine arts.' Indeed it will take rank above music, painting, sculpture, &c.; for it combines the charms and benefits of them all." Noyes's Oneida community was denounced by the whole country. In 1881 the "Perfectionists" finally agreed to give up their nonconforming ways, settle down, one wife to one husband, and concentrate on wordly affairs, which included making silverplate and mousetraps.

John Humphrey Noyes

Male continence was given further currency in the books of Dr. Alice Bunker Stockham, published in the late eighties and nineties. She called the method "Karezza" (an exotic-sounding word that was probably a corruption of the Italian word for caress), and promised that its practice would bring visions, spiritual companionship, and the consciousness of unsuspected powers, provided each act was preceded by an interval of two to four weeks of "thoughtful preparation."

A surgeon in the United States Navy, Thomas Ewell, is given credit for the earliest (1806) and most imaginative new "remedy or corrective for fruitful nature." Negroes, it seemed to him (erroneously), were highly fertile; Negroes were in the habit of copulating outdoors; thus he deduced that "coition will always be unfruitful unless it be done in pure air." Ergo, couples who did not

The naughty ladies above unveil their charms in the service of a beer ad, c. 1897. The silver-buckled garters below were for very special affairs.

wish to be fruitful should embrace in "vessels filled with carbonic acid or azotic gas." Whether any couple ever tried this out is not recorded.

In 1873 the spread of birth control information received an immense set-back: under Section 211 of the Federal Criminal Code, better known as the first Comstock Law, it was classified with pornography and prohibited from circulation through the United States mails. Anthony Comstock, the stern Victorian citizen who propelled the law through Congress (and was rewarded with an appointment as special agent to the Post Office Department), was a self-appointed guardian of public morals. His theory was, "If you open the door to anything, the filth will all pour in and the degradation of youth will follow." From his combined position as postal watchdog and secretary of the New York Society for the Suppression of Vice, Comstock continued to cast his shadow across science, the arts, and religious thought in America even after his death in 1915. Toward the end of his life, he said with satisfaction, "In the forty-one years I have been here I have convicted persons enough to fill a passenger train of sixty-one coaches, sixty coaches containing sixty passengers each and the sixty-first almost full."

The passengers who looked from the windows of Comstock's remarkable dreamtrain, bound presumably straight for hell, were an oddly mixed lot: Madame Restell, a Fifth Avenue abortionist; Bernarr Macfadden, arrested for displaying pictures of twelve women in union suits; the editors of the sedate *Chautauquan* magazine, who had ventured to depict on one of its covers an ancient statue of a naked faun; a belly dancer, captured on the Midway at the Chicago Exposition of 1893; the directors of the New York Art Students League, for printing a booklet showing students' life-class sketches; painters of such shrinking-violet nudes as "September Morn"; the Broadway producers of George Bernard Shaw's *Mrs. Warren's Profession* (Comstock called Shaw an "Irish smut dealer," and Shaw, retaliating, coined the word *comstockery* to deal with overzealous censorship); a number of freethinking intellectuals, notably the atheist Robert G. Ingersoll; a raffish collection of madams, purveyors of useless or dangerous quack cures, and publishers of erotic literature and filthy postcards; and a clergyman who had issued a treatise on the propagation of marsupials.

Medical men who continued to write on birth control between the 1870's and the First World War were exceptional. Most doctors said and did nothing to make family planning respectable, and many denounced it as impure and immoral. In 1890 the president of the American Gynecological Society delivered an address advocating large families, condemning birth control on theological grounds, and attacking sex education of children as bound to lead to bad morals. Nevertheless, the birth rate for middle- and upper-class families tapered off enough to become noticeable by the end of the century, when the average family had dwindled to three members.

Gynecologists reported that the treatment of postabortion ailments took up more of their time than maternity cases; an 1887 estimate put the number of women to die from the effects of abortion at not less than six thousand a year. One writer said that fear of conception "makes a mental wreck of many a normal and healthy woman," and another praised "the superior, or at least the more persistent, happiness of couples without children," the reason for it being that the couples could devote themselves to each other's happiness, without the cares of a large household. Critics of this state of affairs blamed the ever-growing woman's rights movement, complaining that native upper-class Americans were the worst offenders because they prized ease and social dissipation above parenthood. The Frenchman Paul Bourget, visiting our shores in 1893, wrote that in America maternity was almost humiliating or vulgar. Another commentator muttered darkly that such evils were all the fault of the Teddy Bear, which came on the market in 1902, shortly after a celebrated incident in which Theodore Roosevelt had spared the life of a bear cub. The critic maintained that the stuffed animal symbolized "the substitution of sterile interests for the cult of motherhood."

An American male who found too meager a sex life at home was exposed to all manner of temptation in the back streets of the cities. Although prostitution was illegal and there were plenty of Comstocks to make periodic raids (Comstock was laughed at for watching a lewd dance in a bawdyhouse before arresting the dancers), every sizable town had its "palatial bagnios," its kept women, and its streetwalkers. In the West, where women were scarce, there was a kind of amiable gallantry on the part of the men toward local "soiled doves" and "nymphs du prairie." When one Alice Chambers of Dodge City, Kansas, lost seven dollars from her stocking in a sudden gust of wind, local yokels helped her look for it but recovered only one dollar. The incident was reported in the Dodge City newspaper, with the comment, "even the wind can be found feeling around in and by forbidden paths." Houses of prostitution East and West were raided regularly, but were rarely fined heavily enough to put them out of business. When Theodore Roosevelt was made police commissioner of New York in 1895, he made a point of treating the male customers apprehended in vice raids no better than the women purveyors—an unusual police commissioner indeed in those days of the hard-and-fast double standard.

New York had the biggest population of prostitutes in the country. In an effort to rescue and rehabilitate these fallen women, some of whom were as young as thirteen, a few charitable souls had founded the Magdalen Society in 1830. The group—and their first annual report—were attacked from many quarters on the grounds that they were libeling the city's good name, and were publishing pornography besides. *Magdalen Facts*, a corroborating book written the following year by a young clergyman, asserted that there were then not less than ten thousand prostitutes in the city—more than the number of marriageable virgins.

The minister quoted the *Christian Advocate* in support of his study: "It is indeed mortifying to a virtuous mind to be under the necessity of believing that so much licentiousness exists. But must it be concealed for fear of offending the ears of delicacy?" He blamed not only men and poverty, but the theater, fairs, and waxworks shows for starting unfortunate girls on the primrose path. "She was humbled" was the euphemism he preferred for describing the crucial downward step, following which it was apparently impossible for a girl to go back home or to be accepted within the portals of outraged society. Even the Magdalen Society could do little for her beyond keeping her out of the river and teaching her how to make a few dollars a week by sewing or cleaning house. Meantime, her betrayer might blithely continue to travel in the most elegant society.

During the 1850's, a doctor at one of New York's hospitals, William Sanger (no relation to the twentieth-century birth control advocate Margaret Sanger),

Anthony Comstock on a moral crusade

concerned over the high incidence of venereal disease he saw daily, made a study of the extent of prostitution in America. Like Dr. Kinsey nearly a century later, Dr. Sanger based his report on interviews. He also wrote letters to the mayors of large cities, asking for estimates on local prostitution. Some of the mayors' figures were obviously low. The mayor of Newark, for instance, stated that in a population of 55,000 there were only fifty cases of prostitution, and they were "private"—whatever that was. The mayor of Buffalo, where the population was only 20,000 more than that of Newark, acknowledged a total of 384 prostitutes. Even taking the mayors' reports at face value, Sanger estimated that if all the prostitutes in the United States "were walking in a continuous line, thirty-six inches from each other, they would make a column nearly thirty-five miles long."

Dr. Sanger ranked houses of prostitution in several classes. "Parlor houses" constituted the top class. They occupied expensive but unobtrusive premises in the most fashionable part of large cities. To become a client of such a house, an introduction was usually needed, although a well-dressed, quiet-mannered person, an obvious gentleman, might gain admittance without one. A servant ushered the new arrival into an elegant parlor, where he would find a number of beautifully dressed young women, engaged in polite conversation. Joining in their talk for a while, the gentleman would order champagne and begin to concentrate his conversational gambits on one of the young women in particular. After a leisurely glass or two of champagne and more well-turned phrases, she would suggest continuing the chat in a more sequestered part of the house. The price of her company might run as high as sixty dollars.

"Parlor house" girls usually were well-educated, came from middle- or upper-class homes, and had been seduced and abandoned by gentlemen. Once seduced, they had crossed the yawning gulf that separated good women from bad ones. They were thoroughly ruined in the eyes of the world, and the occupation of high-class whore could hardly ruin them further. Dr. Sanger gave a few case histories: "Miss Margaret ____, of Neilson Place, is a beautiful blonde, of graceful figure and attractive mien, remarkable both for her distinguée appearance and manner, and dresses with charming taste—not gaudily, but always richly, and in the latest fashion. She is a native of Providence, Rhode Island, and is now in the twenty-fourth year of her age, and is thoroughly educated, having graduated from one of the leading ladies' seminaries of New England. She speaks French as fluently as English, and is accomplished in music. She is not only elegant and refined in her manners, but possesses conversational powers and mental culture that would fit her for any sphere."

Many a Victorian married man sought an afternoon's or evening's dalliance with Miss Margaret. Dr. Sanger had an explanation: ". . . the full force of sexual desire is seldom known to a virtuous woman. In the male sex, nature has provided a more susceptible organization than in females, apparently with the beneficent design of repressing those evils which must result from mutual appetite equally felt by both. In other words, man is the *aggressive* animal, so far as sexual desire is involved. Were it otherwise, and the passions in both sexes equal, illegitimacy and prostitution would be far more rife in our midst than at present."

A house of the second class was less dignified and exclusive than the parlor

Hooking a victim by gaslight, c. 1850

house. The ability to play the piano or to read Molière in the original was not required of the girls, many of whom were foreign-born and had met their downfall through being seduced on board an immigrant ship or in an immigrant boardinghouse. While parlor houses took great precautions against venereal disease, in second-class houses and below it was common.

A third-class house was often found in conjunction with a bar or beer garden, the latter mostly owned and operated by German immigrants. The establishment was usually run by a husband and wife, the husband tending bar and the wife acting as madam. Brothel- and bar-keeping was also a vocation of the Irish, but their houses had the reputation of being less clean and orderly than the German ones, and considerably more alcoholic. There were also saloons that maintained accommodations for streetwalkers. The lowest category of brothel, a filthy slum basement, was the last stop in degradation for "old" prostitutes. Twenty-five was old in this line of work. Dr. Sanger reported: *"The average duration of life among these women does not exceed four years from the beginning of their career! . . .* It is a tolerably well-established fact that one-fourth of the total number of abandoned women in this city die every year." A woman shrewd enough to save her money, and lucky enough to escape venereal disease or a fatal abortion, usually ended her days as a madam.

A New York police chief of 1887, in a book of recollections of the city's dens of iniquity, described the French Ball, held annually at the Academy of Music and two adjacent halls on then-fashionable Fourteenth Street. "The French ball," wrote the chief, "is an assemblage of the higher class demimonde and the club men of New York City. . . . It is taken for granted that most of the *jeunesse dorée* will go . . . and that respectable women will not go. Yet respectable women do attend the ball. There are usually more than a hundred on the floor and in the dress circle, deeply and thoroughly masked beyond recognition, except to those who know their forms and methods of walking. Husbands and wives often go—generally with somebody's else wives and husbands." The chief goes on to describe the bacchanal: "If it was lively at twelve, what adjective will describe it at two? . . . A woman approaches us, attired in a brocaded pink silk dress, shirred down the front with pink satin, ornaments, laces and diamonds, and tries to kick our hats off. We quit the terrible person, and retreat to the stairs, where a gentleman, well known in New York parlors, is tugging away at something. It is a woman, apparently; a very heavy weight. He has clasped her wrists over his shoulders, and is trying to carry her up stairs on his back.

" 'O, Harry! Drop that mountain of loveliness!' shouted an acquaintance to him, and the 'mountain' rolls off and rushes for the speaker, who flees."

Not all the chief's recollections were so merry. He described the most villainous dives of New York, where, "under the brilliant glare of gas-jets," innocent factory girls came, lured by "the fascination of the waltz," and took their first false steps, "as surely as a displaced stone goes tumbling down a hillside. . . . Shop girls go to Armory Hall to dance, and just as surely as they become habitués of the place their horrible fate as prostitutes is settled. The can-can dance is the favorite one here, and the debauchery and licentiousness exhibited is terrible."

The low life of the great cities teemed with abortionists, and from the 1840's to the 1870's, the most notorious, evil, and successful was Madame Restell of

High life among the low, especially if they were Irish, was centered in the neighborhood saloon. These sketches record a gay night in 1871.

New York. Madame, born a working-class girl in Gloucestershire, England, came to America as a young wife in 1831, was left a widow, and, casting about for a means of livelihood, fell in with an old crone on Chatham Street who sold "peculiar medicines" to women who wished to abort. These peculiar medicines had the advantage of being absolutely ineffective, so that in case of arrest no charge beyond swindling could be made, and in any event no victim was likely to bring a complaint. Setting herself up as a "female physician," Madame Restell did a lively business. Besides selling fake abortive pills, she also performed real abortions, delivered babies, and undertook to get rid of unwanted ones—ideally by means of adoption, but sometimes by criminal neglect and, it was suspected, by murder. She became so successful that she moved to an elegant brownstone at the corner of Fifth Avenue and Fifty-second Street, then the most fashionable part of town. It was there, in 1878, that she was served with a search warrant by none other than Anthony Comstock. Two days before her trial was set to open, Madame Restell cut her throat in the bathtub, thus joining the growing list of suicides for which Mr. Comstock claimed credit. The editors of *Puck* predicted a local population explosion within the year.

Madame Restell obviously had had enough prosperous clients to pay for a brownstone and a carriage, which is perhaps an indication of skeletons in a good many respectable closets. Women of good social position sometimes managed to lead a secret love life by means of meeting their lovers at houses of assignation. Such places were open in the daytime rather than in the evening, during the hours when ladies went shopping or visiting. The lover made all the arrangements beforehand, so that when the lady arrived, heavily veiled, no one saw her except the servant who answered the door and showed her to a luxuriously furnished bedroom. No gentleman unknown to the management was admitted, nor were prostitutes allowed. Payment for the room was in cash; no names were asked for or given except false ones. It was vital to the success of the house to allay its patrons' fears of blackmail or discovery.

Houses of assignation seemed to the Victorian American mind even more wicked than houses of prostitution, for they indicated unthinkable proclivities on the part of well-bred women, whose interest in sex was supposed to be minimal. Dr. Sanger, in his 1858 report, blamed the whole thing on Europe. "Such houses must be regarded as the connecting link between the licentious excesses of the capitals of Europe and this city of the New World. . . . As yet they are rare, and it speaks well for the morals of our upper classes that they are so. It shows that the majority of people in the higher walks of life are untainted. But the course of deterioration has commenced. Will not American good sense and American morality check this base imitation of a foreign custom?"

That women of the middle and upper classes were beginning to get restless and dissatisfied with their lot as child bearers and docile helpmates is more surely indicated by the rising divorce rate. Before the Civil War, divorce was exceptional. In cases of adultery on the part of the husband, the wife was supposed to keep her eyes shut, though if the wife were the guilty party, no jury would convict her husband if he shot either her or her lover or perhaps both. A famous example of a *crime passionnel* occurred in Washington in 1859 when Congressman Daniel Sickles shot and killed his wife's lover in a duel. Sickles readily admitted the murder—it was the first time a defendant

(Continued on Page 234)

This stereopticon scene of wild abandon was titled "Better than Champagne."

Cheyenne: 1873

The Wild West, as seen by Isabella Bird in A Lady's Life in the Rocky Mountains. *Miss Bird warned fellow Englishmen that it was "no region for tourists."*

Cheyenne is described as "a God-forsaken, God-forgotten place." . . . it forgets God is written on its face. . . . A short time ago it was a perfect pandemonium, mainly inhabited by rowdies and desperadoes, the scum of advancing civilization; and murders, stabbings, shootings, and pistol affrays were at times events of almost hourly occurrence in its drinking dens. But in the West, when things reach their worst, a sharp and sure remedy is provided. Those settlers who find the state of matters intolerable, organize themselves into a Vigilance Committee. "Judge Lynch," with a few feet of rope, appears on the scene, the majority crystallizes round the supporters of order, warnings are issued to obnoxious people, simply bearing a scrawl of a tree with a man dangling from it, with such words as "Clear out of this by 6 A.M., or ____." . . . Piety is not the *forte* of Cheyenne. The roads resound with atrocious profanity, and the rowdyism of the saloons and barrooms is repressed, not extirpated. The population, once 6,000, is now about 4,000. It is an ill-arranged set of frame houses and shanties; and rubbish heaps, and offal of deer and antelope, produce the foulest smells I have smelt for a long time. Some of the houses are painted a blinding white; others are unpainted; there is not a bush, or garden, or green thing. . . . It is utterly slovenly looking and unornamental, abounds in slouching barroom characters, and looks a place of low, mean lives . . . be-

yond the railroad tracks are nothing but the brown plains, with their lonely sights—now a solitary horseman at a traveling amble, then a party of Indians in paint and feathers, but civilized up to the point of carrying firearms . . . then a drove of ridgy-spined long-horned cattle, which have been several months eating their way from Texas, with their escort of four or five much-spurred horsemen, in peaked hats, blue-hooded coats, and high boots, heavily armed with revolvers and repeating rifles, and riding small wiry horses. A solitary wagon, with a white tilt [canvas hood], drawn by eight oxen, is probably bearing an emigrant and his fortunes to Colorado. . . . Everything suggests a beyond. . . . [Among westerners] all courtesy and gentleness of act or speech seem regarded as "works of the flesh," if not of "the devil." They knock over all one's things without apologizing or picking them up, and when I thank them for anything they look grimly amazed. . . . I wish I could show them "a more excellent way." This hard greed, and the exclusive pursuit of gain, with the indifference to all which does not aid in its acquisition, are eating up family love and life throughout the West. [Having] seen a great deal of the roughest class of men . . . the more important I think the "mission" of every quiet, refined, self-respecting woman [and] the more mistaken I think those who would forfeit it by noisy self-assertion, or fastness. I have written that this scenery is not lovable, but I love it.

The ideal woman allowed her man ample room to pursue his own life. The clinging vine above and the self-sufficient divorcée below were not playing by the rules.

pleaded temporary insanity—and was acquitted amidst courtroom cheers. By the 1870's, however, the public would have thought Sickles uncivilized and would rather have seen him take his grievance to a divorce court. Sixteen thousand divorces were granted in 1878; nearly twenty-nine thousand in 1888, and nearly forty-eight thousand in 1898, an increase much greater than that of the population growth. Grounds for divorce varied from none, in South Carolina, to any cause "deemed by the court sufficient," in the state of Washington. North Dakota required but ninety days' residence, and Nevada and Wyoming six months. In the South, where women seldom were able to earn their own living, divorce was more often sought by husbands than by wives.

A pioneer for liberal divorce laws was the noted suffragist and woman's rights leader Elizabeth Cady Stanton. Unfortunately, she had one fault generally considered to be typically feminine—the inability to keep her mouth shut when she knew a good piece of gossip. Her crusade for divorce suffered through her part in letting loose the most sensational scandal of the century. To review the story briefly, among the parishioners of the eminent Henry Ward Beecher at Plymouth Church, in Brooklyn, was a couple named Theodore and Elizabeth Tilton. Beecher had married them in 1855 and had made Tilton, who was a successful writer, editor, and orator, something of a protégé. He was a frequent visitor at the Tilton home. In 1870 Mrs. Tilton told a friend that Beecher's calls, for the past two years, had been directed to herself, not her husband, and that they had not been platonic. The friend told Mrs. Stanton, who told the free love advocate Victoria Woodhull. The latter was editing a newspaper whose slogans were "Progress!" "Free Thought!" "Untrammelled Lives!" "Breaking the Way for Future Generations!" After pondering Mrs. Tilton's story for a couple of years, Woodhull published it, not as scandal (she said), but in defense of free love. As a result, the Tiltons separated; Tilton threatened suicide but thought better of it and became Woodhull's lover instead; Woodhull and her sister were arrested for sending obscene literature through the mails; Beecher was tried by his church and exonerated; Tilton sued Beecher, the trial resulting in a hung jury; the Tiltons were reunited; and Beecher went on preaching to packed congregations, just as before.

Arthur Schlesinger, Sr., in *The Rise of the City*, is of the opinion that the great increase in divorce resulted from urban conditions: "the anonymity of city life, its distractions and temptations, the growing practice of living in boarding houses and flats, the harsh struggle for existence, the opportunities for self-support afforded women. . . . Since twice as many divorces in the period 1878–1898 were granted upon the wife's complaint as on the husband's, it is likely that the increase reflected, in part, a greater self-respect among women and an unwillingness to put up with conditions which their mothers would have accepted in silence." Monetary difficulties were said to be the major cause of divorce, although the prime complaint in court was desertion. Adultery was not a usual charge; whether because it was not committed, or because it was hard to prove, or because people did not wish to talk about it, is a moot question.

It seems surprising that late-nineteenth-century freedom for women did not extend to their clothing. Yet the thousands of women who marched to court to get rid of their irksome husbands were encumbered by whalebone and steel corsets, wire "forms," like two inverted sieves, over the bosom, and steel bustles behind. Ladies of the 1890's omitted the bustle; the corset, though lighter, was still there; and skirts still dusted the pavement. Other underpinnings included multiple petticoats, a chemise, a corset cover, hose supporters, and cotton or silk stockings. Underpants or drawers, originally a masculine garment, had been adapted around the beginning of the 1800's.

For decades, doctors and reformers had been trying vainly to get women to stop compressing themselves with steel and whalebone. The use of padding and India rubber bosoms was apparently common; many a Victorian bridegroom must have been in for an unhappy surprise. Lola Montez, the renowned international courtesan, who published a book of beauty hints in 1858, advised women to leave their breasts as nature made them. "The bosom, which nature has formed with exquisite symmetry in itself, and admirable adaptation to the parts of the figure to which it is united, is often transformed into a shape, and transplanted to a place, which deprive it of its original beauty and harmony with the rest of the person. . . . I have known ladies to take a preparation of iodyne internally to remedy a too large development of the bosom. But this must be a dangerous experiment for the general health."

An 1893 article in *The Ladies' Home Journal* begs ladies not to put their daughters into corsets at the age of eleven or twelve, and hopes that they will themselves find the courage to do without them. "Until very recently it has required great courage to adopt dress reform, . . . because propriety was outraged by any departure from the strict rules laid down by fashion, and a woman to achieve freedom of body was almost obliged to endure social ostracism." Very few women must have heeded *The Ladies' Home Journal*, for that much-emulated beauty, the Gibson Girl, headed into the twentieth century laced to the nines. Though corsets and other underclothes were widely advertised in magazines, shop windows, and on billboards, they were strictly unmentionable between the sexes.

Bloomers in full flower, 1851

Perhaps the most taboo subject of all was homosexuality—so unmentionable that many Americans lived and died without ever hearing of it. That it existed and was not rare is obvious from the fact that there were laws against it and had been ever since early colonial days. The penalty was no longer death, as it had been in the days when Governor Bradford had noted in *Of Plimoth Plantation* that "sodomie and bugerie (things fearfull to name) have broak forth in this land, oftener than once"; but in most states, homosexual offenses brought sentences of up to ten years. There were no American books on the subject, but in England, toward the close of the century, the historian John Addington Symonds broached it in a privately printed book, *A Problem in Modern Ethics*. In it, he quoted a letter written by a German homosexual: ". . . I went to North America [in 1871] to try my fortune. There the unnatural vice in question is more ordinary than it is here [in Germany]; and I was able to indulge my passions with less fear of punishment or persecution. The American's tastes in this matter resemble my own; and I discovered, in the United States, that I was always immediately recognised as a member of the confraternity."

If the German was right, no American cared to admit it—at least, not in writing. Symonds wrote to Walt Whitman, apparently asking whether certain passages in *Leaves of Grass* had homosexual connotations. The reply was indignant. Whitman spoke of "morbid inferences—which are disavowed by me and seem damnable." Nevertheless, some Americans seem to have suspected Whitman of unorthodox behavior. A parody of his "Song of Myself" appeared

in *Vanity Fair* in 1860. It was called "Counter-Jumps"—a counter-jumper being a slang word for a dry goods salesman, an occupation thought suitable only for the most effete men. The "poemettina" ran:

> *I am the Counter-jumper, weak and effeminate.*
> *I love to loaf and lie about dry-goods.*
> *I loaf and invite the Buyer.*
> *I am the essence of retail. . . .*
> *I am the crate, and the hamper, and the yard-wand,*
> *And the box of silks fresh from France,*
> *And when I came into the world I paid duty,*
> *And I never did my duty,*
> *And never intend to do it,*
> *For I am the creature of weak depravities;*
> *I am the Counter-jumper;*
> *I sound my feeble yelp over the woofs of the World.*

During the nineties, the daring proponent of male continence Dr. Alice Stockham brought out a book on sex written by an Englishman, Edward Carpenter; but she omitted one chapter called "The Intermediate Sex," dealing with homosexuality. The full text of the book was not printed in this country until 1911, after it had been through many editions in a number of languages. Homosexuals, said Carpenter, "are by no means so very rare; but . . . form, beneath the surface of society, a large class."

An equal wall of silence surrounded the bathroom and the water closet. Women who worked in stores or factories were often deeply embarrassed by having to ask a male overseer if they might visit the water closet, or by having to walk past men and boys to get there. A study called *Women Wage Earners* reported, "All physicians who treat this class testify to the fact that many become seriously diseased as the result of unwillingness to subject themselves to this ordeal." Such delicacy could not have existed in colonial times or even in rural nineteenth-century America; large families in small houses may not have allowed the privy and the chamber pot to come into the conversation, but there must have been little question about where they were or who was using them. A prevalent rural custom of disguising the outhouse with sunflowers made that building especially easy to identify. During the corn season, a provident housekeeper saved all the well-chewed corncobs and stacked them neatly by the privy—there being no toilet paper in those days. It was not until the facilities were moved indoors that it was possible to ignore them.

As far as is known, the first household bathroom in the country was installed by George Vanderbilt, who added one to his New York residence in 1855. It had a porcelain tub, a super luxury in a time when bathtubs were usually metal. The pipes were undisguised—the explanation being that the bathroom was not a proper place for ostentation. Other rich people followed suit. Plumbing became an expected feature of the best American hotels, with the Mount Vernon Hotel in Cape May, New Jersey, being first, in 1853, to provide a private bath with every bedroom. But indoor bathrooms in the private house remained a luxury until this century. The earliest running-water bathtub had its own heater, a boiler connected with the kitchen range.

As late as the 1880's, five out of six city dwellers had no bathroom at home and used a public bath. When plumbing was introduced into tenements and

The poet Walt Whitman, above, and the visiting English aesthete, Oscar Wilde, below, represented varieties of male eccentricity quite beyond the ken of most Victorian Americans.

apartment houses, there was usually but one bath and one water closet for several families—possibly a whole building. As soon as a city acquired a water-supply system, water was run to kitchen sinks first, then to wash basins, then to bathtubs, and finally to toilets. (The word *toilet* was borrowed from the French *toilette*, and was adopted in this country as a euphemism for *water closet*. The English were satisfied with shortening *water closet* to *W.C.*) A daily bath was not considered necessary—once a week was more like it. Mrs. Mary Baker G. Eddy once made the pronouncement, "The daily ablution of an infant is not more natural or necessary than to take a fish out of water and cover it with dirt once a day, that it may thrive better in its natural element. Cleanliness is next to godliness, but washing should be only to keep the body clean, and this can be done with less than daily scrubbing the whole surface."

Mrs. Eddy may have been right to avoid the bathroom, for imperfect plumbing soon became a source of lethal diseases. An article written in 1883 for the staid *North American Review* bore the forthright title "The Unsanitary Homes of the Rich." According to the author, "the defects of the costliest houses on Murray Hill rival those of the tenements of Dexter street. . . . [They are] mere whited sepulchers, and their luxurious inmates are exposed to constant risk of disease and death. . . . In the best houses, the provisions kept in refrigerators are exposed to the chance of contamination when the drip-pipe connects directly with the house-drains. Frequent cases of sickness have been traced to this cause. . . . The space behind the woodwork of basins, sinks, and other fixtures [the author hesitates to name the other fixture] is almost invariably foul. Slop sinks are sources of offensive odors, and all these evils are intensified by the lack of water for flushing purposes, owing to the deficient pressure. . . . In Washington the sanitary defects in the White House, which are believed to have contributed to President Garfield's death, are equaled by those in several public buildings, where trapless water-closets, leaky drains, furnaces with polluted air-supply abound." This abysmal state of affairs was apparently largely due to a shortage of well-trained and honest plumbers ("some one has said that a man cannot handle lead without moral deterioration"). Architects and builders failed to understand the requirements of plumbing and did not allow for proper facilities in their plans. One splendid New York mansion had a bathroom in the center of the house with no ventilation except through a transom opening into a bedroom. "The occupant of that bedroom died of typhoid fever."

Heads of families were exposed to lurking death every time they went to work. In old buildings, where basements were often rented out as offices, the cellars were damp and the antique drains had never been intended to cope with sewage. "Hence such buildings are found saturated with sewer-gas, and their occupants, too absorbed in business cares to heed their unsanitary surroundings, learn only too late what are the physical effects of such exposure." Escape to the country was no answer, for things were still worse there. Country plumbers were even less competent than city ones and had no objection to installing an unventilated cesspool next to a well. "The risks of a summer spent at so-called health resorts are of a serious nature."

But at least the country had fresh air to offer, while city dwellers drooped in fetid houses, particularly in New York, where the long, narrow brownstone houses offered no air circulation. "Such air as does enter the seldom opened

A breath of fresh air on a city rooftop

windows is redolent with scents from stables, soot from elevated railroads, vapors from factories, or odors from Hunter's Point refineries; the careful housekeeper therefore closes the windows tightly, and the sole source of air is the furnace register, which is supplied from a leaky cold-air box, filled with cellar-damp and street-dust. When ignited, the latter smells like burnt feathers, and on analysis it yields twenty per cent of organic matter.... After passing through the furnace registers, it mingles with the vapors from the kitchen and laundry, or with gases from leaky drains or foul plumbing fixtures and the products of combustion from scores of gas-jets, forming what Professor [Thomas] Huxley aptly calls 'a stirabout of solid particles,' and a poor substitute for nature's atmosphere.... In the vast majority of houses, the air from the lower floors stagnates in the rooms next the roof, whose occupants are in a constant state of stupor."

Because people were ignorant about matters of sanitation and hygiene and were embarrassed to ask questions, they suffered in silence from ailments great and small. Even reputable physicians did not know answers that are now common knowledge, and there were no laws to control patent medicines. Thus from 1708, when Daffy's Elixir Salutis was advertised in the *Boston News-Letter*, to 1906, when the federal government moved in, any quack with a talent for salesmanship, or "puffery" as it was called, could get rich. No threat or claim was too preposterous to print, particularly if it concerned an "unmentionable" subject, for few readers would try to check on the truth of it. The purveyors of a cancer "cure," for example, wrote in their advertisement, "In any woman's breast, any lump is *cancer*."

Loss of manhood and female weakness seem to have worried a large part of the population. Lydia E. Pinkham, self-proclaimed "mother to the women of the world," put her wonder-working vegetable compound on the market in 1875. She promised, among other things, to cure "falling of the womb" with a tablespoon of her syrup taken every four hours. Like many panaceas of its genre, it was high proof, but as Mrs. Pinkham, an earnest W.C.T.U. member, put it, alcohol was added "solely as a solvent and preservative."

An electric belt for "weak men"

Men had a wider choice of curatives. With health belts, purporting to send charges of alternating electrical current through all their vital organs, men suffering from "Nervous Debility, Lack of Nerve Force, Wasting Weaknesses and all those diseases of a Personal Nature resulting from Abuses" were guaranteed a speedy recovery of their manhood. Prevention of "abuses," a Victorian euphemism for masturbation, was promised by one Michael McCormick of San Francisco. In 1896 he received a United States government patent for a male chastity belt which delivered very painful sensations to the wearer when, "through forgetfulness or any other cause his thoughts should be running in lascivious channels.... Voluntary self-abuse will be checked, presuming the wearer be desirous of benefit, as he will not take the trouble to relieve himself of the appliance, and he cannot continue his practice without removing it." Since self-abuse was widely believed to be a cause of insanity, Mr. McCormick probably found a few takers.

Victorian gentlemen were also invited to "private lectures" at which learned doctors could explain to them in clinical detail some of the mysteries of their physiology. Advertised with the same sort of ballyhoo that made P. T. Barnum famous, the lectures of a Dr. Warner dwelt on "The Functions of Man ... and How false delicacy has led to ignorance and Ignorance to injurious and sinful Practices." His story unfolded with such visual aids as "Manikens, Skeletons, and a great number of Costly and Beautiful Models, Oil Paintings and Natural Preparations." Patent medicine cures included Dr. Red Wing's bottled Mexican Herbs of Joy and Mormon Damiana Wafers, which capitalized on the supposed super vigor of that polygamous society.

Another subject that was stringently taboo, from the earliest colonial times well into the twentieth century, was insanity. In Puritan times, the insane were thought to be possessed by the Devil; once this explanation ceased to be believed, there was for years no other to take its place. The insane were no longer beaten, racked, or sent to the gallows in order to drive the Devil out, but they were treated with brutal indifference, believed to have no human sensibilities or deserve any human rights. By the end of the eighteenth century a handful of public hospitals cared for the insane, notably in Philadelphia, Williamsburg, and New York. Dr. Benjamin Rush was the first to promote a measure of kindness, cleanliness, and occupational therapy for his patients, but for years he had few followers. Rush and many of his contemporaries believed that terror was a cure for insanity. One terror-inducing device was to pour cold water down the patient's sleeves, "so that it may descend into the arm pits and down the trunk of the body," for fifteen or twenty minutes. If this failed, Rush tried death threats; or starving the patient until nearly dead; or "the bath of surprise," wherein a trap door suddenly opened and plunged the patient into a pool of cold water; or the "well-cure," which called for chaining the patient in the bottom of an empty well and slowly pouring water on him until he nearly drowned. For Rush and his colleagues, all this was kindness; the unkindly treated insane were left in chains, untended, with no attempt made to cure them or make them comfortable.

The hospitalized insane were usually violent cases. Those who were relatively harmless but without families to care for them were treated by most communities as paupers. One way of dealing with paupers — and consequently, the insane — was to auction them off to the lowest bidder, who would house them and use their labor in return for a pittance from the town or state. This custom, called the New England System, lasted throughout the nineteenth century and in some states into the twentieth. "Strong backs and weak minds" were considered assets for farm laborers, and there was lively bidding for the harmless insane and feeble-minded. The insane were also put into almshouses along with impoverished but sane men, women, and children. For example, a New York almshouse in 1838 was reported to accommodate, in one ten-bed chamber, nineteen persons — two married couples, one aged colored woman, two male idiots, one very old man, and eleven children. The insane were also lodged in jails. As no community liked this state of affairs, efforts were made to "pass on" insane paupers to wherever they had come from, or to dump them illegally and by night in another town, provided they were too confused to be able to recall who they were or what had happened.

Families with an insane or retarded member faced a most agonizing decision, and faced it in secrecy, for mental illness was a disgrace. Even if they could find a hospital that would take the ill person, they would be condemning their own flesh and blood to misery. The alternative was to keep him at home, out of sight and under restraint — perhaps in an attic, cellar, closet, or cage. Not a few families lived with such burdens, made heavier by compulsive

"Bust beauty" and an hourglass figure were guaranteed to every flat-chested client willing to invest in a ten-dollar home course.

secrecy and by the belief that close relatives of the insane must not marry.

A fragile old-maid Boston schoolteacher, Dorothea Lynde Dix, working almost alone throughout the forties and fifties, changed the prevailing attitude toward the insane to one of humanity and hopefulness. Her first humanitarian act was in an East Cambridge jail, where she had gone to teach Sunday school to the inmates. When she saw insane, noncriminal inmates lodged in unheated cells, she asked the jailer to provide heat and received the answer, "The insane need no heat" (in the belief that they were insensitive to temperature). Miss Dix took her request to the East Cambridge court, which enjoined the jail to provide heat for the insane. For the next forty years—she died at eighty-five—Dorothea Dix toured facilities for the insane both here and abroad, and at the end of her life had caused thirty-two mental hospitals to be founded or enlarged, and humanely operated. She uncovered not only brutality in public institutions but cases of private cruelty as well, in which insane relatives kept at home were subjected to the most inhuman suffering. In one Rhode Island house, she found an insane pauper shut into an unventilated, unlit vault. He had survived there through the winter cold, lying on wet straw under two comforters that were stiff with frost. The publicity Miss Dix gave this story led to the founding of Providence's Butler Hospital, for which she persuaded one of Rhode Island's richest but theretofore most tightfisted manufacturers, Cyrus Butler, to give the funds.

Country lass in a sweet seduction

Few single human beings have so changed a prevailing moral attitude as Miss Dix managed to do. Whether she could have accomplished as much if she had been born fifty years earlier is an interesting question. Perhaps mid-nineteenth-century America was ready for humanitarianism as it had not been earlier. The complexities of urban life were clearly beyond the control of working people, and the idea that pauperism, sickness, and degradation were personal faults was at least beginning to be questioned. Phrenology and mesmerism, while pseudosciences, led to scientific thinking about criminals and other social outcasts. Even if bumps on the skull did not indicate a man's destiny, perhaps other factors, equally outside his control, might be held responsible. The novels of Dickens helped, too, to awaken the sympathy of the prosperous for their less fortunate neighbors. Even fallen women received a certain amount of gingerly solicitude. The magazines ran stories and poems about women who were more to be pitied than censured:

> *But let us now enter the city,*
> *Pass down through this dark, filthy street;*
> *Do you hear the wild cry of that lost one,*
> *A child lost from chastity, sweet?*
> *Perhaps you may think her self-honor*
> *Should keep her from crime, base and low,*
> *When starving and naught left to live for,*
> *Think you would in uprightness go?*

A sentimental story entitled "The Umbrella Girl," about the near seduction of a country lass with glossy black hair and "lips like wet coral," actually permits a happy ending—at the last moment, the heroine hangs on to her virginity and eventually finds a suitable husband. If she had lost it, of course, there would have been no hope for her, or at least not in ladies' literature and not in the nineteenth century's code of behavior.

Paradigms
of
Vice and Virtue

Obedience and rebellion were, for the purposes of John Hailer's 1862 morality picture, the fundamental choices in life, and they were confronted not in church but at the schoolhouse door. In reality, however, even those who elected the path of rectitude found the going rough. America turned out to be a land where Virtue and Vice made more congenial bedfellows than anyone had supposed.

Race, Creed, and Color

RUTHERFORD B. HAYES LIBRARY

Whatever lip service might be paid to the melting pot idea, white Anglo-Saxon Protestants felt in their hearts that they alone had the right to rule. They were especially antagonistic toward Catholics, who, they charged, were plotting a Vatican takeover by undermining the country with intemperance, ignorance, poverty, and crime. To counter these un-American activities, secret Know-Nothing societies were founded in the 1840's and 1850's. Rabble-rousing members, elected to public office in Massachusetts, even snooped in nunnery bedrooms for "evidences" of priestly presence and other moral corruption. *Harper's Weekly*, one of the few publications to make intolerance an issue, depicted religious bigotry in the cartoon above, and later, in 1874, decried racial prejudice. The editors described the postbellum Ku Klux Klan as "wild gangs of murderous villains . . . hunting the white and black Republicans from their homes . . . destroying the first principles of free government, forcing free citizens to abstain from voting by terror, committing barbarous murders and crimes. . . ." California nativists made the Chinese their whipping boys; and a law was enacted in 1882 to bar the "yellow menace." As Mark Twain charged when a lad was arrested for stoning an Oriental, "Everything conspired to teach him that it was a high and holy thing. . . ."

Cloaked and pillowcased Alabamians in the 1868 Klan (left) aim to keep the newly freed Negro in his place.

LIBRARY OF CONGRESS

This jaundiced ad for cleaning fluid, c. 1886, implies that America can get along without recourse to cheap Chinese labor.

In a Manner Of Speaking

In a nation that glorified its oratorical tradition, even ordinary citizens could hope someday to address the masses, or at least, a local lyceum. Guides, providing formulas for all facets of Victorian living—how to dress, write, act, think—also made sure that people were never at a loss for words. An 1855 elocution manual for young ladies cautioned against mispronouncing "tobacco" as "tub-ac-cur," and slurring, so that "an ice house" became "a nice house." It advocated using pure, orotund, aspirated, and guttural tones, inflections, and rhetorical pauses to avoid the monotony of which women were evidently guilty. A later anthology of set speeches warned that "in . . . church, broad humor is not advisable"; for the parlor, "simple narratives or stories are the most suitable, high tragedy and declamation being decidedly inappropriate." Thomas Hill's 1881 *Album of Biography and Art* noted that a seasoned talker could spew forth more than seven thousand words an hour. His illustrations and literary selections reproduced on these pages show how actions speak louder than decibels in conveying a mood. *Horror* (right), gesticulated with "shrinking, repulsive movements," supposedly aroused "a similar emotion in the breasts of the audience."

Horror.

EXAMPLE—" Which of you have done this?
Avaunt and quit my sight! Let the earth hide thee!
Thy bones are marrowless, thy blood is cold;
Thou hast no speculation in those eyes,
Which thou dost glare with.
Hence, horrible shadow!
Unreal mockery, hence!"

IN this illustration, representing the emotion of **Love,** the whole being is subdued, the head and body inclining forward; the forehead is tranquil; the eyebrows droop; the eye sparkles with affection; the palm of the right hand is pressed over the heart, and the left hand, with open fingers, is folded over the right wrist; the lower limbs stand together in easy position, with the right foot in advance; the voice is low and musical, and often there is an air of melancholy thought.

Love.

EXAMPLE—"I love you, Margery dear, because you are young and fair,
For your eyes' bewild'ring blueness, and the gold of your curling hair.
No queen has hands that are whiter, no lark has a voice so sweet,
And your ripe young lips are redder than the clover at our feet.
My heart will break with its fullness, like a cloud o'ercharged with rain,
Oh!—tell me, Margery darling, how long must I love in vain?"

THE head is either erect or thrown slightly back, in **Laughter** and **Mirth;** the forehead is smooth; the eyes are partly closed and full of cheerful expression, sometimes filled with tears of joy; the mouth is open and extended; the shoulders are elevated; the elbows are spread, the hands resting on the sides of the body below the waist; and the voice is loud and joyous in tone. Should the mirth, however, be inward and silent, the form is convulsed with emotion, as in the expression of grief.

Laughter—Mirth.

EXAMPLE—"So he took me for a Priest, did he?
Ha! Ha!! Ha!!! Ha!!!!
Couldn't he tell the difference between a saint and a sinner?
Ha! Ha!! Ha!!! Ha!!!!
Why, that man don't know the difference between his heels and his head,
Ha! Ha!! Ha!!! Ha!!!!"

THE height of enthusiasm, the wildness of **Madness** or insanity, the struggle going on within, are manifested in this character. The head is dishevelled and uneasy; the arms and hands are moved about—now pressing the head, now thrown convulsively from it. Every movement of the body is irregular, rapid and reckless; the eyes, with fearful effect, turn uneasily from object to object, dwelling on none; the countenance is distorted, and the world is a blank.

Madness—Insanity.

EXAMPLE—"Mark how yon demon's eyeballs glare.
He sees me; now, with dreadful shriek,
He whirls a serpent high in air.
Horror! the reptile strikes its tooth
Deep in my heart, so crushed and sad.
Aye, laugh, ye fiends, I feel the truth,
Your work is done—I'm mad!—I'm mad!!"

WITH the sense of **Dignity,** or self-valuation, the head is held erect, or thrown slightly back; the form is straightened and raised to its fullest height; the forehead is expanded; the eyebrows are raised; the eyes indicate a subdued fierceness; the lips are compressed, and the countenance firm; the arms are folded across the chest, or the left hand is thrust into the bosom; the lower limbs are straight and together, with the feet at right angles; the movements are slow and methodical.

Dignity.

EXAMPLE—"I am a Roman citizen.... Here, in your capital, do I defy you. Have I not conquered your armies, fired your towns, and dragged your generals at my chariot wheels, since first my youthful arms could wield a spear? And do you think to see me crouch and cower before a tamed and shattered senate? The tearing of flesh and rending of sinews is but pastime compared with the mental agony that heaves my frame."

Saints and Sinners

Rev. Henry Ward Beecher

Dr. Charles Parkhurst

Since the gospel of gloom was no longer converting its quota of souls, preachers in the second half of the nineteenth century provided something more optimistic for sentimental Americans. The religion of joy, as spoon-fed to middle-class audiences, struck emotional chords in lieu of thought, glorified mother, home, and heaven, soothed those guilt-ridden about amassing wealth, and made sensational disclosures about social conditions. Dr. Charles Parkhurst exposed New York's corrupt police in vitriolic sermons. Henry Ward Beecher's flair for drama, his human foibles, versatile mind, and Midas touch on lecture tours, epitomized another type of minister. At the Plymouth Church in Brooklyn, Beecher had the pulpit removed and spoke to *his* worshipers from a platform "built on . . . the principle of social and personal magnetism, which emanates reciprocally from a speaker and from a close throng of hearers. . . . I shall be in the center of the crowd, and have the people surge all about me." On Sundays, listeners flocked to hear the Barnum of religion thunder out life's glittering generalities or appeal for reform by staging abolitionist spectaculars in which Negro women cringed in chains, while Beecher went through the motions of a slave auction. His popularity was such that Mrs. Beecher complained: "When I married him, I merely had to share him with the congregation, but since then he has married the Platform and the Press and the Goddess of Liberty, and I miss him a good deal." Unbeknownst to her, the pastor spent much time with one of his ewe lambs, wife of his protégé, Theodore Tilton. In 1872 the alleged affair was "ventilated" in various scandal sheets: the *Police Gazette* reported that Mrs. Tilton's "sexual commerce with Mr. Beecher had never proceeded from low or vulgar thoughts . . . but always from pure affection and a high religious love." Though tried and acquitted by church and civil courts, the divine's innocence was never established. No need, however. Americans regarded Beecher "as a national institution" and supported him, right or wrong.

This 1883 cartoon pokes fun at those muckraking ministers who, ostensibly to wage campaigns against vice, offer the public Sabbath melodramas, instead of more sober forms of worship.

247

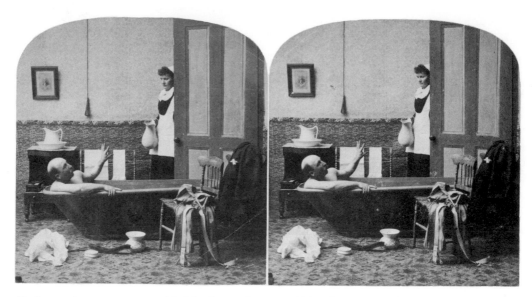

Embarrassing moments provided bathroom humor c. 1890, this one titled "Did You Ring, Sir?"

Next to Godliness

Most hotels could be expected to provide washstands like the patented model at left, with fold-up lavatory and a cabinet for a chamber pot in its base. But the fastidious traveler did well to make his own provisions for a tub. The rubberized hammock above could be packed in his luggage, and slung between chairs.

Linking cleanliness with godliness was nothing new; but for etiquette books to associate proper toilette with inward purity suggests that Victorians recognized a timely persuasion in the old Biblical metaphor. Hygiene became a *cause célèbre* of preacher, doctor, and layman alike as portable showers, or "rainbaths," and tubs came on the market and indoor plumbing began to climb stairs. The sick adopted baths—"cold, sea, warm, hot, vapour, gas, and mud"—as the latest cure-all. The healthy insisted that vigorous use of soap and water had more to do with duty than vanity. To improve the lot of the masses and effect a general "advance from physical to moral amelioration and progress," Victorian reformers revived the institution of public baths. By the nineties, five cents would entitle any city dweller to hot and cold water, a cake of soap, and a clean towel. Public "necessaries" were also becoming common, the reason most often cited being that without them virtuous citizens were driven into saloons for relief. A vogue, an art, plumbing had become another Yankee obsession to confound the world.

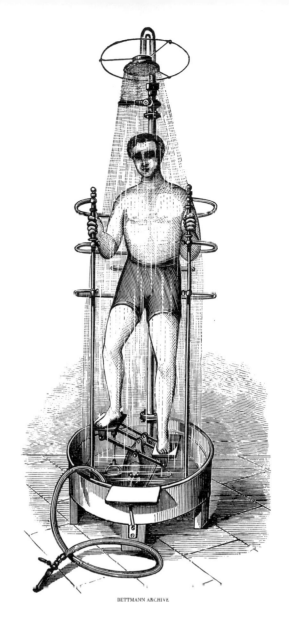

BETTMANN ARCHIVE

The public might yearn for the sort of luxury enjoyed by the lady at left, but indoor plumbing was too costly for most. Compromises abounded, as in the "earth closet" below, where stove ashes or charcoal obviated the need for flushing water: "much cheaper, besides being an accumulator of valuable matter." The pedaldriven "rain bath" above was recommended only for those bathers who were in the best of health.

BEECHER, AMERICAN WOMAN'S HOME, 1869

249

Struttin' Their Stuff

1ST PRIZE

Negro music and dances, like the stylish "walk for the cake" strutted above, fascinated white observers—though at a genteel distance. Beginning in the 1840's, dozens of white troupes in black face toured the nation in versions of that uniquely American invention—the minstrel show. Based on broad parodies of slave entertainments and set forth by stock characters in a routine that seldom varied, it offered just the sort of comfortable fun Victorians wanted.

MUSEUM OF THE CITY OF NEW YORK, J. CLARENCE DAVIES COLLECTION

*Christy's troupe, seen in formal attire and stage costume, introduced
many of Stephen Foster's "Ethiopian Songs," including "Swanee River."*

251

Soiled Doves
And Painted Cats

This house was home for Cripple Creek's naughty ladies c. 1900. Lil Powers, in the striped dress, had "no regrets."

Lou Bunch (left) operated in Central City, Colorado. Mattie Silks (above) wears her trademark, a diamond-studded cross. As Denver's "Queen of the Tenderloin," she boasted of having never been a "boarder," always a "madame."

Spurred by tales of vast riches and a preponderance of men, hordes of pretty girls in the 1870's went out West to dispense their much-needed social services. At railheads like Dodge City, Kansas, "nymphs du prairie" set up housekeeping and received cordial visits from trainmen, who left their red signal lights outside. By 1878, gamblers, pimps, and every sort of parasite thronged the cow town, described by an upright citizen as the "Beautiful Bibulous Babylon of the Frontier . . . her code of morals is the honor of thieves, and decency she knows not." Denver's district, however, had an aura of semirespectability; "august lawmakers" daily frequented the Row, a line of brothels situated near the main street, and madams took an active interest in public affairs. Society on the Row was as rigidly stratified as in proper Victorian sectors of the city. Lowest on the scale were "crib" girls who displayed their charms from windows or doorways and operated on the quick turnover principle. Rates, as advertised, were cheap: "10¢ Lookee, 25¢ Feelee, 50¢ Dooee,"

and customers purchased tokens like those above to exchange for a lady of their choice. When business boomed, a prostitute might take in fifty brass checks for a night's work. Handsomely furnished Parlor Houses employed more discreet means to attract a clientele — usually by sedate calling cards, or by word of mouth. Orchestras entertained in downstairs ballrooms, champagne flowed freely, and satisfied patrons paid up to thirty dollars. Whether a red-hot mamma or a refined type, a madam had her share of occupational headaches: she often supported a paramour who gambled away earnings; she hired servants and bouncers and maintained the liquor license; she bribed the police (providing a major source of municipal revenue); and she consoled those suicidal "soiled doves" to whom the path of easy virtue seemed the path of no return. The liquor prohibition of 1915 helped eradicate Denver's social evil. Recalling the rip-roaring red-light district, an old-timer mused, "It was a day of hard living. Men took their liquor neat and women took what they could."

Recruiting teetotalers seemed to many militants an unsure route to saving the nation. William Dodge of the National Temperance Society and Frances Willard of the W.C.T.U. wanted to dry up the flow at its source. "The Whiskey Dragon," above, which Dodge purchased abroad for home consumption, depicts still owners as the real villains.

NATIONAL WOMAN'S CHRISTIAN TEMPERANCE UNION

To early humanitarians, who liked their issues and answers simple, "ardent spirits" were clearly at the root of all evils, but it was not until the 1820's that temperance was equated with teetotalism and the crusade became nationwide. Militant religionists argued that everyone, even the moderate drinkers, must renounce liquor or be an accessory to the crimes of weaker men. Songs, lurid sermons and lectures, and a spate of journals devoted to temperance poured forth. The Cold Water Army pledged thousands of youngsters to "perpetual hate to all that can intoxicate" as soon as they could write their names, and etiquette books warned mothers lest they develop unnatural appetites in their sons. "All that is necessary to make a drunkard is a good healthy boy . . . and plenty of candy, pastry, pickles, and medicine," was one pre-Freudian's analysis. Fortunately, there were remedies in adulthood for a poor upbringing. The Sons of Temperance enlisted more than 250,000 dues-paying reformed; semifraternal orders also catered to Irish immigrants, wronged wives, and other special interest groups. Even those sinners who had no intention of renouncing spirits could have the vicarious pleasure of watching other men wrestle with the demon on stage. W. H. Smith's *The Drunkard, or The Fallen Saved* enjoyed a sensational run from coast to coast following its opening in 1850, and a tidier version, "the delirium scene," turned up regularly as a single act in traveling minstrel shows. Successful efforts to enact state prohibition laws in the 1850's and the movement's association with the cause of abolition were its final undoing. With the end of the Civil War and of slavery, the idea of government imposing another sort of servitude on those who liked their liquor was insupportable. Though many women, such as Kansas' own Carry Nation, would continue the fight into this century, the tide had, at least temporarily, turned.

The Temperance Ferment

American ladies' acceptance of smoking and America's acceptance of smoking ladies was gradual. The 1837 cartoon at right shows women clutching at their noses in protest as the men persist. The belle below was an 1897 harbinger of today.

LEFT AND RIGHT: LIBRARY OF CONGRESS

Going Down in Smoke

"Almost all confirmed smokers will go so far as to admit that they wish they had never acquired the habit. Few of them desire their boys to acquire it. None recommend it to other men." So wrote historian James Parton in an 1868 issue of the *Atlantic Monthly.* Tobacco had been a fact of life in America from the beginning, its indispensable pleasure creating an indispensable industry. Pipes, cigars, cigarettes, snuff, and chews all had their advocates. As a man advanced in society, he could look forward to finer fumes in finer rooms, but the basic pleasures of tobacco were available in some form to all classes. And the bad effects of tobacco affected smokers and nonsmokers alike. Parton's primary objection to the habit was that men seemed to prefer the weed to women. "Smoking lures and detains men from the society of ladies. . . . That community is already far gone in degeneracy in which men prefer to band together by themselves. . . . The Turks shut women in; we shut them out. . . . Humiliating as the truth is, it must be confessed, tobacco is woman's rival, her successful rival. When men are sensual, women will be frivolous. . . . The

NEW-YORK HISTORICAL SOCIETY

wonder is that they confine themselves to the innocent delights of the toilet. A husband who spends one day and seven evenings of every week at his club ought to expect that his wife will provide herself both with fine clothes and some one who will admire them. Remove from every club-house . . . all the wine and tobacco,—and seven out of every ten of them would cease to exist in one year. One of the worst effects of smoking is that it deadens our susceptibility to tedium, and enables us to keep on enduring what we ought to war against and overcome. . . . Tyrants and oppressors are wrong in drawing so much revenue from tobacco; they ought rather to give it away, for it tends to enable people to sit down content under every kind of oppression." But for the aware, Parton offered his personally endorsed smoking cure. "I managed it in this way: whenever my time came to smoke, which was four times a day, I drank a good stiff glass of whiskey and water. . . . Before one bottle of Bourbon had been imbibed, I had forgotten both the pipe and the liquor, and have never since had an uncomfortable desire to indulge in either."

Scotch oil, at right, seemed so effective an equine elixir that it was later recommended for the human species. The product of medical knavery below made the weaker sex less weak.

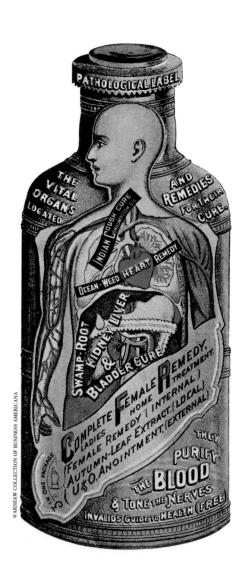

WARSHAW COLLECTION OF BUSINESS AMERICANA

NEW YORK HISTORICAL SOCIETY, BELLA C. LANDAUER COLLECTION

If the patent medicines sold in the nineteenth century were any indication, the nation's health was indeed precarious. In surprisingly candid language, pitchmen warned the gullible that infirmities—baldness, "humiliating eruptions," and bad breath—left untreated would result in social ostracism, moral decay, and death. Lydia Pinkham's Vegetable Compound, a best-selling herb syrup featuring the grandmotherly lady on every package, was nature's remedy for the "worst forms of Female Complaints . . . particularly adapted to the Change of Life." Erotically suggestive advertisements promised cures for male debility as well as unmentionable diseases. Hucksters of Orchis Extract, "the Greatest Known Treatment for Weak Men," claimed that their product contained "a substance from the testicles of rams." Such restorers of potency were usually fraudulent. The relaxation of Victorian decorum would doubtless have benefited "lost manhood" more.

Potent Medicines

Public figures were not immune from being falsely quoted in testimonials. At right, Governor Robinson of Massachusetts is shown at his inauguration, chiding the loser: "At the beginning of the campaign I was all broken down . . . but 'Sulphur Bitters' gave me strength to beat you." The vermifuge ad below promised to purge the nation of worms.

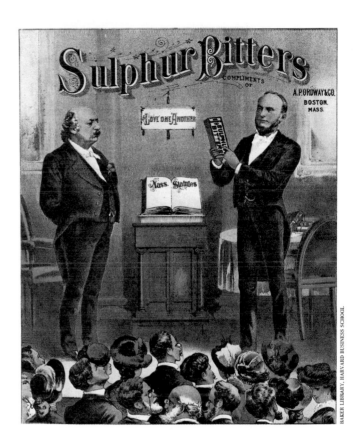

BAKER LIBRARY, HARVARD BUSINESS SCHOOL

259

AMERICAN ANTIQUARIAN SOCIETY

The Confidence Game

The American as eternal greenhorn was a favorite subject of native satire. Some moralists attacked the cities as breeding grounds for sophisticated swindlers and warned away country boys. A more cynical Herman Melville concluded that the not-so-innocents, prompted by their own greed, went willingly to slaughter, seeking out the confidence men. The creator of "Vive la Humbug," a catalog of fads and follies c. 1850, above, takes a lighter view.

Suspenders for heavy skirts

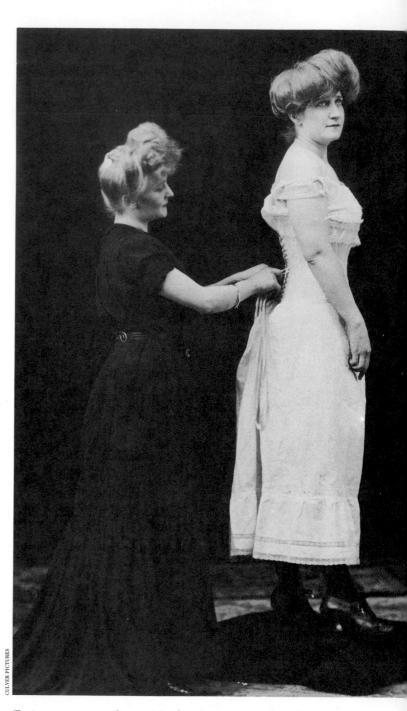

Up Tight

CULVER PICTURES

Wire dress pads for the underendowed

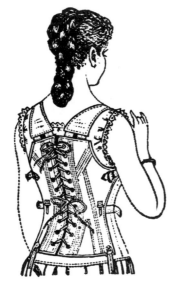

An 1880 curvature corrective

An "unmentionable" combination

Trying on corsets often required assistance; once laced in, women even sleep in them. The lady above, oblivious to the need for dress reform, can breathe a sigh of satisfaction, if she can breathe at all, in knowing that her waistline is thereby reduced as much as fifteen inches.

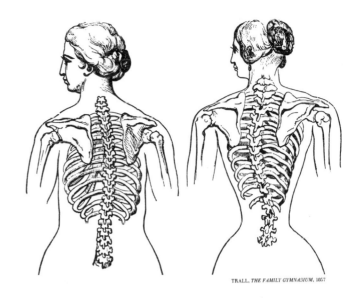

In a before and after diagram of 1857 (right), a doctor shows how the likes of the corset above make "internal viscera . . . injuriously compressed."

TRALL, THE FAMILY GYMNASIUM, 1857

Playing a major supporting role in the life of the Victorian woman, the corset improved upon nature by creating a wasp-waisted, hourglass figure. Though steel and whalebone made the wearer virtually impregnable to male assault, it left an embracing feeling, described by one female as "delicious sensations, half pleasure, half pain," which may have been a sort of sex substitute. Rich ladies, who had no need to engage in labor, wore the tightest lacings and most voluminous dresses; indeed, the slightest exertion for a woman thus attired was apt to bring on a fainting spell. Feminists, however, were not content to be useless. In 1851 they donned trousers with knee-length skirts "to attain a position side by side with man . . . his co-worker in life and its duties." As the costume's champion Amelia Bloomer pointed out, Adam's and Eve's fig leaves were identical. After becoming the butt of vilification, "female pantaloonery" was abandoned, and even diehards went back to stays and long skirts, which lasted until women were granted the vote in 1919.

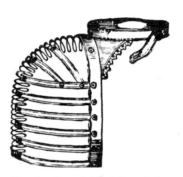

Bustle that folded for sitting

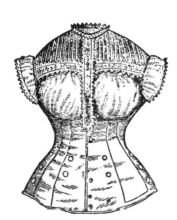

"Emancipation Waists" of 1875 which expanded with the wearer

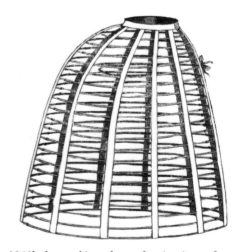

1860's hoop skirt, eleven feet in circumference

Victoria Woodhull

Out of Harness

Had the authors of the Declaration of Independence heeded Abigail Adams' warning that women, denied rights, would "foment a rebellion," feminism might never have taken root. Instead, the drafters proclaimed all men free and equal and paid dearly for their oversight. Though Victorian American females had pedestals, lord protectors, and the best theater seats, they still were considered intellectual inferiors, were dispossessed of property after marriage, and were subordinated to husbands who could legally beat them "with a reasonable instrument." By mid-century, woman-power advocates were agitating for total emancipation—equal job opportunities, suffrage, and divorce. Crusaders were generally treated with contempt. In one extremist's view, "the day which invests women with the elective franchise . . . would consign the race to a night of degradation and horror infinitely more appalling than a return to primeval barbarism." Shortly after the Civil War, however, western states began to grant women the vote. At the same time, factories provided women with a means of self-support, and divorce (alimony was rarely awarded) became an increasingly popular remedy for marriages where, as one feminist remonstrated, the "unholy passion of a master" was endured nightly. Victoria Woodhull, who campaigned against the double standard, not only ran for President in 1872, but ran through three spouses. To this new breed of woman, the double standard that allowed promiscuous men fresh from "polluted beds . . . to be . . . fellowshiped by virtuous men and chaste women" was intolerable.

Suffrage, as interpreted by Currier & Ives in 1869, creates masculine, aggressive women who make milquetoasts of men.

MUSEUM OF THE CITY OF NEW YORK, HARRY T. PETERS COLLECTION

According to this 1879 cartoon, divorcées had no problem remarrying. A matrimonial tree, drawn on the prospective bride's curvaceous posterior, is "for the benefit of intending lovers," who are seen examining the alliances, apparently nipped in the bud, as well as the merchandise.

PUCK, JANUARY 22, 1879

When a group of businessmen in New York's genteel Murray Hill area adopted rules for hitting a little ball with a big stick in 1845, they had no idea that their diversion would become the national pastime. Indeed, the nattily dressed Knickerbocker Club tried to monopolize baseball by keeping "outsiders" away from matches and refusing to play with a Brooklyn team of "greasy mechanics." However, as one member of the elite noted, "The great mass, who are in a subordinate capacity, can participate in this healthgiving and noble" sport, requiring only the great outdoors, bat, and ball. Democratization inevitably occurred, and soon urban workers, disadvantaged by long factory hours, were scheduling "morning-glory" games at dawn. Unlike wrestling or cockfighting, baseball was suitable for spectators of every age, class, and sex—though before the days of grandstands a lady might be offended by a frantic player looking for a stray ball under her hoop skirts. After the Civil War, baseball became a mania; professionals toured the country; amateurs neglected their jobs; and rooters either became rabid over victory or mourned. As the ballad ran: "somewhere men are laughing and somewhere children shout, But there is no joy in Mudville—Mighty Casey has struck out."

YALE UNIVERSITY ART GALLERY, WHITNEY COLLECTION OF SPORTING AR

Diamonds
for
Everyone

At the 1866 championship match at left, the Philadelphia Athletics defeat the Brooklyn Atlantics. Wealthy aficionados sit in a shaded grandstand, while poorer fans meander or sunbathe in the "bleachers." Studio poses, perhaps for baseball cards that would be sold with cigarettes, are struck by two players: James Fogarty (top) exhibits truly suspended animation—the ball hangs from a wire. Deacon McGuire (above), resembling a Greek statue, hurls a ballistic missile.

BOTH: NEW YORK PUBLIC LIBRARY, SPALDING COLLECTION

A Man's Best Friend

Everyone from "big wheels" to the common man enjoyed this healthful form of recreation. The roster of enthusiasts even included President Rutherford B. Hayes's children, two of whom, in the 1888 photograph above, are about to commence a tricycle trip on the secluded family estate in Fremont, Ohio.

Inspired by snappy foreign models, freewheeling men on this side of the Atlantic were peddling variations of the bicycle as early as the 1860's. However, unicycles, tricycles, and the compact "pedespeeds," above, were but fleeting fads. It was the invention of the "safety" in 1888, with low wheels and pneumatic tires, that made bicycling "an abiding national habit." Despite opposition from the Women's Rescue League which demurred that riding created invalids as well as fallen women, and from piano manufacturers who lost half their sales when the gentle sex went outdoors, by 1893 females were included in the million people enjoying the new mode of rapid transit. A girl could at long last escape parental surveillance and get together in tandem with a beau, but she was plagued with advice. A physician cautioned: after riding, "do not think of sitting down to table until you have changed your underclothing." A screen attachment for the bicycle was recommended to keep feet and ankles, which she now admittedly possessed, from view. An etiquette book advocated that she wear modest attire instead of bloomers "so inartistic, so ugly and so 'loud'"; carry an ammonia gun "for the benefit of barking dogs"; and "above all else . . . maintain an upright position."

RUTHERFORD B. HAYES LIBRARY

The Arizona lad above poses with his bicycle, which may have cost his parents over one hundred dollars.

The Naked Truth

KENNEDY GALLERIES, INC

Professional strongman Eugene Sandow profited from the tableau vivant *trade. Live Biblical and literary scenes had as much appeal in the late 1800's as nude statues.*

LIBRARY OF CONGRESS

Though a mid-century Victorian would never admittedly gaze at a female's erogenous zones in a painting, it was quite permissible to examine a nude statue with more than furtive interest. At a time "when husbands left the room when their wives changed stockings," moral standards were skin deep at best, and often contradictory. While painted flesh tones were considered indecent, marble surfaces were not. Popular taste in pictures ran to sentimental, amply attired "Floras and Doras, with big eyes and little mouths . . . big busts and little waists, big bustles and little feet." Concurrently, sculpture in the raw was fashionable, provided it had some literary purpose, as did Hiram Powers' "Greek Slave." A toplofty name like "Purity" or "The Triumph of Chastity," or features modeled after antique prototypes rather than real, recognizable people, also made a statue acceptable. Not even the Puritan conscience of Nathaniel Hawthorne was offended by the chilly nudity of Powers' "America," "warmed out of the cold allegorical sisterhood who have generally no merit in chastity, being really without sex." Miniature copies of neoclassic ladies, a genre described by Henry James as "so undressed, yet so refined, even so pensive, in sugar-white alabaster, exposed under little glass covers," adorned American parlors for nearly fifty years. For those who did not deem verbal fig leaves sufficient coverage for nakedness, plaster ones could

John Inman's oil of 1887, "Bathing on the Hudson," was a masterpiece of der-ring-do. This was probably the first time in America that realistic nudes rather than Grecian goddesses were painted.

always be added. The Ladies' Academy of Art in Cincinnati hired a Mr. Fazzi to conceal the "parts" of their European statuary. As late as 1890, a magazine reported that at a college in Ada, Ohio, the sight-unseen purchase and subsequent unveiling of an Apollo caused "wild screams and a precipitate scattering of the students, who fled in all directions, leaving the god master of the situation. . . . It was decided . . . to resort to heroic measures. . . . When a pair of fine velvet knee breeches were completed the famed Apollo was decently clothed with them; and there he stands, clad as no god was ever before adorned, a monument to the . . . ingenuity of the students." A small clique of "art missionaries" had been trying to steer Americans away from such appalling Philistinism, and to set the country on the road to sophistication. They advocated establishing art schools as well as a national gallery, which would serve as touchstones for taste. New York's Metropolitan Museum and the Art Students League, both founded in the 1870's, were among the first to undertake the all but impossible task of eliminating the public's prudery, ignorance, and self-consciousness regarding the fine arts. Would-be connoisseurs were lured away from the evil temptations of the city to these institutions where they could see old and new masters and also study art in the original from live models, posing, as one put it, in the "toot and scramble."

Hiram Powers' "Eve" is not the usual sexy temptress. Her polished apple, discreetly modeled bosoms, and circumspect stance bespeak the modesty of a fully clothed lady.

SMITHSONIAN INSTITUTION, NATIONAL COLLECTION OF FINE ARTS

271

Rich Men's Idylls

❧

In which New Money and Old Family Position arrange a Gilt-Edged Merger; Fun and Games for the Few are Developed, & some Society Leaders make Culture a Private Trust

New York society before the 1870's was "the most exclusive and brilliant upon this hemisphere." At least so said an old New Yorker, Mrs. John King Van Rensselaer, looking back on those cherished days from the crass 1920's. There had been only one way to get into the inner circle: to be born in the right brownstone or brick mansion. Society had been a citadel, "an austere and carefully guarded structure, the sentinels of which admitted none but those who approached along the sanctioned pathway of birth and breeding." Alas, according to Mrs. Van Rensselaer, on the fateful date of December 26, 1874, the citadel had been betrayed. On that evening, a group of socially impeccable but reckless bachelors had held a fancy-dress ball at Delmonico's and included among the guests various persons who, although "reputable," had never before shared a dance floor with Van Rensselaers, Beekmans, Livingstons, Rhinelanders, or Roosevelts. "Since that epoch-making dance," Mrs. Van Rensselaer went on morosely, "New York Society has continued to break up. Before that time, one either was socially acceptable everywhere or one was not recognized anywhere. He was definitely within the pale or uncompromisingly out of it. To-day [1924] no one can tell whether a person is socially prominent or not, because no one can be sure exactly what social prominence is."

Why did these young men betray the citadel? Perhaps they felt as one of their peers, Edith Wharton, felt when she was young: "the group in which I grew up was like an empty vessel into which no new wine would ever again be poured." At any rate, the breakup of New York society cannot be wholly blamed on the traitorous bachelors. The real betrayal began two or three generations before, when daughters of impecunious but highly respectable old families began to marry sons of pecunious new ones. Among the first

❧

New York's Hoffman House, boasting the longest bar and the most resplendent Bouguereau nudes in America, was home away from home for the city's wealthy playboys.

Social arbiter Ward McAllister

Blue bloods and their red-blooded forebears

young men to marry into the inner circle was John Jacob Astor, a German immigrant who was on his way to making a fortune in fur trade and real estate; he married an impoverished relative of the Brevoort family. Their son, William Backhouse Astor, married a descendant of Livingstons and Beekmans. The first son of this union, John Jacob III, married a member of the "proud, but threadbare" Gibbes family, originally of South Carolina; and a second son, William Backhouse Astor, Jr., married Caroline Schermerhorn, of one of New York's leading families.

Whereas in Europe the husband's rank set the social tone for his family, in America, much, if not all, depended on the wife. Caroline Schermerhorn Astor was a born guardian of the citadel; and perhaps to compensate for the fact that she was without beauty, intellect, charm, or wit, set out in the early seventies to install herself as Queen of Society. Her first move was to compile a rigid list to show who was in society, for since the Civil War there had been numerous parvenus hanging around the citadel gates, hoping that a lavish outlay of money would get them in. It was hard enough to keep track of those with a legitimate hereditary claim to social rank without having to fend off interlopers armed with cash and etiquette books.

To assist her in her mission, Mrs. Astor was fortunate in finding Ward McAllister, a southern gentleman who had resettled in New York to devote his life to "social" causes. Mrs. Astor and "Make-a-lister," as some wags later called this dedicated snob, composed their first list in the winter of 1872–73; it included the names of the twenty-five foremost gentlemen in New York. Mrs. Astor designated them "Patriarchs," and asked each to invite four ladies and four gentlemen to a subscription ball to be held in the elegant rooms of Delmonico's restaurant. As McAllister later wrote, "Patriarchs were chosen solely for their fitness, on each of them promising to invite to each ball only such people as would do credit to the ball. We then resolved that . . . if any objectionable element was introduced it was the duty of the management [of which McAllister was the prime mover] to at once let it be known by whom such objectionable party was invited, and to notify the Patriarch so offending that he had done us an injury, and pray him to be more circumspect."

Thus, the guest list made a solid, safe inner core of society, for the Patriarchs were mature citizens, not hotheaded youngsters, and could be depended upon to man the defenses. However, ten years later, Mrs. Astor was guilty of breaking her own rules: she let in the Vanderbilts, who had been vainly battering at the inner gates for decades.

"Commodore" Cornelius Vanderbilt, founder of the Vanderbilt fortunes, had been born in 1794, a generation later than the original John Jacob Astor; unlike John Jacob, he had not chosen a wife of gentle birth. However, his son William had married the socially acceptable daughter of a Brooklyn clergyman, and *their* sons, Cornelius and William, had married, respectively, Alice Gwynne, of Cincinnati society, and Alva Smith, a belle from Mobile. Alva later told the world, "I always did everything first. I was the first girl of my set to marry a Vanderbilt."

Despite the handicap of a fortune only three generations old—albeit larger than the four-generations Astor pile—Alva set out to scale the Astor heights. She gave lavish balls in New York, but, ungraced by Mrs. Astor, they might as well have been fish frys at Coney Island. At last her big chance came: in March, 1883, Alva planned a housewarming for the three-million-dollar Vanderbilt town house, newly risen at Fifth Avenue and Fifty-second Street. It was to be the most expensive fancy-dress ball yet seen in America. Mrs. Astor's youngest daughter, Caroline, anticipating an invitation, joined with a group of other young girls to rehearse a special quadrille for the ball. Whereupon, Mrs. Vanderbilt let it be known that it was a shame to disappoint the young lady but it would be impossible to invite her, since her mother had never called. Mrs. Astor was a doting mother even more than she was a watchdog of society. She sent for her carriage, drove to the Vanderbilts' Fifth Avenue home, and left the all-important pasteboard rectangle, worth more to its recipient than pearls and diamonds. The ball was a triumph.

Ward McAllister was still at his patroness' side in 1888 when he devised the term "the Four Hundred." He told a New York *Tribune* reporter that the Astor ballroom would contain no more than four hundred people and that this number also happened to be that of the socially acceptable of New York. "If you go outside that number you strike people who are either not at ease in a ballroom or else make other people not at ease." The *Tribune* pressed him for a list of the Four Hundred, and after thinking the matter over for several years, he announced a list of considerably fewer than four hundred names, a somewhat amplified version of the list for the Patriarchs' Ball. It included Mr. and Mrs. Cornelius Vanderbilt and George Vanderbilt, but not Alva and William K. By this time, however, Alva Vanderbilt and Caroline Astor had become friends, and McAllister was on his way out. "The Autocrat of Drawing-Rooms" accelerated his own exit by publishing a book of memoirs, *Society As I Have Found It*, which even his oldest friends and admirers found fatuous. It contained such advice as: "A dinner invitation, once accepted, is a sacred obligation. If you die before the dinner takes place, your executor must attend the dinner." And, "If you want to be fashionable, be always in the company of fashionable people. . . . If you see a fossil of a man, shabbily dressed, relying solely upon his pedigree dating back to time immemorial, who has the aspirations of a duke and the fortunes of a footman, do not cut him; it is better to cross the street and avoid meeting him."

In a review of McAllister's book, *The New York Times* commented sourly, "It must be borne in mind that the distinction of the social leader is that what other men do for lucre he does for love. . . . When a man of mature years betakes himself to organizing tea parties and dances as a career he becomes an interesting object. The first requisite for success, as in so many other things, is intense moral earnestness. No suspicion that he is making a continental laughing stock of himself must disturb his mind or interfere with the singleness of his devotion. It would be fatal. . . . The degree of fervor that the author puts into undertakings that adults commonly leave to adolescents is really wonderful."

By the time McAllister died, in 1895, the society he had so earnestly loved had passed him by: only five Patriarchs bothered to attend his funeral. There was a new and giddier tone to society now. No one had succeeded McAllister as Mrs. Astor's prime minister; apparently that office no longer existed. Instead, she had a court jester, a lively, skipping young man named Harry Lehr. Lehr, penniless but well connected, had a flair for doing impudent things that amused and stirred up the rather too sedate upper crust. Some of his behavior sounds sophomoric, but it seems to have been marvelously successful with those he aimed to entertain. When he first met diamond-sparkling Mrs.

Caroline Schermerhorn Astor

Sand racing on a stretch of Florida beach

Astor, he seized a bunch of flowers from a vase and handed them to her, saying, "Here, you look like a walking chandelier." She found this gambit charming and from that moment his fortune was made. Female impersonations were one of his specialties, and another was the arrangement of outlandish parties. At one, for instance, male guests came dressed as cats and handed white mice to the ladies. At another, given by Mrs. Stuyvesant Fish, the guest-of-honor was announced as a prince, and turned out to be a monkey dressed in evening clothes. Lehr even persuaded Mrs. Astor to dine with him at Sherry's, an event that made headlines as it marked the first time that lady had ever appeared in a public restaurant.

While the women of America's high society were struggling for supremacy or occasionally relaxing enough to giggle over Harry Lehr's antics, their husbands appeared at parties as appropriate though not entirely essential adjuncts, perhaps classifiable with the gold plate and the orchid centerpieces. William Backhouse Astor (his wife made him drop the "Backhouse") was absent more than most; he went off for months at a stretch on his ocean-going yacht. Stuyvesant Fish, it is said, used to come home late from the office, find a party going on, and say mildly, "It seems I am giving a party. Well, I hope you are enjoying yourselves."

When Henry James revisited New York in 1904, after an absence of almost thirty years, he was struck by the all-pervasive dominance of the female in society and the emptiness of the ritual amusements to which the upper class was addicted. "This failure of the sexes to keep step socially is to be noted in the United States, at every turn," he wrote in *The American Scene*. Attending a dinner party at an elegant house, he found "the scene of our feast was a palace and the perfection of setting and service absolute; the ladies, beautiful, gracious and glittering with gems, were in tiaras and a semblance of court-trains." The trouble, in James's view, was that the occasion did not really demand a tiara. "There was nothing for us to do at eleven o'clock—or for the ladies at least—but to scatter and go to bed. There was nothing, as in London or in Paris, to go on to; the going on is . . . always the stumbling-block. A great court-function would alone have met the strain, met the terms of the case—would alone properly have crowned the hour. . . ." James did not think the husbands were up to it, in any case. "Had there been a court-function the ladies must have gone on to it alone, trusting to have the proper partners and mates supplied them on the premises—supplied, say, with the checks for recovery of their cloaks."

Vastly wealthy husbands of the period were usually too busy all day and too weary at night to take much pleasure in the activities of "the leisure class," which were often staged in far-off summer colonies to which the men went only on long weekends. Some New Yorkers, however, were not preoccupied with money-making; they did not make money, they had it, usually due to the happy accident of having inherited Manhattan real estate. Edith Wharton tells us in *A Backward Glance* that only one of her near relations and none of her husband's was "in business," and that among the first precepts she learned from her mother was "Never talk about money and think about it as little as possible." When, after the Civil War, Mrs. Wharton's father found himself in straitened circumstances, instead of going to work, as a middle-class American would have done automatically, he rented his houses to war profiteers and took his family on a six-year sojourn abroad.

Club life was a favorite form of relaxation for the tired tycoon. Every gentleman worthy of the name belonged to clubs, some of which were at least as difficult to get into as Mrs. Astor's ballroom. Perhaps the epitome of exclusiveness was reached by Newport's Gooseberry Island Fishing Club, whose membership was traditionally limited to fourteen. On a tiny island off Ocean Drive the members swam and sunbathed *au naturel*, and perhaps gloried in being triply safe from female intrusion: in a men's club, on an island, and naked.

Yachting and horse racing were fine ways to advertise one's vast wealth, for they were too expensive for all but multimillionaires. The first Cornelius Vanderbilt, though frugal in most ways, splurged on a yacht and took his family to London aboard it in 1853, where they were snubbed by London society and by the American ambassador. Catching a glimpse of Queen Victoria and Prince Albert at Covent Garden, Vanderbilt is said to have remarked that they looked "anything but aristocratic." The family's visit, which Vanderbilt announced had cost him half a million dollars, inspired the London *Daily News* to a recklessly un-English mood: "Those who ought to be the Vanderbilts of England would shrink from employing their wealth in the magnificent manner employed by their American friend. They would dread the effect of making any unusual display, which would surely subject them to the reproach of being millionaires and parvenus. Here is the great difference between the two countries. . . . It is time that *parvenu* should be looked on as a word of honor."

Less expensive than yachting and horse racing, but still a rich man's pastime, was coaching. Following English example, young New York "swells" found it vastly amusing to operate a sort of public transport, up and down the most fashionable avenues. Anyone who cared to pay an exorbitant three dollars could ride in an old-fashioned four-in-hand coach, and the young people of their set were more than willing, even though it meant reserving a place weeks in advance to ride a few blocks. Predictably, the gentlemen-hacks formed a club to keep out unsuitable competition, prescribed an official uniform — dark green cutaway coats and white top hats — and devised an annual coaching parade, to be held every autumn. The coaches were brightly painted, the horses wore flowers, and the society people on top were decked out in their gayest clothes. The coaching parade was as near as ordinary people in the streets ever came to a good view of the quality. So satisfactory was it on all counts that society of other cities were soon mobilizing coaching clubs and learning to wind the horn from imported English experts, too.

For the enjoyment of all the sports of polite society, the country club was invented during the 1880's. Boston's Brookline was probably the first. The concept was uniquely American, and although it was imitated in England, it never became really popular there, possibly because the ancient custom of house parties in country houses was not to be dislodged. In 1888, a golfing club was organized and the first course laid out, ushering in the era of golf as a gentleman's game (ladies did not invade the golf courses until years later). The first players wore the costume traditional in Scotland: red coats, visored caps, and leg wrappings to protect their legs from gorse, though it does not grow in America. The country club became a status symbol. Society's highest echelons kept its country clubs as sacrosanct as Mrs. Astor's lists, and still contrive to do so.

Bicycling was a "gay nineties" diversion for everyman, but when automobiles appeared on the market, the very rich had them first, and there was

Gay blades do the "Philadelphia Twist" in a detail from W. L. German's water color, above. The elegant ladies below shoot a few for an 1882 advertisement.

great cachet in driving down Fifth Avenue, Beacon Street, or Lake Shore Drive in one's own horseless carriage. At Newport, during the turn-of-the-century years, there were parades of motorcars decorated all over in flowers so that they looked something like floats or bassinets. The socially prominent passengers were at least as dressed up as their conveyances. For the first few years of the automobile age, only the rich could afford automobiles because of the expense of upkeep, which in one year would very nearly equal the cost of purchasing the car. A verse published in the old *Life* weekly in 1904 shows who were in the drivers' seats:

> *Half a block, half a block,/Half a block onward,*
> *All in their automobiles,/Ride the Four Hundred.*
> *"Forward!" the owners shouted,/"Racing car!" "Runabout!"*
> *Into Fifth Avenue/Rode the Four Hundred.*

In comparison with the national population, the social elite of America's cities added up to a minuscule number, to which their fame and influence was out of all proportion. The reason was that the newspapers had discovered an unfailing stimulus to circulation in tales of the rich and their doings. A musicale at the Vanderbilts' was reported on the front page, and all details of the floral decorations, the menu, and the costumes of hostess and guests were dwelt upon at length. Apparently, it was impossible to be too ostentatious, nor was there anything vulgar about displaying one's wealth. On the contrary: "No wealthy man has any business to live in a cottage," said the pious author of *Our Home, or The Key to a Nobler Life*. ". . . those who possess wealth and will not spend it in being served, are the thieves and robbers of society. . . . There are poor people enough to live in cottages. It is [the rich man's] business to live in a palace, and to hire those to build it who live in cottages."

The society page in daily newspapers was an American innovation. In England and Europe, the comings and goings of the elite were reported in brief and formal language, unembellished by the number of diamonds in tiaras or the amount of asparagus fern festooning the chandeliers. Most of the new society pages were purely admiring—fawning might be a better word. And the plain American might pick up French vocabulary by reading them: Mrs. Astor was *soignée* in a magnificent *robe de bal*, the Fish reception was *un succès fou*, and so on. The pioneer in the presentation of social chitchat was James Gordon Bennett's New York *Herald*, a paper also known for its vivid descriptions of murder and mayhem. The *Herald*'s success led more respectable papers to follow its example. Society people were apparently ambivalent as to whether they wanted publicity. When the *Herald* inadvertently confused one of Mrs. Stuyvesant Fish's reception lists with a list of people holding ringside seats for a prize fight, Mrs. Fish was so disagreeable about it that the *Herald*'s managing editor decided to mention her no more; whereupon she went in person to the paper's owner, Bennett, Jr., and had herself reinstated.

Women were the chief readers of the society pages, and it was for the most part about women that the pages were written. Women reporters were first admitted to the fourth estate for their ability to describe ball gowns and memorize family trees, and gradually the society pages were put into feminine hands. In their naïve way, social columns were probably responsible for an eventual public reaction against wild extravagances, and a lowering of esteem for those flighty people who indulged in them. A case in point is that of the

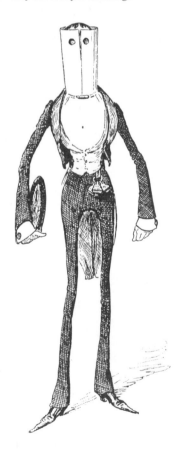

An 1878 Scientific American *marvelled at the adjustable hat form diagramed above.* An 1888 Harper's Monthly *satirized the new extremes in men's fancy dress fashions for evening.*

Bradley Martin Ball, held in New York in February, 1897. Descriptions of society balls of the eighties and nineties might fill volumes, but this particular event is a prime example. Bradley Martin was an extremely rich lawyer from Troy, New York. He and his wife wished to outdo other partygivers and advance their social position by throwing the most lavish ball in New York history. Newspaper reporters leaped to attention, and for weeks before the appointed evening they could scarcely speak of anything else.

The Waldorf Hotel ballroom was decorated with some five thousand orchids, arranged in clusters to conceal electric lights and "richly but not heavily garlanded in a curtain effect" around five mirrors as well as over the chandeliers. Roses trailed from a balcony, and there was not an empty space that had not been "festooned, banked, showered with American beauty, and pink roses, or lilies-of-the-valley or orchids." Garlands of mauve orchids streamed "carelessly to the floor, like the untied bonnet strings of a thoughtless child." Among several orchestras was the Twenty-second Regiment Band of fifty players. The Bradley Martins hired four hundred carriages for the convenience of guests who did not want to keep their own coachmen up all night. As for the costumes, Mrs. Bradley Martin appeared as Mary, Queen of Scots, in black velvet and cerise satin over a white satin petticoat, topped off with a ruby necklace formerly owned by another beheaded queen, Marie Antoinette; a cluster of diamond grapes, once the property of Louis XIV; and a fabulously jewelled stomacher. (For the very rich, *stomach* does not seem to have been a taboo word as long as it formed part of the word *stomacher* and was preceded by the adjective *jewelled*.) There were several Louis XVs at the ball, including Mr. Bradley Martin. Anne Morgan, the debutante daughter of J. P. Morgan, was Pocahontas, and James Lawrence Breese, of Tuxedo Park, who not long before had had a little adverse publicity because of a stag party he gave at which a scantily clad and underage damsel had appeared out of a pie, was resplendent as Henry VIII in white satin, seed pearls, and a fascinating leer. August Belmont wore a full suit of armor inlaid with gold, reputed to have cost ten thousand dollars.

As tidings of the ball and its high cost continued to be reported—$369,200 was the final figure—newspapers began running editorials critical of the expenditure of so much money in depression times. The Panic of '93 was still being felt, but Mrs. Bradley Martin had been quoted as saying that she was giving the ball as "an impetus to trade." Commenting on Mrs. Astor's costume, the *World* wrote disapprovingly, "It was perfectly astonishing how Mrs. Astor managed to find a place for so many jewels [her jewelled stomacher was worn on the bosom rather than the logical place]; they covered her like a cuirass. She was gowned as a Venetian lady in a dark-blue velvet costume. It was laden with $200,000 worth of jewels." (Ten years before, Mrs. Astor would not have given the Bradley Martins the time of day; but roguish Harry Lehr had persuaded her to accept their invitation.) Criticisms rained down on the Bradley Martins from both editorial page and pulpit, and they found that instead of making their name, the ball had given them a bad one. Adding insult, the New York tax authorities doubled the Bradley Martin real estate tax assessments. Crestfallen and indignant, the couple moved permanently to England, and their ball went down in history as a classic example of conspicuous consumption.

Possibly Thorstein Veblen had the debacle in mind when he wrote, in *The*

Mrs. Stuyvesant Fish at home

Theory of the Leisure Class (1899), "Conspicuous consumption of valuable goods is a means of reputability to the gentlemen of leisure. As wealth accumulates on his hands, his own unaided effort will not avail to sufficiently put his opulence in evidence. . . . The aid of friends and competitors is therefore brought in by resorting to the giving of valuable presents and expensive feasts and entertainments. Presents and feasts had probably another origin than that of naïve ostentation, but they acquired their utility for this purpose very early, and they have retained that character to the present; so that their utility in this respect has now long been the substantial ground on which these usages rest. Costly entertainments, such as the potlatch or the ball, are peculiarly adapted to serve this end. The competitor with whom the entertainer wishes to institute a comparison is, by this method, made to serve as a means to the end. He consumes vicariously for his host at the same time that he is a witness to the consumption of that excess of good things which his host is unable to dispose of single-handed, and he is also made to witness his host's facility in etiquette."

A vital question in New York and in many other cities was certainly "How much are you worth?" But in Philadelphia "Who was your grandfather?" was even more important, and in Boston "How much do you know?" demanded a satisfactory answer. Edith Wharton recalled that she had always been considered too fashionable in Boston and too literary in New York. Her New York relatives never mentioned her books to her—"the subject was avoided as though it were a kind of family disgrace." But in Boston the upper crust were not embarrassed to number in their midst Oliver Wendell Holmes, James Russell Lowell, William James, Charles Eliot Norton, and other wellborn persons who used their brains.

Bostonians were, however, embarrassed by the potlatch mentality that pervaded the rest of the country. Even at the height of the Gilded Age, the richest families of Boston lived on the incomes from their incomes. No Boston family owned any of the marble "cottages" at Newport; and since the New Yorkers had taken that resort over, many of the Bostonians preferred the simpler atmosphere of Bar Harbor or Nahant, where big, gray shingle houses and meals with a recurrent theme of baked beans, fish balls, and Indian pudding, advertised nothing of wealth. The only Bostonian noted for extravagance was Mrs. Jack Gardner, and she was born and brought up in New York. Apparently shades of Cotton Mather and his Puritan cohorts still troubled Boston women when they selected their wardrobes. "I wish Mother would look like a New York mother," was the complaint of a rebellious Boston girl. As for New Yorkers, if they could, they ordered their clothes, sometimes semiannually, from Worth or one of the other great Paris houses.

The arrival of the Paris trunks was a moment of excitement for even the most blasé society woman. Each garment was packed in a snowbank of tissue paper and supported by tapes, so as to put no weight on the dresses packed beneath. The Paris *couturière* may never have seen her American client (commissions could be handled by mail if exact measurements were sent), but if the lady had been prudent about her daily intake of champagne and *pâté de foie gras*, the clothes fitted to perfection. For a summer season in Newport, some women ordered up to a hundred dresses, complete with matching shoes, hats, and parasols. A winter season required an even greater supply. Maintenance was a further problem, for which a ladies' maid was a necessity. "Where

(Continued on Page 282)

A lady's beast of burden

Salt Lake City: 1880

"Zion of the Mountains," as seen by George Augustus Sala. An Englishman, he shared the prejudice of many Americans that the Mormon capital was sin city.

The architectural lions of Salt Lake City are not numerous, nor . . . are they very interesting. Behind a high wall is the far-famed Tabernacle . . . a monstrous structure. From the roof . . . hang a multitude of ingeniously interlaced festoons . . . certainly curious and almost pretty. . . . the one oasis in a Desert of Ugliness. In the church . . . the sermons are on bee-culture, or on the manufacture of "sorgham" molasses; then will come addresses on infant baptism, and on the best manure for cabbages; upon the pious perseverance of the Saints; upon the wickedness of skimming milk . . . upon abstinence from tobacco; upon chignons, twenty-five yard dresses, and plural marriages; all these being mingled with fierce . . . invocations of wrath on the heads of Gentile enemies of the Mormons. At the Sunday school celebrations . . . within the Tabernacle . . . "voluntaries" on the organ . . . are sometimes varied by . . . "Home, Sweet Home!" . . . the gallery fronts are decorated with gay mottoes, among which the following is conspicuous: "Utah's best Crop:—Children." The Mormon sisterhood . . . don a garment during the celebration of the mysteries . . . made to envelope the whole body, and . . . worn night and day. Male Mormons are all dressed in the same kind of undermost garment . . . drawers and shirt all in one. There is no certain test by which a stranger can ascertain the extent to which polygamy actually prevails in Salt Lake City. I was told

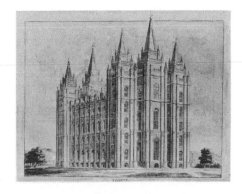

. . . that it was always feasible to estimate the numerical strength of the seraglio of a Mormon Elder by the number of front doors, with windows to correspond, of his house . . . but it would be of course imprudent to accept this as a sure test. In some cases there may not be a front door for every wife. The great pluralists in the way of spouses are the Mormon Bishops and Elders, many of whom are very wealthy. . . . The rank and file of the Mormons are a most laborious, peaceable, law-abiding and deservedly thriving community, and . . . they are kept in a state of spiritual subjection by a select ring of "nasty" old men who, by aid of a preposterous theological humbug, are enabled to fill their purses and to gratify with impunity their libidinous propensities. There was one individual indeed, attached to a livery stable . . . who appeared to regard the proximate decay of polygamous Mormonism as a far from improbable contingency. "I thought," he remarked . . . "that this city was a moral place until I druv a 'ack. . . . There's a deal of . . . carryin' on by moonlight here . . . wiolet powder u'd do it." "Why violet powder?" I asked. "They slaps it on, sir . . . the gals; they powders and paints theirselves, and they don't mind what their pa's and their ma's say, and they aint whacked 'arf enough; and then they camels up [wear bustles], goes to 'ops and helopes with Gentiles. Whether cosmetics are to be factors in overthrowing Mormonism time will show.

and how all these innumerable ball and dinner dresses, tea-gowns and *robes de chambre*, opera wraps, street costumes, and reception dresses are kept, is an important question," says the author of a housekeeper's guide, *Millionaire Households*. "Who cares for them? Certainly not the wearer. It will take all of her time to wear them." A well-planned house for a millionaire provided closets big enough to live in; ranks of drawers for lingerie, and rows of cupboards for platter-sized hats. The ladies' maid needed a workroom where she could iron, mend, sew buttons, and cope with the street dirt that Madam tracked in on her pretty little kid shoes and on her majestic trains.

I n the hierarchy of servants, the ladies' maid ranked high, and perhaps this was compensation for being in constant attendance except when her mistress was asleep or out. "The hired companion's position is heaven by comparison," says *Millionaire Households*, "although in both instances, luxury and bondage go hand in hand—both are joyless." Evenings were seldom her own. She went along to parties and waited in the dressing room, ready to administer first aid should Madam's hair come undone or her ruffles get into the soup. "If she can manage also to be deaf, dumb, and blind . . ." says *Millionaire Households* delicately, "she will greatly enhance her own personal comfort, as well as her desirability as an attendant at all hours and under varied circumstances." Her talents and tact brought her $25 to $40 a month, plus her keep. Compared with the shopgirl's $3 a week this was good money, but compared with the pay of men servants, it was grossly unfair. Footmen in livery earned from $35 to $50 a month, slightly more if they could wear a powdered wig with dignity, and a butler demanded $75 a month or more. The chef expected to augment his pay of at least $100 a month with a 10 percent gratuity from the butcher and other tradesmen in return for his patronage. The housekeeper, who acted as official prime minister for her preoccupied mistress, earned the best salary—up to $150 monthly.

Liveried servant playing a buss-boy

The master of the house retained a valet to take charge of his clothing, which, according to *Millionaire Households*, reposed in wardrobe closets as big as small shops. A man of lofty standing in the business world wore a frock coat and a high silk hat to the office. Lesser breeds wore dark sack suits, always with a waistcoat. It was unthinkable to go without a hat of some kind: in winter, a derby; in summer, a hard straw hat. For a really informal occasion, such as a picnic, white duck or white flannel trousers might be worn with a jacket and waistcoat of blue serge. But for the races or for milling around the Newport Casino on a summer morning, a gentleman's attire was as dressy as his lady's.

A book called *The Ultra-Fashionable Peerage of America* (1904), records the outfit chosen by one Newport social leader for watching a tennis tournament: "a suit of purplish gray cheviot, with a double-breasted vest of bright brocaded purple satin, a long flowing scarf, of a bit brighter shade of purple, a white felt *chapeau-la-ville* hat, with heavy folds of purple corded-silk girded around it." The author adds a cautionary note: "With the men . . . a steadily increasing picturesqueness and poetic license in personal attire are en regle. . . . A man or woman brought into social contact with the magic circle needs to be solidly well placed socially, to indulge in inventive vagaries in dress. . . . We will condone Mr. Thomas Suffern Tailer's green suits of clothes at Newport last season, for they had very modish transatlantic precedents to fall back upon, besides, when one has the blood of both a Suffern and a Tailer coursing through his veins, he can do a variety of things with impunity."

Those whose blood was less dazzlingly blue could rely on *The Ultra-Fashionable Peerage of America*'s recommendations for "an ultra-smart man's wardrobe: It contains a fur-lined top coat for the opera; an Inverness fur-lined, without the fur showing; a Chesterfield, in black or dark gray, or a Newmarket, to be worn over dress clothes ordinarily; a long, loose sack over-coat, silk-faced for Spring and early Autumn; a double-breasted Newmarket, a single-breasted Prince Henry coat, a Strand coat, which is single-breasted with tails; rain and steamer coats, yachting suits, a double-breasted ulster, made of homespun; golf costumes and a short covert coat for between seasons. For golfing, only a few incurable Anglomaniacs among our society men still persist in wearing Knickerbockers with rough stockings and Norfolk jackets, the outfit being voted exasperatingly trying in midsummer. Driving and automobile coats, of course, vary with the season. For four-in-hand driving, the Newmarket coat must disport a flaring skirt."

Dandies on the make at a summer resort

Gentlemen of society must have spent a tiresome amount of time with their tailors, but, once suitably dressed, they were freer to do as they liked than were their wives, who bore the brunt of fulfilling social obligations. "What with having to keep *en evidence* the year round, we society women simply drop down in harness," said one of them, Mrs. John R. Drexel. No amount of inconvenience or bad weather could detain these plucky creatures in their rounds of distributing calling cards. Edith Wharton wrote that "the onerous and endless business of 'calling' "took up every spare hour.

Driving was another way of keeping *en evidence*, and at Newport there was nothing more evident every afternoon than the ladies as they trundled down Ocean Drive in victorias or barouches. "For this drive," said Mrs. Wharton, "it was customary to dress as elegantly as for a race-meeting at Auteuil or Ascot. A brocaded or satin-striped dress, powerfully whale-boned, a small flower-trimmed bonnet tied with a large tulle bow under the chin, a dotted tulle veil and a fringed silk or velvet sunshade, sometimes with a jointed handle of elaborately carved ivory, composed what was thought a suitable toilet for this daily circuit between wilderness and waves." Mrs. Harry Lehr, in a none-too-kind book she wrote about her late husband, described an average eleven o'clock scene at the Newport Casino: "Such clothes! How they swished and rustled over the Casino lawn! Petticoats embellished with elaborate designs of plump cupids playing gilded lyres, true-love knots interspersed with doves embroidered in seed pearls. White gloves to the elbow, priceless lace ruffles at throat and wrists!"

To solve the perennial shortage of male partners at dances, one cartoonist suggested that hotel management provide puppet gigolos.

A young lady might take a drive with a young man, provided a groom went along in the carriage rumble. "The dress of the young ladies . . . was no less elegant than that of the dowagers," wrote Mrs. Wharton, "and I remember, one hot summer afternoon, seeing one of the damsels . . . appear for the drive arrayed in a heavy white silk dress with a broad black satin stripe, and a huge hat wreathed with crimson roses and draped with a green veil against the sun. It is only fair to add that my brother, who helped her to the giddy summit of the T-cart [a high, four-wheeled conveyance] . . . was arrayed in a frock-coat, a tall hat and pearl-gray trousers."

The "damsel" may well have been a debutante; a girl's wardrobe for a coming-out year was as elaborate as if for a trousseau. The tradition of "coming out" dates back to the eighteenth century when the fifteen- or sixteen-year-old daughters of prosperous families were given parties, ostensibly to introduce them to polite-society people of all ages but actually to call attention to the fact that they were now nubile and available. After the Civil War, with the years of schooling extended and girls marrying somewhat later, debuts were usually at eighteen and the parties more elaborate. In New York, the "season" began in mid-November and closed with Lent. There were also seasons at the resorts, and a girl of wealth might well be tendered several parties throughout the year, usually meeting the same people over again. July and August were the fashionable months at Newport and Bar Harbor, and in September the stately houses of Long Island and Tuxedo Park and on the banks of the Hudson had their share of excitement. "Indeed," gushed a contemporary etiquette book, "with the gayety of country-house life, hunting, lawn tennis and driving, it is hard to say when the American season ends."

A debutante ball, cautions that arbiter of deportment, Mrs. Sherwood, should never be called by that name on the invitation, which should simply give the names of the young lady's parents and the day and place of the party. "Dancing" should be engraved in the left-hand corner, and the card of the debutante may be enclosed. Until the 1880's, it was considered bad form to send an invitation through the mail. But Mrs. Sherwood, in 1884, decreed, "the post is now freely used as a safe and convenient medium, and no one feels offended if an invitation arrives with a two-cent stamp on the envelope." A public but very exclusive place such as Delmonico's was *de rigueur* as a setting for a coming-out ball, unless the debutante's parents had a house big enough to accommodate several hundred guests, or were willing—as Ward McAllister thought they should be—"to build an addition . . . to be used but for one night, and to be made large enough to comfortably hold, with the house, one thousand or twelve hundred people."

All age groups were invited to a coming-out ball, but as Mrs. Sherwood sadly pointed out, older women had to be prepared for a dull time. "Such is the limbo of the woman of forty or over, who in Europe would be the belle, the person just beginning to have a [social] career. For it is too true that the woman who has learned something, who is still beautiful, the woman who has maturity and experience, is pushed to the wall in America, while in Europe she is courted and admired. Society holds out all its attractive distractions and comforts to such a woman in Europe; in America it keeps everything, even its comforts, for the very young."

Probably the chief reason why older women were ignored was that men were afraid of situations remotely suggesting scandal. While in Europe a ballroom flirtation would pass almost unnoticed, in America Mrs. Grundy lurked behind every portiere. Eagle-eyed chaperons prevented young girls from committing indiscretions, but an older woman had to watch her own step. "No unprotected woman can do the least thing that is unconventional without having Mrs. Grundy shouting to everyone the worst possible things about her." Emily Post wrote that sentence in 1922, but it could as well date from fifty years earlier. "If she is a widow her conduct must be above criticism, but if she is young and pretty and divorced, she must literally live the life of a Puritan spinster of Salem." Edith Wharton's *The Age of Innocence*, set in the 1870's, shows its heroine, Ellen Olenska, causing her conventional relatives terrible anxiety. Among her offenses are living alone, being separated from her husband, and actually contemplating divorce. Worse still, she is admired

Youth cult, as seen by Charles Dana Gibson

Folding opera glasses for a lady's purse

by a married duke, and goes with him to a party, given by a woman considered "common," where there is smoking, champagne, and music-hall songs — and on Sunday, too. "People should respect our ways when they come among us," complains one old New Yorker. "Ellen Olenska especially. . . . Countess Olenska is a New Yorker, and should have respected the feelings of New York."

As for the young daughters of the rich, a close degree of chaperonage distinguished them from ordinary middle-class Americans. The Age of Innocence was also the Age of Chaperons, and for many it lasted into the twentieth century. A young woman in a Henry James short story is convinced that a gentleman acquaintance ought to marry her because they have been left alone together in an opera box. Mrs. Post, in 1922, cites a case of a man and girl who went out in a sailboat from Bar Harbor, and did not get back until the next day. "Everyone knew the fog had come in as thick as pea-soup, and that it was impossible to get home; but to the end of time her reputation will suffer for the experience."

The code of behavior for rich people also included attendance at church, and the Episcopal communion was the fashionable one nearly everywhere except in Boston, where the oldest families were Unitarian or Congregationalist. In New York, Grace Church was for decades the most socially desirable place of worship. Climbers competed for the privilege of renting a pew there, and its sexton, Isaac Brown, became an unofficial social arbiter. He delivered invitations and opened carriage doors; he advised hostesses as to who was in town, who was in mourning, and who had houseguests; and, if a party-giver was socially insecure, he would advise her what to serve and what decorations were the latest thing. As New York's fashionable world became bigger and less manageable, he announced that he could only "run society" as far north as Fiftieth Street. At one party, where a nervous newcomer had asked him to be on hand to receive the carriages as they arrived, he advised certain of the old guard who drove up to drive away again, whispering confidentially, "This is mixed, very!" A ubiquitous figure at all society's important moments — and an unmistakable one, since he weighed three hundred pounds — Brown retained his self-carved niche for thirty-five years.

Pew holders at Trinity Church in Newport had their pews upholstered to match their servants' liveries and the cushions in their carriages. A member of the Morgan family had his pew done in crimson damask, with two comfortable armchairs for the parents and swivel chairs for the children. The pew was known in the parish as "the parlor car." Society editors did not hesitate to follow rich and prominent worshipers through the sacred portals. "Mrs. Burke Roche stood in a romantic and graceful attitude," came a reporter's tidings from Trinity Church. "Her big black hat had a drooping black plume; her gown was of heavy Irish lace. There were many velvet fleur de lis in life size on Mrs. Prescott Lawrence's hat, matching her purple cloak; she followed the service devoutly, the gardenias in her corsage making sweet perfume in all the adjacent pews. On her knees on the carpet she listened to the last prayer. Mrs. Richard Stevens was in dark blue moiré, picturesque in effect. Mrs. O.H.P. Belmont wore an exquisite gown of ecru and black, very modish."

By and large, the pew holders at Newport's Trinity were the same people who held boxes at the opera. Social cachet demanded patronage of the opera,

The "Soc et Tuum" ideal at posh colleges

which, before 1883, was given at the old Academy of Music on Fourteenth Street; the *crème de la crème*, for some long-forgotten reason, always patronized it on Monday evenings. As the waiting list for the eighteen boxes on Monday evenings at the academy never seemed to get shorter and did not include any of the newly arrived, a group of the latter, headed by the Vanderbilts, got together to construct the Metropolitan Opera House—with a generous 110 boxes. On the night of the opening, many socialites were perplexed as to whether to join the glitter and excitement of the sumptuous new opera house, or to remain loyal to the shabby but more exclusive older one. At least one *grande dame*, Mrs. Paran Stevens, spent part of the evening at one, part at the other, and part in a mad dash by carriage.

A growing appetite for opera, as well as for painting, European manners, and the French language—many society ladies spoke English with a slight French accent—all came about in the last decades of the century, as ocean travel gradually became reasonably comfortable and safe. According to the social historian Dixon Wecter, "the zenith of European influence upon American society came from about 1895 up to the Great War." Those wishing to remain *en evidence* had to be seen on both sides of the Atlantic, especially in Paris, London, and the German spas. Wherever they went, they took along their own bed linen and towels, as well as a few personal servants.

Since, for the very rich, to live was to acquire, they no sooner set foot in Europe than they began to buy things. From Worth gowns and Savile Row suits they branched out to jewels, dogs, horses, wines, dinner services, *objets de virtu*, and very soon to the world of art. One of the first of the very rich to buy good paintings was Mrs. Potter Palmer, queen of Chicago society and chatelaine of a $700,000 castle on Lake Shore Drive that had a lot of empty wall space. Money and empty wall space do not insure a fine art collection, but Mrs. Palmer had two more necessary ingredients—taste and the good sense to follow the counsel of people more knowledgeable than herself. She trusted Mary Cassatt, possibly because Miss Cassatt was not only a painter but an authentic Philadelphia socialite; following her advice, Mrs. Palmer acquired paintings by Monet, Degas, Pissarro, and Renoir at a time when such French salon painters as William Bouguereau and Carolus Duran were fashionable. Her Chicago peers followed suit, with the result that today the Art Institute of Chicago has the finest public collection of impressionist paintings in America.

An indirect result of the growing sophistication of its rich was that Chicago's leading citizens got together and outbid New York, St. Louis, and Washington for the privilege of holding the Columbian Exposition of 1893. Mrs. Potter Palmer, whose social position in Chicago suffered not at all from her husband's having made his fortune with a dry goods emporium and a hotel, was in the forefront as chairman of the Board of Lady Managers. In this capacity she corresponded with or visited the august women of the world, from Queen Victoria to the Queen of Siam, and through them reinforced their countries' interest and cooperation in the fair. The Infanta Eulalia of Spain, while attending the fair, rudely tried to avoid one of Mrs. Palmer's receptions, saying, "I prefer not to meet this inn-keeper's wife." Berthe Palmer, not one to be defeated by a snub, was later appointed by President McKinley to be the only woman on the United States commission to the Paris Exposition of 1900, and she had the pleasure of turning down a reception for the Infanta. "I cannot

American tourists "doing" the Continent

meet this bibulous representative of a degenerate monarchy," was her returning salvo. Mrs. Palmer's contacts with other royalty, however, improved her shaky position in Newport, where Potter Palmer's credentials were regarded with suspicion. The list of royal visitors at their Newport mansion in subsequent years read like the *Almanach de Gotha*. By 1918, when she died, she had become the acknowledged social leader of Newport, and had married off her niece to a Russian prince.

Princes, dukes, and other noblemen were a popular European import throughout the Gilded Age. Such articles had long been admired in America, largely because they seemed rare and exotic; the visit of the future King Edward VII in 1860 made that year a stellar one to society. In New York the ranks of the old guard closed around him, shutting all others out of a ball at the Academy of Music.

The awe of Americans for titles and royalty has probably been exaggerated because of the immense publicity attached to a few marriages of heiresses into noble houses. That of Consuelo Vanderbilt to the Duke of Marlborough, in 1895, appears to have been an arrant case of title-buying: the bride was late to her magnificent wedding, looking pale and teary-eyed; years later, when the marriage was dissolved, the duchess' mother, Alva Vanderbilt Belmont, admitted that she had forced her daughter to marry the duke. Another bad example that year was the union of Anna Gould and Count Boni de Castellane, who spent over five million dollars of his wife's money before they were divorced eleven years later. In 1909 someone calculated that more than five hundred American heiresses had married titled foreigners who had thus raked in a total of about $220,000,000. The majority of American parents, however, probably preferred to see their children marry mates of similar backgrounds. Most sympathized with the Quaker mother who, when told that her son, an American attaché in London, had danced with Queen Victoria at her Coronation Ball, remarked, "I hope my son Richard will not marry out of meeting."

If most upper-class Americans were happy to live in a republic, it is probably fair to say that they also took a deep interest in genealogy. When they could unearth a coat of arms in their ancestries, they were quick to have it engraved on their writing paper or silver or to have it painted on their carriage doors. Historians believe that not fifty colonial families had a right to armorial bearings. Yet in the late nineteenth century, their descendants appeared to have proliferated so remarkably that Tiffany had to set up a department of "Blazoning, marshalling, and designing of arms complete." An "Office of Heraldry" did a flourishing business in New York, and numerous books to aid self-styled genealogists were published. *The Blazon of Gentry* assured its readers, "Christ was a gentleman, as to the flesh, by the part of his mother . . . and might have borne coat-armor." *Americans of Royal Descent*, which went into several editions in the 1890's, listed thousands of blue bloods. Persons of distinguished colonial ancestry began organizing themselves into clubs, most of which still exist: the Colonial Dames, the Descendants of the Signers of the Declaration of Independence, the Society of Descendants of the Continental Congress, the Huguenot Society of America, the Order of Colonial Lords of Manors in America, the Society of Mayflower Descendants, and the Daughters of the American Revolution—to name a few. Some had great social cachet, while others, like the D.A.R., were open to too many people to be really exclusive. And so, for better or worse, was American society.

Royalty besieged by the Four Hundred

Poor Men's Dreams

*In which Poverty is seen
to Result from Factors
other than Moral Turpitude;
new Immigrants find
the American Dream elusive,
& Urban Reformers
stir the Nation's Conscience*

Poverty in Victorian America had many guises. There was the kind that fiction writers liked to describe sentimentally—doing without a new pair of gloves, as in *Little Women*, or working stalwartly at humble tasks, like Longfellow's village blacksmith. And there was the sort of poverty that most people preferred not to think or hear about—the abject misery of the slums. The very poor, for the most part, were immigrants of the first or second generation; for them, if they were ignorant and friendless, these shores were bleak indeed. Until after the Civil War, most of them came in the steerage of sailing ships, packed so tightly that after a voyage of six weeks or more they could hardly stand when they debarked. Even the best ships were crowded; the worst were "damned plague ships and swimming coffins," in the words of one reporter; when they dropped anchor in American harbors, they could be identified from a distance by their nauseous smell.

A New York doctor whose duty it was to inspect incoming immigrant ships, wrote after a morning on board a ship from Liverpool, "We passed through the steerage, making a more or less minute examination of the place and its inhabitants; but the indescribable filth, the emaciated half-nude figures, many with the petechial erupture [typhus] disfiguring their faces, crouching in the bunks, or strewed over the decks, and cumbering the gangway; broken utensils and debris of food spread recklessly about, presented a picture of which neither pen nor pencil can convey a full idea. Some were just rising from their berths for the first time since leaving Liverpool, having been suffered to lie there all the voyage, wallowing in their own filth."

Those who survived such a crossing and were able to land with their health, belongings, and spirits reasonably intact often found that their difficulties were just beginning. Native Americans either ignored the newcomers or were

*Late-nineteenth-century immigrants were principally city dwellers. William Glackens'
"Far from the Fresh Air Farm" depicts, perhaps too cheerfully, a transplanted slum.*

actively hostile toward them. People of the same nationality helped when they could, but in the large immigrant ports life was a struggle and there were few who wanted or could tolerate extra burdens. "Sink or swim" was a positively kindly attitude. Some swam, particularly those who were able to leave the port behind and settle in the West. Skilled workers usually found work and eventually became part of "the backbone of America"—honest, hard-working folk who realized the dream, or something like it, for which they had left their homelands. Others, either because they were penniless, untrained, illiterate, sick, crippled, mentally ill, or too young or too old to earn a living, became part of the unwelcome masses of the port city where they had first set foot. Sometimes a city or state in Europe would decide to pay the passage of all its dependent persons in order to get rid of them. In 1847 one Prussian city sent over the sick and destitute of its prisons; most of the unfortunates ended their days in New York's overcrowded workhouses. Not until 1882 would the American government begin to pass laws dealing with such outrages.

"Runners rushed at emigrants like jackals at a dying deer," states a history of German emigration, to sell them "tickets to some wonderful place in the country, a land of milk and honey, and did not rest until the greenhorn had hardly any money left." Consuls and port authorities tried to warn against these sharks who lived off innocent newcomers, but often in vain. A German consul in New York wrote, "The German emigrants seem not to be able to imagine what awaits them. Everything is different from what they expected. When they arrive in New York they are overwhelmed by the noise and the bustle of life; only knowing German life and accustomed to obeying, they believe that every authoritative man who questions them must be an official person; they do everything they are told to do and do not suspect that they are in the hands of a runner."

Later, to avoid the police, immigrant sharks took to operating on board ship. Describing the arrival of Italians in 1900, a reporter for Frank Leslie's magazine said, "Many a wretched widow, who has sold all her household goods to secure the passage money for herself and children, finds before she lands that she has been swindled out of her little fortune by some insinuating stranger." The United States was still a dumping ground for Europe's unwanted, for "there are other cases of women who, with their children, have been literally forced aboard ship by their own husbands, who in this way attempt to shift their burdens upon the hospitable American public."

Yankee—an oddity in a land of aliens

The port of New York received the largest number of immigrants and in consequence the country's worst slums developed. The once-handsome old Dutch houses of Lower Manhattan were subdivided again and again and more stories added, often without regard to safety. Jacob Riis, the Danish-born American reformer, described the phenomenon in *How the Other Half Lives* (1890): ". . . in the old garden where the stolid Dutch burgher grew his tulips or early cabbages, a rear house was built, generally of wood, two stories high at first. Presently it was carried up another story, and another. Where two families had lived ten moved in." The managers of such buildings were seldom the real owners. They leased the properties from wealthy families and then sublet them, room by room, to the poor, often at huge profits of 30 to 40 percent.

The Astors, the Rhinelanders, the Goelets, and others could afford to wait for the inevitable growth of the city to increase land values. There was no one to help the tenant—certainly not the city government, which was run by people who had clawed their way out of the slums and looked upon life as a dog-eat-dog enterprise. The richest slumlord of them all, John Jacob Astor, had arrived in New York in 1784 as a young man with five pounds in his pocket and had accumulated a twenty-million-dollar fortune with nobody's help or guidance. In his opinion, any immigrant could do the same, and if he failed, it was nobody's fault but his own. Astor advised his son, William, to acquire the habit of going to bed early so that he would perform his work well the next day. "It's all a matter of habit, and good habits in America make any man rich." If he wondered at all about the people living ten or more to a room in his tenements, he probably concluded that they did not have good habits. Astor's son and grandson shared the old man's philosophy. However, few slum tenants knew who owned their wretched quarters, or whom to blame for the miserable way they had to live.

Most prosperous Americans shared the Astors' indifference to the poor, and many went even further, suspecting that poverty was the result of sin. That the New York cholera epidemics of 1832, 1849, and 1866 raged most fiercely in the slums seemed to sustain this view. The disease, commented a prominent New York banker during the first epidemic, was "almost exclusively confined to the lower classes of intemperate dissolute & filthy people huddled together like swine in their polluted habitations." The editor of *The Western Sunday School Messenger* told his young readers, *"Drunkards and filthy, wicked people of all descriptions*, are swept away *in heaps* . . . just as we sweep away a mass of filth when it has become so corrupt that we cannot bear it. . . . The cholera is not *caused* by intemperance and filth, in themselves, but it is a *scourge*, a *rod* in the hand of God." The next epidemic began in the spring of 1849 and was traced to a dark and filthy New York cellar occupied by five adults. They all died, and there were soon other cases on the same street.

Cholera moving in on a slum landlord

Old Philip Hone noted in his diary that these people had lived "where water never was used internally or externally, and the pigs [which commonly shared space with their poor owners] were contaminated by the contact of the children." Men and women of Hone's class were not surprised that cholera attacked the "vicious poor," a group set apart in their minds from the "industrious poor." What did surprise them later in that terrible summer was that not only many of the industrious poor but some of their own friends died of cholera. Hone's reaction to this was to blame the immigrants, who through their dirtiness, intemperance, and Sabbath-breaking, had brought the disease, "engendered on shipboard," to virtuous Americans. At least he admitted the possibility that it was the disease itself that killed, not sin.

The epidemic of 1849 attacked every large city in the United States, and gradually the connection between lack of sanitation and the spread of the disease forced itself upon the public mind. Cities had long been considered dangerous to the soul; now their danger to the body became apparent. The concept of cholera as retribution was firmly rooted, however, and most people were now convinced of a dual cause for the disease: "Imperfect ventilation, impure water, and a crowded population, necessarily induce fevers and pestilence," said an Indiana minister, "while evil pleasures and sensual pleasures corrupt the morals, and enfeeble the intellect; and generation after genera-

An English line seeks steerage passengers with the poster above. Below, Polish emigrants are lured by unscrupulous-looking agents of a German company.

tion, fall victims to flagrant and senseless violations of the laws of health."

Noting that cholera usually struck first in low-lying areas where the houses lacked ventilation, the cellars were damp or even flooded, and garbage was never disposed of, many cities tried to order or cajole the poor into cleaning their premises. It was not easy. A continual complaint of reformers was that the poor were their own worst enemy. Having no place else to go and fearing the poorhouse, they had to be dragged out of their fetid cellars. The pigs with which they lived were their only economic asset. Physicians who ordered the poor to keep themselves clean, wear warm clothing, and eat nourishing meals were discouraged by the lack of response. Puritan-minded Protestants found therein a new weapon against Catholicism: "All testimonies agree in affirming that there is scarcely anything more distinctive of paganism than its love of dirt," wrote a Cincinnati Protestant paper. "Catholicism which is but one remove from paganism, shows much of this disgusting character, whether its votaries sun themselves in the streets of Naples, or crouch on the mud floor of an Irish cabin."

In the years between 1849 and the next cholera epidemic, 1866, there were advances both in medical knowledge and social conscience. In 1849 very few physicians had thought that cholera might be contagious, but by 1866 few doubted it, although its precise pathology was unknown. It had also become clear to many native-born Americans that the new immigrants were needed for their labor and that by no means all were "vicious poor." Some were "industrious poor," and an asset to the cities. Charles E. Rosenberg, in his book *The Cholera Years*, notes, "Despite the disdain of the thoughtless, the mechanic in his city workshop was as indispensable to society as the farmer in his fields. And, moralists noted, St. Paul a tentmaker and Jesus a carpenter, had both been mechanics." Americans earnestly undertook the job of cleaning streets, disinfecting privies, and getting rid of urban pigs, once convinced that such measures were worthwhile. Certainly, it was easier than eradicating sin or making Protestants out of Catholics. Wherever citizens worked conscientiously to make their cities sanitary, cholera cases were fewer. In New York City, despite a vast increase in population after 1849, the number of deaths from cholera in 1866 was only one-tenth that of the previous epidemic.

New York's revitalized Board of Health, its powers greatly extended, implemented the Tenement House Act of 1867. Cellars were not to be considered residential; buildings must occupy no more than 60 percent of a lot; and 46,000 windows must be cut in rooms that had none. Unfortunately the first two stipulations were ignored, and although the windows were indeed cut, there was so much garbage and refuse on the ground beneath them that most tenants kept them closed. Rules to control the number of occupants to a room were impossible to enforce; not only were they avoided by the sublandlords but by the tenants as well. Five families—twenty persons—might live in a 12 by 12 room and call itself "a family with boarders." From the 1850's until the early nineties, when Jacob Riis wrote his crusading books, the only remedial effect in the slums was the banning of pigs, chickens, and other farm creatures from houses and city streets.

Immigrant groups set up housekeeping, if it could be called that, in ethnic enclaves, each finding little in common with other nationalities and even less with native Americans. It was usual for the latter to ascribe characteristics to each group and ignore any behavior that belied the stereotype. Even Jacob Riis, unusually perceptive in many ways and himself an immigrant, labeled the Irishman "contentious," the Italian "content to live in a pig-sty," the German "order-loving," and the Jew bent on a "headlong hunt for wealth." As for the Chinese, "there is nothing strong about him, except his passions when aroused." Riis thought the Chinese thoroughly undesirable, but added that "having let them in, we must make the best of it." He thought that if they were required to bring their wives and families with them they might indulge less in gambling and opium.

Certainly the poor did not grasp the possibility of improving their lot via the ballot box. The concept of "one man, one vote" was completely new to European immigrants, and the realities of voting in the big cities were hardly likely to give them an exemplary picture of the process. Native Americans tended to blame immigrants for the corrupt state of city politics; yet the indifference and hostility of long-time Americans toward new ones did its share to drive the newcomers into a mutually helpful coalition with city bosses. In return for votes, a politician would extend credit, pay for funerals, find jobs, and intervene in case of trouble with the police. The friendless immigrant did not know, of course, that the same benevolent politician who stepped in to prevent his eviction from a filthy tenement probably also cooperated with the landlord to prevent laws from being passed to improve tenements, enforce fire precautions, clean streets, outlaw sweatshops, and shorten hours.

A particularly fruitful source of votes was the slum lodginghouse, populated by homeless and nearly penniless men. Their votes went to the highest bidder. Says Jacob Riis, ". . . the two [party] 'machines,' intrenched in their strongholds, outbid each other across the Bowery to open rivalry as to who shall commit the most flagrant frauds at the polls. . . . It must be admitted that the black tramp who herds in the West Side 'hotels' is more discriminating in this matter of electioneering than his white brother. He at least exhibits some real loyalty in invariably selling his vote to the Republican bidder for a dollar, while he charges the Democratic boss a dollar and a half."

Passionate politics c. 1850

Riis believed that crime was not a major problem in the city. "There is nothing to be afraid of. In this metropolis, let it be understood, there is no public street where the stranger may not go safely by day and by night, provided he knows how to mind his own business and is sober." But another prominent reformer, the clergyman Charles Loring Brace, took a more pessimistic view. In his book *The Dangerous Classes of New York* (1872), he warned that the American-born children of immigrants "are far more brutal than the peasantry from whom they descend." The youth formed gangs, with names such as Dead Rabbits or Plug-Uglies. "They are ready for any offense or crime, however degraded or bloody." Brace was not sure whether to blame heredity or environment for this state of affairs. On the one hand, he was sure that "certain appetites or habits . . . come to have an almost irresistible force and no doubt modify the brain. . . . This is especially true of the appetite for liquor and of the sexual passion, and sometimes of the peculiar weakness, dependence, and laziness which make confirmed paupers." On the other hand, he felt that the more self-controlled and virtuous poor tended to survive, passing on "gemmules" of self-control and virtue to their offspring; so that "the natural drift among the poor is toward virtue." He also pointed out that "the separate members of these riotous and ruffianly masses are simply neglected and street-wandering children who have come to early manhood"—illiterate, unskilled, and unchurched. For their predicament he also blamed "the increasing aversion of American children whether poor or rich, to learn anything thoroughly; the boys of the street, like those of our merchants, preferring to make fortunes by lucky or sudden 'turns,' rather than by patient and steady industry."

Apparently people questioned the work of Brace and other reformers among children of the poor, partly because making "facilities for the care of illegitimate children increases the temptation to vicious indulgence." Brace thought not; provided there were a few good "gemmules" in a child, it would be cruel to penalize him for the sins of his parents. The Children's Aid Society, founded by Brace in 1875, opened night schools, lodginghouses, and reading rooms for homeless boys and girls of New York, and sent thousands of lost or abandoned children west to live with foster parents. It was not easy to pry contributions for the society out of millionaires' pockets, even when Brace pointed out the advantages of taking the "dangerous classes" of tomorrow off the streets. Mrs. William Backhouse Astor (mother-in-law of *the* Mrs. Astor) gave him his first donation—fifty dollars. Another daughter-in-law was one of the Society's most generous donors, leaving it $25,000 in her will—a great deal in view of the tight-fistedness of other people of wealth. However, it should be noted that an Englishman who visited New York during this period found rich New Yorkers infinitely more philanthropic than their counterparts in England or on the Continent.

Placing children with western families continued for fifty years and seems to have worked well, despite occasional instances of exploitation. Hundreds of abandoned babies were cared for by the sisters of the New York Foundling Hospital, who nightly placed a bassinet outside their door. Desperate mothers who left babies on the doorsteps of the rich had a misplaced faith in charity; the babies were almost invariably handed over to the city for dispatch to the Infants' Hospital, where the mortality was 65.55 percent.

A slum child who managed to survive infancy and have a home of sorts was usually put to work at any age upwards of three. Many states forbade the employment of children under thirteen and required their attendance (for fourteen weeks of the year) at school. But parents lied about their children's ages or put them to work in sweatshops, where the overworked inspectors could not find them. Sweatshops were tenement rooms given over to a deteriorated form of cottage industry. Children aged five worked ten hours a day, making paper collars; and there was no end to what could be performed by an eight-year-old: plucking feathers from cocks' tails, sewing buttons, making artificial flowers, stripping tobacco. The pay was up to three dollars a week. Most children who were put to work at an early age became so stunted physically and mentally that they were all but unemployable by the time they had reached maturity.

Girls who were able to go to school a few years and stay off the streets had three choices (unless they were lucky enough to find a husband who could support them): employment in the factories and "sweated trades," domestic service, or the shop. Domestic service at least guaranteed a girl warm, dry lodgings, three regular meals a day, and security from the temptations of sin in the outer world. Irish Catholic girls seem to have been especially attracted to the calling. In *Advice to Irish Girls in America*, written

A shopgirl fitting customers for gaiters

in 1872, no alternatives—except marriage—are even discussed. Readers are reminded that even saints were servants and that domestics perform tasks not unlike those of the guardian angels. They are instructed to avoid thoughts about salaries, better positions, and getting ahead. "If she wishes to be rich that she may buy fine clothes, which are not suitable to her station in life, or that she may be able to go to places of amusement which are sinful, and where she may see and hear wickedness, which no Catholic girls should see or hear, then she is doing very wrong . . . in this world and the next."

For others, employment in a shop was by far the most popular job, as it gave a glimpse of another, brighter world. A girl began work at thirteen and made no more than two dollars a week for the first two or three years. During this time she was on her feet nine and a half hours a day in summer and eleven in winter—longer on Saturdays and at holiday time—except for a half-hour "lunch," usually a roll or cookies brought from home. Fines for being late, for sitting down while on the job, and for sundry other offenses, were deducted from her two dollars. It was said that the prettiest girls went into the shops, the cleverest into the factories, and the rest into service. Women's wages were consistently lower than men's. Housewives or farmers' daughters living at home in the country were willing to work for a pittance in order to earn pin money, and their competition drove wages even lower.

A woman's rights worker who had been a mill girl at Lowell during the 1840's returned to Lowell in 1898 and thought that the girls "did not go to their labor with the jubilant feeling that the old mill girls used to have." Their hours were shorter, but the machines more complicated and difficult to run, and after work the girls were too tired to improve their minds. Instead of attending lectures or contributing to the factory's literary magazine, *The Lowell Offering*, as had an earlier generation of girls, they idled about the streets or read story papers. Living conditions, also, had deteriorated since the days when girls had slept two to a feather bed under the superintendence of a motherly boardinghouse-keeper. Now, whole families were apt to be employed by the mills, and they often lived six to a small room—not as bad as city slums but hardly commodious. The factories were not as airy or sunny as they had been, the former mill girl observed. "Would that I could say one word that would lead stockholders to see that it is not from out of such surroundings that the best dividends can be secured!"

To appeal to capitalists through their dividends rather than their hearts seemed the likeliest way to reach them. "It's seas of tears that these men sail on," a sweatshop seamstress told Mrs. Helen Campbell, a New York City missionary and author of *Darkness and Daylight.* "My shortest day has been fourteen hours. . . . For a year [doing] the best that I can do I have earned not over eighty cents a day,—sometimes only seventy-five. I'm sixty-two years old. I've never asked a man alive for a penny beyond what my own hands can earn, and I don't want it. . . . There's nothing left but men that live to grind the faces of the poor; that chuckle when they find a new way of making a cent or two more a week out of starving women and children. . . . if men with money will not heed, the men and the women without money will rise some day. How? I don't know. We've no time to plan, and we're too tired to think; but it's coming somehow, and I'm not ashamed to say I'll join in if I live to see it come." Such aggressive talk was not usual among the poor—or at least was not usually reported. Jacob Riis, however, cautioned that "the sea of a mighty

Darkness and Daylight, *an early exposé on urban life, published these engravings of the poor. Above, a foundling is brought to a police station. Below, an older waif is left to shift for himself.*

population, held in galling fetters, heaves uneasily in the tenements."

The attitude of the poor toward hospitals and doctors was one of deep mistrust. It was widely imagined that to die in the hospital meant that one's body went forthwith to the dissection room. A dying dressmaker told Mrs. Campbell, "I'd rather die here at home when the time comes than at the hospital, where they cut you open before the breath is fairly out of your body. That's the way a friend of mine was served last year—just cut right up. Her folks didn't know no better than let her be took there, and after her death, which I suppose was helped along by the black bottle [medicine], them doctors, without asking leave of nobody, just slashed away at the poor thing, and then they botched her up again, and made a great pucker in the seam, such as I wouldn't allow a little 'prentice girl to make."

In offering solace to the dying, the Catholic clergy were more often on the scene than the Protestant. "In the twenty years preceding 1888," says Arthur M. Schlesinger, Sr., in *The Rise of the City*, "seventeen Protestant churches moved out of the district below Fourteenth Street, New York, though two hundred thousand more people crowded into it. . . . and it was said that in the heart of Chicago sixty thousand people had no church either Protestant or Catholic. It was generally true of large cities that those parts which needed most religious attention got least. . . . American Protestantism, the product of a rural, middle-class society, faced a range of problems for which it had neither experience nor aptitude." One reason for its unpreparedness was that the rich supported the churches and they did not care to hear themselves criticized on Sunday mornings. Thus, most clergymen did not venture to say a great deal about better living and working conditions for the poor while delivering a sermon to their employers. It was easier to collect funds for the heathen overseas than for those a block or two away.

"Where do you go to church, my boy?" Jacob Riis heard a policeman ask.

"We don't have no clothes to go to church," was the answer.

The old established Protestant churches of the city had prosperous parishioners who paid a yearly fee for their pews, and there was no room left for the penniless and the dirty. One of the most fashionable parishes, Trinity, was making a gratifying profit as a slumlord. But this is not to deny that many dedicated Protestants—Charles Brace and Helen Campbell were two examples—labored diligently in the discouraging vineyards south of Fourteenth Street. And they had their counterparts from Boston to San Francisco.

For most poor people, Sunday was for jollity. European immigrants brought the tradition with them and refused to be governed by the strict American blue laws; and urban Americans were quick to embrace this new concept of the Lord's Day. In the worst slums there was neither space nor money for amusement. Singing was free to those who felt like it, and the Italians sometimes did, although their natural exuberance was sorely stifled. An Italian dramatist, Giuseppe Giacosa, who visited New York and Chicago slums in 1898, reported, "They prattle, only not in the lively and witty chatter of the Neapolitan lands, but rather in a sort of painful chirp that strikes the heart." However, working people who made an adequate wage had a choice of leisure amusements: every city had its dime museums, and its imitator of P. T. Barnum, featuring freaks and flea circuses; and a dime or a quarter paid for a ticket to a dance hall, music hall, melodrama, or vaudeville show. In addition, there were shooting galleries, bowling alleys, and billiard parlors. Baseball

(Continued on Page 298)

A German street musician

296

New Orleans: 1874

"The Metropolis of the South," as seen by Mark Twain in Life on the Mississippi. *French sophistication and southern insularity are treated in his mixed review.*

Canal Street was . . . attractive and stirring . . . with its drifting crowds of people, its several processions of hurrying street-cars, and — toward evening — its broad second-story verandas crowded with gentlemen and ladies clothed according to the latest mode. . . . The city, well-outfitted with progressive men — thinking, sagacious, long-headed men . . . . is a driving place commercially, and has a great river, ocean, and railway

business. It is the best lighted city in the Union, electrically speaking. . . . The old French part of New Orleans — anciently the Spanish part — bears no resemblance to the American end. . . . A jog through that old quarter is a vivid pleasure. And you have a vivid *sense* as of unseen or dimly seen things — vivid, and yet fitful and darkling. . . . We visited the old St. Louis Hotel, now occupied by municipal offices. There is nothing strikingly remarkable about it; but . . . if a broom or shovel has ever been used in it there is no circumstantial evidence. . . . We visited also the venerable Cathedral, and the pretty square in front of it; the one dim with religious light, the other brilliant with the worldly sort. . . . We drove a few miles. . . . And by and by we reached the West End, a collection of hotels of the usual summer-resort pattern. . . . Thousands of people come by rail and carriage . . . every evening, and dine, listen to the bands, take strolls . . . and entertain themselves. . . . I found the half-forgotten Southern intonations and elisions as pleasing to my ear as formerly. . . . A Southerner talks music. [He] has no use for an *r*, except at the beginning of a word. He says "Gove' nuh," and "befo' the waw," and so on. . . . Every man you meet was in the war; and every lady you meet saw the war . . . . the war is what A.D. is elsewhere: they date from it. . . . The largest annual event in New Orleans is . . . the Mardi-Gras festivities. I saw the procession of the Mystic Crew of Comus . . . with knights and nobles . . . clothed in silken and golden Paris-made gorgeousnesses . . . and in their train all manner of giants, dwarfs, monstrosities, and other diverting grotesquerie — a startling and wonderful sort of show, as it filed solemnly and silently down the street in the light of its smoking and flickering torches. . . . All these people are gentlemen of position and consequence; and . . . the mystery in which they hide their personality is merely for romance's sake . . . . Mardi-Gras is of course a relic of the French and Spanish occupation; but I judge that the religious feature has been pretty well knocked out of it now. . . . It is a thing which could hardly exist in the practical North. . . . The very feature that keeps it alive in the South — girly-girly romance — would kill it in the North. . . . In our South . . . the genuine and wholesome civilization of the nineteenth century is curiously confused and commingled with the Walter Scott Middle-Age sham civilization and so you have practical . . . progressive ideas, and progressive works, mixed up with the duel, the inflated speech, and the jejune romanticism of an absurd past. . . .

was a common sport since the seventies, and there were frequent boxing and wrestling matches as well as horse racing, rowing, and trotting races. A modest outlay would buy a long trolley ride or a day's excursion by steamboat or railroad. Trolley carnivals (amusement parks owned by trolley companies) were a development of the nineties. The only active sports offered for a small fee were bathing, wherever a beach was available, and roller skating in public rinks. One form of Sunday entertainment was to have a "sundae." The name and the concoction were invented by a drugstore owner who had been forbidden to serve sodas on Sunday. The sundae became so popular that it sold Monday through Saturday as well.

For those who could read, there were story papers, violent or sentimental or both, and the *Police Gazette* (not for females), and a wide choice of "penny dreadfuls" that went into exciting detail on the subject of crime and, according to authorities of the time, gave the poor lurid and unsuitable ideas. In a critique of story papers that appeared in the *Atlantic Monthly* for September, 1879, the author asked himself whether story papers had anything to recommend them, and decided that "the taste for reading, however perverted, is connected with something noble, with an interest in things outside of the small domain of self, with a praiseworthy curiosity about the great planet we inhabit." Even if this curiosity was rewarded with nothing but heroines with purple-black hair, crying, "Oh, how can I repay you, my noble, my generous preserver!" and with villains with names like Death Notch the Destroyer, at least the reader had made connection with the printed page. Story papers also offered advice on housekeeping, child care, problems of the affections, and manners and morals: Edith F. is informed that too many rings on the fingers are vulgar, Emma D. that pie should be eaten with a fork. The circulation of story papers was vast, for they appealed to both sexes and all ages, the only limitation being a degree of simple-mindedness.

One of the most popular, and certainly the most controversial, of poor men's amusements was drinking. The rich man had his club, the middle-class man had his fraternal order, but the poor man had his saloon. Often it was the one bright, cheerful spot in a blighted neighborhood, and "Ladies Not Invited" was a sign frequently seen there. Rather than spend precious leisure in cramped quarters with squalling children and a complaining wife, many men preferred the solace of the saloon, where they could be with friends and enjoy a few hours of fleeting pleasure.

Most reformers of the Victorian age had no patience with the view that dismal social conditions drove men to drink; an editorial writer in the New York *Graphic*, in 1874, was expressing an unpopular opinion when he wrote, "It is not surprising that people who are compelled to live in tenements unfit for horses, or even swine, resort to the dram-shop when the work of the day is over, and try to hide their wretchedness from themselves in the convivialities of a well-lighted saloon and the delirium of intoxication. . . . Health and morals require something more than soup and sentiment." It would be many years before laws were passed to alleviate the poor man's daily lot; but the war on saloons intensified during the 1870's with the establishment of the Woman's Christian Temperance Union.

The woman who took over as its president in 1879, Frances Willard, was not content with temperance lectures and appeals to the conscience. Her goal was legal prohibition, and to this end she connived to insert temperance

Currier & Ives getting sentimental over ice cream and the sweetness of young love

propaganda in the school textbooks of every state and territory so that the rising generation would grow up imbued with a horror of liquor. A representative text read, ". . . sometimes one is sick or suffers very much because of wrong things that his parents or grand-parents did. . . . Over in the poorhouse is a man who does not know as much as most children four years old . . . because he is the child of drinking parents whose poisoned life blood tainted his own. Many men and women are insane because they inherit disordered bodies and minds, caused by the drinking habits of their parents; and the descendants of 'moderate drinkers' differ in this way as well as those of the drunkard. . . . This is called the law of heredity . . . one of God's laws, and just like earthly laws, helps right living and punishes those who disobey." Among other frightening pieces of misinformation was the old one about spontaneous combustion — the theory that a drinker's body could become so saturated with alcohol that it would ignite accidentally and burn up.

In their holy war on the enemies of virtue, women turned their heaviest arms against spirits, as vividly shown in the 1874 print above. Saloon art, like the semi-nude statue below, also received the hatchet treatment.

Ladies armed with hatchets had begun to assault saloons as early as the fifties and such was their success that they continued. Authorities hesitated to lock up females whose husbands were often prominent citizens. Saloonkeepers, on the other hand, were mere nobodys, and the vandalism they endured often went unprosecuted. The most renowned vandal was Carry Nation, who once axed a barroom nude with the explanation that the picture was "hung up in a place where it was not even decent for a woman to be in when she had her clothes on." Prayers and hymn singing accompanied the violence, causing Judge Alphonso Taft of Cincinnati (father of William Howard Taft) to hand down the opinion, "It is an objectionable feature of the present crusade that it intrudes religious observances on those who do not ask for them. Prayer with or for those who desire it is commendable; but when forced upon the unwilling it is a mockery of God."

Temperance found many adherents among the middle class and the moderately poor, but the very poor were hard to convince. In the late 1880's, according to Riis, more than half the city's 7,884 saloons were in the slums — not counting unlicensed "stale-beer dives," whose number Riis estimated at about a thousand. A law forbidding the sale of liquor to children was consistently ignored. A tot bearing a "growler," or pitcher, to be filled with beer was one of the commonest sights of the slums. In the neighborhood of Jane Addams' Hull House, the first settlement house in Chicago, there were nine churches and 250 saloons. Similar situations prevailed in all big urban centers. Ranking lower than the saloons was the sort of drinking place where the dregs of barrels were dispensed at one cent a pint, and "lodgings" let for two or three cents a night. Riis, accompanying a police sergeant on a routine raid, saw seventy-five men and women drinking stale beer in four small rooms of a cellar. "The filth and the stench were utterly unbearable; even the sergeant turned his back and fled after scattering the crowd with his club and starting them toward the door. The very dog in the alley preferred the cold flags for a berth to the stifling cellar."

The story of the poor in nineteenth-century America was most often told by people who, like Riis, made their observations from above. Among the few good writers who actually experienced the life of the poor was Robert Louis Stevenson, who, in 1879, came to America in steerage and traveled by emigrant train to San Francisco. The start of the thirteen-day trip, at Jersey City, was a chaos of pushing people, lost and screaming children, rain-soaked lug-

gage, and harsh treatment for the emigrants, some of whom had given years of savings to pay for their tickets. The conductors were rude, one refusing to answer Stevenson's inquiry about the time of a meal, on the grounds that one question would lead to another and "he could not afford to be eternally worried." In contrast, a newsboy on the train, having bumped into Stevenson several times without apologizing, noticed that he was looking ill and presented him with a large, juicy pear; and from then on lent him newspapers and often came to sit beside him to cheer him up. The incident, Stevenson thought, was a good example "of that uncivil kindness of the American, which is perhaps their most bewildering character to one newly landed." Another national trait that impressed itself on Stevenson (as it had on many a foreign observer before him) was an extreme inquisitiveness concerning one's name and occupation. "Some of them were on nettles till they learned your name was Dickson and you a journeyman baker; but beyond that, whether you were a Catholic or Mormon, dull or clever, fierce or friendly, was all one to them."

Most of the writer's fellow passengers were native Americans moving west in search of "the good land." As the train moved slowly over the plains, from time to time it passed another train, bound eastward. "Come back! Come back!" the eastbound passengers would cry, apparently as disillusioned with the West as the others with the East. "If, in truth," wrote Stevenson, "it were only for the sake of wages that men emigrate, how many thousands would regret the bargain! But wages, indeed, are only one consideration out of many; for we are a race of gipsies and love change and travel for themselves."

In contrast to the plush and gilt trappings of a first-class Pullman, an emigrant train was equipped with nothing but wooden benches, just wide enough for two to sit together in considerable discomfort. At night every other bench was reversed, and boards laid from seat to seat with straw-filled cushions on them. Two could lie side by side on the boards. Food was obtained at the frequent stops—sometimes having to be abandoned when the train capriciously began to move again. "Equality," said Stevenson, "though conceived very largely in America, does not extend so low down as to an emigrant. Thus, in all other trains, a warning cry of 'All aboard!' recalls the passengers to take their seats; but as soon as I was alone with emigrants . . . I found this ceremony was pretermitted; the train stole from the station without note of warning, and you had to keep an eye upon it even while you ate."

Low though these emigrants found themselves, they still looked down as from a great height on the Chinese who were riding the emigrant train in a segregated car. "They declared them hideous vermin, and affected a kind of choking in the throat when they beheld them." Stevenson, on the other hand, thought the Chinese the cleanest people on the train, and was outraged by the snobbish behavior of his fellow Caucasians. "Awhile ago it was the Irish, now it is the Chinese that must go," he wrote. "It seems, after all, that no country is bound to submit to immigration any more than to invasion: each is war to the knife, and resistance to either but legitimate defence."

American hostility toward the Irish was diminishing by the 1870's, but was still strong in the port cities where the poorest of them congregated. "No Irish need apply" was a common phrase in the want ads. A resurgence of anti-Catholicism during the eighties was a burden not only to the Irish but to many of the newer immigrants—Italians, south Germans, Czechs, and Poles. Reviving the Know-Nothing attitudes of antebellum days, an organization

Frederick Douglass, black leader in the civil rights struggle from the 1840's to his death in 1895, appears above. Below, a youngster tries his skill at the horn, in a sketch by J. D. Chalfant.

called the American Protective Association spread rumors of vice among priests and nuns and warned against a papist takeover. It incited scattered mob actions against Catholics and made a brief foray into politics. Theodore Roosevelt and other prominent political figures eventually came out against it, and by the end of the century it was no more. Catholic, Protestant, Jewish, or Buddhist, whatever the religious background, every nationality that immigrated in large, poverty-stricken numbers experienced American prejudice. Those who were able to join the "industrious poor" or climb eventually into the middle class outlived the worst harassment. Unfortunately, like sophomores hazing freshmen, they were likely to turn upon the next comers.

In the case of the oldest minority group of all, the Negroes, there seemed no end to prejudice. Among the educated few, hope was in the ascendancy for ten or fifteen years after the Civil War; then, increasingly during the eighties and nineties, doubt and fear took its place. It was clear that the promises of Reconstruction days were false ones. For the very poor, the struggle had never even slackened. Between 1882 and 1898, sixteen hundred lynchings were recorded in the South. By the end of the century, southern Negroes were virtually disenfranchised, while in the North their worst difficulty was in competing for jobs with working-class whites.

In cities where there were many Negroes, their society was divided into three echelons. At the top were perhaps no more than a few families, who were not only prosperous but had light skins. The heads of families worked in banking, real estate, the professions, or government jobs. Below them was a middle class, usually owners of small businesses; and at the bottom were the uneducated, working at whatever menial jobs they could find. In Washington, D.C., in 1887, two Negroes had fortunes of about $100,000, two had $75,000, one $50,000, and about forty others were worth between $10,000 and $25,000. Their comings and goings were reported in the Negro press just as the white press reported on the Astors and the Vanderbilts. Perhaps because they were more insecure in their wealth than white people, they were even less philanthropic; while whites, indignant at the uncharitableness of Negroes toward their own poor, gave little support to Negro charities. The poor Negroes were the losers. During the last decades of the century, when some Negro socialites were still being invited to government functions (although not cordially welcomed), the Washington press complained of "more discrimination among the colored people than . . . among the white against the colored." As Constance McLaughlin Green points out in *The Secret City*, well-to-do Negroes "were certainly culturally closer to the white community than to the lower-class Negro. In displaying an ungenerous attitude toward their inferiors, they were behaving like most self-made white men who reached positions of eminence in the face of enormous obstacles."

Negroes of the middle class and "industrious poor" were even greater joiners of lodges and fraternal organizations than their white counterparts. Picnics, cakewalks, parades, church affairs, and lavish funerals were a constant source of interest in their communities, causing captious whites to call Negroes irresponsible and childlike. The black leader Frederick Douglass feared that such behavior, "inviting public disgust and contempt, and repelling the more thrifty and self-respecting among us, is a positive hurt to the whole colored population."

Etiquette books, directed to black readers, were no less critical of preten-

Immigrants on a westbound railway coach

*Old folks, little changed by emancipa-
tion, pursue a simple, rural home life.*

tiousness. E. W. Wood's manual, published in 1899, offered down-to-earth counsel on handshaking: "People who extend you one or two fingers or a part of the hand only when they attempt to shake hands with you, expose un-bounded egotism, ignorance, foolishness, and serpentine hypocrisy. . . . A man who shakes a lady's hand with a tight squeeze and holds it unusually long will bear watching." On using cologne: "Oh, how sickening it is to go into a hall or room whose pure, sweet air is poisoned with old, cheap cologne or dirty musk! If you will take the time to read up on 'musk' and learn where it comes from, I promise that you will use considerably less in the future . . . . Good authority says: The more enlightened a people are the less cologne they use." On kissing: "Girls, it is in bad taste for you to be given too much to kissing boys and men. . . . A kiss is nothing more nor less than a physical sounding of a woman's social, mental, and moral strength." Booker T. Wash-ington was sorry to see "young colored men who were not earning more than four dollars a week spend two dollars or more for a buggy on Sunday to ride up and down Pennsylvania Avenue in, in order that they might try to convince the world that they were worth thousands." For the many, whether black or white, who longed for the gilt of the Gilded Age but could not afford it, it was an age of envy and discontent.

By the end of the century, all but a handful of Negroes were either moder-ately or desperately poor. Even worse, the incentive to rise, so much in evi-dence during Reconstruction, had disappeared. There now seemed no way for a Negro to share the good things of the white world. As Mrs. Green points out, "With the dwindling of the attainable external rewards for continuing the struggle, only the strongest individual able to draw upon deep inner resources could withstand the ceaseless battering of his self-respect." Few foreigners settled in Washington, but the sufferings of its very poor Negroes were at least as great as those endured by New York's alien population. The children and grandchildren of "contrabands," fugitive slaves who had flocked to the city during the Civil War, populated the back alleys, within sight of the Capi-tol. The slums were on a par with Calcutta's and so was the death rate. Ne-groes died in such numbers, not only in Washington but in all large cities, that a visiting Englishman wrote, "some [white men] have predicted a solution of the difficulty in the disappearance of the whole colored race in the next fifty years." Yet somehow, despite typhoid epidemics and an infant mortality rate of 338.5 per thousand (in 1890), these people refused to "disappear." Some managed to get a little education, acquire a skill, and become members of the "industrious" rather than the "vicious" poor. According to Riis, Ne-groes were considered good tenants because they were cleaner than immi-grants, and also because, having fewer accommodations available to them than whites, they could be charged several dollars more per wretched room and generally made little or no complaint.

The world of the poor was made up of distinct subcultures, more so than it is today when the whole nation is drawn together by television and other ways of communication. The poor of the South, black and white, lived in a revamped version of antebellum society, a world divided into two. Impoverished whites depended heavily on pride of race and family to buoy them up. One seventy-year-old planter, whom the Civil War had ren-dered penniless, took to doing the family washing, rather than see Sherman's ambition "to bring every southern woman to the washtub" fulfilled. The mountain whites, to whom poverty and illiteracy were nothing new, continued their primitive ways. The women did a good share of the farmwork as well as all the housekeeping, married early, and had numerous children. Unlike the mainstream of American women, they deferred in all respects to their men, who were lords of their miserable castles. Clannish feeling led to the sometimes lethal feuds for which these people have become perhaps unduly notorious. As late as 1918, Arthur W. Calhoun, in his *Social History of the American Family*, called them "our contemporary ancestors."

In the West, the cowboy became a new American legend. Beginning in the 1840's, there was a way of life open to sturdy, self-reliant young men in rounding up the cattle left behind by fleeing Mexican ranchers and driving them to East Texas to be sold, and later, in working for owners of vast cattle ranches. Seldom have the habits of so few been a source of fascination for so many: all America and a good part of the rest of the world knows that a cowboy wore a broad hat, tied a handkerchief round his neck, and prided himself on his boots; lived in the saddle for months at a time; liked to sing; carried a gun and knew how to use it; did not drink on the trail; was bashful with women; and subscribed, at least in theory, to a boy scout-like code of loyalty, honesty, courage, and independence. If not all cowboys were like the stereotype, apparently enough of them were so that their legend, like that of knights in armor, captured the universal imagination.

A less attractive subculture was that of the tramp, who began to roam the country in numbers after the Civil War and particularly after the Panic of 1873. A survey made in 1893 reported that there were 45,845 tramps—that is, men with no fixed address nor fixed employment; that three out of five were native-born and had a skill, and that nearly all were in good health and literate. Like today's hippies and yesterday's beatniks, most tramps were voluntary dropouts from society; unlike them, they had no social axe to grind, or, at least, were not organized to do so. In the early twentieth century, the Industrial Workers of the World ("Wobblies") claimed a large migrant membership. They had a code of behavior toward their own kind and invented a colorful vocabulary to go along with it: *mooch, handout, panhandle, hobo, flophouse,* and some three thousand other words formed their argot.

In the public view, country poverty was never so horrifying nor its victims so "vicious" as the city variety. Nostalgia for the simple farm life of colonial ancestors did not take into consideration the loneliness, the anxiety, and the deprivation, spiritual and physical, of life on an unprosperous farm. The mail-order catalog and the village general store relieved the farmer's family of many chores but increased the need for cash, deprived them of their most creative activities—weaving, whittling, furniture-making—and led to discontent. New England's rural areas became sadly depopulated, as whole communities abandoned the rocky fields for more fertile ones in the West. In the eighties, many a good Vermont farm went begging, even at five dollars or less an acre. New Englanders who stayed prided themselves on exceeding thrift, making a virtue out of necessity: "Use it up, wear it out, make it do." Mary E. Wilkins' stories of New England villages in the last quarter of the century show a courageous but dour and static way of life, dominated by lonely, estimable women. Here, for example, is a little girl, Lucretia, on her way to school: "It was quite a cold day, but she was warmly dressed. She wore her Aunt Lucretia's red and green plaid shawl, which Aunt Lucretia had worn

A graduate of Virginia's Hampton Institute dines with middle-class formality.

Polish couple in their wedding portrait

to meeting when she was herself a little girl, over her Aunt Maria's black ladies' cloth coat. The coat was very large and roomy—indeed, it had not been altered at all—but the cloth was thick and good. Young Lucretia wore also her Aunt Maria's black alpaca dress, which had been somewhat decreased in size to fit, and her Aunt Lucretia's purple hood. . . . She had mittens, a black quilted petticoat, and her Aunt Maria's old drab stockings drawn over her shoes to keep the snow from her ankles."

Provided one was not starving, Victorians tended to deem it a virtue to be poor. "Homes of the poor!" cried the author of *Our Home, or The Key to a Nobler Life*, published in 1889. "Sacred shrines of earth where the altar fires of genius have been lighted. May the world forever be blessed with moderate want." He also pointed out that since "the busy brain of invention" had brought former luxuries within the reach of all, a poor man's home need not be bare, especially if he gave up smoking and saved ten cents a day in tobacco money. After twenty years, he would have amassed enough to buy five hundred books. The simple but cozy cottage, with or without books, was a favorite locale in the period's novels, poems, and sermons. Nevertheless, the national urge to rise in the world made most residents of such cottages ignore their advantages and hurry away to the city, the mill town, or the frontier.

The urban version of the cottage, the workingman's flat, was described in 1898 by the visiting Giuseppe Giacosa after a Sunday afternoon ride through Manhattan on the Ninth Avenue El. Peering into the windows on a level with the El tracks, he saw "copious and commodious" furniture, of a standard found in Italy only in the homes of the higher classes—doctors, lawyers, judges, and merchants. Whole families sat serenely before spacious windows, reading the Sunday paper. "These are settled people," he said, "they neither owe nor are owed; they are not in danger of ruin; and their needs are not limited to that which barely keeps them from dying but also include what is desirable for living." In Chicago the Italian was impressed to see that the slaughter-yard butchers looked clean and well-dressed when they left their bloody work for home. "All are solemn and sober; you would think they were leaving an aristocratic club or a classical concert at twenty *lire* a ticket." He was of the opinion that Italian immigrants were prone to live too frugally and work too hard even after acquiring a little money, and that the American prejudice against Italians would disappear if they would follow the American way of life, accumulate material possessions, and spend money on personal luxuries. "The Americans are the most indomitable, the most ambitious, the most audacious, the most eager for pleasure and for a full life, of any nation that has ever existed."

In spite of the horrors of slum life, the new century saw an awakening of public concern in the life of the common man. By 1914 labor was guaranteed the right to organize, and there were new laws to protect basic rights of the poor. With a touch of good fortune—perhaps a kind employer or the opportunity to learn a skill—the hapless slum dweller might move uptown and sit in an airy window overlooking the El. Despair breeds revolution, but late-nineteenth-century America was a place where optimism prevailed. Better medical care and better diet showed itself in more robust health and in the fact that clothing dealers now had to stock larger sizes, both in length and width. In the overall picture, America was still the land of opportunity, and the "huddled masses yearning to breathe free" continued to pour across the ocean.

A Nation
of
Opposites

*The tragic divisions between rich and poor were rarely
reflected in Victorian art. In this pretty scene, c. 1865,
the smartly dressed mother and child and the street ur-
chins appear to be bent on the same cheery shopping tour.*

The Melting Pot

Immigrants who arrived in the "sweet land of liberty" after 1880, encountered problems that the colonists had never faced. Mainly from southern and eastern Europe, the latecomers quickly discovered that Americanization could be traumatic. As described by one Romanian, it was "a spiritual adventure of the most volcanic variety .... born in one world ... thrust then into the midst of another ... adjusting within one's own being the clash of opposed systems of culture, tradition and social convention." Assimilation for some began at ports of entry where inspectors assigned them Anglicized names: a Czech Mylnář might become Miller. Since land was no longer cheap or plentiful, aliens were generally herded into urban ghettos, whose horrid conditions moved the civic-minded to transform the foreign element in their own American image. Cities offered adults night courses in English and free elementary schools for children. In an effort to hasten the homogenization process, ladies paid calls on families to preach the virtues of naturalization; the D.A.R. provided loyalty lectures to inculcate the "spirit of true Americanism"; and Henry Ford not only required foreign employees to learn the language, but staged a pageant in which workers clad in native costumes entered a huge melting pot and emerged in identical suits, carrying American flags. Immigrants continued to pour in until the restrictive acts of the 1920's gave the lie to Emma Lazarus' Statue of Liberty inscription: "Give me your tired, your poor ... The wretched refuse of your teeming shore, Send these, the homeless, tempest-tost, to me. . . ."

Before the days of Ellis Island, New York's Castle Garden, painted by Charles Ulrich in 1884 (right), gave immigrants their first impression of the land of promise.

THE CORCORAN GALLERY OF ART

Mr. John Lawrence—*Hungarian Hussar*

Mrs. Cornelius Vanderbilt—*Electricity*

Mr. Julian Kean—*Mother Goose's Squire*

In Full Regalia

Mr. Buchanan Winthrop—*Le Comte de Brie*

Mr. Francis Appleton—*Dresden Figurine*

Mrs. Cornelius Lee—*Gypsy Queen*

Miss Katherine Blake—*Puritan Girl*

Mr. Ridgeway Moore—*Court Jester*

Miss Constance Rives—*A Wasp*

For six weeks before The Party—*the costume extravaganza held one Monday night in 1883 for a thousand of Alva Vanderbilt's best friends—New York's blue bloods thought of little else. Some guests were recruited to prepare special quadrilles—the Hobby Horse, Star, Dresden, and Mother Goose. And everyone was urged to pose for Mora, the photographer, lest their efforts be lost to posterity.*

NEW YORK HISTORICAL SOCIETY, HAROLD SETON COLLECTION

Mr. Frederick Beach—*Matador*

Mrs. William K. Vanderbilt—*the hostess*

Mr. Augustus Coe Gurnee—*Arab Prince*

THE SANTA CLAUS OF TO-DAY.

Foreign Exchange

Even at the zenith of America's democratic spirit in the 1830's, *Knickerbocker Magazine* commented on the "abject reverence for foreign titles prevalent in our fashionable society." The writer might also have noted the abject reverence for American money prevalent among titled Europeans; the financial embarrassment of many a noble foreigner coupled with the social insecurity of America's newly rich produced some strange bedfellows. While August Belmont, a Frankfurt tradesman turned "English aristocrat," embellished his Fifth Avenue palazzo with the family crest, the New York *Tribune* thoughtfully published a list of American women it considered "entitled to a place in the nobility of Europe," and the German papers advertised means of putting "impoverished *Junkers* in touch with American heiresses." Every wellborn fortune hunter who set out from Europe to share his title was certain to find a gold-plated American victim of title mania. Blessings were mixed. Leonard Jerome, lawyer, whose sole previous claim to prominence had been his marriage to "the most beautiful girl in Palmyra, N.Y.," blew $10,000 on a Delmonico's debut for his daughter Jennie—an investment that paid off when she married Lord Randolph Churchill (and later became the mother of Sir Winston). Not all brides rejoiced in these marital mergers. Consuelo Vanderbilt became the tearful bride of the Duke of Marlborough only after her mother stationed guards outside her bedroom, and Comte Boni de Castellane pounced successfully on Anna Gould and $5,500,000 of her fortune, though he had no qualifications other than his elegant name.

The Constitution forbade an American nobility, but nothing could keep husband-hunting society belles from peering into the future for a peer, or counting on a count. In this cartoon, Ward McAllister is Santa Claus, offering a tray of nobles to a trio of nubile ladies.

311

DRAMATISCHER CLUB.
ULK.
NIAGARA FALLS
JULY 20 to 24 1891.

MUSEUM OF THE CITY OF NEW YORK, J. CLARENCE DAVIES COLLECTION

Ever on Sundays

Compared to other nineteenth-century immigrants, Germans had little difficulty becoming assimilated, unhyphenated Americans. Though Teutons were not greeted with brass bands, they had several advantages over other new arrivals. They were of the same Anglo-Saxon stock as the "natives," and mainly Protestant. Skilled artisans, sturdy farmers, and professional people composed their ranks. And they had a reputation for being hard working, orderly, submissive -to authority, and politically unambitious. As the *Illinois Journal* of 1855 reported, "Our German settlers are valuable acquisitions to the State. . . . It is seldom, indeed, that we hear of one being in the poor house." Their value—to Chicago, New York, Cincinnati, St. Louis, Milwaukee, and other centers—lay partly in the traditions which these *Kultur*-conscious people brought. Beer gardens,

Christmas trees, and *Volksfests* added *Gemütlichkeit* to an America still inhibited by the kill-joy ethic. Indeed, Germans' love of merriment seems to have been their only quarrel with Victorian life, and their manner of observing the Sabbath perhaps their most controversial characteristic. Anything that interposed itself between a German and his lager was sure to brew trouble. When a Chicago mayor tried to close a "tea garden" on Sundays, he was met with armed resistance and was forced to yield. The defenders of New York's blue laws were no more successful. The Winter Garden, a huge Bowery music hall, was filled to capacity on Sundays with German customers purportedly there to hear "sacred concerts," though the sounds emitting from the orchestra pit were distinctly Strauss-like and the clink of beer mugs suspiciously secular.

Much of German club life was devoted to mental and physical improvement. Culture buffs organized amateur Thespians, like the all-male group taking an outing at left. In the 1854 lithograph above, German athletes participate in a Turnfest.

313

With Pluck and Luck

During the Gilded Age, when success was measured in hard cash rather than heavenly rewards, the self-made millionaire became the American dream incarnate. Seeing endless opportunity in the land of the dollar, poor but plucky youths roamed city streets, selling newspapers and blacking boots. Not all of them made it; disillusioned waifs squandered meager earnings on dance halls and liquor, and others drifted toward the underworld. The more fortunate were rescued from the skids by charitable institutions like New York's Newsboys' Lodging House, which offered bed, board, and hymn singing for a dime a night. Moral sustenance was provided by inspirational literature of the sort found in penny magazines and Horatio Alger's books. Alger's romantic, albeit erroneous, formula ensured riches to the honest lad who rose early and abstained from telling lies, swearing, smoking, and drinking. Ironically, the "strongly made," "well-knit," and "resolute" teen-agers in his novels only climb to the top by virtue, *plus* "the breaks." Though bravery enables one hero to rescue a little old lady from an onrushing cable car, it is pure chance that she is rich and makes the boy her heir. Justifying this short cut to wealth for his hard-working readers, Alger explained: "He has struggled upward from a boyhood of privation and self-denial into a youth and manhood of property and honor. There has been some luck about it, I admit, but after all, he is indebted for most of his good fortune to his own good qualities."

Since bachelor Alger boarded with the newsboys from 1864 to 1894, lads like the one at right were probably real friends. For most New York youths, however, Alger advised going west. As one character reported, "If I had stayed in the city I might be no better off now. But in a lucky moment, I was induced . . . to go West . . . and I hope in time to become rich."

Founded in the 1850's by Teddy Roosevelt's father, the Newsboys' Lodging House gave tenants like the young scrubbers at left "proper discipline, without . . . letting them feel that the restrictions are too severe." The earnest boys below, c. 1910, cajoled customers into buying papers, whether or not they wanted them.

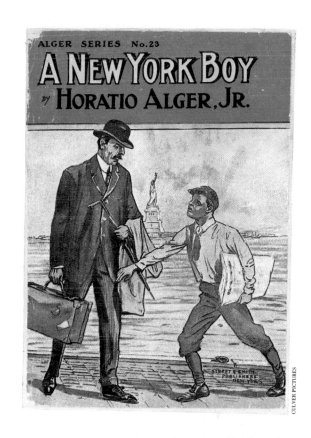

ALGER SERIES No.23
A NEW YORK BOY
by HORATIO ALGER, Jr.

STREET & SMITH
PUBLISHERS
NEW YORK

CULVER PICTURES

GEORGE EASTMAN HOUSE

Playgrounds Of the Privileged

Theatrical societies were among the first extracurricular groups permitted on campuses. At right, members of a Princeton club appear, costumed for a performance of "The Honorable Julius Caesar," in 1893. Author-actor Booth Tarkington sits in the second row, on Caesar's left. Below, sophomores of Vassar College, selected for beauty and perhaps strength, prepare to escort seniors in Class Day ceremonies. The girls have taken time out from studies to harvest some six thousand daisies and weave them into a floral chain—a rite of spring dating from 1889.

PRINCETON UNIVERSITY

Gone were the days of the Yale student who "studied Homer almost ye whole day . . . [and] felt melancholy and dejected on thinking of ye difficulties my Dadde must undergo to provide for me." The prevailing attitude of Victorian collegians was summed up by Henry Adams when he wrote of his class of 1858, "no one took Harvard College seriously. All went there because their friends went there, and the College was their ideal of social self-respect." Struggling for a balance to a classical-theological curriculum and the oppressive regimentation of earlier years, students by the 1870's had been so successful in redefining the institution that a Denison president was won over, urging the faculty "not to exaggerate the importance of the intellectual." As social emphasis grew, the proportion of public school admissions dropped markedly. An 1878 *Harvard Lampoon* portrayed a typical student's day: fencing, boxing with "a fashionable private tutor," dancing lessons, and cotillions in Boston. Football games among the most prestigious eastern colleges, especially those organized into an "Ivy League," were as social as they were sporting. Fraternities, whose memberships hinged on the answer to "Would you want your sister to marry him?" continued to grow. Fads were spawned — canes, top hats, bowlers, moustaches, mandolins. As a Wellesley girl burbled, "For good times, for romance, for society, college life offers unequaled opportunities."

VASSAR COLLEGE LIBRARY

The Police
And the Mob

MUSEUM OF ART, RHODE ISLAND SCHOOL OF DESIGN

H. Schuldt's sentimental painting above depicts the traffic cop of 1878 as he benignly leads children to safety. Irish lads who entered this noble profession became the pride of their neighborhoods; often cited for bravery, they also earned one thousand dollars a year—then a status salary.

318

HARPER'S WEEKLY, AUGUST 1, 1863

During the 1863 draft riots, mobs sacked the drugstore at left. After four bloody days, police restored order to war-torn New York.

As this 1858 cartoon implies, the patrolman intrepid enough to step into public melees was well-advised to dress for the occasion.

The motto "every man his own policeman," served Americans adequately in the early years of the Republic. By 1850, however, crime and violence were rampant in the nation's cities, and civilian watches no longer could maintain law and order. Citizens complained of streets being unsafe and demanded full-time professionals to preserve peace, guard property, and control the volatile poor in their slums. Hastily organized departments adopted cop' (copper) badges, drilled recruits in "military tactics," and supplied uniforms, billy clubs, and revolvers, which, emergencies excepted, were to be kept in hip pockets. Applicants were screened for such traits as physical courage and moral character. Sometimes the latter was overlooked, and many officers received commissions through political pull. Patrolmen occasionally dispensed justice as described in an 1859 *Harper's Weekly*: a rich murderer might get off scot free, but "if a poor wretch . . . steals a loaf for his starving family, the zeal and fury of the . . . police know no bounds, and the fellow is lucky if he be not brained on the spot." New York's fighting Irish, forgetful of their own recent immigrant status, reportedly searched foreign suspects in a manner that "might be mistaken for a set of rowdies robbing an unfortunate inebriate." And Chicago's trigger-happy guardians, in dispersing an 1886 rally of strikers in the Haymarket district, participated in clashes unparalleled in that century for brutality. By 1900, the reform of America's finest had begun.

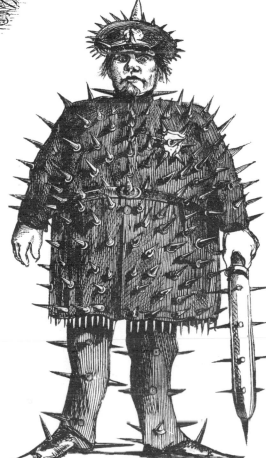

FRANK LESLIE'S ILLUSTRATED NEWSPAPER, NOVEMBER 21, 1858

Onward Christian Soldiers

Ladies denied other emotional outlets could engage in a flurry of philanthropic activity. Evangeline Booth, daughter of the Salvation Army's founder, distributes Christmas handouts below. The condescendingly sympathetic volunteer at right takes a break from her beat.

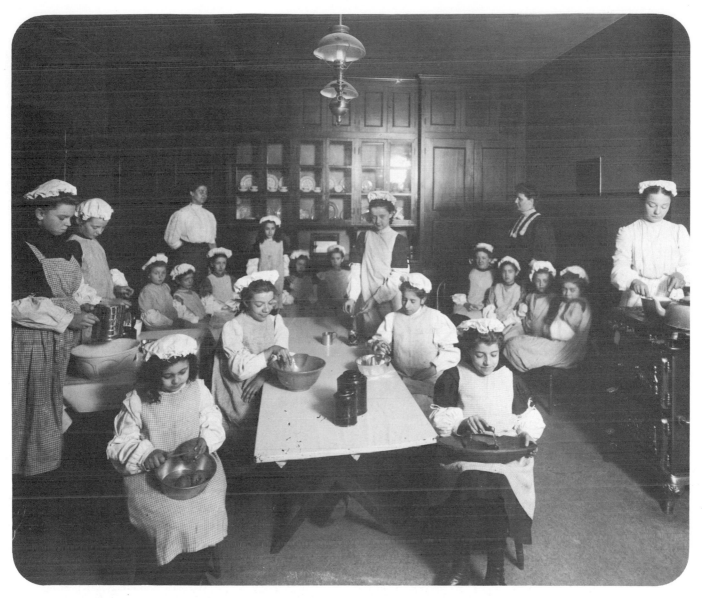

The children of working mothers are cared for at a day nursery in the 1915 photograph above.
The tots are taught such useful trades as cooking to keep them off the relief rolls later in life.

Throughout most of the nineteenth century, rugged individuals shared Henry Ward Beecher's conviction that "no man in this land suffers from poverty, unless it be more than his fault—unless it be his *sin*." However, as city slum conditions worsened, people began to realize that the other half was not morally corrupt, but rather losers in the struggle for survival. According to one professor in the 1880's, a seemingly "unlimited supply of reformers, philanthropists, humanitarians, and would-be managers-in-general of society," arose to declare a full-scale war on poverty. Leading the ranks was William Booth's English Salvation Army, which on these shores spread the social gospel to "rumdom, slumdom and bumdom"; it also ran employment bureaus, supplied families with caseworkers, and rescued fallen women. And a few industrialists with more money than they could possibly spend in a life-

time, assumed the rich man's burden: John D. Rockefeller made benevolence big business by donating some $530,000,000 to worthy causes, and promoted the new idea of welfare agencies run by professionals. People with less money, but equally dedicated to human uplift, joined the settlement movement. In the wilderness of a Chicago tenement district, Jane Addams founded Hull House in 1889, and resided there to "learn of life from life itself." Inviting urchins from off the streets to attend clubs and classes, this pioneer made the venture so successful that she later added a "little theater," lessons in music and art, and a neighborhood orchestra. As another social servant, Lillian Wald, leader of New York's Henry Street settlement, explained the concept, "We . . . live in the neighborhood . . . identify ourselves with it socially, and, in brief, contribute to it our citizenship."

LIBRARY OF CONGRESS

Mixed Doubles

Try as they might, the rich could not keep sports to themselves. As with baseball, they would no sooner take to the playing fields with some new game than the democratizing process would set in, a galaxy of poor boys would outstrip the gentlemen in prowess, and society would have to look elsewhere. *Outing* magazine smugly endorsed such sports as tennis, golf, yachting, and polo in the hope that they would not "offer any attractions to the more vulgar elements." These upper-class sports also had the added cachet of having been imported from Britain, where touring Americans had first seen them played by the aristocracy, and they could be pursued in stylish dress. Croquet, offering unlimited possibilities for flirtations and whispered asides, was among the first well-bred amusements to be taken up, followed by "rinking" on roller skates. Tennis, decreed the *Tribune Book of Open-Air Sports* in 1886, was "essentially . . . for ladies and gentlemen," and golf, that compromise between "the tediousness of croquet and the hurly-burly of lawn tennis," was in the opinion of an 1895 reporter, "pre-eminently a game of good society." Yet time was running out. Eventually, little but dollars separated the sporting tastes of America's classes, and the common man must have gained some satisfaction in seeing New York's nabobs take up the bicycle in the 1890's. However, lest members of the exclusive Michaux Cycling Club be confused with the common variety of road runners, they always took along their uniformed instructors and, on cue, could be led through a series of aristocratic cotillion figures — on wheels.

Lawn tennis, imported from England in 1874, emerged at once as an "elegant and pleasant pastime" suited (as first played) to the requirements of the long-skirted female participant. Tournaments were largely social events; the ladies were concerned more with securing male partners (as in the 1886 lithograph at left) than with rules of play.

The Servant Problem

By creating a democracy, the Founding Fathers precipitated an insoluble domestic crisis. Perhaps George Washington had second thoughts after he had to advertise a month and a half to find a cook "perfect in the business." Notions of equality, as an Englishman observed, had made republicans loathe to "submit to the degradations of wearing a livery, or any other badge of servitude. This they would call becoming a man's man." In the late 1800's, immigrants partially resolved the help problem. However, room, board, and $3.80 a week, the going rate in 1890, did not satisfy Irish Bridgets or German Gretchens. They tyrannized homes by breaking heirlooms, and gave substance to the *Harper's Bazar* joke: "Do you spoil *every* piece of meat you cook?" "No, mum. Sometimes it comes bad from the butcher." Snobbish servants would only work for the Four Hundred or for employers who owned carriages and pianos. And maids demanded folding beds, so as not to receive gentlemen callers in circumstances that might compromise their virtue.

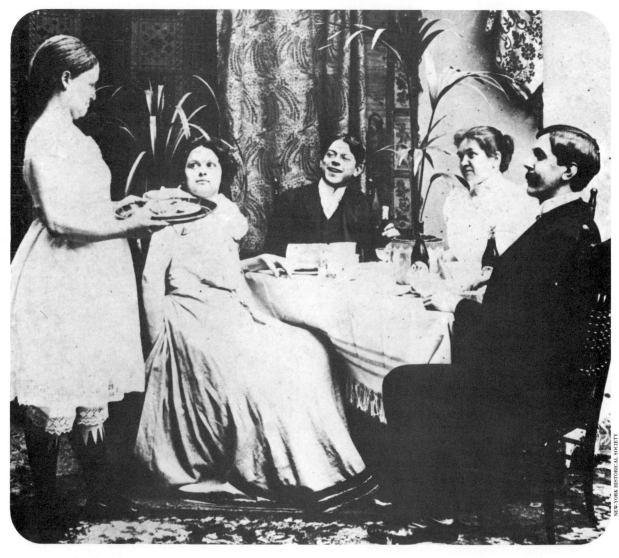

324

In the above example of stereopticon humor, Biddy misinterprets an order for "potatoes undressed," and clad in her pantaloons and petticoats, she serves spuds in their skins.

The domestics in the drawing above congregate belowstairs on their day off and amuse themselves by mimicking the pretensions of their parvenu masters. The roles of servant and served are reversed in the 1873 cartoon below. An agent assures a persnickety maid that the would-be mistresses, seated in a row, have impeccable character references.

Thespian Thrills

No American melodrama became a theater classic, but many won gaudy fame on the Victorian stage. With exaggerated plots and uncomplicated heroes, the spectaculars filled a void in humdrum lives. Enticed by breathtaking poster advertisements, audiences flocked to gasp at a nearly nude Adah Menken lashed to a "wild horse" in Mazeppa (right), at bloodhounds chasing Eliza in dramatizations of Uncle Tom's Cabin (below), and at daring rescues made on the brink of disaster, as at left. Spotless virtue was pitted against soulless villainy, and a loyal audience gave the Devil his due.

ADAH ISAACS MENKEN

CULVER PICTURES

JAY RIAL'S IDEAL UNCLE TOM'S CABIN.

ELIZA PURSUED BY BLOOD-HOUNDS

CHICAGO HISTORICAL SOCIETY

Heaven on Wheels

Railroads outdated coach travel in most areas by the 1870's, but a zest for the esoteric turned it into an urban status sport. Following British example, an oversized four-in-hand, or "tallyho," was introduced to New York's swells, who promptly formed a coaching club. The Chicago socialites above, photographed c. 1890, followed suit. Lady passengers also dressed for the occasion.

329

Profiting from the mass appeal of freaks, the barkers in this 1908 photograph ballyhoo one of the grossest shows on earth.

MUSEUM OF THE CITY OF NEW YORK, BYRON COLLECTION

Penny Pleasures

The electric trolley enabled working classes in the 1890's to pursue happiness beyond city limits. At the ends of lines from New York to San Antonio, amusement resorts offered beaches, boardwalks, and a gamut of gaslight delights. Towers and minarets at Coney Island's Luna Park bedazzled crowds; broadening novelties included hot dogs and rides, provocatively named Barrel of Love, Blow Hole, and Electric Seat. For the morally fastidious, acts were touted where "performers [avoid] Vulgarity or Slang or the words Damn or Liar or any saying not fit for Ladies and children."

MUSEUM OF THE CITY OF NEW YORK

THE MUSEUM OF MODERN ART, NEW YORK, FILM STILLS ARCHIVE

"Little Egypt" (above left) performs the hootchy-kootchy at Coney Island c. 1910. San Francisco kinetoscopes (above right) provide girly peep shows. A mini-skirted bathing suit of 1898 draws official disapproval (below).

LIBRARY OF CONGRESS

Packing the Saratoga trunk with sufficient "Saratogery" to last the holiday required careful planning.

Posh Resorts

Getting away from it all, for the rich Victorian, rarely happened. When he vacationed—which was customarily often and long—he chose his retreat from a small list of genteel resorts, preferably eastern and exclusive. Bar Harbor, Newport, the Berkshires, and Southampton were preeminent in summer, the scene shifting southward to Palm Beach and other warm meccas in winter. Saratoga Spa was the most popular of all, to the distress of a few Knickerbockers who feared that too many social swimmers—Jews among them—were roiling the waters. "Hundreds," commented one of the prominents, "who in their own towns could not find admittance into the circles of fashionable society . . . come to Saratoga where they may be seated at the same table . . . with the first families of the country." And seated they were, much of the time. Before horse racing took hold, in 1863, the hours between breakfast and supper offered only such diversions as cards, backgammon, concerts, billiards, and changing clothes—carried to extreme by one dandy who appeared in forty different outfits in a day. "Hops" were the evening fare. Effused a visitor, "Saratoga is all things to all men."

Getting there was half the fun. At a dangerous 20 mph, train passengers might have been extra-attentive to a Sunday church service (opposite). Right, a group takes the waters at Saratoga.

333

The Four Hundred

"*You can never be absolutely certain whether people are in society or not until you see them at four or five of the best houses,*" *decreed Ward McAllister. Under that stern mandate, society belles whirled wearily through an "unceasing round of gaiety and dissipation." One could not say no to a bid which might lead to the best houses. Besides, to miss a party might—horrors!—imply not having been invited. Woe to the miss, therefore, who missed a step on Fashion's social treadmill.*

PUCK, SEPTEMBER 14, 1892

Daring Decades

*In which the Old Queen passes,
taking with her much that
is Stuffy & Retrograde
in American Behavior; and a
New Century is turned over
to the Babbitts and Bohemians
for their Mutual Disposal.*

In January, 1900, old Queen Victoria had only a year more to live, but the age that bore her name appeared in abundant health and promised (or threatened) to go on forever. Placid self-satisfaction characterized the late Victorians. Beyond a financial panic or two, nothing really bad had troubled the middle class since the Civil War. "Laws are becoming more just, rulers humane," announced a minister, as he looked back on the century just closed. "Music is becoming sweeter and books wiser; homes are happier, and the individual heart becoming at once more just and more gentle." In this best of all possible worlds, most people saw little need or possibility for improvement, nor did they perceive some of the changes that were about to overtake them. For example, the editors of the *Literary Digest* predicted that the horseless carriage would "never, of course, come into as common use as the bicycle." And when Dr. S. P. Langley, secretary of the Smithsonian Institution, intimated that he saw a future for flying machines and that they would someday "travel at speeds higher than any with which we are familiar," *The Popular Science Monthly* took him to task for speaking irresponsibly.

To predict the modern airplane in 1900 seems almost clairvoyant, but not even Dr. Langley went so far as to forecast or imagine the speakeasy, short hair for women, petting parties, "nice" women smoking, drinking, and wearing make-up, or the knee-high skirt, all of which were coming in twenty years or less. The contrast between the manners and morals of 1900 and those of the twenties appears so absolute that it is hard to believe we are dealing with one country, one people, and a difference of only one generation. Surely, the flapper was not the child of the Gibson Girl; she must have appeared from the sea like Aphrodite, perhaps floating to shore on a barrel of bootleg whiskey. Yet, the years between 1900 and 1920 were filled with portents.

The sixty-year-old fight for the emancipation of women had been gathering momentum. By 1900 most states allowed women to control their own prop-

In the revolt against Victorianism, the Ford flivver was a juggernaut. Here it transports a modern-day Omar Khayyám to an afternoon of "near beer, chickens, and jazz."

erty and their own earnings. A divorce was easier to get, although in many states there was still a double standard when it came to divorce for adultery, the man suffering no penalties and the woman forfeiting property and children. And in the realm of daily behavior women were changing profoundly. For instance, in 1900 all but very old-fashioned mothers allowed their girls to ride bicycles, and might even run them up a pair of culottes to do it in. Ping-pong, an innovation of 1902, offered women another outlet for self-expression, if we are to believe a poet in the Baltimore *American*, who wrote,

> . . . *She led him away to the ping-pong net;*
> *And then came an hour he'll never forget;*
> *For his shoulders ache from the many stoops*
> *To pick up the balls, and his eyelid droops,*
> *Where she smote him twice with her racket small,*
> *Which left her hand as she struck the ball;*
> *And he'll never ping where she pongs again,*
> *For she heard him swear when she pinged him then.*

(Ping-pong was still being played in the twenties; the flapper was likely to be an expert player and perhaps an expert swearer as well.)

The ideal belle of the turn-of-the-century years loved active games and was bursting with energy, a distinct contrast to the delicate, languid maiden of an earlier day. Here, from the 1906 play *The New York Idea*, by Langdon Mitchell, is a description of the heroine: "Cynthia enters, absorbed in reading a newspaper. [As it turns out, she is reading the racing section.] She is a young creature in her twenties, small and high-bred, full of the love of excitement and sport. Her manner is wide awake and keen and she is evidently in no fear of the opinion of others. Her dress is exceedingly elegant, but with the elegance of a woman whose chief interests lie in life out of doors. There is nothing horsey in her style, and her expression is youthful and ingenuous."

The philosopher William James observed that the American girl was full of "'bottled lightning'. . . . Bottled lightning, in truth, is one of our American ideals, even of a young girl's character!" James feared that this trait was "not wholly good," and recommended that women seek "not the exacerbation, but rather the toning-down of their moral tensions. Even now I fear that some one of my fair hearers may be making an undying resolve to become strenuously relaxed. . . .'"

Bottled lightning seems to have been congenital in girls of all classes; those who did not have the leisure for an energetic ping-pong game vigorously threw themselves into gainful employment. Since the advent of the typewriter in the 1870's and the discovery that women were not only bright enough to handle it but would do so for considerably less pay than men, typing had become almost exclusively a woman's province. In the year 1900, 206 out of every thousand girls over the age of sixteen worked in offices. "Heaven Will Protect the Working Girl" was a popular song of 1909, and there were many wives who hoped that heaven would keep an eye on their husbands as well. But whether wives liked it or not, the female secretary was becoming as much a part of the office scene as the roll-top desk.

The day had not yet arrived when women worked even when they did not need the money. But if wealthy women did not invade the business world, they were pioneers in other freedoms for the female, such as smoking and using

"I Love My Wife, But OH! You Kid"

A very personal secretary, c. 1910

rouge and powder. Having seen such things done in the best European circles, a few intrepid souls determined to show their native country a thing or two. When Mrs. Teresa Fair Oelrichs, of San Francisco, smoked in public, a newspaper reported, "San Francisco women have now an unquestioned precedent for smoking if they feel so inclined. In Tait's Café, Mrs. Oelrichs and Mrs. McCreery lighted their cigarettes after dinner and puffed their smoke rings with the men as if there had not been anything to disapprove in their action." For a time, less advanced New York City forbade women to smoke in public places. Not long after, a headline in the New York *Herald* announced: "WOMEN SMOKE ON WAY TO OPERA, Are Discovered Puffing Cigarettes When Electric Light Beams Into Their Carriage."

"It is needless to say that women who paint their faces put themselves on a level with savages," wrote one irate citizen in 1902. During the previous century, most women who countenanced make-up at all, wore whitening powders. Rouge was for actresses and Jezebels. But at the turn of the century, women who painted their faces were, or wanted to be, on a level with the *grandes dames* who affected the manners of European society. By 1905 the fashion had filtered down to people who ordered from the Sears, Roebuck catalog, which offered *rouge de théâtre* for the first time that year, as well as hair bleaches and dyes. Five years later, the catalog was devoting several pages to cosmetics of all kinds. "There are very few who are hopelessly homely," said Sears encouragingly; adding, in a sterner vein, "Because You Are Married Is No Excuse for Neglecting Your Personal Appearance." However, it was not until the First World War that the mass of American women became acquainted with the allurements of French powder and perfume, sent to them by soldier sweethearts.

Rich women joined their husbands in making the automobile a favorite toy. In 1906 Woodrow Wilson, then president of Princeton, warned that this foolish and expensive plaything was sure to cause a spread of socialist sentiment. An ecclesiastical paper reminded its readers that "In the Paris of 1789 the coaches of the wealthy, arrogantly driven through crowded streets, were at last halted, overturned and the horses cut from them." And a medical journal reported breathlessly that driving an automobile caused "nervous symptoms traceable to excitement and nervous tension of rapid travelling with the emotional repression necessary to secure a reasonable feeling of enjoyment, while speeding rapidly with risks and dangers constantly at hand." The effect of speed, said the journal, was not unlike that of indulgence in alcohol and tobacco. However, *The New York Times* rather sadly predicted that the terrible apparatus "has come to stay . . . sooner or later they will displace the fashionable carriage. . . . Sensitive and emotional folk cannot view the impending change without conflicting emotions. Man loves the horse and he is not likely ever to love the automobile."

If not so lovable as a horse, the automobile was easier to manage, especially the self-starting electric model. A car made it possible for a woman to get out of the house at a moment's notice, call on friends, take daughter to a dancing lesson and son to the dentist, perhaps join a suffragette picket line for an hour or two, and still be home in time to lay out her husband's slippers. Whereas in Europe license holders were required to understand the engine and be able to change a tire, in America such an idea was impracticable. Women could not be expected to know a carburetor from a spark plug, and

Pre-dating silent movies, nickelodeon theaters offered short reel "flickers," interspersed with colored lantern slides of song lyrics and helpful bits of advice, like those shown above.

Emancipated ladies of 1906 were of-
fered courses in self-defense. A furled
umbrella, a stiletto hatpin, or a well-
aimed kick in the shins supposedly
kept the highwayman at bay.

it was a foregone conclusion that they would demand the right to drive.

Instructions on "Motor Manners" began to be a regular feature in etiquette books. Readers were coached that the guest of honor was to be seated to the right of the host; that "the ordinary polite conversational tone of the motor horn should be a series of chuckles" and not a rude blast; that the courteous driver always carried a towrope to aid fellow motorists; that "the dignified stop" should be executed by coasting to a halt without applying the brakes; and that flying the Stars and Stripes on the hood was bad form when touring abroad. One mentor even offered some party advice: "Let the car's first year in the family circle . . . . supply the motive for a pleasant social gathering . . ." with the garage as dance floor.

Getting in and out of cars and operating the foot pedals made full, heavy skirts a nuisance, and in 1908 female dress was streamlined by the introduction of the slinky sheath gown, which dispensed with the voluminous petticoats and waist-squeezing corset that had been in fashion for nearly a hundred years. "The sheath gown uncovers a multitude of shins," said a jokester; while a fashionable ladies' club in Connecticut denounced it as "but one big step backward toward the fig-leaf." Some years later, the war brought women a further excuse for shortening and simplifying dresses. Nurses and female ambulance drivers had a practical reason to discard unnecessary petticoats, and women on the home front lost no time in following suit.

The theories of Freud, which were to have immense bearing on the metamorphosis of women, were cautiously noted in 1906 by a staid American medical journal. Not for years would Freud be known to the general public (Webster's Dictionary would not accept the word *Freudian* until 1927), but in intellectual circles sex gradually became open to discussion in mixed company. Initially treated with solemnity and clinical detachment, discussions grew more frivolous as the novelty wore off.

If Freud's works were too heavy-going for the average reader, an easier book that jolted Puritan and Victorian standards was *The Rubáiyát of Omar Khayyám*, as translated by the Englishman, Edward FitzGerald. The heady sentiments of a twelfth-century Persian tentmaker's son found an astonishingly wide audience among respectable middle-class Americans, particularly young ones. From the nineties through the twenties, it was a favorite gift between sweethearts. One can only suppose that parents did not take it seriously, for it undermined the most cherished moral principles of the land. "Come, fill the cup, and in the fire of Spring Your Winter garment of repentance fling." "A jug of wine, a loaf of bread—and thou Beside me singing in the wilderness." What kind of language was that for young unmarried people to be reading together in the porch swing?

Gradually, other stringent Victorian taboos were broken down. *Double entendre* songs began to be heard in vaudeville houses and other places of public entertainment. "Mary took the Calves to the Dairy Show" was a hit of 1908. Snickers greeted the chorus, which ended: "The farmers joked, said they'd never, never stroked Such beautiful calves as Mary's." The following year young wags were humming "I love my Wife, But OH, You Kid."

In 1910 there was a newspaper campaign attacking prostitution and venereal disease. Plain words like syphilis and gonorrhea, previously unmentionable, were used. Belief that white slave trade threatened the nubile youth of America was the excuse for description in print of another once unmentionable subject. The Mann Act, making it illegal to transport women across a state line for immoral purposes, was one result. Three years later, in 1913, *My Little Sister*, concerning two victims of white slavery, became a best seller. A reviewer in the old *Life* commented, "A generation ago no one but a few particularly daring parents would have read such a book if it had existed, and they would either have burned it afterwards or have hidden it behind 'Fox's Book of Martyrs' . . . whereas, to-day the chances are that most of the parents who read it will do so because . . . it has been recommended to them by their daughters." Many a woman who grew up in that era remembers being told to avoid crowded streetcars and department store elevators, lest some little old lady should jab her with a needle and spirit her away to Buenos Aires.

Another new development, sinister or benign, depending on one's viewpoint, was ragtime jazz. A Negro "ragged-time" dance, the Cakewalk, was sometimes imitated by high-spirited young whites, but it was not regarded as proper ballroom behavior. Booth Tarkington voiced a popular opinion when he wrote that ragtime belonged "to the underworld or circles where nature is extremely frank and rank."

Artist in the grips of his libido, c. 1922

Had Tarkington been up on his classics, he might have seen some future significance in the new dance. Plato once wrote, as if ragtime were on his mind, "The introduction of a new kind of music must be shunned as imperilling the whole State; since styles of music are never disturbed without affecting the most important political institutions. . . . In the guise of amusement, and professing to do no mischief . . . it does none, except that gradually gaining a lodgment it quietly insinuates itself into manners and customs; and from these it issues in greater force, and makes its way into mutual compacts: and from compacts it goes on to attack laws and constitutions, displaying the utmost impudence . . . until it ends by overturning every thing, both in public and in private." Respectable America must have had a secret yearning for the frank, rank, and impudent, for in 1911, Irving Berlin's "Alexander's Ragtime Band" caused the biggest revolution in dance manners since the waltz. Suddenly, dancers were calling for syncopated tunes. Since there were not many new ones, musicians jazzed up old standbys. When "Nearer, My God, to Thee" was syncopated as "Nero, My Dog, Has Fleas," one citizen declared, "A halt should be called before this system of ridicule shatters our every tradition and ideal."

New dance steps swept the country: the Turkey Trot, the Grizzly Bear, the Kangaroo Dip, and the Bunny Hug. Partners danced closely entwined ("Snug up close to your lady, Hug up close to your baby," went the words of Irving Berlin's "The Grizzly Bear."). And while it had always been considered bad ballroom form to "back the lady," the lady now consistently backed around the floor and seemed to love it. The new rhythms, said one critic, "are threatening to force grace, decorum, and decency out of the ball-rooms of America." Edward W. Bok, editor of *The Ladies' Home Journal*, fired fifteen young women from his offices for dancing the Turkey Trot during their lunch hour. The Vatican sent word that ragtime dancing would have to stop. But not only did it not stop, it spread to Europe. In 1913, Irving Berlin wrote the "International Rag" ("London dropped its dignity, so has France and Germany . . . Italian opera singers have learned to snap their fingers.").

Mark Sullivan, writing in his six-volume history *Our Times*, completed in 1935, thought that "the triumph of rag-time and jazz was merely another case of a new vogue taking root like a weed in the heterogeneous welter that [New York] was, and from there inundating the country; and that the genuinely American thing was not rag-time, but the instinctively defensive—and pathetically futile—effort of the older generation in the rural parts of the country to ward off this assault on the older American melodies at which rag-time jeered."

New York, as this passage shows, had long been looked upon with grave suspicion by the rest of the country, because it was a city of many aliens. By 1910, 41 percent of its population was foreign-born. The Irish, constituting more than 13 percent, had now moved up in public estimation in the face of the mass entry of immigrants from eastern and southern Europe. Ever since the days of the Know-Nothings, there had been an American minority who feared foreigners in general, and especially Papists and Radicals. The greatest apprehension existed, as always, among those whose social or financial status was shaky and who were looking for someone to blame for their situation. However, even the lofty and wellborn were often concerned about the dilution of the old Anglo-Saxon stock. "Who shall respect a people who do not respect their own blood?" cried New York's eminent Bishop Potter. "Pan, who was the son of everybody, was the ugliest of the gods." Chauncey M. Depew, president of the New York Central Railroad, politician, and socialite, suspected immigrants of wishing "to destroy our government, cut our throats, and divide our property." The Immigration Restriction League, formed in 1895, was headed by a half dozen or more noted citizens of colonial descent.

The First World War put a temporary stop to immigration but not to the dislike of "hyphenated Americans" of recent arrival. The feeling was intensified by the Russian Revolution. Ever since the 1880's the Chinese had found it all but impossible to immigrate to the United States. As a result of a succession of immigration agreements and laws, the Japanese were excluded after 1924, and quotas for other nationalities favored immigrants from northern Europe and the British Isles, without reference to ability, intelligence, or character (provided it was not criminal).

Anti-Semitism in America began much as anti-Irish feeling had begun—out of fear for jobs and prospects. With more education than the Irish and a longer experience in the ways of city life and in financial dealings, many immigrant Jews became prosperous and invaded precincts where theretofore only "old" Americans had presided. In the West, where Jews were only a handful compared with the rest of the population, there was little friction. In the East, high society would not, as a rule, receive these outlanders, and the middle class, ever eager to ape society, followed suit. In New York, Jews established their own circles, with as many gradations and snobbisms as their Gentile counterparts. Social exchange between Jew and Gentile at all levels was standoffish; intermarriage was rare. Christian hotels and neighborhoods were often avowedly "restricted," and were unabashed to advertise "Gentiles Only." Nobody seemed to think dialect jokes in poor taste, and rafters rang to condescending laughter over Izzie and Ike, as well as Mike and Pat, Rastus and Remus, and Giuseppe and Sal.

During the early twenties, the Ku Klux Klan had a membership of several million and was respectable enough to hold a parade on Washington's Pennsylvania Avenue, traditional scene of inaugural parades and heroes' welcomes. The fact that its influence began to wane later in the decade cannot be attributed to a diminishing of bigotry but to the disgrace of the Klan's "Grand

Suffragette parade marshal, 1912

Dragon of the Invisible Empire for the Realm of Indiana," who was convicted of rape and manslaughter. The mentality of the Know-Nothings, the American Protective Association, and the Ku Klux Klan did not vanish.

The Negro seemed to be in an even worse predicament than the immigrant, for he had no place to go back to and he was virtually precluded from advancement by the color of his skin. In 1901, Theodore Roosevelt stirred up a hornets' nest when he invited Booker T. Washington to dine with him at the White House. The Richmond *Times* said that obviously the President favored miscegenation. Senator "Pitchfork Ben" Tillman of South Carolina told his constituents, "The action of President Roosevelt in entertaining that nigger will necessitate our killing a thousand niggers in the South before they will learn their place again." Many northerners joined in criticizing this breach of tradition, and as far away as Hong Kong, a British colonial said to an American visitor, "I hear that your President believes in breaking down all the barriers between the races."

Finley Peter Dunne, a very popular newspaper columnist, who wrote as the pseudonymous Irish bartender "Mr. Dooley," commented on the controversy: "I don't mind sayin' that I'd rather ate with a coon thin have wan wait on me. I'd sooner he'd handle his own food thin mine. F'r me, if anny thumb must be in th' gravy, lave it be white if ye please." Dooley said that the President's position was similar to his own—both were public servants. "If it wint th' rounds that Dooley was handin' out rayfrishment to th' colored population, I might as well change in me license. . . . I—an' th' Prisidint—is public sarvants, an' manny iv our customers have onrais'nable prejoodices. . . . 'Tis not me that speaks . . . 'tis the job."

If little love was lost between the races, there was a perceptible increase in the compassion of rich for poor whites. Andrew Carnegie set the pattern for the model multimillionaire when, in 1901, he retired from business and concentrated on performing good works with his money. After initial surprise and suspicion, the American public warmed to the Carnegie image, and the millionaire of the Gilded Age, known for conspicuous waste, went quickly out of style. For example, Alva Vanderbilt, now Mrs. O. H. P. Belmont, no longer gave balls that cost hundreds of thousands of dollars. She dedicated herself to the fight for woman's rights. If lavish balls were given, they were usually for charity. When Mrs. Astor died in 1908, no social arbitress arose to take her place. Henry James called Newport's palaces white elephants. "They look queer and conscious and lumpish—some of them, as with an air of the brandished proboscis, really grotesque—while their averted owners, roused from a witless dream, wonder what in the world is to be done with them." James found American high society peculiarly insecure and baseless, like "a small child set on a mantel-shelf and about to cry out."

Andrew Carnegie was of the opinion that "of every thousand dollars spent in so-called charity to-day, it is probable that nine hundred and fifty is unwisely spent—so spent, indeed, as to produce the very evils which it hopes to mitigate or cure." He gave $311,000,000 to establish, among other philanthropies, more than 2,500 libraries, several concert halls, and the Carnegie Endowment for International Peace. But he severely criticized an acquaintance for giving away a quarter to a man on the street, because "he knew nothing of the habits of this beggar." Like Carnegie, most of the new breed of philanthropists were paternalistic. Within that pattern, reform and improve-

Irene and Vernon Castle, professional ballroom dancers in the teens, execute a genteel tango, above. The couple below dip to a more strenuous, "vulgar" version.

ment went forward as never before: slum clearance, safe working conditions in mines and factories, workmen's compensation, research on tuberculosis (with new knowledge of the causes of T.B., spitting was at last discouraged), care of poor children, and better schools. Looking back at those days, Mark Sullivan wrote, "whether because it is in times of well-being that men become kindly and open-handed and only in times of economic depression and spiritual fear that they become wolfish toward each other—for whatever cause the period was characterized by concern with the fortunes of fellowmen, a desire to make the world better, an awakening to the possibility of a finer way of life, a fervor of many souls to bring in a juster, more lovely era, a super-sensitive, over-eager determination like the conscience of a fifteen-year-old boy."

Henry Ford was not one of those who gave money away, but he made a very favorable impression on most Americans when, in 1914, he raised the wages of his thirteen thousand employees to $5 per eight-hour day. The plan made headlines. Some thought that the workers would "spend their money foolishly"; others said that Ford was merely showing shrewd self-interest. Rivals called him a socialist. Socialists held a mass meeting to denounce him, resolving that "Ford had purchased the brains, life and soul of his men by a raise in pay of a few dollars a week." Whatever his motives, with one gesture Ford had changed America's conception of what a workingman's wages should be. If publicity was what he wanted, he got it.

The press found him to be a rugged individualist and a dedicated businessman—the kind of man that Americans of that day held in highest esteem. He lived simply, cherished such adages as "Chop your own wood and it will warm you twice," and was fond of the out-of-doors, but above all he was concerned with producing the Ford as cheaply and in as great a number as possible. His paternalistic attitude toward his employees seemed the right one to most Americans. He was urged to run for President. His prestige was indestructible, even when he made fatuous remarks like "History is bunk," or did simple-minded things, like going to Europe in 1915 to stop the war single-handedly. Ford was the man of the age: his name was synonymous not only with the automobile but with mass production, and it was these factors, plus the emancipation of women, that most profoundly changed American life and indirectly prepared the way for that phenomenal decade, the twenties.

When the First World War ended, people spoke of "returning to normalcy," but if they meant the unruffled days of the early part of the century, that kind of normalcy had vanished forever. "The older generation had certainly pretty well ruined this world before passing it on to us," wrote a young contributor to the *Atlantic Monthly* in September, 1920—sounding very much like young people of forty and fifty years later. "They give us this thing, knocked to pieces, leaky, red-hot, threatening to blow up; and then they are surprised that we don't accept it with the same attitude of pretty, decorous enthusiasm with which they received it, way back in the 'eighties." Also in the *Atlantic* that year, an anonymous writer who admitted to being middle-aged remarked gloomily, "We must advance along the road where the new generation is leading us, or we must travel alone—and backwards."

To cheer his older readers, he pointed out that manners might change, but certain human qualities were permanent—among them, the desire to be liked. "A hundred years ago the young girl who wished to ensnare the heart of a man would blush, and tremble, give a side glance and look down, and care-

Poster in a 1917 labor newspaper

(Continued on Page 346)

344

Chicago: 1899

The "Boss Town," as seen by Rudyard Kipling. His report, for a Calcutta journal, evinces the dislocation of a Victorian confronting twentieth-century life.

I have struck a city,—a real city,—and . . . having seen it, I urgently desire never to see it again. It is inhabited by savages . . . and its air is dirt. . . . They told me to go to the Palmer House, which is a gilded and mirrored rabbit-warren . . . crammed with people talking about money and spitting about everywhere. . . . I went out into the streets . . . and . . . looked down interminable vistas . . . crowded with men and women, and the show impressed me with a great horror. . . . A cab-driver volunteered to show me the glory of the town. . . . He conceived that all this turmoil and squash was a thing to be reverently admired; that it was good to huddle men together in fifteen layers, one atop of the other, and to dig holes in the ground for offices. . . . [He] showed me business-blocks, gay with signs and studded with fantastic and absurd advertisements . . . it was as though each vender stood at his door howling: "For the sake of money, employ or buy of *me* and me only!" . . . I had sooner watch famine-relief than the white man engaged in what he calls legitimate competition. . . . The cabman said that these things were the proof of progress. . . . I was expected to do more than listen or watch. . . . I should admire; and the utmost that I could say was: "I am very sorry for you." That made him angry, and he said that insular envy made me unresponsive. . . . Sunday brought me the queerest experience of all—a revelation of barbarism complete. I found a place that was officially de-

scribed as a church. . . . To a congregation of savages, entered suddenly a wonderful man. . . . With a voice of silver and with imagery borrowed from the auction-room, he built up for his hearers a heaven on the lines of the Palmer House . . . and set in the centre of it a loud-voiced, argumentative, and very shrewd creation that he called God. One sentence . . . caught my delighted ear: "No! I tell you God doesn't do business that way." He was giving them a deity whom they could comprehend. . . . But I don't think it was the blind hurry of the people, their argot, and their grand ignorance of things beyond their immediate interests that displeased me so much as a study of the daily papers of Chicago. . . . In these papers, were faithfully reproduced all the war-cries and "back-talk" of the . . . bar, the slang of the barbers' shops, the mental elevation and integrity of the Pullman-car porter, the dignity of the Dime Museum, and the accuracy of the excited fishwife. I am sternly forbidden to believe that the paper educates the public. . . . I went off to see cattle killed by way of clearing my head. . . . There . . . each man carried a knife . . . and from bosom to heel he was blood-red. . . . Women come sometimes to see the slaughter. . . . And there entered that vermilion hall a young woman in flaming red and black. . . . She looked . . . with hard, bold eyes, and was not ashamed. Then said I: "This is a special Sending. I have seen the City of Chicago." And I went away to get peace and rest.

THE STARCHED COLLAR SET

In town, about the office, and clubs during the evening, town or country, starched collars are it.

The Noon Day Clubs, the Club Cars, the offices of Banks, Insurance Companies—

Wherever appearance is an asset, the starched collar is required. Men will wear starched collars, white or of very modest colored patterns, in town and to business.

Soft collars on shirts will be the thing for the country and the car.

The Starched Collar Class is the Gentleman's Class

ARROW COLLARS

CLUETT, PEABODY & CO. Inc. Makers

J. C. Leyendecker's idealized "Man in the Arrow Collar" (top) was one of the most famous advertising images of the period. "The Starched Collar Set" (above) flattered men who could afford to wear linen rather than celluloid or rubber collars.

lessly drop a rose from her bosom in the path of her pursuer. Her granddaughter seeks popularity by another path. At a dinner-party she seizes a roll of bread, dexterously slings it across the table, avoiding intervening heads, and with a raucous cry of 'Hi there! Catch it, you boob!' has flung her gauntlet into the arena of popularity. One may prefer the fallen rose to the hurled roll, but the motor-power behind both is the same."

One person who deplored the hurled roll was Mrs. Emily Price Post, who, in 1922, published *Etiquette—The Blue Book of Social Usage*, and thereby installed herself as America's high priestess on the subject. Mrs. Post was to the manner born. At the time of her New York debut, in the early nineties, Ward McAllister numbered her among "the ten ladies in New York who could gracefully cross a ballroom floor alone." Crossing a ballroom was only one of thousands of social graces that were of transcendent importance to Mrs. Post. "Etiquette is the science of living," she once said. "It embraces everything. It is honor. It is everything."

Etiquette sold out its first printing of ten thousand copies almost overnight. Arthur M. Schlesinger, Sr., in his study of the literature of American etiquette, *Learning How to Behave*, attributes Mrs. Post's success to "the need many earnest souls felt for a steadying hand in a period of bewildering flux in social conventions. Puzzled and disturbed by the négligé state of manners, they disliked being thought old fogies and hence losing touch with their children; yet, on the other hand, they wanted to make certain that youth was not headed straight for perdition. Some, to be sure, itched to learn whether they too, despite their different upbringing, might not adopt the freer, franker ways of the rising generation."

One sign of youth's take-over was the entry of slang into the conversation of supposedly well-bred people. Frederick H. Martens, in his *Book of Good Manners*, cautioned readers to be on guard against vulgar speech. His list of phrases that "will not pass muster" began with *Aggravating papa* (meaning a refractory lover) and continued for several scolding pages with such citations as *Big bug* (a person of prominence); *Cake-eater* or *Lounge Lizard* (an effeminate young man); *Finale hopper* (one who always stays to the last dance); *Frail* (a girl); *Glad rags* (best clothes); *Heavy-sugar papa* (an elderly lover); *Jazz hound* (a young society idler); *Peel* (to disrobe); *Plunk* (a silver dollar); *Prune* (a tiresome person); *Tickle the tusks* (to play the piano); and *Wild woman* (a girl who is no better than she should be).

Mrs. Post gave little encouragement to freer, franker ways. Much of the 1922 edition of *Etiquette* might have been written years earlier. It spoke of the indispensability of chaperons, the importance of card-leaving, how to look one's best riding sidesaddle, and how to manage without a personal maid while camping out. Nothing in the book intimated that there might be a social revolution in progress. In a revised edition, published in 1927, she countenanced smoking and admitted that the chaperon was a vanishing institution. But through many more revised editions until her death in 1960, her standards were both conventional and conservative. Mrs. Post had written novels before she became the leading arbiter of manners, and she enlivened the pages of *Etiquette* with cautionary tales. She described every detail of a weekend with the Oldnames (who had more taste than money) or dinner with the Gildings (who did everything in the grand manner and did it impeccably), so that the reader could imagine himself there and with Mrs. Post look down his nose at the egregious *faux pas* of some of the other guests, such as Mr. Richan Vulgar and Mr. and Mrs. Unsuitable. In this way, she offered something that could not be found in the average behavior manuals—a sense of what it took to be a snob. Mrs. Post not only provided explicit instructions on manners but graciously conducted a sort of guided tour into a world that would normally be closed to the public. Setting aside the velvet rope and unlocking the Inner Sanctum, she allowed her readers to peep at Mrs. Oldname's exquisitely appointed breakfast tray, to pull open Miss Wellborn's delicately scented bureau drawers, and to join in those ladies' well-bred amusements over Mr. Vulgar's efforts to make friends. Mrs. Post's world was that of Edith Wharton, J. P. Marquand, and Louis Auchincloss—but unlike the novelists, she endorsed it wholeheartedly.

If, in 1922, thousands of Americans were enjoying vicarious snobbery with Mrs. Post, a great many others were ignoring her and daring to carry out a manners revolt. The instigators of the uprising were young men and women who had grown up with the century and who were now setting out to put their own stamp on it. Their disapproving elders labeled them "flaming youth," an epithet originally used by Horace to describe hell-raising young Romans of his day. In 1923 a best-selling novel of that name by Samuel Hopkins Adams, alias Warner Fabian, was dedicated "To the woman of the period . . . restless, seductive, greedy, discontented, craving sensation, unrestrained, a little morbid, more than a little selfish, intelligent, uneducated, sybaritic, following blind instincts and perverse fancies, slack of mind as she is trim of body, neurotic and vigorous . . . fit mate for the hurried, reckless and cynical man."

This giddy girl was popularly known as a flapper. (The word does not, as has been supposed, derive from her habit of walking about in unbuckled galoshes; it was appropriated from nineteenth-century English slang for an unruly girl.) She wore a short skirt that gave a glimpse, or more than a glimpse, of the tops of her silk stockings, rolled just above or below her knees. Her hair was also short, and either marcelled in stiff waves or tortured into wiry curls by the new permanent-wave machine. Like Clara Bow, the "It" girl, and other screen sirens, she made up her mouth in the shape of a Cupid's bow. Rouge adorned her cheeks and even her knees. Underneath her scrap of a dress she wore nothing much—perhaps only a one-piece garment called a teddy. But, curiously, she clung to hat and gloves—taking seriously her mother's dictum that a lady would as soon be seen on the street without her shoes and stockings as without hat and gloves. However, a cloche pulled down over the ears took the place of the hatpinned flower-and-bird extravaganzas of an earlier day. Wrote Frederick Lewis Allen, in *Only Yesterday*, these girls of the 1920's were "men's casual and light-hearted companions; not broad-hipped mothers of the race, but irresponsible playmates."

Just how irresponsible they were is not quite clear. Sexual surveys in those days were not as scientific as Dr. Kinsey's, and respondents were undoubtedly reticent. Mrs. Post did not recognize unchaperoned dating, and as for necking and petting, the Oldnames and the Gildings had never heard of such things. A more realistic observer was Scott Fitzgerald, who wrote, "As far back as 1915 the unchaperoned young people of the smaller cities had discovered the mobile privacy of that automobile given to young Bill at sixteen to make him 'self-reliant.' At first petting was a desperate adventure even under such favorable conditions, but presently confidences were exchanged

Garter buttons, like the Boop-Boop-a-Doop model above, were designed to draw attention to feminine knees, an anatomical asset rediscovered by the flappers. Fashion also called for bobbed hair, often curled to a frazzle, as shown below.

and the old commandment broke down. As early as 1917 there were references to such sweet and casual dalliance in any number of issues of the *Yale Record* or the *Princeton Tiger*. But petting in its more audacious manifestations was confined to the wealthier classes — among other young people the old standard prevailed until after the War, and a kiss meant that a proposal was expected, as young officers in strange cities sometimes discovered to their dismay. Only in 1920 did the veil finally fall — the Jazz Age was in flower."

The flapper's date — "sheik," he was called — was apt to have a flask of bootleg liquor in his hip pocket. Before the advent of prohibition, most American girls had avoided drinkers; having been told over and over again, in magazines, newspapers, speeches, and sermons, that even moderate drinkers made unreliable husbands, that drink could make men impotent, and if it did not, that children could be impaired by the taint of alcohol. But no sooner had prohibition become law than the public began to turn against it. In 1922 a *Literary Digest* poll uncovered much sentiment in favor of repeal or at least modification of the Eighteenth Amendment. Prohibition represented a victory of rural over urban America, but now that the automobile, the radio, and the movies were bringing the city to the country, even the most isolated country people were beginning to hanker for city ways. Flaming youth led the way in flouting the law, and excused itself with talk of A-World-We-Never-Made, as the young have often done before and since.

A young man just starting out in the twenties was likely to enter the world of business, which was blossoming as never before. The businessman was the ideal citizen. Said George Babbitt, the anti-hero of Sinclair Lewis's novel, "The modern American business man knows how to talk right up for himself, knows how to make it good and plenty clear that he intends to run the works. . . . With all modesty, I want to stand up here as a representative business man and gently whisper, 'Here's our kind of folks! Here's the specifications of the Standardized American Citizen! Here's the new generation of Americans: fellows with hair on their chests and smiles in their eyes and adding-machines in their offices."

The modern reader who finds such adulation of the businessman too absurd to be believed might look into *The Man Nobody Knows*, by Bruce Barton, a nonfiction best seller of 1925 and 1926. Jesus, wrote Barton, was "the founder of modern business." He was "the most popular dinner guest in Jerusalem," and "picked up twelve men from the bottom ranks of business and forged them into an organization that conquered the world." The parables, Barton went on, were "the most powerful advertisements of all time." Proof that Jesus was indeed a businessman lay in the words, "Wist ye not that I must be about my father's business?"

Salesmanship in the twenties was highly competitive, and manufacturers and advertisers counted on the salesman to keep products selling as never before; for if the consumer should suddenly balk, the whole dizzying structure of twenties prosperity would totter. "You can't be an order-taker any longer — you've got to be a *salesman*," was the command that went round and round in a salesman's head. In *Only Yesterday*, Frederick Lewis Allen quotes the manager of a company that offered a Christmas turkey to every salesman who beat his quota for the year: "We asked each man to appoint a child in his family as a mascot, realizing that every one of them would work his head off to make some youngster happy at Christmas. The way these youngsters took hold of

"Just a song at twilight"
gets a noisy co-ed rendition
at a John Held jam session.

the plan was amusing, and at times the intensity of their interest was almost pathetic."

A salesman's textbook advised, "*Do not permit the Prospect to reason or reflect. The expert fisherman tries out the fish—if one kind of bait doesn't get the strike, he changes. And if one kind of hook doesn't land them he changes hooks. If he is alert, aggressive, masterful, persistent, and a thorough psychologist he perseveres. He carefully lays his snares, places his bait, and, then the unsuspecting Prospect falls into the trap.*" One go-getting salesman reported success through making the prospective buyers angry. "It was up to me to get their attention. What did I do? I tramped on their corns. I reached over and plunked down on their corns. I really did this; I am not stuffing you. When they got red and mad all over, I knew that I had their attention. Then I would say: 'I was clumsy, wasn't I? But profits, profits for you today and profits you haven't dreamed of. . . .'"

One useful lure that had not been available to most salesmen of an earlier day was the installment plan. A few purveyors of expensive products, such as sewing machines or pianos, had done installment business for years, but until the second decade of the twentieth century, the practice of buying what one could not immediately pay for was generally regarded as both immoral and a public admission that one was in poor financial shape. Said *The Ladies' Home Journal* in 1909, "What then is the remedy for the evils of the installment business? . . . There is but one safe and sure one; have nothing to do with such a business."

In 1910, Sears, Roebuck had sold nothing on credit, not even their $370 to $495 line of automobiles. But by 1920, competitors were selling so many automobiles on time-payment plans that even Sears had to follow suit. Very quickly, so did manufacturers of other expensive products, and by 1923 there was little prejudice against installment buying. The salesmen loved it, as it made their work much easier. However, one harrassed Ford dealer, writing in *Harper's Monthly* in 1927, told how the company kept raising his quota and how it took him to task when he did not make enough sales. "If Mr. Ford knew personally some of the things that go on I am sure he would call a halt to his branch managers riding the local agents the way they do."

With business growing in productive capacity and seeking wider markets, enormous funds became available for advertising. Automobile manufacturers and large department stores led the way in running full-page ads—which, in turn, caused an increase in the size and circulation of magazines and newspapers. In 1925, Stuart Chase estimated, in a *New Republic* article, that over a billion dollars a year was being spent on advertising, about half of which went to advertise products nationally.

Held's flaming youths, with characteristic costumes and slouches

The advertisers played on the public's longing to succeed, to do the right thing, to be popular, and to improve. There was the girl who was "often a bridesmaid but never a bride," because she failed to use Listerine; the rejected suitor who had B.O.; the housewife who risked her family's health by failing to shake Sani-Flush into the toilet. A *Harvard Classics* advertisement showed a disconsolate couple, "One year married and all talked out." If they would only buy the Five-Foot Shelf and study it fifteen minutes a day, they might "turn their silent, lonely hours into real human companionship." An ad for an etiquette book showed another unhappy pair who had just said goodnight to dinner guests, and had apparently done everything wrong. "When

Your Guests Are Gone," says the caption, "Are You Sorry You Ever Invited Them? . . . Be Free From All Embarrassment! Let the Famous *Book of Etiquette* Tell You Exactly What to Do, Say, Write, or Wear on Every Occasion."

As it grew apparent that women were increasing their grip on the nation's purse strings, advertisers slanted their material more directly to catch their attention. Since women formed most of the readership of society pages, manufacturers paid society people to endorse products. Back in the eighties, the Reverend Henry Ward Beecher, a great favorite with the ladies, had allowed his picture to be used in a soap ad. Henry M. Stanley had discovered the efficacy of a patent medicine in the nineties, and half a dozen senators had given their support to Ivory Soap. But it took the twenties to put socialites to work. Anyone who said that such endorsements were in questionable taste was reminded that the King of England had been doing it for years—"By Appointment to His Majesty the King" having long been the cherished boast of certain favored British tradesmen. What was good enough for His Majesty was good enough for America's social queens, especially since checks for up to $10,000 underlined the advertisers' appreciation. Mrs. Oliver Harriman endorsed Hardman pianos. She also came out for Pond's Cold Cream, as did Mrs. Nicholas Longworth (Theodore Roosevelt's daughter Alice), and Mrs. August Belmont. Camel cigarettes received the accolade of a good part of the social register. Some of the ladies endorsed products in order to contribute their take to favorite charities. Others were simply acquisitive and were thrilled at the idea of earning money on their own rather than having it handed to them at the bank.

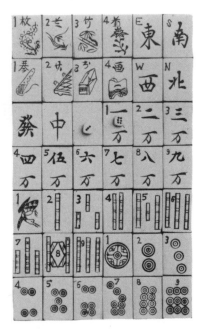

Millions of sets of mah-jongg, the Chinese gambling game above, were imported to America in the twenties.

The eagerness among salesmen and advertisers to sell had its counterpart in the eagerness of consumers to buy, otherwise known as Keeping-Up-With-The-Joneses. The impulse was not new, but now, in the twenties, more people strove to keep up than ever before. *Middletown*, the study of an American town, published in 1929 by Robert and Helen Lynd, is filled with examples. For instance, the wife of a workingman told the Lynds, "No girl can wear cotton stockings to high school. Even in winter my children wear silk stockings with lisle or imitations underneath." A white-collar-class woman said, "The dresses girls wear to school now used to be considered party dresses." In the manner of a *Herald* report on Mrs. Astor's doings, the Middletown newspaper gravely described the elaborate dresses seen at high-school dances. Inability to have the "right" clothes was a common cause for dropping out of school.

The houses being built in Middletown in the twenties were smaller than older ones, not only because of rising building costs but also because the housewife sought escape from drudgery. The old-time front porch was disappearing, and Middletown's Joneses were replacing it with the sleeping porch, the glassed-in sun porch, and the den. Electric light, central heat, a telephone, and at least one bathroom were now available to all but the poor. In Middletown, the Lynds found that many working-class families would rather have a car than running water, and most chose to mortgage their houses in order to buy one. "According to an officer of a Middletown automobile financing company, 75 to 90 percent of the cars purchased locally are bought on time payment, and a working man earning $35.00 a week frequently plans to use one week's pay each month as payment for his car." The mother of nine children informed the interviewers, "We'd rather do without clothes than give up the car." Those who had no car were likely to tell the Lynds that they opposed it on moral grounds: Sunday motor trips interfered with going to church; courting in automobiles rather than in the family parlor endangered the home. A judge of Middletown's juvenile court called the automobile "a house of prostitution of a Ford Dealer." The expense of keeping a car running (estimated at $100 a month by one Middletown businessman) prevented most people from saving.

The newest status symbol of the twenties was the radio. Broadcasting to the public began in 1920. Less than two years later, a wide audience was listening in—if the sale of $60,000,000 worth of equipment is any indication. At first, it was a novelty, just another fad like mah-jongg and the Charleston in 1923, the crossword puzzle in 1924, and contract bridge and the Black Bottom in 1926. It was logical to suppose that the craze for hearing a static-filled rendition of "Yes, We Have No Bananas" would go the way of other fads. But reception improved, advertisers moved in to provide a gamut of entertainment, and by 1929 a radio was another example of a luxury that many Americans thought more important than clothing, savings, or running water.

Another new drain on family incomes was the annual vacation. In Middletown one citizen told the interviewers that in the nineties local businessmen "never took a vacation." Now vacations for the middle class were common, although they were seldom with pay; the idea of paid holidays had scarcely been thought of. Most vacationers traveled by automobile, either to visit relatives far away or just to wander about. In 1926 Florida was the goal of thousands who used their vacations to drive there and take part in the gigantic land boom that was going on. "From everywhere came the land-seekers, the profit-seekers," reported *Harper's Monthly*. "Automobiles moved along the eighteen-foot-wide Dixie Highway, the main artery of East Coast traffic, in a dense, struggling stream. . . . Most of the cars brimmed over with mother, father, grandmother, several children, and the dog." Early buyers did well, provided they sold again. Late comers got caught when hurricanes and bankruptcies turned the boom to a bust. In a sense, Florida was the last frontier, awakening in Americans the old urge to seek out greener pastures, to improve their lot, to succeed in a big way.

The twenties saw a notable increase in travel abroad. New luxury liners and the introduction of tourist class brought Europe within reach of teachers, students, and moderately well-off businessmen. The trend had started before 1914, but accelerated after the war until in 1929 nearly 300,000 Americans visited Europe. Some of them behaved badly, offending local custom, boasting, and getting noisily drunk. "By 1928, Paris had grown suffocating," wrote Scott Fitzgerald. "With each new shipment of Americans spewed up by the boom the quality fell off, until toward the end there was something sinister about the crazy boatloads. . . . I remember the Judge from some New York district who had taken his daughter to see the Bayeux tapestries and [wrote to] the papers advocating their segregation because one scene was immoral." In the Place de l'Opéra one day, a mob converged angrily on a covey of tourists in sight-seeing buses. Although no bloodshed resulted, President Coolidge broke his customary silence and sent word that Americans had better either mind their manners or come home. Europeans in those days had not yet thought of writing "Yankee Go Home" on walls, but Americans were making their first painful discovery that they could not have everything their own way.

Party games were often elaborate affairs, requiring costumes, props, and high art. Rea Irvin depicts two "Pastimes of the Intelligentsia": Detective, above, and Charades, below.

Toward A New Morality

In which a chastened America emerges from the Depression & a Global War to find that the World has been permanently altered & Multitudes demand a Philosophical Retooling of our Social & Ethical Conduct

The whirlwind of the stock market crash left behind it a sober, contemplative, and bewildered America. It was as if the country had been on a binge—drunk too much, acted loud and silly at a party, and ended by wrecking the family car. The hangover was painful, and no one wanted to be reminded of that long, giddy carousal. At the same time, the "normalcy" of the pretwenties was beyond return, and few mourned its passing. For better or for worse, America had begun "the World a New" perhaps even more drastically than the Puritans had done three centuries before.

If the thirties revived some old-time decorum and elegance, it was more in a sense of a nostalgic backward glance than of an about-face. Skirt lengths dipped, but never became lower than nine inches from the ground. There was less talk of sex, both in print and in general conversation, but the day when sex was unmentionable had passed, as had the day when the very enunciation of the word was daring. Young people took their comparative freedom for granted. As Frederick Lewis Allen wrote in his study of the thirties, *Since Yesterday*, "the revolution was being consolidated. The shock troops were digging in in the positions they had won." Robert and Helen Lynd, in their follow-up story of Middletown, were struck by the lack of consistency in sex attitudes. The mores of the twenties vied with those of an earlier time for sway over young people, who, in turn, were looking for a pattern of their own. "A girl should never kiss a boy unless they are engaged," decreed a columnist in Middletown's daily newspaper; but, judging by the Lynds' interviews, such advice was widely ignored. On the other hand, a Middletown businessman who had been young in the twenties, told the interviewers, "At the 1934 Christmas dances I remarked to my wife that we people of the older generation behaved much less well than the high-school kids. We got tighter and let

With our whole code of human behavior coming under relentless scrutiny, Everyman finds himself face to face with some very basic moral imperatives. Love springs eternal.

In 1930, when William Gropper drew these cartoons for the leftist monthly the New Masses, *American individualism seemed in danger of capitulating to conformity.*

ourselves go more." According to the Lynds, "the range of sanctioned choices confronting Middletown youth [had become] wider, the definition of the one 'right way' less clear."

In 1936, *Fortune* made a study of college youth, a more sophisticated group than the Middletowners, and concluded that "sex is no longer news. And the fact that it is no longer news is news." *Fortune*'s interviewers found that about half the young men and slightly more of the girls hoped to marry soon after graduation, and about half of each sex hoped that children would soon follow. Forty percent of the girls feared that housewifery would bore them and wanted to combine marriage with a career, while 85 percent of the men opposed that notion. Both sexes craved security—whatever was safe and permanent interested most of them far more than anything adventurous or radical. "[The student] doesn't think he will attain great heights in the world as it is constituted . . . and he doesn't think he can make that world over. He may deplore war, but he can't see himself thwarting the forces that make for war." He was not, however, an ostrich. Professors reported that college students in 1936 took more courses in economics, history, and the social sciences than their counterparts of the twenties; that they read the papers more carefully and knew much more about what was going on in the world. Predicted *Fortune*, "Intellectual curiosity born of caution may, indeed, result in the crusades of tomorrow."

For college students and for many other Americans, one of the new pleasures and/or problems of the thirties was what to do with leisure. Some of the free time was a direct result of the Depression. Among students, as Don Congdon says in *The Thirties*, "there was a hell of a lot of waiting—waiting to get an education, waiting to find a job, waiting to get married." Most workingmen had a five-and-a-half-day week as well as a summer vacation of a week or two. During the Depression, those who were not laid off were likely to have had their hours (and pay) reduced. Housewives found their workdays shortened by the ever-increasing variety of new technological aids and service industries: frozen foods, nylon products, cellophane, a bounty of small electric appliances, and dry cleaners.

Older urban amenities such as electric lights, plumbing, and telephones were rapidly spreading to rural areas. The Sears, Roebuck catalog used unprecedentedly plain language in recommending the DeLuxe Handee Indoor Toilet: "much of the stomach disorders and intestinal ill-health suffered by our adult rural population can often be traced to lack of convenient toilet facilities and the resultant development of the 'deferring habit.'" A mere $7.79 would correct this evil. Only 10 percent of American farms had electricity in 1935 (today, fewer than 10 percent are without it), but farmers' lives were eased by the automobile, which took them in and out of town quickly, and by motorized farm equipment.

In town and country alike, the most popular diversion was listening to the radio. Even in the worst Depression years, 1930–32, four million sets were sold. In 1930 there were twelve million sets in use; in 1940, forty million, including five million in automobiles. Most Americans who remember the thirties at all will remember Eddie Cantor, Lowell Thomas, Myrt and Marge, Amos 'n' Andy, Kate Smith, Jack Benny ("Jell-*O* again"), Fred Allen, Major Bowes' Amateur Hour, the Aldrich Family ("Coming, Mother"), and Rudy Vallee ("Your time is my time"). Their voices were as familiar as those of one's own family. One counted on finding friends at home on Sunday evening—that was when the best programs were on. For those who stayed at home during the weekdays, there were the fifteen-minute soap operas, heralded by swelling organ music and an earnest voice extolling soap and other humble adjuncts to the household. One of the treats of a trip to New York, along with a visit to the Statue of Liberty and the Empire State Building (completed in 1931), was seeing a real, live radio show.

Radio's most important effect on American mores was the beginning of the breakup of regional isolation—a job now being done with far greater effectiveness by television. The radio programs themselves seem to have left no permanent impression, perhaps because they aimed to please everybody. They were as bland as Jell-O and as ephemeral as soapsuds, and most have vanished into the thin air whence they came.

While the radio burbled on in the background, people plunged into new recreational activities, bringing to them the same dedication that characterized the American approach to business. In 1935, 8 percent of the national income went to recreation, the highest amount in the nation's history. (The present estimate is roughly 6 percent.) More than half was spent for vacation travel. Trailers and trailer camps appeared. Given the migratory traditions of Americans, there were those who predicted that half the country would soon take to the open road in trailers. By 1940 there were 100,000 of them in use.

Texas farmers tuning in on the world, 1939

The other half of the nation's recreation money went for movies, plays, radios, books, magazines, musical instruments, and equipment for indoor and outdoor games and sports. During the darkest days of the Depression, miniature golf courses did a rousing business—they were cheaper than real golf courses, and brought the prestigious country-club game to every level of society. Gardening and knitting were popular Depression hobbies, for they not only were diverting but produced something. Amateur photography also flourished, despite the cost of equipment; *Life*, which began publication in 1936, followed by *Look* the next year, presented a fresh conception of how life might be recorded with a camera. To give one example, at the beginning of the decade, pictures taken at weddings had always shown simply the bride with her flowers or perhaps the wedding party, stiffly posed. By 1940 every bride wanted a scrapbook filled with candid shots of cake-cutting, bouquet-throwing, and mother in beige lace and orchids having a little cry.

The nation made heroes of star sportsmen in baseball, football, tennis, and the 1936 Olympics. And more Americans than ever before were trying sports themselves. The decade brought great expansion of public facilities for swimming, ice-skating, and golf. Bowling, an inexpensive pastime for city dwellers, acquired eight million devotees. Bicycles sold well—they not only provided exercise but an alternate means of getting about in case the family car was repossessed. Skiing, which was far from inexpensive, became a popular sport, helped by the trend toward winter holidays and the steadily increasing freedom of young girls, who now made the Rubicon-crossing decision to board an overnight ski train without a chaperon.

Other fun included games-playing, a form of entertainment that suited the tightening budget of the era. *The Ladies' Home Journal* gave its blessing to the boom in word games: "Clerks and plumbers and school teachers and school children go home elbow to elbow in the Subway, muttering five letter words that mean 'commonplace' or trying to supply the Laddergram links between Bride and Groom. Amusement, once the prerogative of royalty and wealth, is everywhere now, and with this wave of games the nation gains a great lifting of the spirit, a sort of universal heightening per capita of the country's average enjoyment." A particularly appealing board game for people short on cash was Monopoly, the brain child of a salesman thrown out of work by the Depression. Minor forms of gambling for money and prizes also became more popular than ever, with people spending long nights over bridge and bingo. Sweepstakes tickets were in great demand, and movies enticed customers with "Dish Night," at which one might win a set of dishes, and the still more exciting "Bank Night," when cash was awarded.

Toward the end of the decade, the movies reached their all-time peak of popularity: eighty-five million Americans were attending a movie every week. Two double features weekly were common fare for many a high-school student, and children stood in line for an hour or more to get into Saturday matinees. Intellectuals complained (but few heard them) of the witlessness of most movies and of the absurdity of the movies' self-imposed moral code. These rules permitted, for example, a character in *Dead End* to be named Spit, but forbade his acting in accordance with his name. Still, the "talkies" were much slicker and more artfully put together than the "silents" of the twenties; and to the citizens of a drab, Depression-ridden America nothing could be more satisfying than a magic-carpet ride among alluring girls with arched eyebrows, like Carole Lombard and Ann Sheridan, and debonair he-men like Robert Taylor and Clark Gable. Such beings suffered, of course—it was only fair—but a happy ending could be counted on, except occasionally, as in *Smilin' Through*, in which Norma Shearer and Leslie Howard uncharacteristically died and walked off hand-in-hand, with the garden gate showing through them. Youngsters and simple-minded grownups followed the lives of their favorite stars on screen and off in the pages of movie magazines which obligingly told all. These paragons of the silver screen projected an image (to use modern jargon that would have been unintelligible in the thirties) that influenced everything. When, for example, in *It Happened One Night*, Clark Gable removed his shirt and was seen to wear nothing underneath, the men's underwear industry shivered.

During the thirties movie stars and their private lives replaced society people as idols of the masses. Mrs. Gilding and Mrs. Toplofty were simply not very exciting any more, not when there was Joan Crawford's next wedding to plan for or Franchot Tone's broken romance to worry about. The Depression prevented even those who managed to hold on to their money from spending lavishly for pleasure, either out of a sense of economy or a sense of appropriateness; it was almost embarrassing to be terribly rich when so many were terribly poor. They closed their great houses and moved to apartments. They entertained by giving small dinners in restaurants, where they began to meet and associate with stage and screen celebrities. It was the beginning of café society, later known as the Jet Set and, more recently, as the Beautiful People.

Very conservative members of the Oldname circle continued to avoid publicity, as they always had, guided by the principle that a gentleman is mentioned three times in the press during his lifetime: when he is born, when he marries, and when he dies. Henry Dwight Sedgwick, a Bostonian who wrote, in 1935, *In Praise of Gentlemen*, complained that the gentlemanly tradition in America had been wrecked by science, which "lifted democracy into the

Clark Gable shedding tradition and his shirt

saddle." Specialization, he said, had done away with the "completeness" of the gentleman. Gone was the well-bred dilettante who took style, taste, and good manners seriously and who "had rather read comedy than tragedy, and books about good fellows than subtle psychological analyses concerning characters one would fight shy of in life." "It appears that, in the present phase of our civilization, reticence in the matter of sex is to go the way of style, of manners, and a good riddance it is thought to be." "Equality loves company and is exasperated by an aristocratic aloofness." These changes were a shame, Mr. Sedgwick thought, for the life of society had always provided such "a pleasant diversion to the lookers-up."

"Bombing Civilian Populations"

Cleveland Amory, in *Who Killed Society?*, pinpoints the thirties as the time of society's doom. "Starting in the 1930's," he says, "with the obituary of the very word 'gentleman,' with the rise of Publi-ciety, with the Glamour Debutante No. 1's and the Poor Little Rich Girls, and perhaps above all with the change from the root basis of money, one is faced with a kind of all-embracing breakdown." Dixon Wecter, who wrote his admirable study *The Saga of American Society* in 1937, in the midst of the debacle, thought that there was a future for "true aristocracy" but perhaps not for "society" as it was then constituted. The world needed gentlemen, he thought, and would be poorer without them. As for society, it was the flimsy product of "industrialism, competition, insecurity, and [the] whirligig of quick riches today and poverty tomorrow. In this hasty exchange of identifications, society is the chevron worn on the sleeve rather than the inner grace." The word *snob*, Wecter pointed out, originally meant "a cobbler's helper, a person of low birth and breeding, and then came to signify a person ashamed of his low birth and breeding. That snobbery and eminent rank have become linked, at least in the popular mind, is an irony due largely to the mediation of society."

"War Exempt Sons of the Rich"

Snobbery is always with us in one form or another, but in the thirties it was beginning to be unacceptable to show it openly. For one thing, some of the erstwhile "best people" had lost their money. Their sons were working their way through college, perhaps waiting on tables. Their daughters were taking jobs, often in shops—thereby making the once much-scorned job of "little shopgirl" respectable and even desirable. There were many Gentiles who were snobbish to Jews, but the events in Germany were causing a reappraisal of such attitudes. Above all, the Depression had brought about an unprecedented social awareness. Poverty had always been in evidence, but now it was very close to home, even for those who were comfortably off. Former white-collar workers were selling apples on the street corners. Officers of failed banks were taking jobs as vacuum-cleaner salesmen or anything else they could get. A former President of the New York Stock Exchange, a Harvard man and socialite, was tried for grand larceny and sent to jail. Middle-class housewives gave their time to ladle out soup to long lines of hungry people, or to collect clothing for babies who had none. And these frightening developments were not happening in faraway countries nor were they confined to the poor sections of town. A good many long-time convictions were shaken: that it was a man's own fault if he failed to make good; that hard work was the key to success; and that nothing could defeat private enterprise and American know-how. The leading shaker of old convictions was Franklin D. Roosevelt, himself a Mr. Oldname, who was accused by his fellows of having deserted the traditions and principles of his class.

"Private Law and Order Leagues"

"Medals for Dishonor," designed by David Smith as a bitter antiwar protest, 1937–40

"Rosie the Riveter" at work on a B-17

The thirties are neatly bracketed in time between October, 1929, and September, 1939: the stock market crash and the declaration of war in Europe. The manners and morals peculiar to that decade were thrown into upheaval by a national emergency. Wars always change behavior patterns, but the Second World War brought deeper changes than any war before. It scooped up millions of people from every class and corner of the country, jumbled them up together and sent them all over the world under one unifying title: Americans. No longer were the top jobs reserved for the white Anglo-Saxon Protestants. As far as the white population was concerned, the war effort was thoroughly democratic. For Negroes, there was less discrimination than there had been in the First World War, and after 1944, the Navy, the Marines, and the Coast Guard were commissioning Negro officers. However, not until after the war was there more than token desegregation of the Armed Forces.

Some women went into military service and many worked for the war effort in civilian jobs; either way they were more on their own than ever and ready to improvise new rules of personal behavior. Going to work in war plants, they wore pants and did men's jobs. Army wives followed their husbands from camp to camp, showing unprecedented adaptability in living where they could and hobnobbing with all manner of fellow Americans. Women's fashions during wartime, with their square, heavily padded shoulders, projected an image of supercompetent womanhood.

For the third decade in a row, young people questioned the sex mores of their elders and looked for answers of their own. As Margaret Mead pointed out not long ago in a *Life* article, "We are always very poor at teaching the last 25 years of history." Anyone can see that things have changed since the war, but it is not easy to be sure which changes are significant and which are just the to-and-fro motion of the pendulum. "Swings between puritanism and license are as old as Methuselah," she continues. "The present change is really a very different one—having recognized the population explosion, society will no longer have to make women's reproductivity of prime importance. Once we have realized this, we free women to be people, and whether we free them to copulate oftener or with more partners is less relevant. . . . We are making an evolutionary change. This is just as important a change as the discovery of nuclear energy, and I think it is here to stay. But I wish people would realize what the change is. All this talk about who is sleeping with whom where is of relatively less importance."

Dr. Mead comments that as many families were disrupted by death fifty years ago as by divorce today, and that divorce should no more be considered indicative of failure than death. "Pretending marriage is for life was fine when people died young and vigorous men could bury three wives and put nice gravestones over all of them. . . . I think the longer people live and the more diverse their experience, the less likely it is that two people will stay married a lifetime. You see, if people get married at 20, they then have a reasonable expectation of being married for 50 years. The contemplation of 50 years together makes people less willing to tolerate an unsatisfactory marriage."

A Gallup Poll taken in 1968 in the United States and eleven other western countries asked the question: "Do you believe that life today is getting better or worse in terms of morals?" Americans were the most pessimistic. Seventy-eight percent thought morals were getting worse; 8 percent thought they were getting better; 12 percent saw no change; and 2 percent had no opinion. In

(Continued on Page 360)

Lake Forest: 1953

Suburbia U.S.A., as seen by James Morris. To the Englishman, the informal way of life at the end of a commuter line was one of the finest features of America.

The word "suburbia" has not acquired those overtones which taint it in England. In the hubbub of American urban life it is only common sense to live in a suburb. . . . Each evening at Lake Forest, when the club train pulls in, a most cheerful and well-acquainted group of businessmen emerges from its cushioned recesses, and parts with fond expressions of fraternity. . . . And

parked beside the line are the long polished rows of their limousines . . . a well-dressed wife at each wheel, an expectant child or two skipping about the seat, a huge lugubrious mastiff peering through the back window. . . . The wife in her black nylon looked very nice from the station platform, but inside the car there is a dauntingly purposeful air to her ensemble. . . . They need only run back and drop the children while he freshens up . . . and he is therefore able to step with scarcely a pause from club car to cocktails. . . . The evening is likely to be an agreeable one. The guests will find themselves in one of two kinds of houses: a comfortable and well-preserved little mansion built by some complacent plutocrat in the early days of the century, and having . . . an atmosphere if not actually horsy, at least distinctly doggy: or a house of uncompromising modernity, with mobiles floating about the drawing room, a hostess who keeps Abyssinian cats, and a host who talks about the G-factor of the roof. . . . There is a determined rejection of formality, a vestigial relic of frontier times or an inherited reaction (which they would fervently disclaim) against the imperial splendors of Europe. . . . It is the custom to serve the meal in the manner of a buffet. . . . Having received your portion, you must then dispose yourself about the house to eat it; and for some reason . . . there are not enough chairs to go round, so that the more girlish of the ladies, and the more resigned or flirtatious of the men, must sit on the carpet. I know of few less relaxing exercises than that of eating a plate of curried prawns with one hand, clutching the support of a neighboring chair leg with the other, trying to avoid destroying a priceless china dog with one's feet, and discussing the Meaning of Truth with one's companion. . . . There is always an encyclopedia in such a house as this; and the children, poor things, sometimes seemed to me to be weighed down with reference books and inducements to learning . . . for expertise is sacrosanct, the specialist is never doubted. . . . You can meet your thrusting self-made Americans in Lake Forest, proud embodiments of the old legend about office boy to high executive; but you can meet at least as many who will drop a hint about "the old place" in England, or assiduously preserve the faintly European accent they acquired at Harvard. . . . This tight little community . . . no longer feels the magnetic pull of the big city, nor the call of the land, but has evolved its own polished and intricate civilization. It has its failings . . . but it shares a grace and an easy style that is one of the more attractive American contributions to social progress.

Sweden, land of permissive sex, the figures were 52 percent "worse," 12 percent "better," 29 percent "no change," and 7 percent "no opinion."

Most Americans think immediately of sex when the word *morals* is mentioned, and many an immigrant is confronted with this national fixation when he applies for citizenship and is subjected to a battery of personal questions. Under the terms of the Immigration and Naturalization Act, "no person shall be regarded as . . . a person of good moral character," hence eligible for citizenship, who has committed adultery within five years of application. Homosexuals were, until recently, excluded under the medical classification of "psychopathic personality"; they are now refused for "sexual deviation," a sin of moral turpitude. The U. S. Customs regularly seizes "immoral articles," which can be anything from pornographic novels to contraceptive devices found in tourists' luggage.

Every state has its share of odd prohibitions, rarely enforced, which are holdovers from a more imaginative age: one of the most notorious is South Dakota's law against fornicating with a bird—a capital offense. Many states are intrepid enough to extend their moral jurisdiction even into the bedrooms of married couples, forbidding certain sexual acts. Laws are enforced more vigorously against individuals who are either unwilling or unable to live according to the community's standards in the areas of abortion, homosexuality, gambling, prostitution, alcoholism, and drug addiction, "crimes" that are considered by a large part of the medical and social professions to have causes and effects outside the province of the law. By treating these problems as crimes, we have only insured the underworld a monopoly on millions of dollars of irrepressible trade. The equation seems to be borne out in Europe: only in France and Italy, where comparable morality legislation exists, does organized crime operate on an American scale.

Another survey, this one made only in the United States, discovered that most adults think teen-agers have "less morals" and "less modesty" than they themselves did when teen-agers. Of a group of adolescents questioned along similar lines, 52 percent were critical of adult moral conduct, particularly in connection with drinking, adultery, and divorces. Teen-agers also criticize parents for putting too much pressure on them to get good grades and to be popular and successful.

Some mothers encourage boy-girl parties, with dancing and kissing games, for children in fifth grade. The chaperon still exists for most younger teen-agers, but remains as unobtrusive and permissive as possible, and sometime during the mid-teens is shown the door. The point at which the chaperon should give up seems to vary geographically. *Amy Vanderbilt's Complete Book of Etiquette* (1952) adroitly passes the buck to "the community and the customs of the child's group." It is a biological fact that children are reaching puberty earlier than in former generations; at the same time educational pressures prevent them from becoming self-sufficient until years later.

Harry Silverstein, a sociologist at New York's New School for Social Research, notes that "the more rapidly a society is changing, the more it will be true that parents and children will have been raised in different and, in increasing respects, uncompatible realities, so that each generation tends to see the other as out of touch with that part of the modern world that each likes to think of as the real world."

With the real world so hard to identify, it is small wonder that the spiritual

Children nowadays shed their innocence with their baby teeth. This ad pitches the superfluous to flat-chested Lolitas of nine and ten.

leaders are having difficulty in making religion a part of it. Whether or not our innate capacity for the spiritual life has diminished over the centuries is debatable. But certainly the early colonial churches had two important advantages over their modern counterparts—attendance was compulsory, and the church was the center of community life. Anyone who missed the double dose of church on Sunday or the "Great and Thursday" lecture had no television, movies, radio, or country club as an alternative. Today's churches and synagogues, fighting the competition, offer bingo, sewing groups, teen-age dances, fashion shows, sports programs, and nursery school care in an effort to draw the faithful. More significantly, many religious orders are changing the form of traditional services as well as their interpretation of traditional precepts. Thoughtful clergymen, nowadays, are more concerned with the immorality of violence, war, racial injustice, bigotry, and hatred than with urging a return to former codes of sexual behavior.

That people are still groping for a standard way of doing things, at least as far as *outward* behavior is concerned, is shown by the fact that publishers continue to bring out books of etiquette. At present there are forty books in print on general etiquette, fifty titles on etiquette for children and teenagers, and seven titles directed specifically to men. A volume called *Twixt Twelve and Twenty*, written by singing star Pat Boone (a wholesome fellow who finished college, does not smoke or drink, and is married to his original wife), has sold a million copies. Emily Post's *Etiquette*, now in its ninety-ninth printing, has sold over four million copies, and *Amy Vanderbilt's Complete Book of Etiquette* has exceeded two million.

However, these volumes apparently do not contain all the answers, for the public is turning to new oracles. Ann Landers, the syndicated advice-to-the-lovelorn columnist, will take on almost any question from trifling to cataclysmic (they are all cataclysmic to the questioners). In a typical column, she fielded the following queries: Should a young man who has fathered an illegitimate child mention it to his fiancée? (Answer: yes—"there is an important distinction between 'indiscretions' and live babies.") A second petitioner, who signed himself "Baffled," wanted to know what to do with prune pits when served stewed prunes. The patient Miss Landers came to his rescue: "Dear Baffled: I can't imagine what else you'd do with prune pits but put them on the plate. This should be done as quietly as possible. When a pit hits fine china or thin crystal it makes a pinging sound which creates attention. Maybe that's your problem."

Playboy magazine conducts a helpful column called The Playboy Advisor. J. T., of Akron, Ohio, who had perhaps thumbed vainly through Amy Vanderbilt or Pat Boone, writes, "My girlfriend and I plan to spend a week in New York City. We would like to share a hotel room, but I am not quite sure how to register. Is my name all that is required to make a hotel reservation, or is it necessary to play the game by using 'Mr. and Mrs.'?" Says *Playboy*, "It is unlawful to register falsely, so the safest approach is to reserve a single room for each of you. Once in your rooms, of course, you may visit each other without reservation." Like Ann Landers, *Playboy* stands ready to solve any behavior problem. J. A., of Arlington, Virginia, asks, "Please tell me the correct procedure for handling a tie that drops beneath the belt line. Should it be tucked into the pants or should it be left hanging out?" *Playboy*, with that comforting assurance that always distinguished Emily Post, and tactfully

To the D.A.R. ladies in Grant Wood's painting of 1932, revolution was something done once and for all by their Forefathers and Foremothers. But as these protest buttons show, the winds of change continue to howl.

overlooking the possibility that the writer may be around ten years old, responds: "Neither. Tied correctly, your tie should end just above your belt."

A man or boy who has trouble with his tie will not be thought strange in these times if he decides to throw away his ties and wear beads instead. With the beads he may wear a see-through shirt, flowered corduroy trousers, and green patent-leather shoes with silver buckles. His hair may be any length but certainly not crew-cut, and he may have a beard. None of this should seem alarming to anyone with a sense of history. The Edwardians dressed elaborately, if not so flamboyantly, and before the Victorian Age only Puritans, Quakers, and clergymen wore unadorned, dark clothing. George Washington was clean-shaven but long-haired, and during the last half of the nineteenth century gentlemen wore beads and sideburns and let their hair grow to the collar line. The aging, crew-cut school principal, bent on expelling long-haired students, might reflect that, historically speaking, he is the nonconformist, not the students. Long hair, however, is a 1960's symbol of rebellion, a declaration of independence, and the rebels have no wish to be told that they are historically run-of-the-mill.

A surprising development of the late sixties has been the burgeoning of a market for men's grooming aids. A decade ago there was no such thing as a face cream for men. Now there are nearly thirty to choose from, as well as countless busy beauty salons for men, offering facials, massages, manicures, pedicures, and hair styling and dyeing jobs. *Harper's Bazaar* has taken occasion to admire "The Frankly Beautiful New Young Gentleman," especially his "long, extremely tossable hair," which he brushes "with absorption." He also "chooses his shampoos with the gravity of a connoisseur, and scents himself with enormous care. . . . [He] seriously collects colognes, perfumes, powders, shave creams and shampoos. Tomorrow, almost surely, he will order unguents for his complexion, masks for his circulation, and—who knows?—makeup for his . . . beauty."

Women raid the men's shops, apparently not because they think the clothes are feminine, but because they like the masculine look. The look-alike fad, which may have started some years back when teen-age "steadies" wore matching sweaters, reached high fashion in 1968 when "unisex" fashions were unveiled at New York's most fashionable department stores. (This is not the first instance of a fashion starting far down in society and working its way to the top; England's "mod" clothes traveled the same route.) One designer recommended snakeskin jackets—red for girls, brown for men—and identical V-necked Argyle sweaters. Both sexes were encouraged to wind a long shiny purple scarf around their frankly beautiful necks.

Beautiful, it should be noted, is a word much overworked in the sixties. It can mean wonderful or nice or in any way pleasing, startling, or remarkable, which brings us to the startling, remarkable, and in some ways pleasing group known as the Beautiful People. "The Beautiful People Kick Up Their Heels," announces a newspaper headline, and we find a story about a theater party and supper dance "hosted" by Mrs. Charlotte Ford Niarchos and Mrs. John Mosler. It was as glittering an affair as those of the Gilded Age, but with two important differences: it was for the benefit of a charity (the Police Athletic League); and neither Mrs. Niarchos nor Mrs. Mosler picked up the tab. That was left for the Allied Chemical Company, "in exchange for the International set's efforts to make a soft new material called Touch socially acceptable."

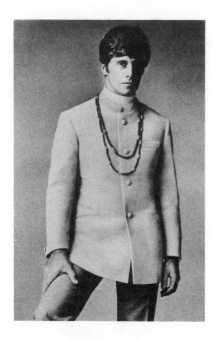

Traditionally somber male attire seems in for drastic changes: the Nehru jacket (top) evinces the trend toward elegant plumage. Designs for women have tended to the "less is more" philosophy, as shown by the flat-chested female mannequin above.

362

Some of the beautiful ladies at the party, including two Vanderbilts and Anne Ford Uzielli, paraded down a runway dressed in yards of "Touch." "Fun and fashion," concludes the reporter, "with plenty of charity for the conscience is the modern social formula for a perfect evening for beautiful people."

When the French Consul in New York gave a farewell dinner for a hundred and fifty "best friends and people who were nice to us," the guests were a typical beautiful mixture—social registrites, fashion designers, and people in the arts. *The New York Times* reported the party in the somewhat saucy style it had begun to use on its society pages, replacing its former straight delivery of the facts: " 'I'm trying Acapulco this year,' Mrs. [Robert] Scull announced, 'I think it will be nice for a change.' Mrs. Scull, who may or may not have known that the Aristotle Onassises are also thinking about Acapulco, usually goes to Barbados. Mrs. Scull's pink chiffon pants got a lot of attention. So did a pink and blue feather boa around her hips. 'I could never do that,' Mrs. Adam Gimbel said, looking at the boa. 'I can't go around with feathers.' "

Barbados, Acapulco, and the rest are commuter stops for the Beautiful, as well as for less beautiful but equally affluent members of today's Affluent Society. They travel far and often. They avoid ordinary tours, of course, but they may, for example, join a group of well-heeled art lovers for a look at the art treasures of the Soviet Union or the stone heads of Easter Island; or they may go bear-hunting in Alaska or hire a famous classics professor to show them Greece. Certain New Yorkers and Bostonians go back and forth to Bermuda every weekend. Angelenos make Acapulco a second home; Chicagoans spend their weekends skiing in Aspen.

Some of today's affluent consider it bad manners to spend ostentatiously and bad morals to stint on charitable donations. Before writing a check for a sable coat or a racing stallion there are those who make a point of writing another check for an equal amount, made out to a favorite charity. But most of the rich spend enthusiastically on a bewildering array of luxuries.

At Christmastime, the affluent man-or-woman-who-has-everything is usually given something he has not from one of the nation's expensive stores. Neiman-Marcus, in Dallas, is especially adept at supplying this sort of thing. In 1968, for example, it offered His and Her jaguars—his car for $5,559, her coat for $5,975. Another gift suggestion at Neiman-Marcus was a Jewel-of-the-Month: for $273,950, the store would deliver every month throughout 1969 a total of four bracelets, four pins, two rings, a watch, and a pair of earrings. Not to be outdone by Big D, New York's Abercrombie & Fitch offered a set of matched luggage covered in zebra for $2,300, and hand-tooled Italian backgammon sets for $1,000. Hammacher Schlemmer could provide a $1,250 music box complete with three chirping birds in a 24-inch gilded cage. Tiffany parted with all their sets of Flora Danica dessert plates, at $1,000 a dozen. Even Sears, Roebuck was bidding for the affluent trade: it advertised a white mink bathrobe for $4,500, plus postage.

Unlike the social monarchs of yesterday—Mrs. Astor and the rest—today's Beautiful People are little interested in family trees. Whether one's grandfather was a gentleman of leisure or a trash collector is a matter of indifference, provided one has charm, personality, *savoir-faire*, the tastes of the Beautiful, and the money to indulge them. As Jacques Barzun has pointed out, "the Fuller Brush man does not introduce himself as a Son of the War of 1812—ask any ten people what the Order of Cincinnati is. Americans may

Unisex fashions, often variations on the pants suit with grudging adaptations to his or her curves, offer a compromise. Fall 1968 gear for the female unigender appears above.

love getting together in costumed brotherhoods, but these impress the membership much more than the nation." Snob society is, in its own way, a costumed brotherhood, and it is important to its members to know the people who walk down the runway dressed in Touch. But it is not important to the nation at large.

The collapse of society as it used to be is a matter of little moment, but the collapse of morality as *it* used to be is a matter of continual concern. Judging by the many articles and books on the subject, we are like a hypochondriac who is constantly taking his own temperature. Or is it that articles about morality, particularly sexual morality, make good reading? Even mother-hen *Reader's Digest* scarcely lets a month go by without an article in which the word *sex* appears in the title — although readers who buy the magazine for prurient reasons will be disappointed: they will find little or nothing that could not have been printed thirty years ago.

Other popular magazines have made startling changes. For instance, *The Ladies' Home Journal*, once dedicated to family, kitchen, and sentimental fiction, now runs such treatises as "When Couples Fight About Extramarital Sex" (in the old days, no husbands, let alone wives, had affairs in the pages of *The Ladies' Home Journal*). *Cosmopolitan* appears to be aimed at the female counterpart of the *Playboy* reader — the swinger, single or married. A typical issue recently offered instructions on achieving an orgasm and an article on "Low-Fidelity Wives." The latter did not endorse adultery, exactly, but it did give us six examples of women who are making adultery work and who would not trade it for high fidelity. "They do not ask to be encouraged or approved of. Nor do they wish to be judged. All that these women, as well as the more conventional cheater . . . seem to be asking with their candor is tolerance, and perhaps our capacity to observe an unconventional way of life with an open mind."

Cosmopolitan has a recipe department, too, just as women's magazines always have — with the difference that its recipes are simple enough to leave a girl time for more amusing things. A breakfast menu suggests vodka and orange juice, scrambled eggs with slices of smoked salmon on the side, brioche from the deep freeze, and creamed spinach (Recipe: Cook one package frozen creamed spinach according to instructions on package). The only other thing that sets *Cosmopolitan's* cookery department somewhat apart is the illustration — an apparently naked young man and woman sitting up in bed and eating off trays. "MARRIED AT MIDNIGHT; BREAKFAST AT NOON," proclaims the caption. "Of course, you don't *have* to be newlywed to serve this scrumptious repast for two. We'll leave *that* up to you. . . . Finish off with plenty of steaming coffee . . . then back to beddybye again . . . ?"

The fascination of the public prints with the world of sex seems to be a characteristic of the late sixties and may be due to the recent demise of censorship. One of the most striking developments of the last thirty years has been the gradual axing of legal bans on what used to be identified as obscenity. In 1930 the Massachusetts courts sheltered the public from Dreiser's *An American Tragedy*, "even assuming great literary excellence, artistic worth and an impelling moral lesson in the story." In 1966 the Supreme Court held that the government could not suppress a book as obscene so long as it had merit as literature. "Hard-core pornography" is still subject to suppression, but the borderline is extremely vague, and, generally speaking, anything goes.

Protesting that body has overtaken soul as a measure of womanhood, militants march on Atlantic City and the Miss America show.

364

When the novelty of being able to say practically anything in print has subsided, many of today's books and magazines may begin to look as quaint and dated, in their way, as *Godey's Lady's Book.*

Says Charles Rembar, the lawyer who fought for *Lady Chatterley's Lover, Tropic of Cancer*, and *Fanny Hill*, "this is indeed a lip-licking, damp-palmed age. . . . But it will pass. It will pass because it is not the freedom itself, but the taboo it displaces, that sets the stage for prurience. . . . The truest definition of pornography requires that the act of reading itself be sinful, or illegal, or authority-defying, or at least sneaky. . . . The response cannot be the same when no book is forbidden. The long refusal to permit honest treatment of sexual subjects has conditioned a nation of voyeurs. As the courts move on their present path, they hustle pornography off the scene, a billy in its back.

"A change, I believe, is already observable. It is the grownups who provide most of the adolescent reaction. They grew up when it took a trip to Paris, or a pass to a locked library alcove, to read Henry Miller. It is they, and not their juniors, who are most likely to be aroused (to sexual response, or to moral indignation, or to both) by the sudden release of forbidden books. The younger generation is much less excited by the new freedom in literature—in both senses: it is less alarmed and it is less titillated."

Magazines like *Cosmopolitan* are aimed at that twentieth-century phenomenon, the woman on her own. Few unattached women now live with relatives. Houses are so small as to preclude the invasion of relatives without the cramping that would take us back to colonial days. The lone woman does not care to be a household drudge for a sister-in-law, nor does the sister-in-law want her taking up space around the house, especially since household mechanization has reduced her usefulness. Elderly parents, aunts, and uncles are also unwanted, not only because they are space-consuming but also because it is generally feared that they will try to impose their superannuated manners and morals on the family. That particular problem has been with us since colonial times, but in our century, full of radical changes even within generations, it has become critical.

The median age of the United States population in 1968 was 27.7 years. There were nearly nineteen million people over 65, and life expectancy had increased since 1900 from 48 to 75 for women and from 46 to 68 for men. A new kind of community has appeared in the land: the "retirement village." Most of these real estate ventures are in California, Florida, or Arizona, where the climate is benign, but they are also scattered throughout the nation. They have enticing names like Leisure Town, Country Club Homes, Sun City, and Dreamland Villa. Their ground rules vary, but most sell small apartments or houses to persons over fifty or so; prohibit children except as short-term visitors, and provide a galaxy of recreational activities, from checkers to woodcraft.

Most retirement villages guarantee to look after the resident for the rest of his days—but those who want to live in such settlements had better not wait too long, for they want elderly people who are not *very* elderly and are in good health. "You can enjoy relaxed country club living amidst beautiful lawns and gardens with complete privacy, or bloom like a rose among the companionship and activities and love you will find offered to you," says one announcement. However, "Residents must be reasonably healthy and able to take care of themselves. Wheel chair and blind persons must be accompanied by spouse

Leisure, a commodity that retired folk find a mixed blessing, is made productive in a woodworking shop (above) and in an adult education class (below).

Proclaiming 1960's mores bank-rupt, flower children do their own thing: the boy celebrates Love at a New York Be-In; the girl has just exchanged wedding vows in a California grove.

. . . . No dogs or cats are allowed. . . . Tenants are permitted overnight visitors, however their visit must be short and not prolonged. . . . Among the activities are the Busy Bee Sewing Club, Bridge Club, Spanish Class, Shuffleboard, Cards, Chess, Dominoes, Checkers, Bingo, Arts and Crafts, Fashion and Variety Shows, Dancing every Saturday night, and special events such as birthdays, Christmas, New Years, Valentine, Hawaiian luaus and Halloween Parties."

Thus, cut off from his family, the "senior citizen" heads for the grave on his own but solaced by all the devices of the New Leisure, and maintaining at all costs the appearance of peppy youthfulness. "Sun City isn't a town of tottering invalids," one retirement village resident is quoted as saying. "Whenever we swim or play golf with friends here, it's just as lively as being with our two daughters and sons-in-law."

In the brightly colored brochures of retirement villages, as well as in the magazine *Modern Maturity*, a publication of the American Association of Retired Persons, there is curiously little said about what becomes of the tottering invalids. (They totter off to nursing homes.) Instead, the emphasis is on a future of perpetual fun and industry. Among the feature articles in a recent issue of *Modern Maturity*, one could read "How to Work After Retirement," "Birthdays Don't Measure Age," "Instant Teeth," "New Hope for Older People," and "They're All Over 100." The senior citizen needs a sizable chunk of cash in order to live in one of the really fun-filled retirement villages; and in some cases, he is contracted to make the management heirs to all that remains of his worldly goods.

The gathering of old people into a sort of nonstop summer camp is indeed something new in our history. Gatherings of hippies, equally detached from the main social body though at the opposite extreme in outlook, attract a great deal more attention but are not really so new a story. We have had Bohemians before and we have had hobo and utopian communities before. Bennett Berger, a sociologist, has pointed out that the Greenwich Village Bohemians of the twenties and today's hippie communities are similar in their devotion to the importance of self-expression, the ideas of paganism, liberty, and female equality, and the love of the exotic. Hippiedom just adds a little mysticism, astrology, anarchism, and drug-taking. Tourists like to drive through the parts of town where hippies live, mostly to shake heads and rail against them—or could it be that the rebels appeal to the secret part of everyone's being that sometimes wants to run away from it all?

Hippies, believing that society has failed, have opted out. Another group of young people, the campus activists, also believe that society has failed, but they intend to browbeat their fellow men into recognizing the failures and correcting them. The position of the members of the New Left—that civil disobedience, riots, and disrupting demonstrations are morally justified—is not new. The Daughters of the American Revolution might reflect that their ancestors responded to the same moral imperative in 1776.

The 1960's breed of college youth poses some interesting problems on the sexual frontiers, too. First it was girls in boys' rooms between certain hours and with doors open. Then the trysting hours were lengthened and the doors closed to "the thickness of a book" (matchbooks were instantly put to use). Now many universities contemplate coed dormitories. "Colleges are supposed to educate, not serve as custodial institutions for students," said a

Harvard dean not long ago. And he quoted the British educator Sir John Wolfenden: "Schoolmasters and parents exist to be grown out of." The Midwest lags behind the two coasts in embracing this point of view. A Bloomington, Indiana, judge recently expressed the fear that Indiana University's new decision allowing men and women to visit each other's dormitory rooms would mean that taxpayers were "maintaining a free love nest." He thought "people under 21 should be subjected to some restraint to control their natural impulses."

Equally dismaying to old grads is the decline in the membership of Greek-letter fraternities. At some colleges, they have been obliged to close their chapters. Some, now willing to open their rolls to Jewish or Negro members, often cannot find any young men at all who will join. At Berkeley, in 1968, Phi Delta Theta sent invitations to 209 prospects and failed to pledge even one. "We were just looking for the kind of guys who'd fit in with the rest of us—the kind of fellow you'd do business with later," the chapter's president wistfully told a *New York Times* interviewer. The *Times* continued, "His attitude was reminiscent of the thirties, when there were some 75 hell-raising Phi Delts in the big house that is being stripped of furniture. It includes dozens of chairs carved with the Greek letters of the fraternity and a great moose head that decorated the living room. . . . The moose head was the gift of alumnus William R. Hearst, Jr., and pledges were required to pray to it."

The counterparts of the young men who thirty years ago would have rejoiced to be allowed inside the Phi Delt house and happy to pray to the moose are now "other directed." They may be student activists or involved in community projects or simply scornful of old-fashioned, rowdy fraternity life in general. As for being "the kind of fellow you'd do business with," many of them do not plan to do business at all, at least not in the foreseeable future. They are off to the Peace Corps, Vista, or other helpful endeavors, or they plan years of graduate study, or they are headed for the professions. Sixty-eight of Harvard's 1,134-man graduating class of 1968, for example, went directly into business.

Contrariwise, the trend of the last two decades has been to send business-men back to learning. Seminars for business executives would astonish George Babbitt and his friends, but those at Colorado's Aspen Institute for Humanistic Studies have been well attended since they began in 1949. A man's company pays about $900 for him to attend two weeks of lectures that call for delving into Socrates, Locke, Thoreau, Marx, Jefferson, Freud, and other thinkers not generally encountered in the business world.

Not only business executives are going back to school these days, but housewives, grandmothers, and illiterate adults. Underprivileged children under kindergarten age are starting school early. "The popular passion of Americans is not politics, baseball, money or material things," Eric Sevareid wrote in a *Look* article. "It is education. Education is now our biggest industry, involving more people even than national defense. The percentage of children in kindergarten has doubled in a rather short period; the percentage of youth in college climbs steeply upward. Today, even a Negro boy in the South has a better statistical chance of getting into college than an English youth. And there are about 44 million full- and part-time *adult* students pursuing some kind of formalized learning on their own! Intelligent foreigners nearly everywhere understand the mountainous meaning of all this for the

Youth in search of a more socially constructive means to express their disaffection with the times can respond to posters like these for the Peace Corps and Vista

world as well as for America. They know that much of the world will be transformed in the American image, culturally if not politically."

So the handful of colonies that turned their backs on the world three centuries ago have ended by dominating that world. It was certainly never their intention, and even now few Americans are interested in actively maintaining the role of top dog. Nevertheless, the American way of life, spread by movies and books and by American troops, industries, and government agencies abroad, is all-pervasive. You can drink Coca-Cola in the Sahara, Bloody Marys in Bangkok, and American coffee on a tea plantation in Ceylon—and in any of these places the waiter will probably say "okay" to you.

Pride of race—one of the healthiest expressions of the Negro revolution—is manifest in a child's banner.

The stay-at-home American is not likely to be conscious of the Americanization of the world, and is more apt to think, looking around him, that the world has taken over America. Thirty years ago the average Midwesterner had never heard of pizza, sukiyaki, or South African lobster tails. He had never seen a foreign car, a Vietnamese, or a reproduction of Van Gogh's "Sunflowers." It would have surprised him to see teak furniture in a neighbor's living room, let alone African tribal masks on the walls, or Thai silk at the windows. Now such former exotica are taken for granted.

As we have seen, twentieth-century America is especially notable for its sharpened social conscience. But if this conscience, both private and governmental, is now greater, so is the necessity. The poor no longer stay in their slums and behave docilely. No longer is it possible to walk along many city streets at night without fear of violence, as Jacob Riis said was possible in the 1890's. At the top of the modern poor man's list of absolute essentials is a TV set; and once he sees what the affluent society is up to, he is no longer resigned to his lot. It is clear to him, judging by the ads and programs he looks at daily, that he is being left out of what millions of his fellow citizens take for granted. "We spend as much for chewing gum as for model cities," said Howard Samuels, Undersecretary of Commerce in the Johnson Administration. "We spend as much for hair dye as for grants to urban mass transit. We spend as much for pet food as on food stamps for the poor. We spend more for tobacco than government at all levels spends on higher education. We spend $300 million for jewelry, and quarrel over $10 million for the Teachers Corps."

In the days before mass communication, especially before television, the social imbalance may have been greater but it was not so obvious. The communications revolution, Eric Sevareid indicates, "brings out every social evil, every human tragedy and conflict immediately and intimately within everyone's ken." The Negro revolution is really just begun, and the woman's revolution is not yet ended. It is small wonder, therefore, that a manners and morals revolution is going on at the same time.

Colonel Frank Borman, on his return from whirling around the moon, said to a world that was ready to make him a hero, "Thousands of people made this possible. I guess you could say we're just proud to be part of this great achievement." In one sense, this was the organization man talking—a phenomenon of the twentieth century. But in another, more significant way, Colonel Borman was showing simple, undated good manners. According to the credo of *The Compleat Gentleman*, modesty and *noblesse oblige* are becoming to the powerful. The old Bostonian Henry Sedgwick, who feared that there would be no more gentlemen now that "science is in the saddle," would be pleased to know that man is taking good manners with him into space.

A World Gone Mod

In a drama that has become a commonplace of the twentieth century, two generations, two opposing systems of behavior, confront each other coldly at Paul Sample's "Church Supper." The prodigal daughter has been changed by life in the larger world—and the old folks who have remained at home regard her risen skirts as a sure sign of fallen morals.

COLLECTION OF DICK LEMEN

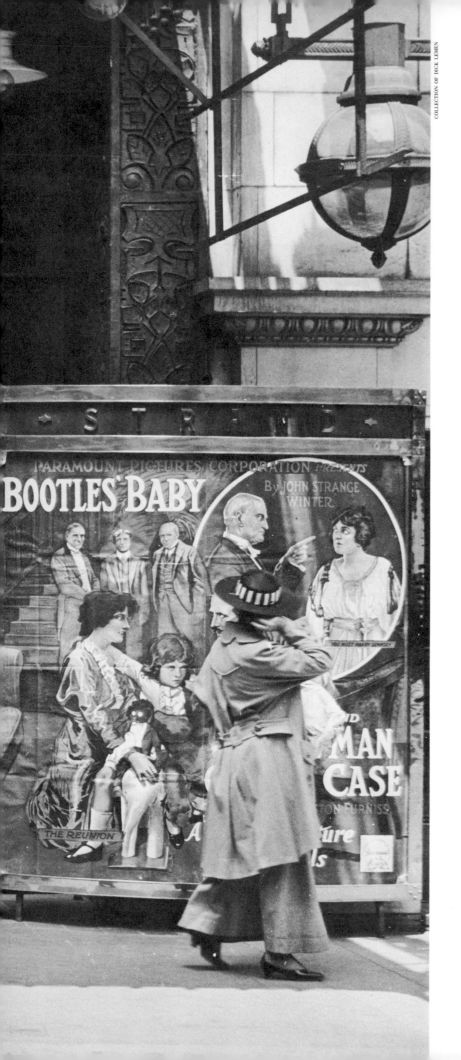

"Sheik" Rudolph Valentino

"It" girl Clara Bow

Mass Media

Motion pictures and radio brought the twentieth century to small-town U.S.A. Merely by turning on receivers, citizens tuned in on city music, speech, and manners. The message was seldom deep, but it implanted in listeners a certain sophistication, group identity, and susceptibility to slogans. When the movies at left were made, censors allowed only thirty-six seconds of film per kiss. By the late 1920's, sex appeal, or "It," was flaunted in scenes of "petting parties in the purple dawn" by stars like Valentino and Clara Bow. "It" affected morals. Said one teenager: "Pictures with hot love-making make boys and girls want to go off somewhere."

KING'S HIGHWAY ELEMENTARY SCHOOL, WESTPORT, CONNECTICUT

*The movie world of 1937 was populated with the idealized stars and
cartoon characters of John Steuart Curry's dreamscape above.*

Baring a shocking amount of anatomy for 1920, winner and runners-up at a California beauty contest pose nervously.

A free spirit tries her wings in the year 1919.

The New Woman

The metamorphosis of the sweet young thing into a hard-boiled, hell-raising "new woman" was all but completed during World War I. Beyond earshot of mother's moral dicta, the American girl serving in Europe adopted a live-for-the-moment code of conduct. Passion and excitement were deemed more than compensation for the impermanence of such liasons. Labor shortages at home gave the weaker sex man-sized jobs in factories and civil service, and "a monstrous regiment of women," as one broker put it, even invaded the stock market. After receiving the vote in 1920, females also became people politically. Though a few militants, not satisfied with mere equality, clamored for an end to "humiliating sex," the flapper style of life offered a more viable alternative to most. Flat-chested, lanky, hipless, and carefree, the new breed of playmate was willing to do anything on a dare. Red-hot babies swore blue streaks and revelled in the disapproving glances of the older generations. According to one *Harper's Monthly* writer, the flapper's very unflappability, her "immunity to the sensation of 'recoil with painful astonishment' is the mark of our civilization."

Wearing mannish uniforms, these intrepid World War I army nurses appear to be a formidable match for any foe.

COLLECTION OF JEAN LIPMAN

Making Whoopee

Artists play hosts to a murmuration of models in Wood Gaylor's uninhibited recollection of "Bob's Party Number One," 1918. The scene is New York's Greenwich Village, which, since the turn of the century, has been a mecca for America's artistic and social rebels. Two of Gaylor's friends, posing for the occasion as a sultan and his wife, are entertaining the crowd with a mock competition for new harem talent, and the girls have joined in with the sort of all-out cooperation that made their flaming generation notorious.

CULVER PICTURES

A champion goldfish gulper demonstrates his knack.

Ralph Waldo Emerson's observation that "Each age has its own follies, as its majority is made up of foolish young people," might well be applied to the 1920's and 1930's. At a time when everything had seemingly been thought of, said, and done, the emotionally jaded "lost generation" lusted after novelty per se. Of the plethora of passing fancies, few had any utility, social value, or sense; most were wacky, worthless, and harmless. Now broadcasted across the nation within a matter of hours, fads-of-the-moment enjoyed a dizzying but brief popularity, then palled on a mercurial public, and vanished as quickly as they had arisen. Much of the foolishness was commercially inspired. Flagpole sitters, for example, were often sponsored by movie theaters, hotels, and resorts. When a Baltimore boy came down from a ten-day, ten-hour, and ten-minute vigil atop Old Glory's standard, the mayor greeted the lad and gushed that he symbolized "the pioneer spirit of early America." Publicizing National Doughnut Week, Shipwreck Kelly even ate thirteen sinkers while standing on his head on a plank perched atop a skyscraper. The forefathers, whose own amusements were inextricably

Begun in fun, marathon dancing developed into one of the more macabre fads of the dizzy era. With occasional fifteen-minute breaks for naps and massage, couples like those at left shuffled for days and miles in search of prize money.

Feats
of
Foolishness

allied with duty, must have turned in their graves. During the Depression, the lure of prizes inspired people with spare time to compete in rocking-chair derbies, kissathons, and non-stop talking, radio-listening, and hand-holding competitions. The dance marathon was the most enduring of the endurance tests. Rules at fallen-arch spectaculars required only that entrants keep moving—the awake half of a team was permitted to "lug" a somnambulant partner around. Though June Havoc broke all records in 1934 by shuffling for 3,600 hours on a dance floor, other contenders did not fare as well. Some collapsed from exhaustion and died. The marathon madness began to wane after doctors warned that it caused a host of heart, nerve, and foot afflictions, and newspapers vented this sort of opprobrium: "No anthropoid ape could possibly have had descendants that could display such hopeless idiocy." People did anything for publicity: a man pushed a peanut up Pike's Peak; thousands of goldfish slid into collegiate stomachs; students also munched on magazines and records. Nunnally Johnson reckoned the nation: "first in war, first in peace, first in . . . peanut pushing."

Shipwreck Kelly, who proudly proclaimed himself "The Luckiest Fool Alive," parlayed his acrophilia into a career as flagpole sitter. In a rare down-to-earth demonstration of his act (above) he lends a little glamour to the sale of used cars.

THE MATING GAME ends and begins at the altar; no sooner have vows been made than new alliances form and partners switch.

Marriage Go-round

'"Till death do us part" had become so meaningless by the late twenties that one marriage in six ended in divorce. Scoffing at Victorian ideals like "marital fidelity" and "mutual esteem," the emancipated flapper was unlikely to stick with an incompatible mate — even for the sake of the children. And the divorcée soon discovered that her aura of scarlet could be even more alluring to men than virgin innocence. As Anne Harriet Fish's cartoons of 1920 suggest, those who failed at marriage the first time could try again and again.

A FIRST DIVORCE is a momentous occasion for the girl who regains her freedom and dreams of being a blushing bride a second time.

GETTING UNHITCHED has its hitches in tedious residence laws which may impede the progress of a diligent husband collector.

THE RENO SPECIAL does a thriving business providing express trains to the land of short-order divorce. Castoff husbands bid their wives mixed farewells at the railroad station.

AFTER THE HONEYMOON the groom is introduced to his bride's repertoire of ex-spouses and boyfriends, giving him the illusion that they are all members of one big happy family.

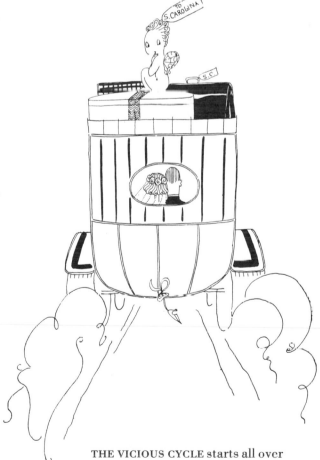

THE VICIOUS CYCLE starts all over with the newlyweds rolling off to their honeymoon; back home, divorce lawyers wait confidently.

In the
Best Cellars

The Eighteenth Amendment and the Volstead Act of 1919, designed to enforce prohibition, only succeeded in making drinking one of the more fashionable ways to demonstrate one's modernity. And, for the first time in the country's history, a large minority of Americans openly defied the Constitution. Lawbreakers used no small amount of ingenuity to circumvent the ban on booze: hoodlums conducted a billion-dollar business supplying bootleg liquor from foreign ports or domestic stills, to be, as Walter Lippmann put it, "consumed by

the flower of American manhood and womanhood"; supposedly "nice" girls got "squiffy," "spifflicated," or "fried to the hat" on the contents of their escorts' hip flasks; and, ordinary middle-class folk brewed bathtub gin, bought "medicinal" alcohol from cooperative druggists, and sipped sacramental wines. Though prohibition temporarily closed an old-time male sanctuary—the corner saloon—it spawned places like the speakeasy painted by Ben Shahn (below), where the drinks as well as the company were mixed. Admittance to these clandestine cabarets was limited to customers who could whisper the right password or present a membership card. Police surveillance became notoriously lax—especially after the customary payoffs—and, in some cities, cops were even so obliging as to inform visitors of the whereabouts of the nearest club. Against such organized resistance, the government's fifteen hundred "hooch-hounds" found enforcing the law impossible; and the nation, convinced that this aspect of morality could not be legislated, gave in to the "wets" in 1933.

MUSEUM OF THE CITY OF NEW YORK

Capital Criminals

Americans' adamant refusal to abide by prohibition in the 1920's bred a disrespect for all law. Underworld entrepreneurs catering to the common man's uncurbable appetites for liquor, gambling, and sex, not only were tolerated by the general public, but were protected and condoned. In a gaudy age which glorified bravado, heroes were as likely to be bank robbers performing daring auto getaways as warriors, athletes, or matinee idols. People lapped up tabloid accounts of their favorite mobsters, who represented adventure, romance, and in brief, everything they themselves would not dare do. Sometimes, however, incidences of crime became too much, even for the most bloodthirsty citizens. Mafia "tough guys," often of Sicilian extraction, caused fear and trembling in many a small businessman by demanding exorbitant fees in return for "protection." Rival gangs jealously guarded their urban fiefdoms, and when one encroached on another's territory a battle was inevitable. In Chicago alone, during the decade, there were some five hundred unsolved gangland slayings, climaxed by the celebrated St. Valentine's Day Massacre of 1929; seven of Al Capone's enemies were wiped out at once. Years later, when a reporter questioned the erstwhile "Public Enemy Number One" about his life of crime, Capone retorted: "The very guys that make my trade good are the ones that yell the loudest. . . . They talk about me not being on the legitimate. Why . . . nobody's on the legit, when it comes down to cases."

Bonnie Parker and Clyde Barrow captured Midwesterners' imaginations in the thirties. The outlaws seemed to be "just ordinary folks" hit by the Depression, who made a livelihood robbing villains of the time—bankers. To promote their gunslinging reputation, the publicity-hungry pair photographed each other in jest, and sent the pictures (left) to newspapers.

BOTH: BROWN BROTHERS

WHITNEY MUSEUM OF AMERICAN ART

The demise of a gangster could usually be attributed to other than natural causes. In 1924 former choirboy gone bad, Dion O'Banion, was murdered by rivals, who then magnanimously gave him a $100,000 send-off, the likes of which Chicago had never seen. Forty thousand of the curious visited the body, lying in state in a bronze and solid gold bier and surrounded by twenty-six truckloads of flowers, including one bouquet "from Al." Jack Levine, in his painting above, captures the garishness and simulated grief of a typical gangster funeral.

The Iconoclast
And the Traditionalist

H. L. MENCKEN was applauded by *Vanity Fair* in 1921 "because he has for years been almost our only bold assailant of the national Puritanism." Mencken's assaults were directed not only at Puritanism ("the haunting fear that someone, somewhere, may be happy"), but at the middle class ("the booboisie"), love ("a state of perceptual anesthesia"), the gentleman ("one who never strikes a woman without provocation"), morality ("the theory that every human act must be either right or wrong, and that 99% of them are wrong"), immorality ("the morality of those who are having a better time"), and every other phase of human behavior. In the more than thirty years that he ruled the national scene as writer, editor, and social critic, Mencken considered everyone and everything fair game. Democracy was to him "the theory that the common people know what they want, and deserve to get it good and hard"; the politician, "any man with influence enough to get his old mother a job as charwoman in the City Hall." But his main attacks were launched against the "sound American"—the "one who has put out of his mind all doubts and questionings, and who accepts instantly, and as incontrovertible gospel, the whole body of official doctrine of his day, whatever it may be. . . ." As the revolution of the twenties gained ground, Mencken looked around at girls. "I do not object to this New Freedom on moral grounds," he said, "but on purely esthetic grounds. . . . If women, continuing their present tendency to its logical goal, end by going stark naked, there will be no more poets and painters, but only dermatologists." And yet there was something praiseworthy in this "charming young creature": "there is music in her laugh. She is youth, she is hope, she is wisdom."

EMILY POST finally had to admit that "no rule of etiquette is of less importance than which fork we use," but she spent a lifetime answering that question for a nation of doubtful diners. Born to wealth and social position in 1873, Mrs. Post's name became synonymous with correct social behavior when her first book of etiquette appeared in 1922. *The Blue Book* was full of those "sign-posts by which we are guided to the goal of good taste" for every social occasion. What, for instance, should one do if invited by the Kindharts to spend a weekend "roughing it" at their Mountain Summit Camp? First, "do not bring a maid"; second, "do not 'dress' for dinner, that is, not in evening clothes"; third, but most important, remember "that well-bred people never deteriorate in manner." For the unsure host holding court at Great Estates or Golden Hall, Mrs. Post left no detail to chance. "You receive your guests with a smile, no matter how inconvenient. . . . Every bedroom has a set of breakfast china to match it. But it is far better to send a complete set of blue china to a rose-colored room than a rose set that has pieces missing. . . . A comforting adjunct to a bathroom that is given to a woman is a hot water bottle. . . ." In a well-appointed guest room, "there should be a candle and a box of matches . . . a palm leaf fan, and . . . a fly killer." The visitor, too, needed guidance. "You must learn as it were not to notice if hot soup is poured down your back. . . . The perfect guest not only tries to wear becoming clothes but tries to put on an equally becoming mental attitude." And one must never forget that "behavior is precisely the same whether at Great Estates or in camp. A gentleman may be in his shirt sleeves actually, but he never gets into shirt sleeves mentally."

Anyone who presumes to advise others on proper social behavior is bound to be more honored than loved. In this caricature for a 1933 issue of Vanity Fair, Miguel Covarrubias *takes a sly—if imaginary—look at the secret side of Mrs. Emily Post.*

In Everett Shinn's drawing of a breadline (above), former businessmen, forced to abandon class distinctions, queue up with vagrants. Conflict between labor and management explodes again in Philip Evergood's 1937 scene of a clash (below).

The Nation's Dispossessed

Even before the Panic of 1929, the American Dream had become a nightmare for millions of people. Rapid industrialization early in the century created a booming economy which provided "pie in the sky" for the middle classes. However, there was only a meager slice for unskilled laborers, pushed to the bottom of the pay scale, and farmers, forced off the land by the high cost of mechanization. Many of them sought a remedy for capitalism's abuses. The Industrial Workers of the World, founded in 1905 on the premise that the "working class and employing class have nothing in common," promised to "bring to birth the new world from the ashes of the old." A classless Utopia never came about, but the union improved the lot of its members and introduced nonviolent tactics, still used by protest groups. "Wobblies" staged sit-down strikes and mass rallies; pickets paraded to tunes from their *Little Red Songbook*; and slowdowns and acts of sabotage humbled many a boss. Though fear of being fired might inhibit a securely settled man from unionizing, Wobbly agitation gained special strength among the nomadic workers of the West. The hobo who beat his way on freight trains from job to job lived a life in contempt of most of society's bourgeois conventions. He worked variously as *pearl diver* (dishwasher), *flunkey* (cookhouse helper), *sewer hog* (ditchdigger), lumberjack, and harvest hand. Other transients tipped him off about the police, panhandling prospects, and local wages by a sort of hieroglyphic code scratched on station walls. During the height of the Depression, when one in four workers was unemployed, hundreds of thousands of down-and-outs joined the floating fraternity. The Okies fled their dust bowl for California in tin lizzies resembling junk yards on wheels. Upon arriving, they discovered that the natives were less than friendly; border patrols turned away families with under $50. As more of the dispossessed took to the road out of necessity, the romance and wanderlust popularly associated with migrant life faded. A woman hitchhiker summed up the plight of practically everybody: "The country's in an uproar now—it's in bad shape.... Do you reckon I'd be out on the highway if I had it good at home?"

Seasonal workers, like the bindle stiffs *above, personified American restlessness. In the nomad hierarchy, these hobos outranked* tramps, *who wandered and mooched, and* bums, *who wandered and drank. Between jobs, hobos camped in* jungles, *where they shared* grub *and* java, *and slept on the ground under* California blankets *(newspapers).*

Search For Self

CULVER PICTURES

MICHAEL ALEXANDER

When Sigmund Freud introduced psychoanalysis to "prudish America" in 1909, he hastened the demise of Victorianism. People erroneously interpreted his Rx for mental health as a license for licence. Self-control was soon considered not only obsolete, but harmful, and "Puritanism" became synonymous with personal restraint. By the 1920's, psychiatry was a national mania, along with mah-jongg and contract bridge. The maladjusted flocked to therapists. Volumes were written: a novel was praised for its "phallic candour"; a Scott Fitzgerald heroine reflected, "I'm hipped on Freud and all that, but it's rotten that every bit of *real* love . . . is 99% passion and one little *soupçon* of jealousy"; and, the *Psychology of Golf*, the *Psychology of Selling Life Insurance*, and Sears, Roebuck's *Ten Thousand Dreams Interpreted*, were big sellers. Cocktail conversations reverberated with "libidos," "Oedipus complexes," and "suppressed desires." Parents learned that children masturbated and experienced "sibling rivalry," and they allowed their darlings to blossom uninhibited at progressive schools. By the 1960's, with the nation's neuroses multiplying and American youth virtually uncontrollable, in their parents' estimation, the question was not whether Freud had been a fraud, but whether psychiatry could cope with the challenges.

388

The psychotherapy practiced at California's Esalen Institute helps people find meaning and even joy in the anxiety-ridden modern world. To awaken dulled senses and heighten self-awareness, participants shed roles and clothing, as evidenced in the photograph above.

389

Credits

The editors wish to express their deep gratitude to the institutions and individuals mentioned below for providing pictorial material and for supplying information and advice.

American Antiquarian Society, Worcester
  James E. Mooney

Booknoll Farm, Hopewell, New Jersey
  Elizabeth Woodburn

Collection of Emily Crane Chadbourne
  Dr. Margaret C.-L. Gildea, St. Louis
  Leo H. Bombard, Stone Ridge, New York

Colonial Williamsburg
  Hugh DeSamper

Leslie Dorsey, Union City, New Jersey

Free Library of Philadelphia
  Ellen Shaffer
  Robert F. Looney

Collection of Edgar William and Bernice Chrysler Garbisch, New York
  Clifford W. Schaefer

Historical Society of Pennsylvania, Philadelphia
  Nicholas B. Wainright
  John D. Kilbourne

James J. Keillor, Wading River, New York

Kennedy Galleries, New York
  Maria Naylor

Library Company of Philadelphia
  Edwin Wolf

Library of Congress, Washington, D.C.
  Virginia Daiker
  Milton Kaplan
  Mrs. Renata Shaw

Fred and Jo Mazzulla, Denver

Metropolitan Museum of Art, New York
  Margaret Nolan
  Harriet Cooper

Museum of American Folk Art, New York
  Mary Black

Museum of the City of New York
  A. K. Baragwanath
  Mrs. Henriette Beal
  Charlotte La Rue

New York Civil Liberties Union
  Burt Neuborne, Staff Counsel

New-York Historical Society
  Wilson G. Duprey
  Martin Leifer

New York Public Library
  Astor, Lenox, and Tilden Foundations
  Lewis Stark
  Mrs. Maud D. Cole
  Mrs. Philomena C. Houlihan
  Elizabeth Roth

Oneida Community Historical Committee, Oneida, New York
  Mrs. Miles E. Robertson
  Mrs. Leslie P. Stone

Smithsonian Institution, Washington, D.C.
  Anne Serio

Henry Francis du Pont Winterthur Museum, Winterthur, Delaware
  Ian M. G. Quimby

Mr. and Mrs. Eugene Van Wye, Johnston, Rhode Island

Yale University Art Gallery
  Caroline Rollins
  Mrs. William Nary

Grateful acknowledgment is made for permission to quote from the following works:

Calhoun, Arthur, *A Social History of the American Family*, Vols. I, II, and III. Copyright 1945 by Arthur W. Calhoun. Published by Barnes & Noble, Inc., New York.

Fitzgerald, F. Scott, *The Crack Up*. Copyright 1945, New Directions Publishing Corp., N.Y.

Furnas, Calista H., "Breakers Ahead." Published in *The Earlhamite*, November, 1888, by Earlham College, Richmond, Indiana.

Handlin, Oscar, ed., *This Was America*. Copyright 1949 by the President and Fellows of Harvard College. Published by Harvard University Press, Cambridge.

Morris, James, *As I Saw the U.S.A.* Copyright © 1956 by Pantheon Books, a division of Random House, Inc., New York.

Rembar, Charles, *The End of Obscenity*. Copyright © 1968 by Random House, Inc., N.Y.

Schlesinger, Arthur M., Sr., *The Rise of the City, 1878–1898*. Copyright 1933 by the Macmillan Company, New York.

Sullivan, Mark, *Our Times*, Vols. I, III, and IV. Copyright 1926 by Charles Scribner's Sons, New York.

Tryon, Warren S., ed., *A Mirror for Americans*. Copyright 1952 by University of Chicago Press.

Wecter, Dixon, *The Saga of American Society*. Copyright 1937, Charles Scribner's Sons, N.Y.

The following subjects appear as illustrations to the City Portraits:

JAMESTOWN: reconstruction of the 1607 settlement, by John Hull; ALBANY: house of the Dutch Governor, 1750; PHILADELPHIA: Independence Hall, from a 1777 map; BOSTON: the Old State House in 1801, from a painting by J. M. Marston; NATCHEZ: the steamboat *Natchez* in 1862; WASHINGTON: the Capitol, photographed by W. F. Langenheim in 1850; NEW YORK: the state seal, engraved by George E. Perine in 1887; CHEYENNE: U.S. cavalryman by Frederic Remington, 1888; SALT LAKE CITY: architect Truman O. Ancell's plan for Mormon Temple, rendered by W. Ward; NEW ORLEANS: costumed figures at Mardi Gras in 1875; CHICAGO: Marine Café, from the World's Columbia Exposition, 1893; LAKE FOREST: detail from "Cocktail Party," by John Koch.

The following is a list of credits for text pictures. Page numbers appear in boldface type.

18 Thomas, *A Little Pretty Pocket Book*, 1787, Free Library of Philadelphia, Rosenbach Collection **19** (top) Princeton University Library, Sinclair Hamilton Collection, (bottom) Bunyan, *The Pilgrim's Progress*, Part II, 1744, Princeton University Library, Sinclair Hamilton Collection **20** (top) Massachusetts Historical Society, (bottom) Billings, *Continental Harmony*, 1794, New York Public Library, Music Division **21** Winterthur **22** *Wonderful Appearance of an Angel, Devil and Ghost*, 1774, American Antiquarian Society **23** A. H. Robins Company **24** By Permission of the Trustees of the British Museum **25** New York Public Library, Arents Collection **26** National Portrait Gallery, Smithsonian Institution **27** (details) Museum of Fine Arts, Boston, M. and M. Karolik Collection **28** Johnson, *History of Pirates*, 1724, New York Public Library, Rare Book Division **30** Haggard, *Devils, Drugs, and Doctors*, 1929 [Harper and Row] **31** Winterthur **34** (top) Metropolitan Museum of Art, Bequest of A. T. Clearwater, 1933, (bottom) Colonial Williamsburg **35** Franklin, *Poor Richard Illustrated*, 1795, Philadelphia Museum of Art **36** American Antiquarian Society **37** (top) American Antiquarian Society, (bottom) Winterthur **38** New York Public Library, Spencer Collection **39** National Gallery of Art, Gift of Edgar William and Bernice Chrysler Garbisch, (bottom) Old Sturbridge Village Photo, Sturbridge, Massachusetts **40** (top) American Antiquarian Society, (bottom) *American Weekly Mercury*, October 23–30, 1735 **41** University of Michigan, William L. Clements Library **42** Collection of Mrs. Paulus Prince Powell **43** Free Library of Philadelphia, Rosenbach Collection **44** (top) American Antiquarian Society, (bottom) Josiah Wedgwood and Sons **45** New-York Historical Society **46** Joseph Badger, "Jonathan Edwards." Yale University, Bequest of Eugene Phelps Edwards for use by Jonathan Edwards College **47** (top) Thomas, *A Little Pretty Pocket Book*, 1787, Free Library of Philadelphia, Rosenbach Collection, (bottom) New-York Historical Society **48** Library Company of Philadelphia **82** Smithsonian Institution, Harry T. Peters *America on Stone* Lithography Collection **83** (bottom) New-York Historical Society **84** (top) *Yankee Notions*, 1852, (bottom) New-York Historical Society, Bella C. Landauer Collection **85** Le Blanc, *The Art of Tying the Cravat*, 1829 **86** *Magazine of American History*, May, 1887 **87** Worcester Art Museum **88** (top) Museum of Fine Arts, Boston, M. and M. Karolik Collection, (bottom) New York Public Library, Prints Division **89** Bryan and Rose, *A History of Pioneer Families of Missouri*, 1876 **90** New-York Historical Society **91** New-York Historical Society **92** (top) *Juvenile Pastimes*, c. 1825, Free Library of Philadelphia, Rosenbach Collection, (bottom) Marine Historical Association, Mystic Seaport, Connecticut **93** (top) Connecticut Historical Society, Morgan B. Brainard Collection, (center) Collection of L. L. Bean, Trenton, (bottom) Mariners Museum, Newport News, Virginia **94** (bottom) New-York Historical Society **95** Chase Manhattan Bank **98** Museum of Fine Arts, Boston,

M. and M. Karolik Collection **99** (top) Culver Pictures, (bottom) Winterthur **100** (top) Library of Congress **101** *Punch*, June 28, 1856 **103** Massachusetts Historical Society **104** Library of Congress **105** (top) *Davy Crockett Almanac*, 1840, (bottom) Yale University Library **106** Leslie, *American Girl's Book*, 1858 **107** New-York Historical Society, Bella C. Landauer Collection **108** Museum of the City of New York **109** (top) *American Comic Annual*, June, 1856, (bottom) (detail) *Living Made Easy*, 1832, American Antiquarian Society **110** American Antiquarian Society **111** *Ladies' National Magazine*, July, 1844 **112** Jennings, *Theatrical and Circus Life*, 1882 **146** (top) New-York Historical Society, (bottom) New-York Historical Society, Bella C. Landauer Collection **147** Collection of Sy Seidman **148** Kenneth M. Newman, The Old Print Shop **149** *Harper's Bazar*, June 20, 1885 **150** (center and bottom) Culver Pictures **151** (detail) New-York Historical Society **152** (top) Collection of Robert Cunningham; Henry Wantland, (bottom) Culver Pictures **153** Smithsonian Institution, Harry T. Peters *America on Stone* Lithography Collection **154** (detail) Albany Institute of History and Art **155** Museum of the City of New York, Harry T. Peters Collection **156** Bassano, London **157** Collection of Ike D. Scharff, Jr.; Courtesy of Leonard V. Huber **158** New-York Historical Society **159** New-York Historical Society, Bella C. Landauer Collection **162** Cooper-Hewitt Museum of Design, Smithsonian Institution **163** New-York Historical Society **164** Museum of the City of New York **165** Library of Congress **166** Collection of Chester Kerr **167** Museum of the City of New York, Harry T. Peters Collection **168** *Hill's Manual of Social and Business Forms*, 1879 **169** (top) Library of Congress, (bottom) Kenneth M. Newman, The Old Print Shop **170** Museum of the City of New York, Harry T. Peters Collection **172** Museum of the City of New York, Harry T. Peters Collection **173** Missouri Historical Society **174** (bottom) Collection of Floyd and Marion Rinhart **175** *Important Events of the Century*, 1878 **176** *Frank Leslie's Illustrated Newspaper*, November 24, 1877 **210** Library of Congress **211** (top) Library of Congress, (bottom) American Telephone and Telegraph Company **213** Library of Congress **214** *Harper's Magazine*, December, 1858 **215** Leslie, *American Family Cook Book*, 1858 **216** (top) Young, *Our Deportment*, 1882 **217** Lossing, *History of New York City*, 1887 **218** *The Ladies' Home Journal*, August, 1901 **219** New-York Historical Society, Bella C. Landauer Collection **220** *Harper's Magazine*, January, 1856 **221** *Frank Leslie's Illustrated Newspaper*, January, 1865 **222** *Harper's Magazine*, December, 1858 **226** Museum of the City of New York, Harry T. Peters Collection **227** (bottom) Culver Pictures **228** (top) Library of Congress **229** *Life*, January 18, 1888 **230** Museum of the City of New York **231** Museum of the City of New York **232** Collection of Wendy Buehr **233** *Century*, April, 1889 **234** *Life*, February 16, 1888, (bottom) (detail) Smithsonian Institution, Harry T. Peters *America on Stone* Lithography Collection **235** Museum of the City of New York, Harry T. Peters Collection **236** (top) Culver

Pictures, (bottom) *Harper's Weekly*, September 9, 1882 **237** *Frank Leslie's Illustrated Newspaper*, September 14, 1878 **239** New-York Historical Society, Bella C. Landauer Collection **240** Princeton University Library, Sinclair Hamilton Collection **274** (top) Library of Congress, (bottom) *Puck*, October 4, 1893 **275** Brown Brothers **276** Library of Congress, Detroit Publishing Company Collection **277** (top) Collection of Philadelphia Skating Club and Humane Society, (bottom) New-York Historical Society, Bella C. Landauer Collection **278** (top) *Scientific American*, March 9, 1878, (bottom) *Harper's Magazine*, April, 1888 **279** Library of Congress **280** *Puck*, September 21, 1892 **281** Church of Jesus Christ of Latter-day Saints **282** Collection of Wendy Buehr **283** *Puck*, August 24, 1892 **284** (top) (detail) *The Gibson Book*, Volume II, 1907, (bottom) Metropolitan Museum of Art **285** *Puck*, December 8, 1886 **286** Lambert (ed.), *Grand Tour*, 1935 **287** (detail) Museum of the City of New York **290** *Frank Leslie's Illustrated Newspaper*, September 8, 1888 **291** *Harper's Weekly*, March 24, 1866 **292** (top) Collection of Frank Johnson, (bottom) Library of Congress **293** Collection of Henrietta L. Hilles **295** Campbell, *Darkness and Daylight*, 1891 **296** (detail) *Harper's Weekly*, April 26, 1879 **297** King, *The Great South*, 1875 **298** Museum of the City of New York, Harry T. Peters Collection **299** (top) Library of Congress, (bottom) Courtesy of Gaslight Clubs **300** (top) Library of Congress, (bottom) Collection of Amanda K. Berls; Hirschl and Adler Galleries **301** Library of Congress **302** The Museum of Modern Art, New York, Gift of Lincoln Kirstein **303** The Museum of Modern Art, New York, Gift of Lincoln Kirstein **338** Library of Congress **339** Collection of John Ripley **340** Museum of the City of New York, Byron Collection **341** (detail) Library of Congress **342** Culver Pictures **343** (top) Brown Brothers, (bottom) Culver Pictures **344** *Solidarity*, August 4, 1917, The University of Michigan Library Labadie Collection **346** (bottom) *Vanity Fair*, August, 1927; Courtesy of Cluett, Peabody and Company **347** (top) Diana Epstein, *Buttons*, Walker and Company, 1968 **348** Held, Jr., and Gilbreth, Jr., *Held's Angels*, 1952; Courtesy of Mrs. John Held, Jr. **349** (top) *Life*, October 7, 1926, (bottom) Held, Jr., and Gilbreth, Jr., *Held's Angels*, 1952; Courtesy of Mrs. John Held, Jr. **350** Chinese Imports Corporation of New York **351** (top) *The New Yorker*, April 20, 1929, (bottom) *The New Yorker*, January 26, 1929 **354** *New Masses*, April, 1930; The Museum of Modern Art Library, New York **355** Library of Congress; Russell Lee **356** Estate of David Smith; Courtesy of Marlborough-Gerson Gallery, New York **357** Columbia Pictures **358** Library of Congress; Andreas Feininger **359** Courtesy of John Koch **360** Teenform **361** (middle) Cincinnati Art Museum **362** (top) Ohrbach's, (bottom) Photo Marc Hispard-Queen; Camera Press from PIX **363** *The New York Times*, December 4, 1968 **364** *The New York Times* **365** National Council on the Aging **366** United Press International, (bottom) Don Snyder **367** (top) Peace Corps, (bottom) Vista **368** *Arts in Society*, Fall/Winter, 1968 (by children of St. Boniface School, Milwaukee)

Index